The
FOOTB
ASSOCIATION
YEARBOOK
1991-1992

The Football Association

Patron

HER MAJESTY THE QUEEN

President

HRH THE DUKE OF KENT KG

The FOOTBALL ASSOCIATION YEARBOOK 1991-1992

LONDON

PELHAM BOOKS

PELHAM BOOKS

Published by the Penguin Group
27 Wrights Lane, London W8 5TZ, England
Viking Penguin, a division of Penguin Books USA Inc.
375 Hudson Street, New York, NY 10014, USA
Penguin Books Australia Ltd, Ringwood, Victoria, Australia
Penguin Books Canada Ltd, 10 Alcorn Avenue, Suite 300, Toronto, Canada M4V 3B2
Penguin Books (NZ) Ltd, 182-190 Wairau Road, Auckland 10, New Zealand

Penguin Books Ltd, Registered Offices: Harmondsworth, Middlesex, England
First published 1991

Copyright © 1991 by The Football Association

Made and printed in Great Britain by
Richard Clay Limited, Bungay, Suffolk

ISBN 0 7207 1980 1

A CIP catalogue record for this book is available from the British Library.

Photo credits
The Publishers are grateful to the following for permission to reproduce
copyright photographs in the book: Action Images pages 116, 117, 124, 125;
Oldham Evening Chronicle page 157; Photographic News Agencies Ltd page 180;
Francis Short page 93; Bob Thomas pages 8, 9, 16, 17, 46, 48, 49, 50, 53, 58, 60, 61, 62,
65, 69, 70, 71, 98, 99, 155, 168; Tony Williams page 94.

Production and advertising sales in association with
Book Production Consultants, 47 Norfolk Street, Cambridge CB1 2LE

Contents

Winning with Style

A Lotto soccer shoe is born from the technology of Lotto's Research and Development Centre and made with all the enthusiasm of those who play the sport themselves. By combining technically innovative features and reflecting the best players' thoughts, Lotto's soccer boots set themselves apart from their rivals.

RUUD GULLIT
LOTTO'S CONSULTANT

The In Stadio shoe is the end result and its characteristics make it a very high quality product to satisfy demands from the World's leading players: Gullit, Hugo, Sanchez, Romario, Clough, Saunders, Thorstedvt, Wright to name just a few.

Official
Sponsors
of:

Crystal Palace   Bristol City

Wolves   Leyton Orient

West Ham   Hartlepool United

Watford   Merthyr Tydfil

St Johnstone   Sevilla

Dundee United   Xerez

Leicester City   Haarlem

Bukta Sportswear Limited

15 Michigan Avenue off Broadway Salford Manchester M5 2GL
Telephone 061 876 5066 Facsimile 061 876 5005

Gary Charles is pursued by New Zealand's Halligan in Wellington.

A Brighter Image For The Game

by Graham Kelly, Chief Executive of The Football Association

Following a very positive World Cup for the England team last summer the game has remained buoyant throughout the season. The national team, now with Graham Taylor in charge, has continued to be successful with an eight-match unbeaten sequence going into the summer tour and top place in the qualifying group for Euro 92. English teams were re-admitted into UEFA club competitions after an exile lasting five seasons and Manchester United celebrated by winning the European Cup Winners' Cup. At home, Barclays League attendances showed another increase against the previous season, albeit a small one. We are now back to the sort of level that we had ten years ago.

The Football Association certainly caused a stir during the season with the decision by the Council to set up the 'FA Premier League'. The plan had as its long-term aims the following: to reduce the number of games for top players, thereby helping the England team, and to take maximum advantage of the commercial opportunities that an élite league would bring.

The merits of the plan seem to brook little argument. By virtue of reducing the top division to 18 clubs, and thereby the number of league matches that each club has to play in a season, the England team will be placed at the pinnacle of our programme for excellence and unprecedented time will be afforded to the Team Manager for the purposes of practice and preparation. We feel that the Premier League

Lee Sharpe survives this challenge from Staunton in the European Qualifying match with the Republic of Ireland on 27th March.

will provide the best future for English football, giving Graham Taylor a free weekend before every competitive international and reducing the wear and tear on the top players. Playing standards at the highest level will be improved and this can only be welcomed as we begin to re-impose ourselves on the European scene.

It is vitally important for the good of the game as a whole that the England team, our flagship, is successful in the major international tournaments like the World Cup and the European Championship. There are figures to prove that there are significant increases in the numbers of people participating in football, both watching and playing, when the national team has done particularly well. Attendances at Football League games shot up by about three million in the two seasons after England's wonderful World Cup of 1966. And, during the same period, thousands more new clubs were becoming affiliated.

The idea of a 'Super League' has been mooted several times in the last few years, but with The Football Association being responsible for the administration of the new league, the commercial benefits of uniting the FA Premier League, the FA Challenge Cup and the England team under one marketing banner will be immense. With the advantage of a unified approach at the top, these benefits will be spread throughout the game. This will mean more investment in stadium facilities and amenities and thus a better deal for the supporters.

When The Football Association brings all the top clubs under its wing, the debilitating power struggle between the FA and the Football League will effectively come to an end. As a result the image and stock of the game will be better and brighter. The FA is football's governing body in England, recognised as such by the World (FIFA) and European (UEFA) authorities, and at last it will now be allowed to govern effectively.

The Government, which has repeatedly called for a unified voice, will be more likely to give its support to football. The game will benefit from independent, objective leadership. In short, the modernisation of the higher echelons has arrived.

There will frequently be opposition to change. The reasoning behind the opposition to a Premier League seems to be that allowing the top 18 to compete in their own division will be detrimental to the other 74 clubs. In other words, the leading clubs in Division One should be held back so that a club three divisions lower and struggling to attract a home gate in four figures can retain a share of the proceeds generated by the existing League structure. But, of course, it is not all about money – it is about pride in performance and the pursuit of excellence. And the benefits will be felt throughout the game. The Football Association gave a categorical assurance that they would look to the financial needs of all clubs.

FUJICOLOR – THE PERFECT MATCH FOR ANY SITUATION!

Whether you're catching the action or shooting the crowd, take Fuji Film.

Available in a range of speeds and formats, it's the perfect choice for stunning shots – both on and off the field!

 **FUJI FILM**

FUJICOLOR FILM. AVAILABLE IN ISO 100, 200, 400 AND 1600 FILM SPEEDS.

World Cup Winners 1930-90

Year	Winners		Runners-up		Venue
1930	Uruguay	4	Argentina	2	Montevideo
1934	* Italy	2	Czechoslovakia	1	Rome
1938	Italy	4	Hungary	2	Paris
1950	Uruguay	2	Brazil	1	Rio de Janeiro
1954	West Germany	3	Hungary	2	Berne
1958	Brazil	5	Sweden	2	Stockholm
1962	Brazil	3	Czechoslovakia	1	Santiago
1966	* England	4	West Germany	2	London
1970	Brazil	4	Italy	1	Mexico City
1974	West Germany	2	Holland	1	Munich
1978	* Argentina	3	Holland	1	Buenos Aires
1982	Italy	3	West Germany	1	Madrid
1986	Argentina	3	West Germany	2	Mexico City
1990	West Germany	1	Argentina	0	Rome

*After extra time

European Football Championship
Henri Delaunay Cup Winners 1960-88

(formerly EUROPEAN NATIONS CUP)

Year	Winners		Runners-up		Venue
1960	USSR	2	Yugoslavia	1	Paris
1964	Spain	2	USSR	1	Madrid
1968	Italy	2	Yugoslavia	0	Rome
			(After 1-1 draw)		
1972	West Germany	3	USSR	0	Brussels
1976	* Czechoslovakia	2	West Germany	2	Belgrade
1980	West Germany	2	Belgium	1	Rome
1984	France	2	Spain	0	Paris
1988	Holland	2	USSR	0	Munich

*Won on penalty-kicks

UEFA Competition for Under-23 Teams
Winners 1972-76

(AGGREGATE SCORES)

Year	Winners		Runners-up	
1972	Czechoslovakia	5	USSR	3
1974	Hungary	6	East Germany	3
1976	USSR	3	Hungary	2

UEFA Competition for Under-21 Teams
Winners 1976-90

(AGGREGATE SCORES)

Year	Winners		Runners-up	
1978	Yugoslavia	5	East Germany	4
1980	USSR	1	East Germany	0
1982	England	5	West Germany	4
1984	England	3	Spain	0
1986	* Spain	3	Italy	3
1988	France	3	Greece	0
1990	USSR	7	Yugoslavia	3

*Won on penalty-kicks

European Champion Clubs' Cup
Winners 1956-91

Year	Winners		Runners-up		Venue
1956	Real Madrid	4	Stade de Rheims	3	Paris
1957	Real Madrid	2	A.C. Fiorentina	0	Madrid
1958	Real Madrid	3	A.C. Milan	2	Brussels
1959	Real Madrid	2	Stade de Rheims	0	Stuttgart
1960	Real Madrid	7	Eintracht Frankfurt	3	Glasgow
1961	Benfica	3	Barcelona	2	Berne
1962	Benfica	5	Real Madrid	3	Amsterdam
1963	A.C. Milan	2	Benfica	1	London
1964	Inter-Milan	3	Real Madrid	1	Vienna
1965	Inter-Milan	1	Benfica	0	Madrid
1966	Real Madrid	2	Partizan Belgrade	1	Brussels
1967	Celtic	2	Inter-Milan	1	Lisbon
1968	Manchester United	4	Benfica	1	London
1969	A.C. Milan	4	Ajax Amsterdam	1	Madrid
1970	Feyenoord	2	Celtic	1	Milan
1971	Ajax Amsterdam	2	Panathinaikos	0	London
1972	Ajax Amsterdam	2	Inter-Milan	0	Rotterdam
1973	Ajax Amsterdam	1	Juventus	0	Belgrade
1974	Bayern Munich	4	Atletico Madrid	0	Brussels
		(After 1-1 draw in Brussels)			
1975	Bayern Munich	2	Leeds United	0	Paris
1976	Bayern Munich	1	St Etienne	0	Glasgow
1977	Liverpool	3	Borussia Mönchengladbach	1	Rome
1978	Liverpool	1	Bruges	0	London
1979	Nottingham Forest	1	Malmo	0	Munich
1980	Nottingham Forest	1	S.V. Hamburg	0	Madrid
1981	Liverpool	1	Real Madrid	0	Paris
1982	Aston Villa	1	Bayern Munich	0	Rotterdam
1983	S.V. Hamburg	1	Juventus	0	Athens
1984	* Liverpool	1	Roma	1	Rome
1985	Juventus	1	Liverpool	0	Brussels
1986	* Steaua Bucharest	0	Barcelona	0	Seville
1987	Porto	2	Bayern Munich	1	Vienna
1988	* P.S.V. Eindhoven	0	Benfica	0	Stuttgart
1989	A.C. Milan	4	Steaua Bucharest	0	Barcelona
1990	A.C. Milan	1	Benfica	0	Vienna
1991	* Red Star Belgrade	0	Marseille	0	Bari

*Won on penalty-kicks

European Fairs' Cup Winners 1958-71

(formerly INTER-CITIES FAIRS' CUP)
(AGGREGATE SCORES)

Year	Winners		Runners-up		Venue
1958	Barcelona	8	London	2	
1960	Barcelona	4	Birmingham City	1	
1961	A.S. Roma	4	Birmingham City	2	
1962	Valencia	7	Barcelona	3	
1963	Valencia	4	Dynamo Zagreb	1	
1964	* Real Zaragoza	2	Valencia	1	Barcelona
1965	* Ferencvaros	1	Juventus	0	Turin
1966	Barcelona	4	Real Zaragoza	3	
1967	Dynamo Zagreb	2	Leeds United	0	
1968	Leeds United	1	Ferencvaros	0	
1969	Newcastle United	6	Ujpest Dozsa	2	
1970	Arsenal	4	Anderlecht	3	
1971	† Leeds United	3	Juventus	3	

*One leg only   †Won on away goals

14

European Cup Winners' Cup
Winners 1961-91

Year	Winners		Runners-up		Venue
1961	A.C. Fiorentina	4	Glasgow Rangers	1	
1962	Atletico Madrid	3	A.C. Fiorentina	0	Stuttgart
	(After 1-1 draw in Glasgow)				
1963	Tottenham Hotspur	5	Atletico Madrid	1	Rotterdam
1964	Sporting Club, Lisbon	1	M.T.K. Budapest	0	Antwerp
	(After 3-3 draw in Brussels)				
1965	West Ham United	2	T.S.V. Munich	0	London
1966	Borussia Dortmund	2	Liverpool	1	Glasgow
1967	Bayern Munich	1	Glasgow Rangers	0	Nuremberg
1968	A.C. Milan	2	S.V. Hamburg	0	Rotterdam
1969	Slovan Bratislava	3	Barcelona	2	Basle
1970	Manchester City	2	Gornik Zabrze	1	Vienna
1971	Chelsea	2	Real Madrid	1	Athens
	(After 1-1 draw in Athens)				
1972	Glasgow Rangers	3	Moscow Dynamo	2	Barcelona
1973	A.C. Milan	1	Leeds United	0	Salonika
1974	Magdeburg	2	A.C. Milan	0	Rotterdam
1975	Dynamo Kiev	3	Ferencvaros	0	Basle
1976	Anderlecht	4	West Ham United	2	Brussels
1977	S.V. Hamburg	2	Anderlecht	0	Amsterdam
1978	Anderlecht	4	Austria Vienna	0	Paris
1979	Barcelona	4	Fortuna Düsseldorf	3	Basle
1980 †	Valencia	0	Arsenal	0	Brussels
1981	Dynamo Tbilisi	2	Carl Zeiss Jena	1	Düsseldorf
1982	Barcelona	2	Standard Liege	1	Barcelona
1983	Aberdeen	2	Real Madrid	1	Gothenburg
1984	Juventus	2	Porto	1	Basle
1985	Everton	3	Rapid Vienna	1	Rotterdam
1986	Dynamo Kiev	3	Atletico Madrid	0	Lyon
1987	Ajax Amsterdam	1	Lokomotiv Leipzig	0	Athens
1988	Mechelen	1	Ajax Amsterdam	0	Strasbourg
1989	Barcelona	2	Sampdoria	0	Berne
1990	Sampdoria	2	Anderlecht	0	Gothenburg
1991	Manchester United	2	Barcelona	1	Rotterdam

*Aggregate scores   †Won on penalty-kicks

UEFA Cup Winners 1972-91

(AGGREGATE SCORES)

Year	Winners		Runners-up	
1972	Tottenham Hotspur	3	Wolverhampton Wanderers	2
1973	Liverpool	3	Borussia Mönchengladbach	2
1974	Feyenoord	4	Tottenham Hotspur	2
1975	Borussia Mönchengladbach	5	Twente Enschede	1
1976	Liverpool	4	F.C. Bruges	3
1977 †	Juventus	2	Atletico Bilbao	2
1978	P.S.V. Eindhoven	3	Bastia	0
1979	Borussia Mönchengladbach	2	Red Star Belgrade	1
1980 †	Eintracht Frankfurt	3	Borussia Mönchengladbach	3
1981	Ipswich Town	5	AZ 67 Alkmaar	4
1982	I.F.K.Gothenburg	4	S.V. Hamburg	0
1983	Anderlecht	2	Benfica	1
1984 *	Tottenham Hotspur	2	Anderlecht	2
1985	Real Madrid	3	Videoton	1
1986	Real Madrid	5	Cologne	3
1987	I.F.K.Gothenburg	2	Dundee United	1
1988 *	Bayer Leverkusen	3	Español	3
1989	Naples	5	VfB Stuttgart	4
1990	Juventus	3	Fiorentina	1
1991	Inter-Milan	2	Roma	1

†Won on away goals   *Won on penalty-kicks

European Champion Clubs' Cup 1990-91

First Round		Second Round		Quarter-Final		Semi-Final		Final	

```
First Round              Second Round           Quarter-Final        Semi-Final        Final

Red Star Belgrade   1:4 ⎱
Grasshoppers        1:1 ⎰ Red Star Belgrade 3:1 ⎱
Valletta            0:0 ⎱                       ⎰ Red Star Belgrade 3:3 ⎱
Rangers             4:6 ⎰ Rangers           0:1 ⎰                       ⎱ Red Star
U.S. Luxembourg     1:0 ⎱                                                ⎰ Belgrade    2:2 ⎱
Dynamo Dresden      3:3 ⎰ Dynamo Dresden  1:1* ⎱                                          ⎰
Malmö               3:2 ⎱                       ⎰ Dynamo Dresden 0:0 ⎰                      ⎱ Red Star
Besiktas            2:2 ⎰ Malmö             1:1 ⎰                                            ⎰ Belgrade   0*
Apoel Nicosia       2:0 ⎱                                                                  ⎰
Bayern Munich       3:4 ⎰ Bayern Munich     4:3 ⎱                                          ⎱
Akureyrar           1:0 ⎱                       ⎰ Bayern Munich   1:2 ⎱                      ⎱
C.F.K.A. Sredetz    0:3 ⎰ C.F.K.A. Sredetz  0:0 ⎰                       ⎱ Bayern Munich 1:2 ⎰  In Bari
Dinamo Bucharest    4:1 ⎱                                                ⎰
St. Patrick's Ath.  0:1 ⎰ Dinamo Bucharest 0:0 ⎱                       ⎰
Porto               5:8 ⎱                       ⎰ Porto           1:0 ⎰
Portadown           0:1 ⎰ Porto             0:4 ⎰
Napoli              3:2 ⎱
Ujpest Dozsa        0:0 ⎰ Napoli            0:0 ⎱
Sparta Prague       0:0 ⎱                       ⎰ Spartak Moscow  0:3 ⎱
Spartak Moscow      2:2 ⎰ Spartak Moscow   0:0* ⎰                       ⎱ Spartak
Odense              1:0 ⎱                                                ⎰ Moscow       1:1 ⎱
Real Madrid         4:6 ⎰ Real Madrid       9:2 ⎱                                          ⎰
Swarovski Tirol     5:2 ⎱                       ⎰ Real Madrid     0:1 ⎰                      ⎱
Kuusysi             0:1 ⎰ Swarovski Tirol   1:2 ⎰                                            ⎰ Marseille  0

A.C. Milan bye           A.C. Milan        0:1 ⎱
                                               ⎰ A.C. Milan      1:0 ⎱
Lillestrom          1:0 ⎱                                            ⎰
Bruges              1:2 ⎰ Bruges            0:0 ⎰                      ⎱ Marseille    3:2 ⎰
Lech Poznan         3:2 ⎱                                             ⎰
Panathinaikos       0:1 ⎰ Lech Poznan       3:1 ⎱                     ⎱
DinamoTirana        1:0 ⎱                       ⎰ Marseille       1:1 ⎰
Marseille           5:0 ⎰ Marseille         2:6 ⎰
```

*Won on penalty-kicks

Red Star Belgrade.

European Cup Winners' Cup 1990-91

First Round		Second Round		Quarter-Final		Semi-Final		Final	
Manchester United	2:1	Manchester Utd	3:2						
Pecsi Munkas	0:0			Manchester Utd	1:2				
Wrexham	0:1	Wrexham	0:0						
Lyngby	0:0					Man. Utd	3:1		
Montpellier	1:0	Montpellier	5:3						
P.S.V. Eindhoven	0:0			Montpellier	1:0				
Glentoran	1:0	Steaua Bucharest	0:0						
Steaua Bucharest	1:5							Man. Utd	2
Famagusta	0:0	Aberdeen	0:0						
Aberdeen	2:3			Legia Warsaw	1:2				
Legia Warsaw	3:3	Legia Warsaw	0:1						
Swift Hesperange	0:0					Legia Warsaw	1:1		
Olympiakos	3:2	Olympiakos	0:1						
Flamurtari	1:0			Sampdoria	0:2				
Kaiserlautern	1:0	Sampdoria	1:3					In Rotterdam	
Sampdoria	0:2								
Viking Stavanger	0:0	Liège	2:0						
Liège	2:3			Liège	1:0				
Estrela da Amadora	1:1*	Estrela da Amadora	0:1						
Neuchatel Xamax	1:1					Juventus	1:1		
P.S.V. Schwerin	0:0	Austria Memphis	0:0						
Austria Memphis	2:0			Juventus	3:3				
Sliven	0:1	Juventus	4:4						
Juventus	2:6							Barcelona	1
Kuopion	2:0	Kiev Dinamo	1:2						
Kiev Dinamo	2:4			Kiev Dinamo	2:1				
Sliema Wanderers	1:0	Dukla Prague	0:2						
Dukla Prague	2:2					Barcelona	3:0		
Fram	3:1	Fram	1:0						
Djurgardens	0:1			Barcelona	3:1				
Trabzonspor	1:2	Barcelona	2:3						
Barcelona	0:7								

*Won on penalty-kicks

Preliminary Round: Bray Wanderers 1:0 Trabzonspor 1:2

Manchester United.

17

UEFA Cup 1990-91

First Round

Glenavon	0:0 }	Derry City	0:0 }	Vejle	1:0 }
Bordeaux	0:2 }	Vitesse Arnhem	1:0 }	Admira Wacker	0:3 }
Avenir Beggen	2:0 }	Norrkoping	0:1 }	Sevilla	0:0* }
Inter Bratislava	1:5 }	Cologne	0:3 }	PAOK Salonika	0:0 }
Roda	1:1 }	Bayer Leverkusen	1:1 }	Magdeburg	0:1 }
Monaco	3:3 }	Twente	0:1 }	Rovaniemen Pall.	0:0 }
Sporting Portugal	1:2 }	Slavia Sofia	2:2 }	Heraklis Saloniki	0:0 }
Mechelen	0:2 }	Omonia Nicosia	1:4 }	Valencia	0:2 }
Hibernians	0:0 }	Roma	1:1 }	MTK-VM Budapest	1:1 }
Partizan Belgrade	3:2 }	Benfica	0:0 }	Luzern	1:2 }
Borussia Dortmund	2:2 }	Katowice	3:1 }	Atalanta	0:1† }
Chemnitzer	0:0 }	Turun Palloseura	0:0 }	Dinamo Zagreb	0:1 }
Hafnfjardar	1:2 }	Dnepr	1:1 }	Partizani Tirana	0:0 }
Dundee United	3:2 }	Hearts	1:3 }	Universitatea Craiova	1:1 }
Lausanne	3:0 }	Torpedo Moscow	4:1 }	Zaglebie Lubin	0:0 }
Real Sociedad	2:1† }	Gais	1:1 }	Bologna	1:1 }
Brondby	5:1 }	Aston Villa	3:2 }	Politehnica Timisoara	2:0 }
Eintracht Frankfurt	0:4 }	Banik Ostrava	1:1 }	Atletico Madrid	0:1 }
Rapid Vienna	2:1 }	Fenerbahce	3:3 }	Chernomorets Odessa	3:1 }
Internazionale	1:3 }	Vitoria	0:2 }	Rosenborg	1:2 }
Anderlecht	2:2 }			Royal Antwerp	0:1 }
Petrolul Ploiesti	0:0 }			Ferencvaros	0:3 }

Second Round		Third Round		Quarter-Final		Semi-Final		Final	
Inter-Milan	0:3 }	Inter-Milan	3:1 }						
Aston Villa	2:0 }			Inter-Milan	0:2 }				
Real Sociedad	1:0 }	Partizan Belgrade	0:1 }						
Partizan Belgrade	0:1* }					Inter-Milan	0:2 }		
Cologne	0:2 }	Cologne	1:0 }						
Inter Bratislava	1:0 }			Atalanta	0:0 }				
Fenerbahçe	0:1 }	Atalanta	1:1 }					Inter-Milan	2:0 }
Atalanta	1:4 }								
Luzern	0:1 }	Admira Wacker	3:0 }						
Admira Wacker	1:1 }			Bologna	1:0 }				
Hearts	3:0 }	Bologna	0:3* }						
Bologna	1:3 }					Sporting Portugal 0:0 }			
Vitesse Arnhem	1:4 }	Vitesse Arnhem	0:1 }						
Dundee United	0:0 }			Sporting Portugal 1:2 }					
Sporting Portugal	7:0 }	Sporting Portugal	2:2 }					First leg	
Politehnica Timisoara	0:2 }							in Milan	
Brondby	3:1 }	Brondby	3:0 }					Second leg	
Ferencvaros	0:0 }			Brondby	1:0* }			in Rome	
Katowice	1:0 }	Bayer Leverkusen	0:0 }						
Bayer Leverkusen	2:4 }					Brondby	0:1 }		
Torpedo Moscow	3:1 }	Torpedo Moscow	2:2 }						
Sevilla	1:2 }			Torpedo Moscow	0:1 }				
Chernomorets Odessa	0:0 }	Monaco	1:1 }					Roma	0:1 }
Monaco	0:1 }								
Omonia Nicosia	1:0 }	Anderlecht	1:1† }						
Anderlecht	1:3 }			Anderlecht	0:2 }				
Univ. Craiova	0:0 }	Borussia Dortmund 0:2 }							
Borussia Dortmund	3:1 }					Roma	0:2 }		
Magdeburg	0:0 }	Bordeaux	0:0 }						
Bordeaux	1:1 }			Roma	3:3 }				
Valencia	1:1 }	Roma	5:2 }						
Roma	1:2 }								

* Won on penalty-kicks   †Won on away goals

England's Full International Record 1872-1991

(Up to and including 12 June 1991)

	HOME				Goals		AWAY				Goals	
	P	W	D	L	For	Agst	P	W	D	L	For	Agst
Albania	1	1	0	0	5	0	1	1	0	0	2	0
Argentina	5	3	2	0	10	6	5	1	2	2	5	5
Australia	—	—	—	—	—	—	5	3	2	0	5	2
Austria	5	3	1	1	18	9	10	5	2	3	36	16
Belgium	4	3	1	0	17	3	14	10	3	1	50	21
Bohemia	—	—	—	—	—	—	1	1	0	0	4	0
Brazil	6	2	3	1	8	6	9	1	2	6	5	14
Bulgaria	2	1	1	0	3	1	3	2	1	0	4	0
Cameroon	1	1	0	0	2	0	1	1	0	0	3	2
Canada	—	—	—	—	—	—	1	1	0	0	1	0
Chile	1	0	1	0	0	0	3	2	1	0	4	1
Colombia	1	0	1	0	1	1	1	1	0	0	4	0
Cyprus	1	1	0	0	5	0	1	1	0	0	1	0
Czechoslovakia	5	4	1	0	13	6	6	3	1	2	10	7
Denmark	5	4	0	1	8	3	7	4	3	0	18	8
Ecuador	—	—	—	—	—	—	1	1	0	0	2	0
Egypt	—	—	—	—	—	—	2	2	0	0	5	0
FIFA	1	0	1	0	4	4	—	—	—	—	—	—
Finland	2	2	0	0	7	1	6	5	1	0	25	4
France	7	5	2	0	21	4	13	9	0	4	39	23
Germany, East	2	2	0	0	4	1	2	1	1	0	3	2
Germany, West	7	5	0	2	15	8	12	4	4	4	21	17
Greece	2	1	1	0	3	0	3	3	0	0	7	1
Holland	5	2	2	1	12	6	5	2	2	1	4	4
Hungary	7	6	0	1	18	9	10	5	1	4	28	18
Iceland	—	—	—	—	—	—	1	0	1	0	1	1
Ireland, Northern	49	40	6	3	169	36	47	34	10	3	150	44
Ireland, Republic of	6	3	2	1	11	6	7	2	4	1	8	6
Israel	—	—	—	—	—	—	2	1	1	0	2	1
Italy	6	3	2	1	9	5	11	3	3	5	16	17
Kuwait	—	—	—	—	—	—	1	1	0	0	1	0
Luxembourg	3	3	0	0	18	1	4	4	0	0	20	2
Malaysia	—	—	—	—	—	—	1	1	0	0	4	2
Malta	1	1	0	0	5	0	1	1	0	0	1	0
Mexico	2	2	0	0	10	0	4	1	1	2	4	3
Morocco	—	—	—	—	—	—	1	0	1	0	0	0
New Zealand	—	—	—	—	—	—	2	2	0	0	3	0
Norway	2	2	0	0	8	0	4	3	0	1	17	4
Paraguay	—	—	—	—	—	—	1	1	0	0	3	0
Peru	—	—	—	—	—	—	2	1	0	1	5	4
Poland	4	2	2	0	7	2	4	2	1	1	4	2
Portugal	6	5	1	0	12	4	9	3	4	2	23	13
Rest of Europe	1	1	0	0	3	0	—	—	—	—	—	—
Rest of the World	1	1	0	0	2	1	—	—	—	—	—	—
Romania	3	0	3	0	2	2	5	2	2	1	4	2
Saudi Arabia	—	—	—	—	—	—	1	0	1	0	1	1
Scotland	53	25	11	17	115	87	54	18	13	23	73	81
Spain	6	5	0	1	19	6	10	5	2	3	16	13
Sweden	4	2	1	1	9	6	9	4	3	2	14	8
Switzerland	5	3	2	0	12	3	10	7	0	3	25	9
Tunisia	—	—	—	—	—	—	1	0	1	0	1	1
Turkey	2	2	0	0	13	0	3	2	1	0	9	0
USA	—	—	—	—	—	—	5	4	0	1	29	5
USSR	4	2	1	1	10	5	7	3	2	2	9	8
Uruguay	3	1	1	1	3	3	5	1	1	3	5	9
Wales	49	32	9	8	126	46	48	30	12	6	113	44
Yugoslavia	7	4	3	0	15	7	7	1	2	4	8	13
TOTAL	287	185	61	41	752	288	389	206	92	91	855	438

GRAND TOTAL

				Goals	
Played	Won	Drawn	Lost	For	Against
676	391	153	132	1607	726

19

England's Full International Goalscorers 1946-91

(Up to and including 12 June 1991)

Charlton, R.	49	Connelly	7	McDermott	3	Bowles	1
Lineker	45	Coppell	7	Matthews, S.	3	Bradford	1
Greaves	44	Paine	7	Morris	3	Bridges	1
Finney	30	Platt	7	O'Grady	3	Chamberlain	1
Lofthouse	30	Charlton, J.	6	Peacock	3	Crawford	1
Robson, B.	26	Johnson	6	Ramsey	3	Dixon, L.	1
Hurst	24	Macdonald	6	Sewell	3	Goddard	1
Mortensen	23	Mullen	6	Steven	3	Hirst	1
Channon	21	Rowley	6	Webb	3	Hughes, E.	1
Keegan	21	Waddle	6	Wilkins	3	Kay	1
Peters	20	Atyeo	5	Wright, W.	3	Kidd	1
Haynes	18	Baily	5	Allen, R.	2	Langton	1
Hunt, R.	18	Brooking	5	Anderson	2	Lawler	1
Lawton	16	Carter	5	Bradley	2	Lee, J.	1
Taylor, T.	16	Edwards	5	Broadbent	2	Mabbutt	1
Woodcock	16	Hitchens	5	Brooks	2	Marsh	1
Chivers	13	Latchford	5	Cowans	2	Medley	1
Mariner	13	Neal	5	Eastham	2	Melia	1
Smith, R.	13	Pearson, Stan	5	Froggatt, J.	2	Mullery	1
Francis, T.	12	Pearson, Stuart	5	Froggatt, R.	2	Nicholls	1
Douglas	11	Pickering, F.	5	Gascoigne	2	Nicholson	1
Mannion	11	Adams	4	Haines	2	Parry	1
Barnes, J.	10	Barnes, P.	4	Hancocks	2	Sansom	1
Clarke, A.	10	Bull	4	Hunter	2	Shackleton	1
Flowers	10	Dixon, K.	4	Lee, S	2	Smith	1
Lee, F.	10	Hassall	4	Moore	2	Stiles	1
Milburn	10	Revie	4	Pearce	2	Summerbee	1
Wilshaw	10	Robson, R.	4	Perry	2	Tambling	1
Bell	9	Watson, D.	4	Pointer	2	Thompson, Phil	1
Bentley	9	Baker	3	Royle	2	Viollet	1
Hateley	9	Blissett	3	Taylor, P.	2	Wallace	1
Ball	8	Butcher	3	Tueart	2	Walsh	1
Beardsley	8	Currie	3	Wignall	2	Weller	1
Broadis	8	Elliott	3	Worthington	2	Wise	1
Byrne, J.	8	Francis, G.	3	A'Court	1	Withe	1
Hoddle	8	Grainger	3	Astall	1	Wright	1
Kevan	8	Kennedy, R.	3	Beattie	1		

England's Full International Caps 1946-91

(Up to and including 12 June 1991)
*Does not include pre-war caps

Player	Caps	Player	Caps
A' Court, A. (Liverpool)	5	Bradford, G. (Bristol R.)	1
Adams, T. (Arsenal)	19	Bradley, W. (Manchester U.)	3
Allen, A. (Stoke)	3	Bridges, B. (Chelsea)	4
Allen, C. (Q.P.R. and Tottenham)	5	Broadbent, P. (Wolves)	7
Allen, R. (W.B.A.)	5	Broadis, I. (Manchester C. and	
Anderson, S. (Sunderland)	2	Newcastle)	14
Anderson, V. (Nottm. Forest, Arsenal		Brooking, T. (West Ham)	47
and Manchester United)	30	Brooks, J. (Tottenham)	3
Angus, J. (Burnley)	1	Brown, A. (W.B.A.)	1
Armfield, J. (Blackpool)	43	Brown, K. (West Ham)	1
Armstrong, D. (Middlesbrough and		Bull, S. (Wolves)	13
Southampton)	3	Butcher, T. (Ipswich and Rangers)	77
Armstrong, K. (Chelsea)	1	Byrne, G. (Liverpool)	2
Astall, G. (Birmingham)	2	Byrne, J. (Crystal Palace and	
Astle, J. (W.B.A.)	5	West Ham)	11
Aston, J. (Manchester U.)	17	Byrne, R. (Manchester U.)	33
Atyeo, J. (Bristol City)	6		
		Callaghan, I. (Liverpool)	4
Bailey, G. (Manchester U.)	2	Carter, H. (Derby)	*7
Bailey, M. (Charlton)	2	Chamberlain, M. (Stoke)	8
Baily, E. (Tottenham)	9	Channon, M. (Southampton and	
Baker, J. (Hibernian and Arsenal)	8	Manchester C.)	46
Ball, A. (Blackpool, Everton and		Charles, G. (Nottm. Forest)	2
Arsenal)	72	Charlton, J. (Leeds)	35
Banks, G. (Leicester and Stoke)	73	Charlton, R. (Manchester U.)	106
Banks, T. (Bolton)	6	Charnley, R. (Blackpool)	1
Barham, M. (Norwich City)	2	Cherry, T. (Leeds)	27
Barlow, R. (W.B.A.)	1	Chilton, A. (Manchester U.)	2
Barnes, J. (Watford and Liverpool)	65	Chivers, M. (Tottenham)	24
Barnes, P. (Manchester City, W.B.A.		Clamp, E. (Wolves)	4
and Leeds)	22	Clapton, D. (Arsenal)	1
Barrass, M. (Bolton)	3	Clarke, A. (Leeds)	19
Barrett, E. (Oldham)	1	Clarke, H. (Tottenham)	1
Batty, D. (Leeds)	5	Clayton, R. (Blackburn)	35
Baynham, R. (Luton)	3	Clemence, R. (Liverpool and	
Beardsley, P. (Newcastle and		Tottenham)	61
Liverpool)	49	Clement, D. (Q.P.R.)	5
Beasant, D. (Chelsea)	2	Clough, B. (Middlesbrough)	2
Beattie, K. (Ipswich)	9	Clough, N. (Nottm. Forest)	4
Bell, C. (Manchester C.)	48	Coates, R. (Burnley and Tottenham)	4
Bentley, R. (Chelsea)	12	Cockburn, H. (Manchester U.)	13
Berry, J. (Manchester U.)	4	Cohen, G. (Fulham)	37
Birtles, G. (Nottm. Forest and		Compton, L. (Arsenal)	2
Manchester U.)	3	Connelly, J. (Burnley and	
Blissett, L. (Watford and A.C. Milan)	14	Manchester U.)	20
Blockley, J. (Arsenal)	1	Cooper, T. (Leeds)	20
Blunstone, F. (Chelsea)	5	Coppell, S. (Manchester U.)	42
Bonetti, P. (Chelsea)	7	Corrigan, J. (Manchester C.)	9
Bowles, S. (Q.P.R.)	5	Cottee, T. (West Ham and Everton)	7
Boyer, P. (Norwich)	1	Cowans, G. (Aston Villa and Bari)	10
Brabrook, P. (Chelsea)	3	Crawford, R. (Ipswich)	2
Bracewell, P. (Everton)	3	Crowe, C. (Wolves)	1

Player	Caps
Lawler, C. (Liverpool)	4
Lawton, T. (Chelsea and Notts. County)	*15
Lee, F. (Manchester C.)	27
Lee, J. (Derby)	1
Lee, S. (Liverpool)	14
Lindsay, A. (Liverpool)	4
Lineker, G. (Leicester, Everton, Barcelona and Tottenham)	68
Little, B. (Aston Villa)	1
Lloyd, L. (Liverpool)	4
Lofthouse, N. (Bolton)	33
Lowe, E. (Aston Villa)	3
Mabbutt, G. (Tottenham)	13
MacDonald, M. (Newcastle)	14
Madeley, P. (Leeds)	24
Mannion, W. (Middlesbrough)	26
Mariner, P. (Ipswich and Arsenal)	35
Marsh, R. (Q.P.R. and Manchester C.)	9
Martin, A. (West Ham)	17
Marwood, B. (Arsenal)	1
Matthews, R. (Coventry)	5
Matthews, S. (Stoke and Blackpool)	*37
McDermott, T. (Liverpool)	25
McDonald, C. (Burnley)	8
McFarland, R. (Derby)	28
McGarry, W. (Huddersfield)	4
McGuinness, W. (Manchester U.)	2
McMahon, S. (Liverpool)	17
McNab, R. (Arsenal)	4
McNeil, M. (Middlesbrough)	9
Meadows, J. (Manchester C.)	1
Medley, L. (Tottenham)	6
Melia, J. (Liverpool)	2
Merrick, G. (Birmingham)	23
Metcalfe, V. (Huddersfield)	2
Milburn, J. (Newcastle)	13
Miller, B. (Burnley)	1
Mills, M. (Ipswich)	42
Milne, G. (Liverpool)	14
Milton, A. (Arsenal)	1
Moore, R. (West Ham)	108
Morley, A. (Aston Villa)	6
Morris, J. (Derby)	3
Mortensen, S. (Blackpool)	25
Mozley, B. (Derby)	3
Mullen, J. (Wolves)	12
Mullery, A. (Tottenham)	35
Neal, P. (Liverpool)	50
Newton, K. (Blackburn and Everton)	27
Nicholls, J. (W.B.A.)	2
Nicholson, W. (Tottenham)	1
Nish, D. (Derby)	5
Norman, M. (Tottenham)	23

Player	Caps
O'Grady, M. (Huddersfield and Leeds)	2
Osgood, P. (Chelsea)	4
Osman, R. (Ipswich)	11
Owen, S. (Luton)	3
Paine, T. (Southampton)	19
Pallister, G. (Middlesbrough and Manchester U.)	4
Parker, P. (Q.P.R.)	16
Parkes, P. (Q.P.R.)	1
Parry, R. (Bolton)	2
Peacock, A. (Middlesbrough and Leeds)	6
Pearce, S. (Nottingham Forest)	41
Pearson, Stanley (Manchester U.)	8
Pearson, Stuart (Manchester U.)	15
Pegg, D. (Manchester U.)	1
Pejic, M. (Stoke)	4
Perry, W. (Blackpool)	3
Perryman, S. (Tottenham)	1
Peters, M. (West Ham and Tottenham)	67
Phelan, M. (Manchester U.)	1
Phillips, L. (Portsmouth)	3
Pickering, F. (Everton)	3
Pickering, N. (Sunderland)	1
Pilkington, B. (Burnley)	1
Platt, D. (Aston Villa)	22
Pointer, R. (Burnley)	3
Pye, J. (Wolves)	1
Quixall, A. (Sheffield W.)	5
Radford, J. (Arsenal)	2
Ramsey, A. (Southampton and Tottenham)	32
Reaney, P. (Leeds)	3
Reeves, K. (Norwich and Manchester C.)	2
Regis, C. (W.B.A. and Coventry)	5
Reid, P. (Everton)	13
Revie, D. (Manchester C.)	6
Richards, J. (Wolves)	1
Rickaby, S. (W.B.A.)	1
Rimmer, J. (Arsenal)	1
Rix, G. (Arsenal)	17
Robb, G. (Tottenham)	1
Roberts, G. (Tottenham)	6
Robson, B. (W.B.A. and Manchester U.)	89
Robson, R. (W.B.A.)	20
Rocastle, D. (Arsenal)	11
Rowley, J. (Manchester U.)	6
Royle, J. (Everton and Manchester C.)	6
Sadler, D. (Manchester U.)	4
Salako, J. (Crystal Palace)	4

Player	Caps
Sansom, K. (Crystal Palace and Arsenal)	86
Scott, L. (Arsenal)	17
Seaman, D. (Q.P.R. and Arsenal)	7
Sewell, J. (Sheffield W.)	6
Shackleton, L. (Sunderland)	5
Sharpe, L. (Manchester U.)	1
Shaw, G. (Sheffield U.)	5
Shellito, K. (Chelsea)	1
Shilton, P. (Leicester, Stoke, Nottm. For., Southampton and Derby County)	125
Shimwell, E. (Blackpool)	1
Sillett, P. (Chelsea)	3
Slater, W. (Wolves)	12
Smith, A. (Arsenal)	7
Smith, L. (Arsenal)	6
Smith, R. (Tottenham)	15
Smith, T. (Birmingham)	2
Smith, T. (Liverpool)	1
Spink, N. (Aston Villa)	1
Springett, R. (Sheffield W.)	33
Staniforth, R. (Huddersfield)	8
Statham, D. (W.B.A.)	3
Stein, B. (Luton)	1
Stepney, A. (Manchester U.)	1
Sterland, M. (Sheffield W.)	1
Steven, T. (Everton and Rangers)	30
Stevens, G. (Everton and Rangers)	42
Stevens, G. (Tottenham)	7
Stiles, N. (Manchester U.)	28
Storey, P. (Arsenal)	19
Storey-Moore, I. (Nottm. Forest)	1
Streten, B. (Luton)	1
Summerbee, M. (Manchester C.)	8
Sunderland, A. (Arsenal)	1
Swan, P. (Sheffield W.)	19
Swift, F. (Manchester C.)	19
Talbot, B. (Ipswich)	6
Tambling, R. (Chelsea)	3
Taylor, E. (Blackpool)	1
Taylor, J. (Fulham)	2
Taylor, P. (Crystal Palace)	4
Taylor, P. (Liverpool)	3
Taylor, T. (Manchester U.)	19
Temple, D. (Everton)	1
Thomas, D. (Coventry City)	2
Thomas, D. (Q.P.R.)	8
Thomas, G. (Crystal Palace)	7
Thomas, M. (Arsenal)	2
Thompson, Peter (Liverpool)	16
Thompson, Phil (Liverpool)	42
Thompson, T. (Aston Villa and Preston)	2
Thomson, R. (Wolves)	8
Todd, C. (Derby)	27

Player	Caps
Towers, A. (Sunderland)	3
Tueart, D. (Manchester C.)	6
Ufton, D. (Charlton)	1
Venables, T. (Chelsea)	2
Viljoen, C. (Ipswich)	2
Viollet, D. (Manchester U.)	2
Waddle, C. (Newcastle U., Tottenham and Marseille)	61
Waiters, A. (Blackpool)	5
Walker, D. (Nottm. Forest)	36
Wallace, D. (Southampton)	1
Walsh, P. (Luton)	5
Walters, M. (Rangers)	1
Ward, P. (Brighton)	1
Ward, T. (Derby)	2
Watson, D. (Norwich City and Everton)	12
Watson, D. (Sunderland, Manchester C., Werder Bremen, Southampton and Stoke)	65
Watson, W. (Sunderland)	4
Webb, N. (Nottm. Forest and Manchester U.)	20
Weller, K. (Leicester)	4
West, G. (Everton)	3
Wheeler, J. (Bolton)	1
Whitworth, S. (Leicester)	7
Whymark, T. (Ipswich)	1
Wignall, F. (Nottm. Forest)	2
Wilkins, R. (Chelsea, Manchester U. and A.C. Milan)	84
Williams, B. (Wolves)	24
Williams, S. (Southampton)	6
Willis, A. (Tottenham)	1
Wilshaw, D. (Wolves)	12
Wilson, R. (Huddersfield and Everton)	63
Winterburn, N. (Arsenal)	1
Wise, D. (Chelsea)	5
Withe, P. (Aston Villa)	11
Wood, R. (Manchester U.)	3
Woodcock, T. (Nottm. Forest, Cologne and Arsenal)	42
Woods, C. (Norwich and Rangers)	24
Worthington, F. (Leicester)	8
Wright, I. (Crystal Palace)	4
Wright, M. (Southampton and Derby County)	40
Wright, T. (Everton)	11
Wright, W. (Wolves)	105
Young, G. (Sheffield W.)	1

IN A WINNING CLASS OF ITS OWN

PHILISHAVE®

THE WORLD'S BEST SELLING ELECTRIC SHAVER

PHILIPS

CLUBCALL

"WE'VE GOT IT COVERED!"

Live match commentary or match reports. Its all on clubcall - the biggest and the best football telephone information service. And you can catch up on all the latest news from your favourite league clubs. Updated Daily. Phone your Clubcall now! Clubcall 24hrs a day

0898 121

THEN ADD THE NUMBER YOU WANT

CLUBCALL

DIVISION 1

ARSENAL	170
ASTON VILLA	148
CHELSEA	159
COVENTRY CITY	166
CRYSTAL PALACE	145
DERBY COUNTY	187
EVERTON	199
LEEDS UTD	180
LIVERPOOL	184
MANCHESTER CITY	191
MANCHESTER UTD	161
NORWICH CITY	144
NOTTINGHAM FOREST	174
Q.P.R.	162
SOUTHAMPTON	178
SUNDERLAND	140
WIMBLEDON	175

DIVISION 2

BARNSLEY	152
BLACKBURN ROVERS	179
BRISTOL CITY	176
BRISTOL ROVERS	631
CHARLTON ATHLETIC	146
LEICESTER CITY	185
MIDDLESBOROUGH	181
MILLWALL	143
NEWCASTLE UTD	190
NOTTS COUNTY	101
OLDHAM ATHLETIC	142
OXFORD UTD	172
PLYMOUTH ARGYLE	688
PORTSMOUTH	182
PORT VALE	636
SHEFFIELD WED	186
SWINDON TOWN	640
W.B.A.	193
WEST HAM UTD	165
WOLVES	103

DIVISION 3

BIRMINGHAM CITY	188
BOLTON WANDERERS	164
BOURNEMOUTH	163
BRENTFORD	108
BURY	197
CAMBRIDGE UTD	141
CHESTER CITY	633
CREWE ALEXANDRA	647
EXETER	634
FULHAM	198
GRIMSBY TOWN	576
HUDDERSFIELD TOWN	635
LEYTON ORIENT	150
PRESTON N.END	173
ROTHERHAM UTD	637
SHREWSBURY TOWN	194
SWANSEA CITY	639
TRANMERE ROVERS	646

DIVISION 4

ALDERSHOT	630
BLACKPOOL	648
BURNLEY	153
CARDIFF CITY	171
CARLISLE UTD	632
CHESTERFIELD	573
DARLINGTON	149
DONCASTER ROVERS	651
GILLINGHAM	107
HALIFAX TOWN	106
HARTLEPOOL UTD	147
HEREFORD UTD	645
LINCOLN CITY	889
PETERBORO' UTD	654
SCARBOROUGH	650
SCUNTHORPE UTD	652
STOCKPORT CNTY	638
TORQUAY UTD	641
WALSALL	104
WREXHAM	642
YORK CITY	643

SCOTTISH

ABERDEEN	551
AYR UNITED	552
CELTIC	888
DUNDEE	649
DUNFERMLINE ATHLETIC	556
FALKIRK	554
HEARTS	183
HIBS	189
KILMARNOCK	557
MOTHERWELL	553
RANGERS	555
ST. MIRREN	885
ST.JOHNSTONE	559
ENGLAND	196
SCOTLAND	681
REP. IRELAND	683
WALES	682
SOCCER SHOW	500
SHOOT NEWSCALL	195

NON LEAGUE

BARNET	544
BOSTON UTD	539
KIDDERMINSTER	547
MACCLESFIELD	546
SUTTON UTD	537
TELFORD	545
GM VAUXHALL CON	653
VAUXHALL LEAGUE	155
BASS N.W COUNTIES	536
BEAZER HOMES LEAGUE	151
HFS LOANS LEAGUE	157
JEWSON LEAGUE	543
NORTHERN LEAGUE	542

For your Free laminated CLUBCALL card please fill
in your name and address and your team and send it to:
Department F.A.Y., BT Supercall,1-9 Downham Road,London N1 5AA.

NAME

ADDRESS

POST CODE

FOOTBALL CLUB

CLUBCALL ⓣ SUPERCALL

Calls cost 33p/minute cheap;44p/minute other times.
BT Supercall, 1-9 Downham Road, London N1 5AA
* Clubcall is a service mark of British Telecom plc.

England Senior Caps 1990-91

	Hungary	Poland	Rep. of Ireland	Cameroon	Rep. of Ireland	Turkey	U.S.S.R.	Argentina	Australia	New Zealand	New Zealand	Malaysia
C. Woods (Rangers)	1	1	1				1		1	1	1	1
L. Dixon (Arsenal)	2	2	2	2	2	2		2				
S. Pearce (Nottingham Forest)	3	3	3	3	3	3		3	3	3	3	3
P. Parker (Queens Park Rangers)	4	4					5		2	2		
D. Walker (Nottingham Forest)	5	5	5	5	5	5		5	5	5	5	5
M. Wright (Derby County)	6	6	6	6	6		6	6	6		6	6
D. Platt (Aston Villa)	7	7	7		8	7	7	7	7	7	7	7
P. Gascoigne (Tottenham Hotspur)	8	8		8								
S. Bull (Wolves)	9	9										
G. Lineker (Tottenham Hotspur)	10	10	10	10	10	10		10	10	10		10
J. Barnes (Liverpool)	11	11		11	11	11	11	11				
T. Dorigo (Chelsea)	*3						3					
C. Waddle (Marseille)	*9	*10										
P. Beardsley (Liverpool)		*9	9		9		*10					
T. Adams (Arsenal)			4		4							
G. Cowans (Aston Villa)			8									
S. McMahon (Liverpool)			11									
D. Seaman (Arsenal)				1	1	1		1				
T. Steven (Rangers)				4								
B. Robson (Manchester United)				7	7							
I. Wright (Crystal Palace)				9	*10		10				10	
G. Pallister (Manchester United)				*7		6						
S. Hodge (Nottingham Forest)				*8		*8						
L. Sharpe (Manchester United)					*4							
D. Wise (Chelsea)						4	4		*10	9	4	
G. Thomas (Crystal Palace)						8	8	8	8	8	8	8
A. Smith (Arsenal)						9	9	9				
G. Stevens (Rangers)						2						
D. Batty (Leeds United)							*4	4	4	4		4
N. Clough (Nottingham Forest)								*11	9			9
D. Hirst (Sheffield Wednesday)									11		*9	
J. Salako (Crystal Palace)									*11	*11	11	11
B. Deane (Sheffield United)										*4	9	
E. Barrett (Oldham Athletic)										6		
M. Walters (Rangers)										11		
G. Charles (Nottingham Forest)											2	2

*Substitute

European Championship 1990-92

Qualifying Competition

GROUP 1

30.5.90	Iceland	2	Albania	0
5.9.90	Iceland	1	France	2
26.9.90	Czechoslovakia	1	Iceland	0
10.10.90	Spain	2	Iceland	1
13.10.90	France	2	Czechoslovakia	1
14.11.90	Czechoslovakia	3	Spain	2
17.11.90	Albania	0	France	1
19.12.90	Spain	9	Albania	0
20.2.91	France	3	Spain	1
30.3.91	France	5	Albania	0
1.5.91	Albania	0	Czechoslovakia	2
26.5.91	Albania	1	Iceland	0
5.6.91	Iceland	0	Czechoslovakia	1
4.9.91	Czechoslovakia		France	
25.9.91	Iceland		Spain	
12.10.91	Spain		France	
16.10.91	Czechoslovakia		Albania	
13.11.91	Spain		Czechoslovakia	
13/20.11.91	France		Iceland	
18.12.91	Albania		Iceland	

	P	W	D	L	F	A	Pts
France	5	5	0	0	13	3	10
Czechoslovakia	5	4	0	1	8	4	8
Spain	4	2	0	2	14	7	4
Iceland	6	1	0	5	4	7	2
Albania	6	1	0	5	1	19	2

GROUP 2

12.9.90	Switzerland	2	Bulgaria	0
12.9.90	Scotland	2	Romania	1
17.10.90	Romania	0	Bulgaria	3
17.10.90	Scotland	2	Switzerland	1
14.11.90	Bulgaria	1	Scotland	1
14.11.90	San Marino	0	Switzerland	4
5.12.90	Romania	6	San Marino	0
27.3.91	Scotland	1	Bulgaria	1
27.3.91	San Marino	1	Romania	3
3.4.91	Switzerland	0	Romania	0
1.5.91	Bulgaria	2	Switzerland	3
1.5.91	San Marino	0	Scotland	2
22.5.91	San Marino	0	Bulgaria	3
5.6.91	Switzerland	7	San Marino	0
11.9.91	Switzerland		Scotland	
16.10.91	Bulgaria		San Marino	
16.10.91	Romania		Scotland	
13.11.91	Scotland		San Marino	
13.11.91	Romania		Switzerland	
20.11.91	Bulgaria		Romania	

	P	W	D	L	F	A	Pts
Switzerland	6	4	1	1	17	4	9
Scotland	5	3	2	0	8	4	8
Bulgaria	6	2	2	2	10	7	6
Romania	5	2	1	2	10	6	5
San Marino	6	0	0	6	1	25	0

28

GROUP 3

12.9.90	USSR	2	Norway	0
10.10.90	Norway	0	Hungary	0
17.10.90	Hungary	1	Italy	1
31.10.90	Hungary	4	Cyprus	2
3.11.90	Italy	0	USSR	0
14.11.90	Cyprus	0	Norway	3
22.12.90	Cyprus	0	Italy	4
3.4.91	Cyprus	0	Hungary	2
17.4.91	Hungary	0	USSR	1
1.5.91	Norway	3	Cyprus	0
1.5.91	Italy	3	Hungary	1
29.5.91	USSR	4	Cyprus	0
5.6.91	Norway	2	Italy	1
28.8.91	Norway		USSR	
25.9.91	USSR		Hungary	
12.10.91	USSR		Italy	
30.10.91	Hungary		Norway	
13.11.91	Italy		Norway	
13.11.91	Cyprus		USSR	
21.12.91	Italy		Cyprus	

	P	W	D	L	F	A	Pts
USSR	4	3	1	0	7	0	7
Norway	5	3	1	1	8	3	7
Italy	5	2	2	1	9	4	6
Hungary	6	2	2	2	8	7	6
Cyprus	6	0	0	6	2	20	0

GROUP 4

12.9.90	Northern Ireland	0	Yugoslavia	2
12.9.90	Faroe Islands	1	Austria	0
10.10.90	Denmark	4	Faroe Islands	1
17.10.90	Northern Ireland	1	Denmark	1
31.10.90	Yugoslavia	4	Austria	1
14.11.90	Denmark	0	Yugoslavia	2
14.11.90	Austria	0	Northern Ireland	0
27.3.91	Yugoslavia	4	Northern Ireland	1
1.5.91	Yugoslavia	1	Denmark	2
1.5.91	Northern Ireland	1	Faroe Islands	1
15.5.91	Yugoslavia	7	Faroe Islands	0
22.5.91	Austria	3	Faroe Islands	0
5.6.91	Denmark	2	Austria	1
11.9.91	Faroe Islands		Northern Ireland	
25.9.91	Faroe Islands		Denmark	
9.10.91	Austria		Denmark	
16.10.91	Faroe Islands		Yugoslavia	
16.10.91	Northern Ireland		Austria	
13.11.91	Denmark		Northern Ireland	
13.11.91	Austria		Yugoslavia	

	P	W	D	L	F	A	Pts
Yugoslavia	6	5	0	1	20	4	10
Denmark	5	3	1	1	9	6	7
Austria	5	1	1	3	5	7	3
Northern Ireland	5	0	3	2	3	8	3
Faroe Islands	5	1	1	3	3	15	3

GROUP 5

17.10.90	Wales	3	Belgium	1
31.10.90	Luxembourg	2	Germany	3
14.11.90	Luxembourg	0	Wales	1
27.2.91	Belgium	3	Luxembourg	0

27.3.91	Belgium	1	Wales	1
1.5.91	Germany	1	Belgium	0
5.6.91	Wales	1	Germany	0
11.9.91	Luxembourg		Belgium	
16.10.91	Germany		Wales	
13.11.91	Wales		Luxembourg	
20.11.91	Belgium		Germany	
17.12.91	Germany		Luxembourg	

	P	W	D	L	F	A	Pts
Wales	4	3	1	0	6	2	7
Germany	3	2	0	1	4	3	4
Belgium	4	1	1	2	5	5	3
Luxembourg	3	0	0	3	2	7	0

GROUP 6

12.9.90	Finland	0	Portugal	0
17.10.90	Portugal	1	Holland	0
31.10.90	Greece	4	Malta	0
21.11.90	Holland	2	Greece	0
25.11.90	Malta	1	Finland	1
19.12.90	Malta	0	Holland	8
23.1.91	Greece	3	Portugal	2
9.2.91	Malta	0	Portugal	1
20.2.91	Portugal	5	Malta	0
13.3.91	Holland	1	Malta	0
17.4.91	Holland	2	Finland	0
16.5.91	Finland	2	Malta	0
5.6.91	Finland	1	Holland	1
11.9.91	Portugal		Finland	
9.10.91	Finland		Greece	
16.10.91	Holland		Portugal	
30.10.91	Greece		Finland	
20.11.91	Portugal		Greece	
4.12.91	Greece		Holland	
22.12.91	Malta		Greece	

	P	W	D	L	F	A	Pts
Holland	6	4	1	1	14	2	9
Portugal	5	3	1	1	9	3	7
Finland	5	1	3	1	4	4	5
Greece	3	2	0	1	7	4	4
Malta	7	0	1	6	1	22	1

GROUP 7

17.10.90	England	2	Poland	0
17.10.90	Rep. of Ireland	5	Turkey	0
14.11.90	Rep. of Ireland	1	England	1
14.11.90	Turkey	0	Poland	1
27.3.91	England	1	Rep. of Ireland	1
17.4.91	Poland	3	Turkey	0
1.5.91	Turkey	0	England	1
1.5.91	Rep. of Ireland	0	Poland	0
16.10.91	Poland		Rep. of Ireland	
16.10.91	England		Turkey	
13.11.91	Turkey		Rep. of Ireland	
13.11.91	Poland		England	

	P	W	D	L	F	A	Pts
England	4	2	2	0	5	2	6
Rep. of Ireland	4	1	3	0	7	2	5
Poland	4	2	1	1	4	2	5
Turkey	4	0	0	4	0	10	0

30

European Championship Finals: Match Schedule

10th–26th June 1992, Sweden

Date	Match	Venue	Time	Teams	Group
10.6.92	1	Stockholm	20.15	1 – 2	I
11.6.92	2	Malmö	20.15	3 – 4	I
12.6.92	3	Göteborg	17.15	5 – 6	II
12.6.92	4	Norrköping	20.15	7 – 8	II
14.6.92	5	Stockholm	20.15	1 – 3	I
14.6.92	6	Malmö	17.15	2 – 4	I
15.6.92	7	Göteborg	20.15	5 – 7	II
15.6.92	8	Norrköping	17.15	6 – 8	II
17.6.92	9	Stockholm	20.15	1 – 4	I
17.6.92	10	Malmö	20.15	2 – 3	I
18.6.92	11	Göteborg	20.15	5 – 8	II
18.6.92	12	Norrköping	20.15	6 – 7	II
21.6.92	13	Stockholm	20.15	I: 1 – II:2	1/2 Final
22.6.92	14	Göteborg	20.15	II: 1 – I: 2	1/2 Final
26.6.92	15	Göteborg	20.15 FINAL		

European Championship for Under-21 Teams 1990-92

Qualifying Competition

GROUP 1

29.5.90	Iceland	0	Albania	0
4.9.90	Iceland	0	France	1
25.9.90	Czechoslovakia	7	Iceland	0
9.10.90	Spain	2	Iceland	0
12.10.90	France	1	Czechoslovakia	2
13.11.90	Czechoslovakia	3	Spain	1
16.11.90	Albania	0	France	0
18.12.90	Spain	1	Albania	0
19.2.91	France	0	Spain	1
29.3.91	France	3	Albania	0
30.4.91	Albania	1	Czechoslovakia	5
25.5.91	Albania	2	Iceland	1
4.6.91	Iceland		Czechoslovakia	
3.9.91	Czechoslovakia		France	
24.9.91	Iceland		Spain	
11.10.91	Spain		France	
15.10.91	Czechoslovakia		Albania	
12.11.91	France		Iceland	
12.11.91	Spain		Czechoslovakia	
17.12.91	Albania		Spain	

	P	W	D	L	F	A	Pts
Czechoslovakia	4	4	0	0	17	3	8
Spain	4	3	0	1	5	3	6
France	5	2	1	2	5	3	5
Albania	6	1	2	3	3	10	4
Iceland	5	0	1	4	1	12	1

GROUP 2

11.9.90	Scotland	2	Romania	0
11.9.90	Switzerland	0	Bulgaria	2
16.10.90	Romania	0	Bulgaria	1
16.10.90	Scotland	4	Switzerland	2
13.11.90	Bulgaria	2	Scotland	0
26.3.91	Scotland	1	Bulgaria	0
2.4.91	Switzerland	0	Romania	2
30.4.91	Bulgaria	1	Switzerland	0
10.9.91	Switzerland		Scotland	
15.10.91	Romania		Scotland	
12.11.91	Romania		Switzerland	
19.11.91	Bulgaria		Romania	

	P	W	D	L	F	A	Pts
Bulgaria	5	4	0	1	6	1	8
Scotland	4	3	0	1	7	4	6
Romania	3	1	0	2	2	3	2
Switzerland	4	0	0	4	2	9	0

GROUP 3

11.9.90	USSR	2	Norway	2
9.10.90	Norway	3	Hungary	1
18.10.90	Italy	1	Hungary	0
18.4.91	Hungary	0	USSR	0

2.5.91	Hungary	0	Italy	1
5.6.91	Norway	6	Italy	0
12.6.91	Italy	1	USSR	0
27.8.91	Norway		USSR	
26.9.91	USSR		Hungary	
16.10.91	USSR		Italy	
29.10.91	Hungary		Norway	
13.11.91	Italy		Norway	

	P	W	D	L	F	A	Pts
Italy	4	3	0	1	3	6	6
Norway	3	2	1	0	11	3	5
USSR	3	0	2	1	2	3	2
Hungary	4	0	1	3	1	2	1

GROUP 4

17.10.90	San Marino	0	Denmark	3
30.10.90	Yugoslavia	1	Austria	0
12.11.90	Denmark	3	Yugoslavia	0
21.11.90	San Marino	0	Austria	2
13.3.91	Yugoslavia	5	San Marino	0
3.4.91	Austria	3	San Marino	0
17.4.91	Denmark	7	San Marino	0
30.4.91	Yugoslavia	2	Denmark	6
4.6.91	Denmark	1	Austria	1
2.10.91	San Marino		Yugoslavia	
8.10.91	Austria		Denmark	
12.11.91	Austria		Yugoslavia	

	P	W	D	L	F	A	Pts
Denmark	5	4	1	0	20	3	9
Austria	4	2	1	1	6	2	5
Yugoslavia	4	2	0	2	8	9	4
San Marino	5	0	0	5	0	20	0

GROUP 5

30.10.90	Luxembourg	0	Germany	3
26.2.91	Belgium	2	Luxembourg	0
30.4.91	Germany	3	Belgium	1
10.9.91	Luxembourg		Belgium	
19.11.91	Belgium		Germany	
17.12.91	Germany		Luxembourg	

	P	W	D	L	F	A	Pts
Germany	2	2	0	0	6	1	4
Belgium	2	1	0	1	3	3	2
Luxembourg	2	0	0	2	0	5	0

GROUP 6

11.9.90	Finland	0	Portugal	1
16.10.90	Portugal	0	Holland	0
18.12.90	Malta	1	Holland	4
8.2.91	Malta	1	Portugal	3
19.2.91	Portugal	2	Malta	0
12.3.91	Holland	7	Malta	1
16.4.91	Holland	1	Finland	0
4.6.91	Finland	1	Holland	7
26.6.91	Finland		Malta	
10.9.91	Portugal		Finland	
15.10.91	Holland		Portugal	
16.10.91	Malta		Finland	

33

	P	W	D	L	F	A	Pts
Holland	5	4	1	0	19	3	9
Portugal	4	3	1	0	6	1	7
Finland	3	0	0	3	1	9	0
Malta	4	0	0	4	3	16	0

GROUP 7

16.10.90	England	0	Poland	1
16.10.90	Rep. of Ireland	3	Turkey	2
13.11.90	Rep. of Ireland	0	England	3
13.11.90	Turkey	0	Poland	1
26.3.91	England	3	Rep. of Ireland	0
16.4.91	Poland	2	Turkey	0
30.4.91	Rep. of Ireland	1	Poland	2
30.4.91	Turkey	2	England	2
15.10.91	England		Turkey	
15.10.91	Poland		Rep. of Ireland	
12.11.91	Poland		England	
12.11.91	Turkey		Rep. of Ireland	

	P	W	D	L	F	A	Pts
Poland	4	4	0	0	6	1	8
England	4	2	1	1	8	3	5
Rep. of Ireland	4	1	0	3	4	10	2
Turkey	4	0	1	3	4	8	1

GROUP 8

31.10.90	Sweden	5	Greece	0
21.11.90	Cyprus	1	Sweden	1
21.11.90	Greece	2	Israel	2
20.3.91	Israel	4	Cyprus	0
17.4.91	Cyprus	1	Greece	0
1.5.91	Sweden	6	Cyprus	0
16.10.91	Sweden		Israel	
30.10.91	Israel		Greece	
14.11.91	Israel		Sweden	
20.11.91	Greece		Sweden	
4.12.91	Cyprus		Israel	
18.12.91	Greece		Cyprus	

	P	W	D	L	F	A	Pts
Sweden	3	2	1	0	12	1	5
Israel	2	1	1	0	6	2	3
Cyprus	4	1	1	2	2	11	3
Greece	3	0	1	2	2	8	1

Under-21 International Matches 1976-91

EC European Under-21 Championship

ENGLAND v ALBANIA

Year	Date		Venue	Goals	
				Eng	Alb
EC1989	Mar.	7	Shkoder	2	1
EC1989	Apr.	25	Ipswich	2	0

ENGLAND v BULGARIA

Year	Date		Venue	Goals	
				Eng	Bulg
EC1979	June	5	Pernik	3	1
EC1979	Nov.	20	Leicester	5	0
1989	June	5	Toulon	2	3

ENGLAND v CZECHOSLOVAKIA

Year	Date		Venue	Goals	
				Eng	Czech
1990	May	27	Toulon	2	1

ENGLAND v DENMARK

Year	Date		Venue	Goals	
				Eng	Den
EC1978	Sep.	19	Hvidovre	2	1
EC1979	Sep.	11	Watford	1	0
EC1982	Sep.	21	Hvidovre	4	1
EC1983	Sep.	20	Norwich	4	1
EC1986	Mar.	12	Copenhagen	1	0
EC1986	Mar.	26	Manchester City	1	1
1988	Sep.	13	Watford	0	0

ENGLAND v FINLAND

Year	Date		Venue	Goals	
				Eng	Fin
EC1977	May	26	Helsinki	1	0
EC1977	Oct.	12	Hull	8	1
EC1984	Oct.	16	Southampton	2	0
EC1985	May	21	Mikkeli	1	3

ENGLAND v FRANCE

Year	Date		Venue		Eng	France
EC1984	Feb.	28	Sheffield Wednesday		6	1
EC1984	Mar.	28	Rouen		1	0
1987	June	11	Toulon		0	2
EC1988	Apr.	13	Besancon		2	4
EC1988	Apr.	27	Highbury		2	2
1988	June	12	Toulon		2	4
1990	May	23	Aix-en-Provence		7	3
1991	June	3	Toulon		1	0

ENGLAND v EAST GERMANY

Year	Date		Venue		Eng	EG
EC1980	Apr.	16	Sheffield United		1	2
EC1980	Apr.	23	Jena		0	1

ENGLAND v WEST GERMANY

Year	Date		Venue		Eng	WG
EC1982	Sep.	21	Sheffield United		3	1
EC1982	Oct.	12	Bremen		2	3
1987	Sep.	8	Lüdenscheid		0	2

ENGLAND v GREECE

Year	Date		Venue		Eng	Greece
EC1982	Nov.	16	Piraeus		0	1
EC1983	Mar.	29	Portsmouth		2	1
1989	Feb.	7	Patras		0	1

ENGLAND v HUNGARY

Year	Date		Venue		Eng	Hung
EC1981	June	5	Keszthely		2	1

ENGLAND v HUNGARY

Year	Date		Venue	Goals	
				Eng	Hung
EC1981	Nov.	17	Nottingham Forest	2	0
EC1983	Apr.	26	Newcastle	1	0
EC1983	Oct.	11	Nyiregyhaza	2	0
1990	Sep.	11	Southampton	3	1

ENGLAND v ISRAEL

Year	Date		Venue	Goals	
				Eng	Israel
1985	Feb.	27	Tel Aviv	2	1

ENGLAND v ITALY

Year	Date		Venue	Goals	
				Eng	Italy
EC1978	Mar.	8	Manchester City	2	1
EC1978	Apr.	5	Rome	0	0
EC1984	Apr.	18	Manchester City	3	1
EC1984	May	2	Florence	0	1
EC1986	Apr.	9	Pisa	0	2
EC1986	Apr.	23	Swindon	1	1

ENGLAND v MEXICO

Year	Date		Venue	Goals	
				Eng	Mex
1988	June	5	Toulon	2	1
1991	May	29	Vitrolles	6	0

ENGLAND v MOROCCO

Year	Date		Venue	Goals	
				Eng	Mor
1987	June	7	Toulon	2	0
1988	June	9	Toulon	1	0

ENGLAND v NORWAY

Year	Date		Venue	Goals	
				Eng	Nor
EC1977	June	1	Bergen	2	1
EC1977	Sep.	6	Brighton	6	0
1980	Sep.	9	Southampton	3	0
1981	Sep.	8	Drammen	0	0

ENGLAND v POLAND

Year	Date		Venue	Goals	
				Eng	Pol
EC1982	Mar.	17	Warsaw	2	1
EC1982	Apr.	7	West Ham	2	2
EC1989	June	2	Plymouth	2	1
EC1989	Oct.	10	Jastrzebie Zdroj	3	1
EC1990	Oct.	16	Tottenham	0	1

ENGLAND v PORTUGAL

Year	Date		Venue	Goals	
				Eng	Port
1987	June	13	Sollies-Pont	0	0
1990	May	21	Six-Fours	0	1

ENGLAND v REPUBLIC OF IRELAND

Year	Date		Venue		Eng	Rep of Ire
1981	Feb.	25	Liverpool		1	0
1985	Mar.	25	Portsmouth		3	2
1989	June	9	Six-Fours		0	0
EC1990	Nov.	13	Cork		3	0
EC1991	Mar.	26	Brentford		3	0

ENGLAND v ROMANIA

Year	Date		Venue	Goals	
				Eng	Rom
EC1980	Oct.	14	Ploesti	0	4
EC1981	Apr.	28	Swindon	3	0

Year	Date	Venue	Goals	
			Eng	Rom
EC1985	Apr. 30	Brasov	0	0
EC1985	Sep. 9	Ipswich	3	0

ENGLAND v SCOTLAND

Year	Date	Venue	Eng	Scot
1977	Apr. 27	Sheffield United	1	0
EC1980	Feb. 12	Coventry......................	2	1
EC1980	Mar. 4	Aberdeen	0	0
EC1982	Apr. 19	Glasgow	1	0
EC1982	Apr. 28	Manchester City	1	1
EC1988	Feb. 16	Aberdeen	1	0
EC1988	Mar. 22	Nottingham	1	0

ENGLAND v SENEGAL

Year	Date	Venue	Eng	Sen
1989	June 7	Sainte-Maxime	6	1
1991	May 27	Arles	2	1

ENGLAND v SPAIN

Year	Date	Venue	Eng	Spain
EC1984	May 17	Seville	1	0
EC1984	May 24	Sheffield United	2	0
1987	Feb. 18	Burgos	2	1

ENGLAND v SWEDEN

Year	Date	Venue	Eng	Swe
1979	June 9	Vasteras	2	1
1986	Sep. 9	Oestersund	1	1
EC1988	Oct. 18	Coventry	1	1
EC1989	Sep. 5	Uppsala	0	1

ENGLAND v SWITZERLAND

Year	Date	Venue	Eng	Swit
EC1980	Nov. 18	Ipswich	5	0
EC1981	May 31	Neuenburg	0	0
1988	May 28	Lausanne	1	1

ENGLAND v TURKEY

Year	Date	Venue	Eng	Turk
EC1984	Nov. 13	Bursa	0	0
EC1985	Oct. 15	Bristol	3	0
EC1987	Apr. 28	Izmir	0	0
EC1987	Oct. 13	Sheffield	1	1
EC1991	Apr. 30	Izmir	2	2

ENGLAND v USA

Year	Date	Venue	Eng	USA
1989	June 11	Toulon	0	2

ENGLAND v USSR

Year	Date	Venue	Eng	USSR
1987	June 9	La Ciotat	0	0
1988	June 7	Six-Fours	1	0
1990	May 25	Toulon	2	1
1991	May 31	Aix-en-Provence	2	1

ENGLAND v WALES

Year	Date	Venue	Eng	Wales
1976	Dec. 15	Wolverhampton............	0	0
1979	Feb. 6	Swansea	1	0
1990	Dec. 5	Tranmere	0	0

ENGLAND v YUGOSLAVIA

Year	Date	Venue	Eng	Yugo
EC1978	Apr. 19	Novi Sad	1	2
EC1978	May 2	Manchester City	1	1
EC1986	Nov. 11	Peterborough	1	1
EC1987	Nov. 10	Zemun	5	1

England Under-21 Caps 1990-91

	Hungary	Poland	Republic of Ireland	Wales	Republic of Ireland	Turkey	Senegal	Mexico	U.S.S.R.	France
A. Miller (Arsenal)	1	1								
G. Charles (Nottingham Forest)	2			*2	2					
L. Sharpe (Manchester United)	3	*6	11							
P. Warhurst (Oldham Athletic)	4	4		2			5	*7	2	*4
D. Lee (Chelsea)	5	5	4		4	4	4		4	4
C. Tiler (Barnsley and Nottingham Forest)	6	6	6		6	.6	6		3	6
J. Ebbrell (Everton)	7	7	7	7		8				
K. Campbell (Arsenal)	8					*10				
I. Olney (Aston Villa)	9	9	9		10	10				
M. Blake (Aston Villa)	10	10	8	4	7					
R. Wallace (Southampton and Leeds United)	11	11			11	11	7	7	7	7
C. Vinnicombe (Rangers)	*3	3	3		3	3	3	3	*11	3
M. Robins (Manchester United)	*8	8								
T. Johnson (Notts County)	*11				*7					
J. Dodd (Southampton)		2	2			2	2	2		2
A. Shearer (Southampton)		*9	10	9	9	9	9	9	9	9
D. James (Watford)			1		1	1	1	1	1	1
J. Cundy (Chelsea)			5		5					
I. Walker (Tottenham Hotspur)				1						
S. Minto (Charlton Athletic)				3						
B. Atkinson (Sunderland)				*4			11	11	*10	11
D. Blackwell (Wimbledon)				5		5	*4	5	5	5
R. Ord (Sunderland)				6				6	6	
C. Ramage (Derby County)				8						
N. Jemson (Nottingham Forest)				10						
S. McManaman (Liverpool)				11				*9		
D. Matthew (Chelsea)					8			4	8	8
M. Draper (Notts County)					*8					
D. Hillier (Arsenal)						7				
G. Stuart (Chelsea)						*7				
G. Watson (Sheffield Wednesday)							8		11	
P. Kitson (Leicester City)							*8	8		10
P. Williams (Derby County)							10	10	10	

* Substitute

37

England Under-21 Caps 1976-91

(Up to and including 3rd June 1991)

Player	*Caps*
Ablett, G. (Liverpool)	1
Adams, N. (Everton)	1
Adams, T. (Arsenal)	5
Allen, C. (Q.P.R. and Crystal Palace)	3
Allen, M. (Q.P.R.)	2
Allen, P. (West Ham and Tottenham Hotspur)	3
Anderson, V. (Nottingham Forest)	1
Andrews, I. (Leicester City)	1
Atkinson, B. (Sunderland)	5
Bailey, G. (Manchester United)	14
Baker, G. (Southampton)	2
Bannister, G. (Sheffield Wednesday)	1
Barker, S. (Blackburn Rovers)	4
Barnes, J. (Watford)	3
Barnes, P. (Manchester City)	9
Barrett, E. (Oldham Athletic)	4
Batty, D. (Leeds United)	7
Beagrie, P. (Sheffield United)	2
Beardsmore, R. (Manchester United)	5
Beeston, C. (Stoke City)	1
Bertschin, K. (Birmingham City)	3
Birtles, G. (Nottingham Forest)	2
Blackwell, D. (Wimbledon)	6
Blake, M. (Aston Villa)	7
Blissett, L. (Watford)	4
Bracewell, P. (Stoke, Sunderland and Everton)	13
Bradshaw, P. (Wolverhampton)	4
Breacker, T. (Luton Town)	2
Brennan, M. (Ipswich Town)	5
Brightwell, I. (Manchester City)	4
Brock, K. (Oxford United)	4
Bull, S. (Wolverhampton)	5
Burrows, D. (W.B.A. and Liverpool)	7
Butcher, T. (Ipswich Town)	7
Butters, G. (Tottenham Hotspur)	3
Butterworth, I. (Coventry and Nottingham Forest)	8
Caesar, G. (Arsenal)	3
Callaghan, N. (Watford)	9
Campbell, K. (Arsenal)	2
Carr, C. (Fulham)	1
Carr, F. (Nottingham Forest)	9
Caton, T. (Man. City and Arsenal)	14
Chamberlain, M. (Stoke City)	4
Chapman, L. (Stoke City)	1
Charles, G. (Nottingham Forest)	5
Chettle, S. (Nottingham Forest)	12
Clough, N. (Nottingham Forest)	15
Coney, D. (Fulham)	4
Connor, T. (Brighton & H.A.)	1
Cooke, R. (Tottenham Hotspur)	1

Player	*Caps*
Cooper, C. (Middlesbrough)	8
Corrigan, J. (Manchester City)	3
Cottee, T. (West Ham United)	10
Cowans, G. (Aston Villa)	5
Cranson, I. (Ipswich Town)	5
Crooks, G. (Stoke City)	4
Crossley, M. (Nottingham Forest)	3
Cundy, J. (Chelsea)	2
Cunningham, L. (W.B.A.)	6
Curbishley, A. (Birmingham City)	1
Daniel, P. (Hull City)	7
Davis, P. (Arsenal)	11
D'Avray, M. (Ipswich Town)	2
Deehan, J. (Aston Villa)	7
Dennis, M. (Birmingham City)	3
Dickens, A. (West Ham United)	1
Dicks, J. (West Ham United)	4
Digby, F. (Swindon Town)	5
Dillon, K. (Birmingham City)	1
Dixon, K. (Chelsea)	1
Dobson, T. (Coventry City)	4
Dodd, J. (Southampton)	6
Donowa, L. (Norwich City)	3
Dorigo, T. (Aston Villa and Chelsea)	11
Dozzell, J. (Ipswich Town)	9
Draper, M. (Notts County)	1
Duxbury, M. (Manchester United)	7
Dyson, P. (Coventry City)	4
Ebbrell, J. (Everton)	12
Elliott, P. (Luton and Aston Villa)	3
Fairclough, C. (Nottingham Forest and Tottenham Hotspur)	7
Fairclough, D. (Liverpool)	1
Fashanu, J. (Norwich and Nottingham Forest)	11
Fenwick, T. (Q.P.R.)	11
Fereday, W. (Q.P.R.)	5
Flowers, T. (Southampton)	3
Forsyth, M. (Derby County)	1
Foster, S. (Brighton & H.A.)	1
Futcher, P. (Luton and Man. City)	11
Gabbiadini, M. (Sunderland)	2
Gale, A. (Fulham)	1
Gascoigne, P. (Newcastle United)	13
Gayle, H. (Birmingham City)	3
Gernon, I. (Ipswich Town)	1
Gibbs, N. (Watford)	5
Gibson, C. (Aston Villa)	1
Gilbert, W. (Crystal Palace)	11
Goddard, P. (West Ham United)	8
Gordon, D. (Norwich City)	4

Player	Caps
Gray, A. (Aston Villa)	2
Haigh, P. (Hull City)	1
Hardyman, P. (Portsmouth)	2
Hateley, M. (Coventry and Portsmouth)	10
Hayes, M. (Arsenal)	3
Hazell, R. (Wolverhampton)	1
Heath, A. (Stoke City)	8
Hesford, I. (Blackpool)	7
Hilaire, V. (Crystal Palace)	9
Hillier, D. (Arsenal)	1
Hinchcliffe, A. (Manchester City)	1
Hinshelwood, P. (Crystal Palace)	2
Hirst, D. (Sheffield Wednesday)	7
Hoddle, G. (Tottenham Hotspur)	12
Hodge, S. (Nottingham Forest and Aston Villa)	8
Hodgson, D. (Middlesbrough and Liverpool)	7
Holdsworth, D. (Watford)	1
Horne, B. (Millwall)	5
Hucker, P. (Q.P.R.)	2
Ince, P. (West Ham United)	2
James, D. (Watford)	7
James, J. (Luton Town)	2
Jemson, N. (Nottingham Forest)	1
Johnson, T. (Notts County)	2
Johnston, C. (Middlesbrough)	2
Jones, C. (Tottenham Hotspur)	1
Jones, D. (Everton)	1
Keegan, G. (Oldham Athletic)	1
Keown, M. (Aston Villa)	8
Kerslake, D. (Q.P.R.)	1
Kilcline, B. (Notts County)	2
King, A. (Everton)	2
Kitson, P. (Leicester City)	3
Knight, A. (Portsmouth)	2
Knight, I. (Sheffield Wednesday)	2
Lake, P. (Manchester City)	5
Langley, T. (Chelsea)	1
Lee, D. (Chelsea)	9
Lee, R. (Charlton Athletic)	2
Lee, S. (Liverpool)	6
Le Saux, G. (Chelsea)	4
Lowe, D. (Ipswich Town)	2
Lukic, J. (Leeds United)	7
Lund, G. (Grimsby Town)	1
McCall, S. (Ipswich Town)	6
McDonald, N. (Newcastle United)	5
McGrath, L. (Coventry City)	1
McLeary, A. (Millwall)	1

Player	Caps
McMahon, S. (Everton and Aston Villa)	6
McManaman, S. (Liverpool)	2
Mabbutt, G. (Bristol Rovers and Tottenham Hotspur)	6
Mackenzie, S. (W.B.A.)	3
Martin, L. (Manchester United)	2
Martyn, N. (Bristol Rovers)	11
Matthew, D. (Chelsea)	7
May, A. (Manchester City)	1
Merson, P. (Arsenal)	4
Middleton, J. (Nottingham Forest and Derby County)	3
Miller, A. (Arsenal)	4
Mills, G. (Nottingham Forest)	2
Mimms, R. (Rotherham and Everton)	3
Minto, S. (Charlton Athletic)	1
Moran, S. (Southampton)	2
Morgan, S. (Leicester City)	2
Mortimer, P. (Charlton Athletic)	2
Moses, R. (W.B.A. and Man. United)	8
Mountfield, D. (Everton)	1
Muggleton, C. (Leicester City)	1
Mutch, A. (Wolverhampton)	1
Newell, M. (Luton Town)	4
Oldfield, D. (Luton Town)	1
Olney, I. (Aston Villa)	9
Ord, R. (Sunderland)	3
Osman, R. (Ipswich Town)	7
Owen, G. (Man. City and W.B.A.)	22
Painter, I. (Stoke City)	1
Palmer, C. (Sheffield Wednesday)	4
Parker, G. (Hull City and Nottingham Forest)	6
Parker, P. (Fulham)	8
Parkes, P. (Q.P.R.)	1
Parkin, S. (Stoke City)	6
Peach, D. (Southampton)	8
Peake, A. (Leicester City)	1
Pearce, S. (Nottingham Forest)	1
Pickering, N. (Sunderland and Coventry)	15
Platt, D. (Aston Villa)	3
Porter, G. (Watford)	12
Pressman, K. (Sheffield Wednesday)	1
Proctor, M. (Middlesbrough and Nottingham Forest)	5
Ramage, C. (Derby County)	1
Ranson, R. (Manchester City)	11
Redmond, S. (Manchester City)	14
Reeves, K. (Norwich and Man. City)	10
Regis, C. (W.B.A.)	6

Player	Caps
Reid, N. (Manchester City)	6
Reid, P. (Bolton Wanderers)	6
Richards, J. (Wolverhampton)	2
Rideout, P. (Aston Villa and Bari)	6
Ripley, S. (Middlesbrough)	8
Ritchie, A. (Brighton & H.A.)	1
Rix, G. (Arsenal)	7
Robins, M. (Manchester United)	6
Robson, B. (W.B.A.)	7
Robson, S. (Arsenal and West Ham United)	8
Rocastle, D. (Arsenal)	14
Rodger, G. (Coventry City)	4
Rosario, R. (Norwich City)	4
Rowell, G. (Sunderland)	1
Ruddock, N. (Southampton)	4
Ryan, J. (Oldham Athletic)	1
Samways, V. (Tottenham Hotspur)	5
Sansom, K. (Crystal Palace)	8
Seaman, D. (Birmingham City)	10
Sedgley, S. (Coventry and Tottenham)	11
Sellars, S. (Blackburn Rovers)	3
Sharpe, L. (Manchester United)	8
Shaw, G. (Aston Villa)	7
Shearer, A. (Southampton)	9
Shelton, G. (Sheffield Wednesday)	1
Sheringham, T. (Millwall)	1
Sherwood, T. (Norwich City)	4
Simpson, P. (Manchester City)	5
Sims, S. (Leicester City)	10
Sinnott, L. (Watford)	1
Slater, S. (West Ham United)	3
Smith, D. (Coventry City)	10
Smith, M. (Sheffield Wednesday)	5
Snodin, I. (Doncaster Rovers and Leeds United)	4
Statham, B. (Tottenham Hotspur)	3
Statham, D. (W.B.A.)	6
Stein, B. (Luton Town)	3
Sterland, M. (Sheffield Wednesday)	7
Steven, T. (Everton)	2
Stevens, G. (Everton)	1
Stevens, G. (Brighton & H.A. and Tottenham Hotspur)	7
Stewart, P. (Manchester City)	1
Stuart, G. (Chelsea)	5
Suckling, P. (Coventry, Man. City and Crystal Palace)	10
Sunderland, A. (Wolverhampton)	1

Player	Caps
Swindlehurst, D. (Crystal Palace)	1
Talbot, B. (Ipswich Town)	1
Thomas, D. (Coventry and Tottenham Hotspur)	7
Thomas, M. (Arsenal)	12
Thomas, M. (Luton Town)	3
Thomas, R. (Watford)	1
Thompson, G. (Coventry City)	6
Thorn, A. (Wimbledon)	5
Tiler, C. (Barnsley and Nottingham Forest)	11
Venison, B. (Sunderland)	10
Vinnicombe, C. (Rangers)	9
Waddle, C. (Newcastle United)	1
Walker, D. (Nottingham Forest)	7
Walker, I. (Tottenham Hotspur)	1
Wallace, D. (Southampton)	14
Wallace, Ray (Southampton)	4
Wallace, Rodney (Southampton)	11
Walsh, G. (Manchester United)	2
Walsh, P. (Luton Town)	7
Walters, M. (Aston Villa)	9
Ward, P. (Brighton & H.A.)	2
Warhurst, P. (Oldham Athletic)	7
Watson, D. (Norwich City)	7
Watson, G. (Sheffield Wednesday)	2
Webb, N. (Portsmouth and Nottingham Forest)	3
White, D. (Manchester City)	6
Whyte, C. (Arsenal)	4
Wicks, S. (Q.P.R.)	1
Wilkins, R. (Chelsea)	1
Wilkinson, P. (Grimsby Town and Everton)	4
Williams, P. (Charlton Athletic)	4
Williams, P. (Derby County)	3
Williams, S. (Southampton)	14
Winterburn, N. (Wimbledon)	1
Wise, D. (Wimbledon)	1
Woodcock, A. (Nottingham Forest)	2
Woods, C. (Nottingham Forest, Q.P.R. and Norwich)	6
Wright, M. (Southampton)	4
Wright, W. (Everton)	6
Yates, D. (Notts County)	5

ONCE DRIVEN, FOREVER SMITTEN.

CALIBRA.

VAUXHALL

PATRICK

NOTHING > LESS

England 'B' Matches 1949-91

England 'B' Caps 1978-91

(Up to and including 20th May 1991)

Player	Caps
Ablett, G. (Liverpool)	1
Adams, T. (Arsenal)	4
Anderson, V. (Nottingham Forest)	7
Armstrong, D. (Middlesbrough)	2
Atkinson, D. (Sheffield Wednesday)	1
Bailey, G. (Manchester United)	2
Bailey, J. (Everton)	1
Barnes, P. (W.B.A.)	1
Barrett, E. (Oldham Athletic)	2
Barton, W. (Wimbledon)	1
Batson, B. (W.B.A.)	3
Batty, D. (Leeds United)	4
Beagrie, P. (Everton)	2
Beardsley, P. (Liverpool)	1
Beasant, D. (Chelsea)	7
Birtles, G. (Nottingham Forest)	1
Bishop, I. (West Ham United)	1
Blissett, L. (Watford)	1
Bond, K. (Norwich and Manchester City)	2
Borrows, B. (Coventry City)	1
Brock, K. (Q.P.R.)	1
Bruce, S. (Norwich City)	1
Bull, S. (Wolves)	5
Burrows, D. (Liverpool)	3
Butcher, T. (Ipswich Town)	1
Callaghan, N. (Watford)	1
Chapman, L. (Leeds United)	1
Clough, N. (Nottingham Forest)	3
Corrigan, J. (Manchester City)	10
Cowans, G. (Aston Villa)	2
Crook, I. (Norwich City)	1
Cunningham, L. (W.B.A.)	1
Curle, K. (Wimbledon)	2
Daley, S. (Wolves)	6
Daley, T. (Aston Villa)	1
Davenport, P. (Nottingham Forest)	1
Davis, P. (Arsenal)	1
Deane, B. (Sheffield United)	2
Devonshire, A. (West Ham United)	1
Dixon, L. (Arsenal)	3
Dorigo, T. (Chelsea)	5
Ebbrell, J. (Everton)	1
Elliott, P. (Celtic)	1
Elliott, S. (Sunderland)	3
Eves, M. (Wolves)	3
Fairclough, C. (Tottenham)	1
Fairclough, D. (Liverpool)	1
Fashanu, J. (Nottingham Forest)	1
Flanagan, M. (Charlton and Crystal Palace)	3
Ford, T. (W.B.A.)	3
Forsyth, M. (Derby County)	1

Player	Caps
Gabbiadini, M. (Sunderland)	1
Gallagher, J. (Birmingham)	1
Gascoigne, P. (Tottenham)	4
Geddis, D. (Ipswich Town)	1
Gibson, C. (Aston Villa)	1
Gidman, J. (Aston Villa)	2
Goddard, P. (West Ham United)	1
Gordon, D. (Norwich City)	2
Greenhoff, B. (Manchester United)	1
Harford, M. (Luton Town)	1
Hazell, R. (Wolves)	1
Heath, A. (Everton)	1
Hilaire, V. (Crystal Palace)	1
Hill, G. (Manchester United and Derby County)	6
Hirst, D. (Sheffield Wednesday)	1
Hoddle, G. (Tottenham)	2
Hodge, S. (Nottingham Forest)	2
Hollins, J. (Q.P.R.)	5
Hurlock, T. (Millwall)	3
Johnston, C. (Liverpool)	1
Joseph, R. (Wimbledon)	2
Kennedy, A. (Liverpool)	7
King, P. (Sheffield Wednesday)	1
Lake, P. (Manchester City)	1
Langley, T. (Chelsea)	3
Laws, B. (Nottingham Forest)	1
Le Saux, G. (Chelsea)	1
Le Tissier, M. (Southampton)	2
Lineker, G. (Leicester City)	1
Linighan, A. (Norwich City)	4
Lukic, J. (Leeds United)	1
Lyons, M. (Everton)	1
McCall, S. (Ipswich Town)	1
McDermott, T. (Liverpool)	1
McLeary, A. (Millwall)	3
McMahon, S. (Aston Villa and Liverpool)	2
Mabbutt, G. (Tottenham)	7
Mackenzie, S. (Manchester City and Charlton)	3
Mariner, P. (Ipswich Town)	7
Martin, A. (West Ham United)	2
Martyn, N. (Bristol Rovers and Crystal Palace)	4
Money, R. (Liverpool)	1
Morley, T. (Aston Villa)	2
Mortimer, D. (Aston Villa)	3
Mountfield, D. (Everton)	1
Mowbray, T. (Middlesbrough)	3
Mutch, A. (Wolves)	3

Player	Caps
Naylor, S. (W.B.A.)	3
Needham, D. (Nottingham Forest)	6
Newell, M. (Everton)	2
Osman, R. (Ipswich Town)	2
Owen, G. (Manchester City)	7
Pallister, G. (Middlesbrough and Manchester United)	8
Palmer, C. (Sheffield Wednesday)	2
Parker, G. (Nottingham Forest)	1
Parker, P. (Q.P.R.)	3
Parkes, P. (West Ham United)	2
Peach, D. (Southampton)	1
Platt, D. (Aston Villa)	3
Power, P. (Manchester City)	1
Preece, D. (Luton Town)	3
Reeves, K. (Manchester City)	3
Regis, C. (W.B.A.)	3
Richards, J. (Wolves)	3
Rix, G. (Arsenal)	3
Roberts, G. (Tottenham)	1
Robson, B. (W.B.A. and Manchester United)	3
Roeder, G. (Orient and Q.P.R.)	6
Sansom, K. (Crystal Palace)	2
Seaman, D. (Q.P.R.)	3
Sims, S. (Leicester City)	1
Sinton, A. (Q.P.R.)	1
Slater, S. (West Ham United)	1
Smith, A. (Arsenal)	2

Player	Caps
Snodin, I. (Everton)	2
Speight, M. (Sheffield United)	4
Spink, N. (Aston Villa)	2
Statham, D. (W.B.A.)	2
Sterland, M. (Sheffield Wednesday and Leeds)	3
Stevens, G. (Everton)	1
Stewart, P. (Tottenham)	4
Sunderland, A. (Arsenal)	7
Talbot, B. (Ipswich and Arsenal)	8
Thomas, G. (Crystal Palace)	2
Thomas, M. (Arsenal)	4
Thomas, M. (Tottenham)	1
Thompson, P. (Liverpool)	1
Waldron, M. (Southampton)	1
Wallace, D. (Manchester United)	1
Wallace, R. (Southampton)	1
Walters, M. (Rangers)	1
Ward, P. (Nottingham Forest)	2
Webb, N. (Manchester United)	2
White, D. (Manchester City)	1
Williams, P. (Charlton Athletic)	3
Williams, S. (Southampton)	4
Winterburn, N. (Arsenal)	2
Wise, D. (Wimbledon)	3
Woodcock, T. (Cologne)	1
Woods, C. (Norwich & Rangers)	2
Wright, B. (Everton)	2
Wright, I. (Crystal Palace)	2

The England team pictured before the friendly with Cameroon in February.

England's International Matches 1990-91

England 3   Hungary 1
(Under-21)
11th September 1990, Southampton

The dawning of a new era for England's national teams, with Graham Taylor and Lawrie McMenemy having been appointed after the World Cup as Team Manager and Manager's Assistant respectively, began with an Under-21 friendly at The Dell. The venue was appropriate in a way, given that McMenemy had guided Southampton to FA Cup Final success in the 1970s.

The match had a less than perfect start for the home team, as Hungary took the lead with Farfas's penalty-kick after only two minutes, and England were still behind as the second half got under way.

Mark Robins, the Manchester United striker and former pupil at the FA's National School at Lilleshall, was introduced for Kevin Campbell at half-time and had swept in the equaliser within six minutes of coming on. But England left it late before finally securing victory, Mark Blake and substitute Tommy Johnson both managing to hit the target in the last four minutes.

England: Miller, Charles, Sharpe (Vinnicombe), Warhurst, Lee, Tiler, Ebbrell, Campbell (Robins), Olney, Blake, Wallace (Johnson).

Hungary: Jegh, Kuttor, Telek, Klausz, Banfi, Geress, Cservenkai, Farfas, Banfoldi (Belvon), Pisont (Komodi), Kaman.

Referee: R. Larsson (Sweden).

Attendance: 9,534.

England 1   Hungary 0
12th September 1990, Wembley

After a heady summer in which Bobby Robson's England had proved themselves to be one of the top four national teams in the world, there was always a possibility that the opening fixture of the new season – a friendly match against Hungary that had been switched at short notice from Budapest (at the Hungarians' request) – would be something of an anti-climax. But the special ingredient that kept the level of interest high was the fact that England had a new manager and this was his first game in charge. The nation expected – and Graham Taylor's England delivered.

England won by virtue of Gary Lineker's goal a minute before the break but the margin of victory could have been much greater as Hungary, 4-1 winners over England's European Championship qualifying opponents Turkey in the previous week, were simply outclassed. There had been great excitement in those memorable World Cup ties with Belgium, Cameroon and West Germany, where England had lived on their nerves by holding on, rather than controlling the situation. Now here was an England team dominating the opposition before an appreciative 50,000-plus crowd at Wembley.

To get the best out of John Barnes, a disappointment in Italy, the new England manager decided to play him in an old-fashioned inside-forward's role, rather than as an out-and-out winger, and there was no doubt that his former charge at Watford revelled in the extra involvement that this position afforded him. In the very first minute

John Ebbrell, captain of England Under-21s, hurdles a Polish leg.

of the match – and of a new era for the England team – Barnes shuffled and swayed past four Hungarian defenders. He put David Platt clear on the left and the Villa midfielder's instant ball into the middle had Lee Dixon rushing in for a shot that was not quite the perfect ending to an exhilarating move.

Managers at all levels are judged on results and England got the one they wanted courtesy of a goal on 44 minutes. Three of the outstanding performers at Italia '90 combined to produce it. Platt's effort was palmed away by Petry and Paul Gascoigne reacted quickly to prod the ball forward for Lineker to roll in his 36th international goal from a few feet.

England: Woods, Dixon, Pearce (Dorigo), Parker, Walker, Wright, Platt, Gascoigne, Bull (Waddle), Lineker, Barnes.

Hungary: Petry, Monos (Simon), Disztl, Keller, Limperger, Garaba (Aczel), Kozma, Bucs (Balog), Gregor, Berczy, Kovacs.

Referee: E. Fredriksson (Sweden).

Attendance: 51,459.

England 0   Poland 1
(Under-21)
16th October 1990, Tottenham

England have a record second to none in the UEFA Under-21 Championship, having won the trophy twice (1982 and 1984) and reached four other semi-finals. Sweden had qualified for the latter stages of the last tournament at their expense and now England were hoping for an encouraging start to the new campaign against Poland, probably their strongest rivals in the four-team qualifying group.

The English tactic of playing long balls through the middle for Ian Olney and Mark Robins to run onto proved fruitless in the first half. The best chance of scoring looked as though it would come from a set-piece and it was a marginally off-target header from Olney following a free-kick that went nearest to counting in that first period. The Poles, favouring a closer passing game, were themselves knocked off the ball too easily, and with David Lee and Jason Dodd commanding at the back it was the home team that dominated.

Lee Sharpe was introduced into the left side of midfield, replacing central defender Carl Tiler, and increasing the emphasis on attack upped the tempo of the English play. Rodney Wallace shot narrowly wide and a Robins volley rebounded to safety off the goalkeeper's knees in this more enterprising and pacy period. But four minutes from time the Poles sneaked a goal that meant the odds were already against England making it to their third final. Alan Miller, the Arsenal reserve goalkeeper, dashed off his line and Adamczuk could even afford a stumble as he deposited a tame shot into the net.

England: Miller, Dodd, Vinnicombe, Warhurst, Lee, Tiler (Sharpe), Ebbrell, Robins, Olney (Shearer), Blake, Wallace.

Poland: Klak, Adamzuk, Lapinski, Kozminski, Bajor, Jalocha, Swierczewski (Jaworek), Brzeczek, Wieszczycki (Gesior), Juskowiak, Grad.

Referee: W. Ziller (Germany).

Attendance: 2,146.

Engand 2   Poland 0
17th October 1990, Wembley

The European Championship is a com-

Steve Bull, with Dixon in support, looks for a shooting opportunity against Poland.

Chris Waddle torments the Polish defence.

petition in which England have never finished higher than in third place (1968). They missed qualifying for the 1984 finals and lost all three ties in West Germany last time round. But two experienced internationals, Gary Lineker and Peter Beardsley, were prominent as England gave Graham Taylor a winning start to the current European Championship campaign. And a win was particularly important after the Republic of Ireland had swamped the Turks 5-0 earlier in the day.

With a crowd very close to capacity there was a highly-charged atmosphere in the stadium and surely the National Anthem has never been sung more lustily. England, however, were continually frustrated in the opening twenty minutes as a very professional Polish outfit closed down space and got as many men as possible behind the ball. The chances did finally come – Lee Dixon shooting just over the bar

and the goalkeeper saving from Steve Bull's header inside the six-yard box – though Wandzik had begun to invite comparison with the legendary Tomaszewski, the scourge of 1973, as he succeeded in blocking everything that England could throw his way.

Then the vital breakthrough came on 39 minutes, as Czachowski handled on the line from Lineker after Mark Wright had headed back a Paul Gascoigne corner. Lineker, the expert penalty-taker at Italia '90 (three out of three), scored confidently from the spot as he sent Wandzik the wrong way. It was his fifth goal in the last five internationals.

England's goalscoring hero took no part in the proceedings after the 53rd minute in which he stooped to head the ball and felt the studs of the guiltless Wdowczyk down the side of his face. The cut needed immediate stitching and Waddle and Beardsley were brought on simultaneously to replace the stricken England captain and the labouring Bull. Into the final few minutes, with England already assured of the points, Beardsley decided that he would double the margin of victory. He collected the ball from Dixon, carried it forward down the right and then struck a 25-yarder that swerved away from Wandzik and into the net. A perfect start for England as they began their attempt to go all the way to Euro 92 in Sweden.

England: Woods, Dixon, Pearce, Parker, Walker, Wright, Platt, Gascoigne, Bull (Beardsley), Lineker (Waddle), Barnes.

Poland: Wandzik, Czachowski, Wdow-czyk, Szewczyk, Kaczmarek, Nawrocki, Tarasiewicz, Warzycha R., Furtok (Warzycha K.), Kosecki (Kubicki), Ziober.

Referee: T. Lanese (Italy).

Attendance: 77, 040.

Rep. of Ireland 0   England 3
(Under-21)
13th November 1990, Cork

England Under-21s partly atoned for the previous month's home defeat against Poland by recording an easy victory at Turner's Cross. They had used their superior strength and experience to provide their senior counterparts with a boost before the big European Championship qualifier in Dublin on the following afternoon.

A very partisan 3,000 crowd and a difficult pitch did nothing to deter England as they quickly settled into their stride and set about securing two UEFA tournament points. It came as no surprise when the visitors went ahead in the 26th minute after O'Dowd had brilliantly turned Alan Shearer's header

behind for a corner. Lee Sharpe, Manchester United's exciting winger who won his place in the record books as England's youngest performer at Under-21 level in 1989, curled the ball towards the far post where Shearer scored from six yards after his initial header had been blocked on the line by O'Donoghue.

David James had to deal with Kelly's rocket of a free-kick before Shearer put the result beyond doubt on 51 minutes, beating O'Dowd with a rising drive at the end of a long advance on goal. Shearer was denied a hat-trick by the width of the crossbar and then Ian Olney added a late third goal with a delightful chip from just outside the box. It had been an almost embarrassingly one-sided contest.

Rep. of Ireland: O'Dowd, Cun-ningham, O'Donoghue, Scully, McCarthy, Poutch, Keane, Roche (Arkins), Power, Cousins, Kelly (Brady).

England: James, Dodd, Vinnicombe, Lee, Cundy, Tiler, Ebbrell, Blake, Olney, Shearer, Sharpe.

Referee: W. Fockler (Germany).

Rep. of Ireland 1   England 1
14th November 1990, Dublin

Not only did the elements conspire against good football – there was a swirling wind and intermittent showers of rain – but the Lansdowne Road pitch itself has rarely been conducive to it. England had come to within ten minutes of clinching the points, when Tony Cascarino, the lanky striker Graham Taylor had once signed to try to help Villa win the League Cham-pionship, punished a rare moment of indecision by England's defence to level the scores.

The England manager had caused a surprise by deciding to omit Paul Gascoigne from midfield, choosing instead another of his former charges at Villa in Gordon Cowans. Tony Adams was pressed into the back four in another tactical switch designed to help nullify the aerial bombardment expected from the Irish. In their previous two matches against Jack Charlton's team, particularly in the European Championship tie in Stuttgart, England had been the better side only to prove wasteful in front of goal. Gary Lineker, who had begun his prolific goalscoring career for England with the one that beat Ireland 2-1 in a Wembley friendly in 1985, had probably been as guilty as anyone. Now, in Dublin, he was in for another frustrating time.

Steve McMahon of Liverpool, brought in to stiffen the midfield, released Stuart Pearce to run at the vulnerable Morris. Once he had lured the Irish full-back out of position, Pearce slipped the ball invitingly into Lineker's path. But at the crucial moment the ball bobbled – another victory for the pitch.

Chris Woods had few alarms as England contained the Irish attacking threat quite comfortably, required only to fist a Whelan effort over the top and carefully watch as McCarthy's long-range free-kick, helped on by the wind, barely cleared the bar. Just at the point when Ireland were starting to wind up for their great push, England suddenly broke with a move of great fluency that culminated in a goal for David Platt, his first since Italia '90. Lineker slipped a short pass to McMahon who made intelligent use of Lee Dixon's overlapping run down the right. The cross came in low and hard and, though

Lineker could not make meaningful contact, Platt had drifted in at the far post and made no mistake. It was only the second goal conceded by Ireland in competitive fixtures under Jack Charlton at Lansdowne Road.

If the score had remained like that, it would have put England firmly on the road to the finals. But then, with ten minutes to go, Staunton's free-kick curled into the heart of England's pressurised defence and Cascarino looped a header away from Woods and into the top corner of the goal. Once again the Irish had taken on England and survived.

Rep. of Ireland: Bonner, Morris, Staunton, McCarthy, O'Leary, Whelan, McGrath, Houghton, Quinn (Cascarino), Aldridge, Townsend.

England: Woods, Dixon, Pearce, Adams, Walker, Wright, Platt, Cowans, Beardsley, Lineker, McMahon.

Referee: P. D'Elia (Italy).

England 0 Wales 0
(Under-21)
5th December 1990, Tranmere

On a cold night at Prenton Park a good-sized crowd witnessed the first meeting between the two countries at Under-21 level since 1979 and the first international fixture (above Youth level) to be played on Merseyside in nine years.

England were without several regulars through injury and manager Lawrie McMenemy was only able to name three players who contributed to the comprehensive victory over the Republic of Ireland in November. England, with John Ebbrell and Craig Ramage performing well at the heart of an orthodox 4-4-2 formation, swiftly established a control of the game. But chances for either team were few and far between. England, in fact, had to wait until the 32nd minute before finding a way through the disciplined Welsh defence. Alan Shearer provided a pin-point cross from the right and Liverpool's Steve McManaman's header drifted just wide of a post.

Shearer and Nigel Jemson enjoyed more space up front in the second half but they were usually let down by the final pass from midfield. Jemson, the Forest striker, had an outstanding game and nearly settled matters on 50 minutes when his first-time shot from McManaman's cross was well saved by the alert Roberts.

England: Walker, Warhurst (Charles), Minto, Blake (Atkinson), Blackwell, Ord, Ebbrell, Ramage, Shearer, Jemson, McManaman.

Wales: Roberts, Perry, Coleman, Melville, Law, Symons, Rees, Nogan L., Nogan K. (Graham), Ebdon (Owen), Speed.

Referee: D. Hope (England).

Attendance: 6,288.

Algeria 0   England 'B' 0
11th December 1990, Algiers

Heavy rain kept the attendance in the Olympic Stadium down to under a thousand. There was a thirteen-minute breakdown of the floodlighting system during the match and Manchester United's Neil Webb, playing his way into the reckoning for a senior team place after his injury in Sweden, became the unlucky thirteenth England player (at Senior, 'B' and Under-21 levels combined) to be sent off the field.

Quality football had been almost

Ian Wright finds the ball slipping away in a damp Algiers.

53

impossible in the conditions, though Haraoui had stood out in an Algerian line-up that had shown good technique. England were generally on top and the home side had to thank Osmani in goal for important stops from an Alan Smith header and a measured shot from Nigel Clough. The Crystal Palace pair, Ian Wright and Geoff Thomas, performed with credit and both made their senior bow later in the season.

Webb tangled with Rahim as the pair attempted to regain their feet near the half-way line in the last minute of the opening half. The Tunisian referee surprised everyone by sending both players off for apparently minor indiscretions.

Algeria: Osmani (Kadri), Bounaas, Adjas, Megharia, Belatoui, Lazizi, Sandjak, Bettadj, Haraoui (Tasfaout), Oudjani (Lounici), Rahim.

England: Martyn (Lukic), Sterland (Thomas M.), Burrows, Webb, Mabbutt, Pallister (Ablett), Robson, Clough, Smith A. (Wallace D.), Wright, Thomas G.

Referee: N. Jouini (Tunisia).

Wales 'B' 0   England 'B' 1
5th February 1991, Swansea

This first ever 'B' fixture between England and Wales was settled by Paul Davis's excellent free-kick close to half-time. A 4,000 crowd on a decidedly chilly evening at the Vetch Field saw the Arsenal midfielder, in the international wilderness for more than two years, give England a victory more slender than might have been expected.

Wales included players from all four divisions of the Barclays League in their line-up, while nine of the England starters were established names in the First Division and six of the players on view had already been capped at senior level. Yet the home team made more of the running in the first half and England were grateful to Nigel Spink for dashing from his goal to save at McCarthy's feet in the third minute and then dealing with worthy efforts from Rees, Allen and Hodges.

At last England managed to find a way past Wales's sweeper system three minutes before the interval. Steve Bull was needlessly brought down by Hodges and Davis curled a superb left-footer into the top corner of the goal from 25 yards' range. After performing well for just over an hour, Davis made way for Geoff Thomas, the Crystal Palace skipper, who was destined to make his senior bow for England three months later. Dave Beasant replaced the slightly injured Spink for the last 19 minutes but had little to do as a Beardsley-inspired England 'B' team called the tune in the second half.

Wales: Norman, Blake, Pembridge, Maguire, Perry, Melville, Rees, Morgan (Nogan), McCarthy, Allen, Hodges.

England: Spink (Beasant), Laws, Burrows, Thomas M., Mabbutt, Barrett, Gordon, Beardsley, Bull, Davis (Thomas G.), Walters.

Referee: L. Mottram (Scotland).

England 2   Cameroon 0
6th February 1991, Wembley

At Italia '90 England and Cameroon had played out a thrilling quarter-final that had brought great credit to both teams. It was entirely appropriate that the African surprise packet at the World Cup should have been invited back for a Wembley 'return'. But an

GUARANTEE

FOR SEATS AT ALL WEMBLEY STADIUM EVENTS

Whether it's football, American football, rugby or hockey you can now enjoy the action without being one of the crowd.
Membership of Club Olympic entitles you to a luxury seat in the high level gallery offering stunning views.
In addition to your regular guaranteed seat you can enjoy:

A hospitality suite to wine and dine guests before and after events, in a relaxed atmosphere.
Designated entrances away from the main turnstiles help you arrive and leave with the minimum of delay.
Bars and restrooms for sole use by visitors to the Olympic Gallery.
Complimentary car park pass helps ease access to the Stadium.

These benefits are available exclusively to Club Olympic members. So if you want to entertain your clients and friends in a unique atmosphere at Wembley Stadium
call the Wembley Club Olympic Line on (081) 902 8833

WATCH OUT FOR THE CROSS.

This is the deadliest cross in football.

It belongs to an Asics boot.

Because when a player puts on a pair of Asics he gets more support, more control and more stability.

And that makes him dangerous.

That's why more and more players are wearing Asics. World class professionals like Franco Baresi and Gianluca Vialli of Italy, Chris Waddle, Peter Beardsley, Tony Dorigo and Paul Parker of England and Maurice Malpas of Scotland.

And with talent like that wearing Asics you'd better watch out.

THE CLASSICO ST

Asics are official sponsors of Norwich City and strip suppliers to Dundee United, Coventry City, Sampdoria and Panathinaikos.

Asics professionals: David Speedie, Lee Sharpe, Gary Speed, Mel Sterland, Vinny Jones and Mike Phelan.

Sole Distributor: Olympian Sports UK Ltd. Tel: (0532) 508486.

arctic Wembley in February is not Naples on a sultry evening in July and the Cameroonians did themselves no favours at all this time. In fact their mercenary and generally undignified attitude lost them a legion of admirers.

This was an entirely different Cameroon side to the one that had captured the hearts of the watching millions during Italia '90. The players were more or less the same ones but their approach was upsetting to the frozen Wembley crowd. Their tackling was malicious, their commitment non-existent and their money-grabbing exploits before the game had probably soured the occasion. Their objective was apparently to achieve as narrow a defeat as possible. 2-0 to England, therefore, was a result.

There was an element of déjà vu about England's first goal on 22 minutes. Ian Wright, the Crystal Palace striker making his England debut, headed down Trevor Steven's cross at the far post, Gary Lineker controlled the ball and was guiding it away from Bell as he was clumsily knocked to the ground. The Cameroon goalkeeper was then as unsuccessful at stopping a Lineker spot-kick as N'Kono had been (twice) in Naples.

Lineker's second goal – his 38th for England – again resulted from England's ability to expose Cameroon's weakness in the air. Mark Wright nudged on Pearce's corner-kick at the near post on 62 minutes and Lineker just beat the other Wright to the final touch a yard or so from the line. At the eleventh hour Cameroon had found themselves without the services of two of their World Cup stars, Milla of the famous wiggle and N'Kono having reportedly held out in vain for some additional 'appearance money' and the disappointing Africans failed through-

out the 90 minutes to mount anything that could have been described as an attack.

England: Seaman, Dixon, Pearce, Steven, Walker, Wright M., Robson (Pallister), Gascoigne (Hodge), Wright I., Lineker, Barnes.

Cameroon: Bell, Ebwelle, Onana, Kunde, Tataw, M'Fede, Mbouh-Mbouh, Pagal, Kana-Biyik (Libiih), Omam-Biyik, Ekeke (Tapoko).

Referee: J. Blankenstein (Holland).

Attendance: 61,075.

England 3   Rep. of Ireland 0
(Under-21)
26th March 1991, Brentford

Needing nothing less than a win to sustain hopes of reaching the latter stages of the UEFA tournament, England made it comfortably in the end with goals from two Southampton players, Alan Shearer and Rodney Wallace, and a third from Jason Cundy, one of three Chelsea players in the England line-up.

The result exactly repeated England's victory in Cork in the previous November. But it was not until they took the lead against determined (but very young) opponents at Griffin Park that their finishing began to match the assurance of their build-ups. In the final minute of the opening half Damian Matthew's accurate pass out to the right found Wallace streaking into acres of space. The Southampton winger, who had cleverly switched flanks, easily outpaced the Irish defence before slipping the ball past the quickly advancing Gough.

Ian Olney missed with a couple of efforts early in the second period and then Shearer outjumped everyone to

Lineker and Moran in a determined tussle for the ball.

power a header into the top corner of the goal from Wallace's flag-kick. With 11 minutes remaining another corner had the ball bouncing around in the box before Cundy smacked it firmly through a few defenders' legs and into the net.

England: James, Charles, Vinnicombe, Lee, Cundy, Tiler, Blake (Johnson), Matthew (Draper), Shearer, Olney, Wallace.

Rep. of Ireland: Gough, Cunningham, Kenna, Scully, Fitzgerald, McGrath, Keane, Collins (Roche), Power, Arkins, O'Donoghue (McCarthy).

Referee: J. Uilenberg (Holland).

Attendance: 9,120.

England 1   Rep. of Ireland 1
27th March 1991, Wembley

England met the Republic of Ireland for the third time inside ten months and once again the result was a 1-1 draw.

The Irish presence in the stadium was huge and tremendously partisan – tickets for the game could have been sold twice over – and the team in green succeeded in matching their best performance at Wembley, where they have never won. If the aim of Kevin Sheedy and Ray Houghton had been more accurate in the second half, England could have found their European Championship ambitions even more threatened.

England started brightly enough and had the boost of a goal after just ten minutes. Staunton's headed clearance from Stuart Pearce's cross set up Lee Dixon for a firm right-footer which ricocheted off the unlucky Staunton's knee and left his own goalkeeper flat-footed and beaten at the near post. The deflection had been a significant one but Dixon was credited with his first England strike.

Rather than employing the sweeper system familiar on the Continent, the trio of Tony Adams, Mark Wright and Des Walker was selected by the

58

England manager to counter the threats posed by Quinn in the air and Aldridge on the ground. But they had their work cut out as the Irish response to going behind so early in the game was to launch wave after wave of aerial attacks and put the English goal virtually under siege.

Peter Beardsley, reunited with Gary Lineker up front, made an important defensive contribution by clearing McGrath's shot off the line. Then, on 27 minutes, the incessant Irish pressure finally caused England to crack. McGrath lofted yet another cross into the penalty area and Quinn stole in behind Adams to guide the ball carefully past Seaman. In the circumstances the Irish could hardly be begrudged their equaliser.

Adams was withdrawn at half-time, the defensive trio thereby becoming a duo, and Lee Sharpe became the first teenager to represent England since John Barnes made his debut against Northern Ireland, also as a substitute, in 1983. Although the home side were clearly more comfortable at the back as a result, the two best chances of the second period both fell to the visitors. Sheedy missed when Dixon's presence caused him to shoot hurriedly and, ten minutes from time, Cascarino nodded the ball down into Houghton's path but the busy Liverpool midfielder steered the ball wide from a central position with only Seaman to beat. England's relief was visible.

England: Seaman, Dixon, Pearce, Adams (Sharpe), Walker, Wright M., Robson, Platt, Beardsley, Lineker (Wright I.), Barnes.

Rep. of Ireland: Bonner, Irwin, Staunton, O'Leary, Moran, Townsend, McGrath, Houghton, Quinn, Aldridge (Cascarino), Sheedy.

Referee: K. Rothlisberger (Switzerland).

Attendance: 77,758.

England 'B' 1   Iceland 0
27th April 1991, Watford

With no First Division fixtures scheduled for the Saturday prior to England's European Championship qualifier in Turkey, an additional international was slotted into the programme to take advantage of the top players' availability. An England 'B' team took on the full Icelandic XI, themselves due for a friendly match against Wales in the following week, and several players performed well enough to impress the watching Graham Taylor.

Steve Hodge, the Nottingham Forest midfielder, probably benefited most from the opportunity presented at Vicarage Road. After missing Forest's FA Cup semi-final success through injury and playing only three hours of reserve-team football, Hodge worked industriously enough in the centre of midfield (his favoured position for Forest) to persuade the England manager to gamble on his experience in Izmir.

Iceland had achieved some surprising results in the last World Cup qualifying competition – a 1-1 draw in Moscow for example – and were never going to be pushovers. The decisive goal was scored two minutes into the second half by Hodge's team-mate at Forest, Nigel Clough. England's display was understandably a little disjointed at times, given that this particular 'B' team had been put together at short notice, but Gary Mabbutt and Paul Stewart, both three weeks away from a Wembley appearance with Tottenham, did their England chances no harm at all.

Paul Stewart finds his way blocked by three Icelandic defenders.

England: Spink, Joseph, Dorigo, Batty, Mabbutt, Pallister (Curle), White, Clough, Chapman (Deane), Hodge, Barton (Stewart).

Iceland: Gottskalksson, Glislasson (Kristjansson), Edvalsson, Kristinsson (Einarsson), Gretarsson, Jonsson, Bergsson, Orlygsson, Gudjohnsen, Thordasson, Gregory (Stefansson).

Referee: K. Burge (Wales).

Attendance: 3,814.

Turkey 2 England 2
(Under-21)
30th April 1991, Izmir

The Under-21s were really looking for a win in the Alsancak Stadium to repair more fully the damage done to their hopes of topping the UEFA Championship qualifying group by the previous October's home defeat against Poland. England had appeared to be heading for a pointless game when

Kevin Campbell, introduced for Ian Olney at half-time, came to England's rescue with 15 minutes left and the Turks 2-1 ahead.

The strong finishing which had made Campbell such a central figure in Arsenal's push for the League title became evident again after he had received a pass from Stuart in space and some 35 yards out from goal. Turning sharply and brushing aside all challenges until he was near enough to goal to try a shot, Campbell drove the ball low into the far corner ultimately to spare England's blushes. It would have been Turkey's first victory against them at Under-21 level.

Alan Shearer of Southampton headed in his fourth goal in five appearances to give England the lead in the 14th minute but Turkey had continued to grow in confidence after a tentative start and Hamdi Cam levelled the scores with a low shot 11 minutes later. England were handed a golden opportunity before half-time when Shearer rounded the goalkeeper only to be brought down by central defender Tugay. Chelsea's David Lee stepped up to take the spot-kick but his shot was poorly placed and Kazim saved easily.

Nine minutes into the second period Osman ran on to a backheeled return pass from Faruk and beat James to score at the second attempt. Despite finally achieving a draw, England now found themselves three points adrift of Poland in the group table with only two games left to play.

Turkey: Kazim, Hamza, Mutlu, Tugay, Feti, Kemalettin, Hamdi Cam, Osman, Hakan, Abdullah (Murat), Faruk.

England: James, Dodd, Vinnicombe, Lee, Blackwell, Tiler, Hillier (Stuart), Ebbrell, Shearer, Olney (Campbell), Wallace.

Referee: A. Wieser (Austria).

Turkey 0   England 1
1st May 1991, Izmir

With the maxim that there is no longer such a thing as an 'easy' international fairly well accepted these days, England could feel satisfied with the scoreline achieved in the Ataturk Stadium. Two precious qualifying points put them in the driving seat in Group 7, because the Republic of Ireland and Poland had taken a point off each other in Dublin earlier in the day.

Gary Pallister was brought in to replace the injured Mark Wright four days after appearing for England 'B' against Iceland, the old Leicester City striking partnership of Alan Smith and Gary Lineker was resurrected and two midfield players were given their first cap – Dennis Wise of Chelsea and Geoff Thomas, the Crystal Palace skipper. Wise got the goal on 32 minutes that won the points and Thomas had a tremendous volley

Kevin Campbell prepares for a shot against the Turkish Under-21s.

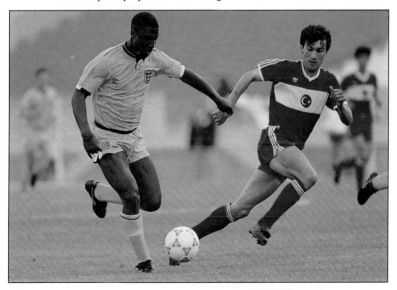

Alan Smith jumps highest in Izmir.

turned over the bar by Hayrettin before he was substituted at half-time.

Fortunately for England their Turkish opponents had virtually forgotten what it was like to score a goal in a competitive international. They have now failed to find the target in their four matches to date in the present European Championship campaign and, equally, have drawn blanks in five games with England dating back to 1984. But, strangely, they created numerous chances in Izmir as Mehmet and Muhammet began to run things in midfield, Riza and Ali combined to turn England's defence on the right and Tanju won several important balls in the air.

Midway through the first half Turkey should have gone ahead. Gokhan launched Mehmet on a counter-attack down the left, Lineker and Walker collided as they attempted to defuse the danger and Seaman had to keep his nerve to block Ridvan's narrow-angled effort as he broke clear in the box. Tanju seized on to the rebound but badly mis-hit his shot. Turkey's best chance of the first half had come and gone.

England's winner came by a traditional route, though the final execution looked rather untidy. Turkey always looked vulnerable in the air against the power of Smith and Pallister at set-pieces and when the latter outjumped the Turks to a high free-kick from Pearce, Hayrettin was slow to react and the alert Wise touched the ball past him from beyond the far post. Turkey continued to show skill and imagination in their approaches to goal in the second period but their confidence seemed to evaporate in the penalty area.

Turkey: Hayrettin, Riza, Ogun, Gokhan, Recep, Muhammet, Unal, Ridvan, Mehmet, Tanju, Ali (Feyyaz).

England: Seaman, Dixon, Pearce, Wise, Walker, Pallister, Platt, Thomas (Hodge), Smith, Lineker, Barnes.

Referee: W. Wiesel (Germany).

England 'B' 2   Switzerland 'B' 1
20th May 1991, Walsall

The new Bescot Stadium at Walsall was packed with a crowd of over 10,000 and, for the players on England duty, there was the chance to impress enough to be chosen to fill one of the two places still available in the party to tour Australasia. Powerful Sheffield Wednesday striker David Hirst, scorer of 32 goals in Wednesday's promotion and Rumbelow's Cup-winning season, improved his own prospects greatly of being drafted into the senior squad by grabbing a brace of goals that won this fourth and final 'B' fixture of the season.

England's hopefuls did not, however, help their cause by conceding a soft goal after only eight minutes. Paul Elliott, the Celtic defender made skipper for the night, put the ball behind for a corner-kick which was blocked on the line by Joseph before Chassot followed up with a close-range header into the net.

The home team gradually worked their way back into the game, with Graeme Le Saux looking dangerous on breaks down the left. Two minutes after Ian Bishop had clipped the crossbar with a lob, the Wednesday trio of King, Palmer and Hirst combined to make a goal for the last-named in the 28th minute. England went close to securing the lead just before the interval, when Swiss goalkeeper Walker dived to make an outstanding save from Bishop.

Hirst, 23, collected his second goal

of the game as he connected with Dale Gordon's cross on 55 minutes and he was unfortunate not to complete his hat-trick when a later effort struck the foot of the post. A minute after that Le Saux also hit the woodwork.

England: Martyn, Joseph (Curle), King, Bishop (Ebbrell), Elliott, Barrett, Gordon (Slater), Hirst, Deane, Palmer, Le Saux.

Switzerland: Walker (Corminboeuf), Camperle, Heldmann, Gambino (Studer B.), Fischer, Sylvestre, Sforza, Penzavalli (Isabella), Douglas, Nadig (Gigon), Chassot (Studer J.).

Referee: J. McCluskey (Scotland).

Attendance: 10,628.

England 3   USSR 1
21st May 1991, Wembley

An England team from which Spurs and Forest players had been excluded was still good enough to beat a young Soviet side in the first match of the 'England Challenge Cup' series. David Platt, Villa's 24-year-old midfielder, gave perhaps his best England performance as he attempted to fill the void in the team left by the absence, enforced or otherwise, of Gascoigne and Robson. Platt netted twice and helped to make it ultimately a successful evening for Mark Wright, appointed England captain for the first time. The Derby defender had un-luckily deflected Tatarchuk's 10th-minute effort past his own goalkeeper to hand the technically impressive Soviets an early lead.

The undeterred Wright had joined the attack whenever possible after that and it was his intervention from a Paul Parker free-kick on the right which led to England's priceless equaliser on 17 minutes. Uvarov, the Moscow Dynamo goalkeeper, flapped at the kick as Wright moved in and Thomas's drive across goal was expertly turned into the roof of the net by Alan Smith – the prolific Arsenal striker's first England goal.

The Soviets entertained the Wembley crowd with some sweet interchanges of passes – Kanchelskis, wide on the right, showing in particular why Manchester United had recently paid £600,000 for his services – but overall they lacked the determination of Graham Taylor's side. Shalimov was too casual as he attempted to play himself out of trouble two minutes before the break and Platt seized the chance to burst into the box between two defenders. There was some contact with Tsveiba's knee, Platt went sprawling and then picked himself up to send Uvarov the wrong way from the spot.

England took command in the second half, with Platt and Barnes prominent in all the best moves, though Chris Woods had to come to the rescue on 55 minutes with a superb diving save to his left to deny Mostovoi, the Soviet substitute, whose firm header had looked a goal all the way. After that the home team were rarely threatened again and deservedly extended their lead with a couple of minutes left on the clock. Peter Beardsley pushed a short pass from new cap David Batty through to Platt on the edge of the area and the Villa player took it confidently in his stride before shooting low into the bottom corner past a flat-footed Uvarov.

Two days later, at Old Trafford, USSR drew 1-1 with Argentina in the second match of the series. Kolyvanov and Ruggeri scored the goals,

Chernishkov was dismissed for a 'professional foul' and the attendance was 23,743.

England: Woods, Stevens, Dorigo, Wise (Batty), Parker, Wright M., Platt, Thomas, Smith, Wright I. (Beardsley), Barnes.

USSR: Uvarov, Chernishkov, Kulkov, Tsveiba, Galiamin, Shalimov, Mikhailichenko, Kanchelskis, Kolyvanov, Tatarchuk (Mostovoi), Kuznetsov.

Referee: E. Aladren (Spain).

Attendance: 23,789.

England 2   Argentina 2
25th May 1991, Wembley

England's last fixture of the season at Wembley saw them achieve the draw sufficient to lift the three-nation 'England Challenge Cup'. For an hour the team had played as effectively as at any time under Graham Taylor and appeared, at 2-0, to be cruising to a comfortable victory. Then Argentina, unpopular finalists at Italia '90, equalised with two free headers from corner-kicks and the match ended tamely from England's point of view. At least they were still unbeaten after eight matches with Taylor in charge.

David Batty, a Leeds United midfielder in the Bremner mould, started his first game for England anchored in central midfield with David Platt and Geoff Thomas pushing forward either side. John Barnes, roaming wherever he wanted in a 'free' role, had a good first half but slowed down after taking a knock on the knee. Gary Lineker, skipper for the fifth time, foraged well up front with Alan Smith and the England captain emphasised his opportunism by punishing goal-

Argentinian captain Ruggeri turns to deal with the threat posed by Barnes.

keeping Goycochea's hesitation for the opening goal on 15 minutes as he moved in behind the defence to head sweetly home from Stuart Pearce's free-kick on the halfway line. It was Lineker's 40th England goal.

With Batty linking defence and attack impressively, England were completely in control and when Platt scored with a typically brave header from Pearce's chip in the 50th minute, and the Forest full-back then lunged forward to miss out on a third goal by inches, a convincing win seemed likely. But a limping Barnes finally went off, to be replaced by Nigel Clough (equalling his father's caps tally), and somehow England's momentum was lost. Lack of concentration at two corners taken inside six minutes by substitute Mohamed cost two goals. Garcia nodded in the first on 66 minutes as he stood almost on the near post and then Franco's towering header from some distance beat Pearce's leap on the line.

Garcia was cautioned for an extremely late tackle on Lee Dixon in the last minute and virtually the whole Argentinian team had surrounded the Yugoslav referee to protest at his controversial decision of a dropped ball on the edge of their penalty area when a spectator ran on to the pitch inside the English half. Otherwise there was little evidence of the 'dirty tricks' seen at Italia '90.

England: Seaman, Dixon, Pearce, Batty, Walker, Wright, Platt, Thomas, Smith, Lineker, Barnes (Clough).

Argentina: Goycochea, Vazquez, Enrique, Basualdo, Gamboa, Ruggeri, Garcia, Franco, Simeone, Martellotto (Mohamed), Boldrini.

Referee: Z. Petrovic (Yugoslavia).

Attendance: 44,497.

regime

The young man's toiletries range

England 2   Senegal 1
(Under-21)
27th May 1991, Arles

England Under-21s began their defence of the Toulon International Tournament trophy with a group match in the Fernand Founier Stadium against Senegal, the African country that they had met in the same competition in 1989 and overwhelmed 6-1. It was a lot harder this time as an England team managed by Ray Harford trailed their 'naïve' opponents for 25 minutes.

In the 16th minute Paul Warhurst had attempted to guide a harmless-looking cross from the right by Gomis back to David James in England's goal. Unfortunately for the Oldham Athletic defender the ball sailed over James's head and into the net. Alan Shearer, the Southampton striker who had been a major success for the Under-21 side this season (four goals before the tournament), then scored twice to ensure victory and make Warhurst feel much better.

After an earlier header had been ruled out for offside and other efforts had also gone close, Shearer's persistence was rewarded with a headed equaliser from Paul Williams's free-kick shortly before half-time. It was equally fitting that he should net the winner 18 minutes into the second period after he and Paul Kitson had sprung a feeble Senegalese offside trap.

England: James, Dodd, Vinnicombe, Lee (Blackwell), Warhurst, Tiler, Wallace, Watson (Kitson), Shearer, Williams, Atkinson.

Senegal: Faye, N'Diane, Diagne, Traore, N'Diaye, Tendeng, Diousse, Sagna, Gomis, Dougnon, Gueye.

Referee: J. Blattman (Switzerland).

England 6   Mexico 0
(Under-21)
29th May 1991, Vitrolles

England gave themselves every chance of reaching the Toulon final by overcoming Mexico 6-0 in a bizarre match in the Jules Ladoumegue Stadium which saw four players shown the red card. The harassed French referee actually blew for time two minutes early.

Delgado, the Mexican defender, had been dismissed in the first half for spitting, with England already 4-0 up, and the Mexican discipline collapsed completely after the interval when Pineda went off for punching Warhurst and skipper Trejo went for persistent arguing. There had been a real danger that the match would be abandoned with the Mexican team having less than the minimum seven players required to continue. Southampton's Jason Dodd joined them, perhaps unluckily, after a rash challenge on Martinez.

The dismissals tended to overshadow an excellent display of attacking football by England, which featured the scoring of a hat-trick by Alan Shearer (nine goals in seven appearances for the Under-21s this season) and additional strikes from Paul Kitson, Rodney Wallace and Damian Matthew. Two of Shearer's had been spot-kicks.

England: James, Dodd, Vinnicombe, Matthew, Blackwell, Ord, Wallace (Warhurst), Kitson, Shearer (McManaman), Williams, Atkinson.

Mexico: Quintero, Enriquez, Trejo, Pena, Delgado, Garcia, Pineda, Martinez, Villalon, Hernandez, Mendoza.

Referee: R. Harrel (France).

68

England 2 USSR 1
(Under-21)
31st May 1991, Aix-en-Provence

England, the holders, moved into their second final in a row by making it three group wins out of three in the G. Carcassonne Stadium. Chris Vinnicombe headed back a long cross from Paul Warhurst with only four minutes to go and Alan Shearer scored the winner with a volley that struck the underside of the bar on its way into the net. It was the Southampton striker's sixth goal of the tournament and his tenth in eight matches at Under-21 level – a very impressive record.

England had led from the seventh minute, when Sheffield Wednesday's Gordon Watson headed home from close range. The Soviets equalised shortly before half-time, when Sharan easily beat James in England's goal, and they had looked the better side for long periods.

England: James, Warhurst, Tiler, Lee, Blackwell, Ord, Wallace, Matthew, Shearer, Williams (Atkinson), Watson (Vinnicombe).

USSR: Pomazoun, Krbashian, Minko, Boushmanov, Klimovitch (Guschin), Balaryan, Korsakov, Drozdov, Manchur (Grishin), Konovalov, Sharan.

Referee: D. Ziober (Poland).

Australia 0 England 1
1st June 1991, Sydney

Graham Taylor extended his unbeaten run as England manager to nine games, equalling the record set by Don Revie in 1975, as his side started their four-match Australasia/Far East tour with a win against the 'Socceroos' in Sydney. The result was satisfactory, especially after the England team had endured a 22-hour flight with a nine-hour time

Salako starts a dribble into the heart of the Australian defence.

69

Australia's Tobin attempts to check Pearce's progress.

difference at the end and only a couple of days to recover before this tough international.

The match turned on a four-minute spell towards the end of the first half. Gray looked certain to put the hosts ahead when he met Vidmar's left-wing cross with a diving header on 37 minutes, but Chris Woods reacted superbly to push the ball away as it came at him from point-blank range. Then, after Durakovic had clumsily felled Gary Lineker out wide on the right, Stuart Pearce's inswinging free-kick found its way into the net via the unfortunate Gray's head. Geoff Thomas had lunged at the ball in front of the goalkeeper but Gray had definitely got the touch that counted.

Jet-lagged England had spurned several chances early on to take a grip on the game. The unmarked Mark Wright headed wide from Pearce's cross, Lineker and Platt were off target

with shots from inside the box, and Clough side-footed wide from close in when it seemed easier to score. Australia had produced a surprising level of skill to delight the 35,000 crowd. They must have been pleased with everything except the result.

Australia: Zabica, Gray, Durakovic, Zelic, Tobin, Vidmar T., Wade, Petersen, Arnold, Tapai (Brown), Vidmar A.

England: Woods, Parker, Pearce, Batty, Walker, Wright, Platt, Thomas, Clough, Lineker (Wise), Hirst (Salako).

Referee: B. Tasker (New Zealand).

New Zealand 0   England 1
3rd June 1991, Auckland

England's second match of the summer tour resulted in another single-goal victory against highly-motivated

70

New Zealand's Declan Edge crosses in front of Barrett.

opponents, though the tourists had to wait until the third minute of stoppage time for the all-important goal from Gary Lineker – his 41st for England. A team which eventually included three players making their senior debut – Earl Barrett, Mark Walters and Brian Deane – had to adjust to another significant time difference only 36 hours after the Australia match and achieved a satisfactory scoreline in the circumstances.

England had failed to cause New Zealand many problems before the closing minutes of the first-ever senior international between the two countries. Dennis Wise's curling centre into the far-post area was nodded down by Deane and Palace's John Salako, having a good tour so far, thumped his shot against the face of the crossbar from six yards. Then, just when we thought there was insufficient time to engineer another scoring chance, Paul Parker's cross at speed was turned in at

the near post by Lineker. The England skipper was destined to miss the next Kiwi encounter, having to fly to Japan to play for his club.

New Zealand: Gosling, Ridenton, Gray, Dunford, Evans, Ironside, McGarry, Halligan, Edge, De Jong, Ferris.

England: Woods, Parker, Pearce, Batty (Deane), Walker, Barrett, Platt, Thomas, Wise, Lineker, Walters (Salako).

Referee: D. Voutsinas (Australia).

England 1   France 0
(Under-21)
3rd June 1991, Toulon

Alan Shearer, the Southampton striker, had netted six times in three matches to help guide Ray Harford's England Under-21 side into the final against the host country in Toulon's Mayol Stadium. It was fitting, therefore, that he should maintain his record of hitting the target in every match by scoring the late goal that won the trophy for the holders.

Extra time had looked a distinct possibility, with neither team able to show any penetration near goal, when Shearer controlled Paul Kitson's centre from the left and volleyed fiercely into the net after cleverly flicking the ball over the most adjacent defender. Shearer won the 'player of the tournament' award and Watford's David James, who had been forced to make a brilliant stop to deny Nouma in the last minute, took the 'best goalkeeper' honour.

Before the late flurry of excitement there had been little for the 6,000 crowd to enthuse over. England's only threat in the opening period had predictably come from ace marksman Shearer as he tested Warmuz with a low drive. Warhurst and Wallace also went close after half-time.

England: James, Dodd, Vinnicombe, Lee (Warhurst), Blackwell, Tiler, Wallace, Matthew, Shearer, Kitson, Atkinson.

France: Warmuz, Dangbeto, Foulon, Thetis, Manach (Piton), Loko, Pabois, N'Gotty, Viaud, Francois, Pickeu (Nouma).

Referee: H. Reygwart (Holland).

New Zealand 0   England 2
8th June 1991, Wellington

England made it three tour wins out of three in Athletic Park and Graham Taylor's unbeaten sequence was extended to eleven matches, two clear of the previous mark. The tourists handled the difficult conditions well and might have managed half a dozen goals with steadier finishing.

Playing with the gusting wind at their backs in the first half, England were under orders to test the goalkeeper whenever possible. John Salako tried his luck with a 25-yarder that brought Schofield to a leaping save and there was an early English goal to cheer for the first time on the tour. Salako, a major success so far, crossed from the right an instant before being tackled. Brian Deane let the ball pass by him and Stuart Pearce came steaming in to thump in a left-footer along the ground that just beat Schofield's dive. England's skipper on the day had registered his second goal in 40 internationals.

Deane's height up front would have been wasted playing against the wind, so David Hirst was introduced at half-time and he made a quick impact with England's second strike on 50 minutes. Ian Wright's measured ball inside the full-back had Gary Charles sprinting clear on the right. Hirst pushed the Forest defender's slide-rule pass away from the goalkeeper with his first touch and then shot confidently home with his second.

New Zealand had two excellent scoring chances in the second period – Declan Edge lobbed miles over when clear of the defence and McGarry narrowly failed to capitalise on Charles's casual back-pass. But this was a much better England performance on a day when the spiritual home of the 'All Blacks' saw the 'All Whites' play in all red.

New Zealand: Schofield, Ridenton, Gray, Dunford, Evans, Ironside, McGarry, Halligan, Edge D. (Edge T.), De Jong, Ferris.

England: Woods, Charles, Pearce, Wise, Walker, Wright M., Platt,

Thomas, Deane (Hirst), Wright I., Salako.

Referee: R. Lorenc (Australia).

Malaysia 2   England 4
12th June 1991, Kuala Lumpur

The closing game of the tour turned into a personal triumph for Gary Lineker, back in the fold after a brief period on club duty in Tokyo. The Tottenham striker scored all four goals in the 4-2 victory, thereby overtaking Jimmy Greaves's England total (44) and leaving himself a tantalising four short of Bobby Charlton's all-time record (49).

As a capacity 45,000 crowd in the Merdeka Stadium sweltered in 100 per cent humidity, the national team rated the fourteenth strongest in Asia were already a goal behind after 42 seconds. Geoff Thomas released Lineker on the left and a rising shot beat Hassan all the way. Midway through the half Mark Wright back-headed Pearce's corner-kick into the goalmouth and Lineker reacted quickly to prod home for 2-0.

Lineker completed his fifth England hat-trick, one less than Greaves in the 1960s, with a glancing header on the half-hour from David Platt's chip to the near post. He completed his one-man scoring show on 70 minutes with a simple header from John Salako's cross in from the right. Either side of England's fourth goal, Malaysia's Matlan took advantage of momentary gaps in concentration in the English defence to register two goals and clinch celebrity status.

Malaysia: Hassan (Khairul), Serbegeth, Lee, Zaid, Jayakanthan, Chow, Ahmad, Nasir, Matlan, Zainal Abidin, Dollah.

England: Woods, Charles, Pearce, Batty, Walker, Wright, Platt, Thomas, Clough, Lineker, Salako.

Referee: A. Letchumerabamy (Malaysia).

England's Full International Teams 1946-91

(Up to and including 12 June 1991)

Captain   †Own goal   Small numerals goals scored   Number after sub. player replaced   Substitutes

versus	Result	1	2	3	4	5	6	7	8	9	10	11	Substitutes
Season 1946-47													
Northern Ireland	7-2	Swift	Scott	Hardwick*	Wright, W.	Franklin	Cockburn	Finney[1]	Carter[1]	Lawton[1]	Mannion[3]	Langton[1]	
Republic of Ireland	1-0	Swift	Scott	Hardwick*	Wright, W.	Franklin	Cockburn	Finney[1]	Carter	Lawton[1]	Mannion[2]	Langton[1]	
Wales	3-0	Swift	Scott	Hardwick*	Wright, W.	Franklin	Cockburn	Finney[1]	Carter[2]	Lawton[4]	Mannion[1]	Langton[1]	
Holland	8-2	Swift	Scott	Hardwick*	Wright, W.	Franklin	Johnston	Matthews, S.	Carter[2]	Lawton[4]	Mannion[1]	Mullen	
Scotland	1-1	Swift	Scott	Hardwick*	Wright, W.	Franklin	Johnston	Matthews, S.	Carter[1]	Lawton	Mannion[1]	Mullen	
Switzerland	0-1	Swift	Scott	Hardwick*	Wright, W.	Franklin	Lowe	Matthews, S.	Carter	Lawton[4]	Mannion	Langton[1]	
France	3-0	Swift	Scott	Hardwick*	Wright, W.	Franklin	Lowe	Finney[1]	Carter[1]	Lawton	Mannion[1]	Langton[1]	
Portugal	10-0	Swift	Scott	Hardwick*	Wright, W.	Franklin	Lowe	Matthews, S.[1]	Mortensen[4]	Lawton[4]	Mannion	Finney[1]	
1947-48													
Belgium	5-2	Swift	Scott	Hardwick*	Ward	Franklin	Wright, W.	Matthews, S.	Mortensen[1]	Lawton[2]	Mannion	Finney[2]	
Wales	3-0	Swift	Scott	Hardwick*	Taylor, P.	Franklin	Wright, W.	Matthews, S.	Mortensen[1]	Lawton[1]	Mannion[1]	Finney[1]	
Northern Ireland	2-2	Swift	Scott	Hardwick*	Taylor, P.	Franklin	Wright, W.	Matthews, S.	Mortensen[1]	Lawton[1]	Mannion[1]	Finney	
Sweden	4-2	Swift	Scott	Hardwick*	Wright, W.	Franklin	Cockburn	Finney	Mortensen[3]	Lawton[1]	Mannion	Langton[1]	
Scotland	2-0	Swift	Scott	Hardwick*	Wright, W.	Franklin	Cockburn	Matthews, S.	Mortensen[1]	Lawton[1]	Pearson	Finney[1]	
Italy	4-0	Swift*	Scott	Howe, J.	Wright, W.	Franklin	Cockburn	Matthews, S.	Mortensen[1]	Lawton[1]	Mannion	Finney[2]	
1948-49													
Denmark	0-0	Swift*	Scott	Aston	Wright, W.*	Franklin	Cockburn	Matthews, S.	Hagan	Lawton	Shackleton	Langton	
Ireland	6-2	Swift	Scott	Howe, J.	Wright, W.*	Franklin	Cockburn	Matthews, S.[1]	Mortensen[3]	Milburn	Pearson[1]	Finney	
Wales	1-0	Swift	Scott	Aston	Ward	Franklin	Wright, W.*	Matthews, S.	Mortensen	Milburn	Shackleton	Finney[1]	
Switzerland	6-0	Ditchburn	Ramsey	Aston	Wright, W.*	Franklin	Cockburn	Matthews, S.	Rowley, J.[1]	Milburn	Haines[2]	Hancocks[2]	
Scotland	1-3	Swift	Aston	Howe, J.	Wright, W.*	Franklin	Cockburn	Matthews, S.	Mortensen	Milburn	Pearson	Finney	
Sweden	1-3	Ditchburn	Shimwell	Aston	Wright, W.*	Franklin	Cockburn	Finney[1]	Mortensen	Bentley	Rowley, J.	Langton[1]	
Norway	4-1	Swift	Ellerington	Aston	Wright, W.*	Franklin	Dickinson	Finney[1]	Morris[1]	Mortensen	Mannion	Mullen	
France	3-1	Williams	Ellerington	Aston	Wright, W.*	Franklin	Dickinson	Finney	Morris[2]	Rowley, J.	Mannion	Mullen	†
1949-50													
Republic of Ireland	0-2	Williams	Mozley	Aston	Wright, W.*	Franklin	Dickinson	Harris, P.	Morris	Pye	Mannion	Finney	
Wales	4-1	Williams	Mozley	Aston	Wright, W.*	Franklin	Dickinson	Finney	Mortensen[2]	Milburn[3]	Shackleton	Hancocks	
Northern Ireland	9-2	Streeten	Mozley	Aston	Watson, W.	Franklin	Wright, W.*	Finney	Mortensen	Rowley, J.[4]	Pearson[2]	Froggatt, J.[1]	
Italy	2-0	Williams	Ramsey	Aston	Watson, W.	Franklin	Wright, W.*[1]	Finney	Mannion	Rowley, J.[1]	Pearson	Froggatt, J.	
Scotland	1-0	Williams	Ramsey	Aston	Wright, W.*	Franklin	Dickinson	Finney	Mortensen[1]	Mortensen	Bentley[1]	Langton	
Portugal	5-3	Williams	Ramsey	Aston	Wright, W.*	Jones, W.H.	Dickinson	Milburn	Mortensen[1]	Bentley[1]	Mannion[1]	Finney[4]	Mullen(7)[1]
Belgium	4-1	Williams	Ramsey	Aston	Wright, W.*	Jones, W.H.	Dickinson	Milburn	Mannion[1]	Bentley[1]	Mortensen[1]	Finney	
Chile	2-0	Williams	Ramsey	Aston	Wright, W.*	Hughes, L.	Dickinson	Finney	Mannion[1]	Bentley	Mortensen	Mullen	
USA	0-1	Williams	Ramsey	Aston	Wright, W.*	Hughes, L.	Dickinson	Finney	Mannion	Bentley	Mortensen	Mullen	
Spain	0-1	Williams	Ramsey	Eckersley	Wright, W.*	Hughes, L.	Dickinson	Matthews, S.	Mortensen	Milburn	Baily, E.	Finney	
1950-51													
Northern Ireland	4-1	Williams	Ramsey	Aston	Wright, W.*[1]	Chilton	Dickinson	Matthews, S.	Mannion[1]	Lee, J.[1]	Baily, E.[2]	Langton	
Wales	4-2	Williams	Ramsey*	Smith, L.	Watson, W.	Compton, L.	Dickinson	Finney	Mannion[1]	Milburn[1]	Baily, E.[2]	Medley	
Yugoslavia	2-2	Williams	Ramsey	Eckersley	Watson, W.	Compton, L.	Wright, W.*	Hancocks	Mannion	Lofthouse[2]	Baily, E.[1]	Medley	
Scotland	2-3	Williams	Ramsey	Eckersley	Johnston	Froggatt, J.	Wright, W.*	Matthews, S.	Mannion	Mortensen	Hassall[1]	Finney	
Argentina	2-1	Williams	Ramsey	Eckersley	Wright, W.*	Taylor, J.	Cockburn	Finney[1]	Mortensen[1]	Milburn[2]	Hassall[1]	Metcalfe	
Portugal	5-2	Williams	Ramsey*	Eckersley	Nicholson[1]	Taylor, J.	Cockburn	Finney[1]	Pearson	Milburn[2]	Hassall[1]	Metcalfe	

74

Opponent	Score												Subs
1951-52													
France	2-2	Williams	Ramsey	Willis	Wright, W.*	Chilton	Cockburn	Finney	Mannion	Milburn	Hassall	Medley[1]	†
Wales	1-1	Williams	Ramsey	Smith, L.	Wright, W.*	Barrass	Dickinson	Finney	Thompson, T.	Lofthouse	Phillips	Medley	
Northern Ireland	2-0	Merrick	Ramsey	Smith, L.	Wright, W.*	Barrass	Dickinson	Finney	Sewell	Lofthouse[1]	Baily, E.	Medley	
Austria	2-2	Merrick	Ramsey[1]	Eckersley	Wright, W.*	Froggatt, J.	Dickinson	Finney	Broadis[2]	Lofthouse	Pearson[2]	Medley	
Scotland	2-1	Merrick	Ramsey	Garrett	Wright, W.*	Froggatt, J.	Dickinson	Finney	Broadis	Lofthouse	Pearson	Rowley, J.[1]	
Italy	1-1	Merrick	Ramsey	Eckersley	Wright, W.*	Froggatt, J.	Dickinson	Finney	Sewell[1]	Lofthouse[1]	Baily, E.	Elliott	
Austria	3-2	Merrick	Ramsey	Eckersley	Wright, W.*	Froggatt, J.	Dickinson	Finney	Sewell[1]	Lofthouse[2]	Baily, E.	Elliott	
Switzerland	3-0	Merrick	Ramsey	Eckersley	Wright, W.*	Froggatt, J.	Dickinson	Allen, R.	Sewell[1]	Lofthouse[2]	Baily, E.	Finney	
1952-53													
Northern Ireland	2-2	Merrick	Ramsey	Eckersley	Wright, W.*	Froggatt, J.[1]	Dickinson	Finney	Sewell	Lofthouse[1]	Baily, E.	Elliott[1]	
Wales	5-2	Merrick	Ramsey	Smith, L.	Wright, W.*	Froggatt, J.[1]	Dickinson	Finney	Froggatt, R.	Lofthouse[2]	Bentley	Elliott[2]	
Belgium	5-0	Merrick	Ramsey	Smith, L.	Wright, W.*	Barrass	Dickinson	Finney	Bentley[1]	Lofthouse[2]	Froggatt, R.[1]	Elliott[2]	
Scotland	2-2	Merrick	Ramsey	Eckersley	Wright, W.*	Froggatt, J.	Dickinson	Finney	Broadis[2]	Lofthouse	Froggatt, R.	Froggatt, J.	
Argentina	0-0	Merrick	Ramsey	Eckersley	Wright, W.*	Johnston	Dickinson	Finney	Broadis	Lofthouse	Taylor, T.[1]	Berry	
Chile	2-1	Merrick	Ramsey	Eckersley	Wright, W.*	Johnston	Dickinson	Finney	Broadis	Lofthouse	Taylor, T.[1]	Berry	
Uruguay	1-2	Merrick	Ramsey	Eckersley	Wright, W.*	Johnston	Dickinson	Finney[2]	Broadis	Lofthouse	Taylor, T.[1]	Berry	
USA	6-3	Ditchburn	Ramsey	Eckersley	Wright, W.*	Johnston	Dickinson	Finney[2]	Broadis[1]	Lofthouse[2]	Froggatt, R.[1]	Froggatt, J.	
1953-54													
Wales	4-1	Merrick	Garrett	Eckersley	Wright, W.*	Johnston	Dickinson	Finney	Quixall	Lofthouse[2]	Wilshaw[2]	Mullen[1]	
FIFA	4-4	Merrick	Ramsey[1]	Eckersley	Wright, W.*	Ufton	Dickinson	Matthews, S.	Mortensen[1]	Lofthouse[1]	Quixall[2]	Mullen[2]	
Ireland	3-1	Merrick	Rickaby	Eckersley	Wright, W.*	Johnston	Dickinson	Matthews, S.	Quixall	Lofthouse[1]	Hassall[2]	Mullen	
Hungary	3-6	Merrick	Ramsey[1]	Eckersley	Wright, W.*	Johnston	Dickinson	Matthews, S.	Taylor, E.	Mortensen[1]	Sewell[1]	Robb	
Scotland	4-2	Merrick	Staniforth	Byrne, R.	Wright, W.*	Clarke, H.	Dickinson	Finney	Broadis[1]	Nicholls[1]	Mullen[1]	Allen, R.[1]	
Yugoslavia	0-1	Merrick	Staniforth	Byrne, R.	Wright, W.*	Owen	Dickinson	Finney	Broadis	Allen, R.	Nicholls	Mullen	
Hungary	1-7	Merrick	Staniforth	Byrne, R.	Wright, W.*	Owen	Dickinson	Harris, P.	Sewell	Jezzard	Broadis[1]	Finney	
Belgium	4-4	Merrick	Staniforth	Byrne, R.	Wright, W.*	Wright, W.*	Dickinson	Matthews, S.	Broadis[2]	Lofthouse[2]	Taylor, T.	Finney[1]	
Switzerland	2-0	Merrick	Staniforth	Byrne, R.	McGarry	Wright, W.*	Dickinson	Finney	Broadis	Taylor, T.	Wilshaw[1]	Mullen[1]	
Uruguay	2-4	Merrick	Staniforth	Byrne, R.	McGarry	Wright, W.*	Dickinson	Matthews, S.	Broadis	Lofthouse[1]	Wilshaw	Finney[1]	
1954-55													
Northern Ireland	2-0	Wood	Foulkes	Byrne, R.	Wheeler	Wright, W.*	Barlow	Matthews, S.	Revie[1]	Lofthouse	Haynes[1]	Pilkington	
Wales	3-2	Wood	Staniforth	Byrne, R.	Phillips	Wright, W.*	Slater	Matthews, S.	Bentley[3]	Allen, R.[1]	Shackleton[1]	Blunstone	
West Germany	3-1	Williams	Staniforth	Byrne, R.	Phillips	Wright, W.*	Slater	Matthews, S.	Bentley[1]	Allen, R.[1]	Shackleton	Finney	
Scotland	7-2	Williams	Meadows	Byrne, R.	Armstrong	Wright, W.*	Edwards	Matthews, S.	Revie[1]	Lofthouse[2]	Wilshaw[4]	Blunstone	
France	0-1	Williams	Sillett, P.	Byrne, R.	Flowers	Wright, W.*	Edwards	Matthews, S.	Revie	Lofthouse	Wilshaw	Blunstone	
Spain	1-1	Williams	Sillett, P.	Byrne, R.	Dickinson	Wright, W.*	Edwards	Matthews, S.	Bentley[1]	Lofthouse	Quixall	Wilshaw	
Portugal	1-3	Williams	Sillett, P.	Byrne, R.	Dickinson	Wright, W.*	Edwards	Matthews, S.	Bentley[1]	Lofthouse	Wilshaw	Blunstone	Quixall(9)
1955-56													
Denmark	5-1	Baynham	Hall	Byrne, R.	McGarry	Wright, W.*	Dickinson	Milburn	Revie[2]	Lofthouse[2]	Bradford[1]	Finney	
Wales	1-2	Williams	Hall	Byrne, R.	McGarry	Wright, W.*	Dickinson	Matthews, S.	Revie	Lofthouse	Wilshaw[2]	Finney	
Northern Ireland	3-0	Baynham	Hall	Byrne, R.	Clayton	Wright, W.*	Dickinson	Finney[1]	Haynes	Jezzard	Wilshaw[2]	Perry[2]	†
Spain	4-1	Williams	Hall	Byrne, R.	Clayton	Wright, W.*	Dickinson	Finney	Atyeo[1]	Lofthouse	Haynes[1]	Perry[2]	
Scotland	1-1	Matthews, R.	Hall	Byrne, R.	Dickinson	Wright, W.*	Edwards	Finney[1]	Taylor, T.	Lofthouse[1]	Haynes	Perry	
Brazil	4-2	Matthews, R.	Hall	Byrne, R.	Clayton	Wright, W.*	Edwards	Matthews, S.	Atyeo	Taylor, T.[2]	Haynes	Grainger[2]	
Sweden	0-0	Matthews, R.	Hall	Byrne, R.	Clayton	Wright, W.*	Edwards	Berry	Atyeo	Taylor, T.	Haynes	Grainger	
Finland	5-1	Wood	Hall	Byrne, R.	Clayton	Wright, W.*	Edwards	Astall[1]	Haynes[1]	Taylor, T.	Wilshaw[1]	Grainger[1]	
West Germany	3-1	Matthews, R.	Hall	Byrne, R.	Clayton	Wright, W.*	Edwards[1]	Astall	Haynes[1]	Taylor, T.	Wilshaw	Grainger[1]	Lofthouse(9)[2]
1956-57													
Northern Ireland	1-1	Matthews, R.	Hall	Byrne, R.	Clayton	Wright, W.*	Edwards	Matthews, S.[1]	Revie	Taylor, T.[1]	Wilshaw	Grainger	
Wales	3-1	Ditchburn	Hall	Byrne, R.	Clayton	Wright, W.*	Dickinson	Matthews, S.	Brooks[1]	Finney[1]	Haynes	Grainger	

ENGLAND'S FULL INTERNATIONAL TEAMS 1946-91 (cont'd)

versus	Result	1	2	3	4	5	6	7	8	9	10	11	Substitutes
1956-57 (cont'd)													
Yugoslavia	3-0	Ditchburn	Hall	Byrne, R.	Clayton	Wright, W.*	Dickinson	Matthews, S.	Brooks[1]	Finney	Haynes	Blunstone	Taylor, T.(10)[1]
Denmark	5-2	Ditchburn	Hall	Byrne, R.	Clayton	Wright, W.*	Dickinson	Matthews, S.	Brooks	Taylor, T.[3]	Edwards[2]	Finney	
Scotland	2-1	Hodgkinson	Hall	Byrne, R.	Clayton	Wright, W.*	Edwards[1]	Matthews, S.	Thompson, T.	Finney	Kevan[1]	Grainger	
Republic of Ireland	5-1	Hodgkinson	Hall	Byrne, R.	Clayton	Wright, W.*	Edwards	Matthews, S.	Atyeo[2]	Taylor, T.[3]	Haynes[1]	Finney	
Denmark	4-1	Hodgkinson	Hall	Byrne, R.	Clayton	Wright, W.*	Edwards	Matthews, S.	Atyeo[1]	Taylor, T.[2]	Haynes[1]	Finney	
Republic of Ireland	1-1	Hodgkinson	Hall	Byrne, R.	Clayton	Wright, W.*	Edwards	Finney	Atyeo[1]	Taylor, T.	Haynes	Pegg	
1957-58													†
Wales	4-0	Hopkinson	Howe, D.	Byrne, R.	Clayton	Wright, W.*	Edwards	Douglas	Kevan	Taylor, T.	Haynes[2]	Finney[1]	
Northern Ireland	2-3	Hopkinson	Howe, D.	Byrne, R.	Clayton	Wright, W.*	Edwards[1]	Douglas	Kevan	Taylor, T.	Haynes	A'Court[1]	
France	4-0	Hopkinson	Howe, D.	Byrne, R.	Langley	Wright, W.*	Edwards	Douglas[1]	Robson, R.[2]	Taylor, T.[2]	Haynes	Finney	
Scotland	4-0	Hopkinson	Howe, D.	Langley	Clayton	Wright, W.*	Slater	Douglas	Charlton, R.[1]	Kevan	Haynes	Finney	
Portugal	2-1	Hopkinson	Howe, D.	Langley	Clayton	Wright, W.*	Slater	Douglas	Charlton, R.[2]	Kevan	Haynes	Finney	
Yugoslavia	0-5	Hopkinson	Howe, D.	Banks, T.	Clamp	Wright, W.*	Slater	Douglas	Charlton, R.	Kevan	Haynes	Finney	
USSR	1-1	McDonald	Howe, D.	Banks, T.	Clamp	Wright, W.*	Slater	Douglas	Robson, R.	Kevan[1]	Haynes	Finney[1]	
USSR	2-2	McDonald	Howe, D.	Banks, T.	Clamp	Wright, W.*	Slater	Douglas	Robson, R.	Kevan[1]	Haynes	Finney[1]	
Brazil	0-0	McDonald	Howe, D.	Banks, T.	Clamp	Wright, W.*	Slater	Douglas	Robson, R.	Kevan[1]	Haynes	A'Court	
Austria	2-2	McDonald	Howe, D.	Banks, T.	Clamp	Wright, W.*	Slater	Douglas	Robson, R.	Kevan[1]	Haynes[1]	A'Court	
USSR	0-1	McDonald	Howe, D.	Banks, T.	Clayton	Wright, W.*	Slater	Brabrook	Broadbent	Kevan	Haynes	A'Court	
1958-59													
Northern Ireland	3-3	McDonald	Howe, D.	Banks, T.	Clayton	Wright, W.*	McGuinness	Brabrook	Broadbent	Charlton, R.[2]	Haynes[1]	Finney[1]	
USSR	5-0	McDonald	Howe, D.	Shaw, G.	Clayton	Wright, W.*	Slater	Douglas	Charlton, B.[1]	Lofthouse[1]	Haynes[3]	Finney	
Wales	2-2	McDonald	Howe, D.	Shaw, G.	Clayton	Wright, W.*	Flowers	Clapton	Broadbent[2]	Lofthouse	Haynes	A'Court	
Scotland	1-0	Hopkinson	Howe, D.	Shaw, G.	Clayton	Wright, W.*	Flowers	Douglas	Broadbent	Charlton, R.[1]	Haynes	Holden	
Italy	2-2	Hopkinson	Howe, D.	Shaw, G.	Clayton	Wright, W.*	Flowers	Bradley[1]	Broadbent	Charlton, R.[1]	Haynes	Holden	
Brazil	0-2	McDonald	Howe, D.	Armfield	Clayton	Wright, W.*	Flowers	Deeley	Broadbent	Charlton, R.	Haynes	Holden	Flowers(6, Bradley(7)
Peru	1-4	Hopkinson	Howe, D.	Armfield	Clayton	Wright, W.*	Flowers	Deeley	Greaves[1]	Charlton, R.	Haynes	Holden	
Mexico	1-2	Hopkinson	Howe, D.	Armfield	Clayton	Wright, W.*	McGuinness	Holden	Greaves	Kevan[1]	Haynes	Charlton, R.[1]	
USA	8-1	Hopkinson	Howe, D.	Armfield	Clayton	Wright, W.*	Flowers[2]	Bradley[1]	Greaves	Kevan[1]	Haynes[1]	Charlton, R.[3]	
1959-60													
Wales	1-1	Hopkinson	Howe, D.	Allen, A.	Clayton*	Smith, T.	Flowers	Connelly[1]	Greaves[1]	Clough	Charlton, R.[1]	Holliday	
Sweden	2-3	Hopkinson	Howe, D.	Allen, A.	Clayton*	Smith, T.	Flowers	Connelly[1]	Greaves	Clough	Charlton, R.[1]	Holliday	
Northern Ireland	2-1	Springett, R.	Howe, D.	Allen, A.	Clayton*	Brown, K.	Flowers	Connelly	Haynes	Baker	Parry[1]	Holliday	
Scotland	1-1	Springett, R.	Armfield	Wilson	Clayton*	Slater	Flowers	Connelly	Broadbent	Baker	Charlton, R.[1]		
Yugoslavia	3-3	Springett, R.	Armfield	Wilson	Clayton*	Swan	Flowers	Douglas[1]	Haynes*	Baker	Greaves[1]	Charlton, R.	
Spain	0-3	Springett, R.	Armfield	Wilson	Robson, R.	Swan	Flowers	Brabrook	Haynes*	Baker	Greaves	Charlton, R.	
Hungary	0-2	Springett, R.	Armfield	Wilson	Robson, R.	Swan	Flowers	Douglas	Haynes*	Viollet	Greaves	Charlton, R.	
1960-61													
Northern Ireland	5-2	Springett, R.	Armfield	McNeil	Robson, R.	Swan	Flowers	Douglas[1]	Greaves[2]	Smith, R.[1]	Haynes*	Charlton, R.[1]	
Luxembourg	9-0	Springett, R.	Armfield	McNeil	Robson, R.	Swan	Flowers	Douglas[1]	Greaves[3]	Smith, R.[2]	Haynes*[1]	Charlton, R.[3]	
Spain	4-2	Springett, R.	Armfield	McNeil	Robson, R.	Swan	Flowers	Douglas[1]	Greaves[2]	Smith, R.[2]	Haynes*[1]	Charlton, R.[1]	
Wales	5-1	Hodgkinson	Armfield	McNeil	Robson, R.[1]	Swan	Flowers	Douglas	Greaves[2]	Smith, R.[1]	Haynes*[1]	Charlton, R.[1]	
Scotland	9-3	Springett, R.	Armfield	McNeil	Robson, R.[1]	Swan	Flowers	Douglas[1]	Greaves[3]	Smith, R.[1]	Haynes*[2]	Charlton, R.[3]	
Mexico	8-0	Springett, R.	Armfield	McNeil	Robson, R.	Swan	Flowers	Douglas[2]	Kevan	Hitchens[1]	Haynes*	Charlton, R.	
Portugal	1-1	Springett, R.	Armfield	McNeil	Robson, R.	Swan	Flowers	Douglas[1]	Greaves	Smith, R.[2]	Haynes*	Charlton, R.	
Italy	3-2	Springett, R.	Armfield	McNeil	Robson, R.	Swan	Flowers	Douglas	Greaves[1]	Hitchens[2]	Haynes*	Charlton, R.	
Austria	1-3	Springett, R.	Armfield	Angus	Miller	Swan	Flowers	Douglas	Greaves[1]	Hitchens	Haynes*	Charlton, R.	

1961-62

Luxembourg	4-1	Springett, R.	Armfield*	McNeil	Robson, R.	Swan	Flowers	Douglas	Fantham	Pointer[1]	Viollet[1]	Charlton, R.[2]
Wales	1-1	Springett, R.	Armfield	Wilson	Robson, R.	Swan	Flowers	Connelly[1]	Douglas	Pointer	Haynes*	Charlton, R.
Portugal	2-0	Springett, R.	Armfield	Wilson	Robson, R.	Swan	Flowers	Connelly[1]	Douglas	Pointer	Haynes*	Charlton, R.[1]
Northern Ireland	1-1	Springett, R.	Armfield	Wilson	Robson, R.	Swan	Flowers	Douglas	Byrne, J.	Crawford[1]	Haynes*	Charlton, R.
Austria	3-1	Springett, R.	Armfield	Wilson	Anderson	Swan	Flowers	Connelly[1]	Hunt[1]	Crawford[1]	Haynes*	Charlton, R.
Scotland	0-2	Springett, R.	Armfield	Wilson	Anderson	Swan	Flowers	Douglas	Greaves	Smith, R.	Haynes*	Charlton, R.
Switzerland	3-1	Springett, R.	Armfield	Wilson	Robson, R.	Swan	Flowers	Connelly[1]	Greaves	Hitchens	Haynes*	Charlton, R.
Peru	4-0	Springett, R.	Armfield	Wilson	Moore	Norman	Flowers	Douglas	Greaves[3]	Hitchens	Haynes*	Charlton, R.
Hungary	1-2	Springett, R.	Armfield	Wilson	Moore	Norman	Flowers	Douglas	Greaves	Hitchens	Haynes*	Charlton, R.[1]
Argentina	3-1	Springett, R.	Armfield	Wilson	Moore	Norman	Flowers	Douglas	Greaves[1]	Peacock	Haynes*	Charlton, R.[1]
Bulgaria	0-0	Springett, R.	Armfield	Wilson	Moore	Norman	Flowers	Douglas	Greaves	Peacock	Haynes*	Charlton, R.
Brazil	1-3	Springett, R.	Armfield	Wilson	Moore	Norman	Flowers	Douglas	Greaves	Hitchens[1]	Haynes*	Charlton, R.

1962-63

France	1-1	Springett, R.	Armfield*	Wilson	Moore	Norman	Flowers[1]	Hellawell	Crowe	Charnley	Greaves[1]	Hinton, A.
Northern Ireland	3-1	Springett, R.	Armfield*	Wilson	Moore	Norman	Flowers	Hellawell	Hill, F.	Peacock	Greaves[1]	O'Grady[2]
Wales	4-0	Springett, R.	Armfield*	Shaw, G.	Moore	Labone	Flowers	Connelly[1]	Hill, F.	Peacock[2]	Greaves[1]	Tambling
France	2-5	Springett, R.	Armfield*	Henry	Moore	Labone	Flowers	Connelly	Tambling[1]	Smith, R.[1]	Greaves	Charlton, R.
Scotland	1-2	Banks, G.	Armfield*	Byrne, G.	Moore	Norman	Flowers	Douglas[1]	Greaves	Smith, R.	Melia	Charlton, R.
Brazil	1-1	Banks, G.	Armfield*	Wilson	Milne	Norman	Moore	Douglas[1]	Greaves	Smith, R.	Eastham	Charlton, R.
Czechoslovakia	4-2	Banks, G.	Armfield*	Wilson	Milne	Norman	Moore*	Paine	Greaves[2]	Smith, R.[1]	Eastham	Charlton, R.[1]
East Germany	2-1	Banks, G.	Shellito	Wilson	Milne[1]	Norman	Moore*	Paine	Hunt[1]	Smith, R.	Eastham	Charlton, R.[1]
Switzerland	8-1	Springett, R.	Armfield*	Wilson	Kay[1]	Moore	Flowers	Douglas[1]	Greaves	Byrne, J.[2]	Melia[1]	Charlton, R.[3]

1963-64

Wales	4-0	Banks, G.	Armfield*	Wilson	Milne	Norman	Moore	Paine	Greaves[1]	Smith, R.[2]	Eastham	Charlton, R.[1]
Rest of the World	2-1	Banks, G.	Armfield*	Wilson	Milne	Norman	Moore	Paine[1]	Greaves[1]	Smith, R.	Eastham	Charlton, R.
Northern Ireland	8-3	Banks, G.	Armfield*	Thomson, R.	Milne	Norman	Moore	Paine[3]	Greaves[4]	Smith, R.[1]	Eastham	Charlton, R.
Scotland	0-1	Banks, G.	Armfield*	Wilson	Milne	Norman	Moore	Paine	Hunt	Byrne, J.	Eastham	Charlton, R.
Uruguay	2-1	Banks, G.	Cohen	Wilson	Milne	Norman	Moore*	Paine	Greaves	Byrne, J.[2]	Eastham	Charlton, R.
Portugal	4-3	Banks, G.	Cohen	Wilson	Milne	Norman	Moore*	Thompson, P.	Greaves	Byrne, J.[3]	Eastham[1]	Charlton, R.
Republic of Ireland	3-1	Waiters	Cohen	Wilson	Milne	Flowers	Moore*	Paine	Greaves[1]	Byrne, J.[2]	Eastham	Charlton, R.
USA	10-0	Banks, G.	Cohen	Thomson, R.	Bailey, M.	Norman	Flowers*	Paine[2]	Hunt[4]	Pickering[3]	Eastham	Thompson, P.
Brazil	1-5	Waiters	Thomson, R.	Wilson	Milne	Norman	Moore*	Thompson, P.	Greaves[1]	Byrne, J.	Eastham	Charlton, R.
Portugal	1-1	Banks, G.	Thomson, R.	Wilson	Flowers	Norman	Moore*	Paine	Greaves	Byrne, J.[1]	Eastham	Charlton, R.
Argentina	0-1	Banks, G.	Thomson, R.	Wilson	Milne	Norman	Moore*	Paine	Greaves	Byrne, J.	Eastham	Charlton, R.

Charlton, R.(10)[1]

1964-65

Northern Ireland	4-3	Banks, G.	Cohen	Thomson, R.	Milne	Norman	Moore*	Paine	Greaves[3]	Pickering[1]	Charlton, R.	Thompson, P.
Belgium	2-2	Waiters	Cohen	Thomson, R.	Milne	Norman	Young	Thompson, P.	Greaves	Pickering[2]	Venables	Hinton, A.
Wales	2-1	Waiters	Cohen	Thomson, R.	Bailey, M.	Norman	Flowers*	Thompson, P.	Hunt	Wignall[2]	Byrne, J.	Hinton, A.
Holland	1-1	Waiters	Cohen	Thomson, R.	Mullery	Norman	Moore*	Thompson, P.	Greaves	Wignall	Venables	Charlton, R.[1]
Scotland	2-2	Banks, G.	Cohen	Wilson	Stiles	Charlton, J.	Moore*	Thompson, P.	Greaves[1]	Bridges	Byrne, J.[1]	Connelly
Hungary	1-0	Banks, G.	Cohen	Wilson	Stiles	Charlton, J.	Moore*	Paine	Greaves[1]	Bridges	Eastham	Connelly
Yugoslavia	1-1	Banks, G.	Cohen	Wilson	Stiles	Charlton, J.	Moore*	Paine	Greaves	Bridges[1]	Ball	Connelly
West Germany	1-0	Banks, G.	Cohen	Wilson	Flowers	Charlton, J.	Moore*	Paine[1]	Ball	Jones, M.	Eastham	Temple
Sweden	2-1	Banks, G.	Cohen	Wilson	Stiles	Charlton, J.	Moore*	Paine	Ball[1]	Jones, M.	Eastham	Connelly[1]

1965-66

Wales	0-0	Springett, R.	Cohen	Wilson	Stiles	Charlton, J.	Moore*	Paine	Greaves	Peacock	Charlton, R.	Connelly
Austria	2-3	Springett, R.	Cohen	Wilson	Stiles	Charlton, J.	Moore*	Paine	Greaves	Bridges	Charlton, R.[1]	Connelly[1]
Northern Ireland	2-1	Banks, G.	Cohen	Wilson	Stiles	Charlton, J.	Moore*	Thompson, P.	Baker[1]	Peacock[1]	Charlton, R.	Connelly

77

ENGLAND'S FULL INTERNATIONAL TEAMS 1946-91 (cont'd)

versus	Result	1	2	3	4	5	6	7	8	9	10	11	Substitutes
1965-66 (cont'd)													
Spain	2-0	Banks, G.	Cohen	Wilson	Stiles	Charlton, J.	Moore*	Ball	Hunt[1]	Baker	Eastham	Charlton, R.	Hunter(9)
Poland	1-1	Banks, G.	Cohen	Wilson	Stiles	Charlton, J.	Moore*[1]	Ball	Hunt	Baker	Eastham	Harris, G.	
West Germany	1-0	Banks, G.	Cohen	Newton, K.	Moore*	Charlton, J.	Hunter	Ball	Hunt[2]	Stiles[1]	Hurst, G.[1]	Charlton, R.	Wilson(3)
Scotland	4-3	Banks, G.	Cohen	Newton, K.	Stiles	Charlton, J.	Moore*	Ball	Greaves[1]	Charlton, R.[1]	Hurst, G.[1]	Connelly	
Yugoslavia	2-0	Banks, G.	Armfield*	Wilson	Stiles	Charlton, J.[1]	Hunter	Paine	Greaves[1]	Charlton, R.	Hurst, G.	Tambling	
Finland	3-0	Banks, G.	Armfield*	Wilson	Peters[1]	Charlton, J.[1]	Hunter	Callaghan	Hunt[1]	Charlton, R.	Hurst, G.	Ball	
Norway	6-1	Springett, R.	Cohen	Byrne, G.	Stiles	Flowers	Moore*[1]	Paine	Greaves[4]	Charlton, R.	Hunt	Connelly[1]	
Denmark	2-0	Bonetti	Cohen	Wilson	Stiles	Charlton, J.[1]	Moore*	Ball	Greaves	Hurst, G.	Eastham[1]	Connelly	
Poland	1-0	Banks, G.	Cohen	Wilson	Stiles	Charlton, J.	Moore*	Ball	Greaves	Charlton, R.	Hunt[1]	Peters	
Uruguay	0-0	Banks, G.	Cohen	Wilson	Stiles	Charlton, J.	Moore*	Ball	Greaves	Charlton, R.	Hunt[1]	Connelly	
Mexico	2-0	Banks, G.	Cohen	Wilson	Stiles	Charlton, J.	Moore*	Paine	Greaves	Charlton, R.[1]	Hunt[2]	Peters	
France	2-0	Banks, G.	Cohen	Wilson	Stiles	Charlton, J.	Moore*	Callaghan	Greaves	Charlton, R.	Hunt	Peters	
Argentina	1-0	Banks, G.	Cohen	Wilson	Stiles	Charlton, J.	Moore*	Ball	Hurst, G.[1]	Charlton, R.[2]	Hunt	Peters	
Portugal	2-1	Banks, G.	Cohen	Wilson	Stiles	Charlton, J.	Moore*	Ball	Hurst, G.[3]	Charlton, R.	Hunt	Peters	
West Germany	4-2	Banks, G.	Cohen	Wilson	Stiles	Charlton, J.	Moore*	Ball	Hurst, G.[3]	Charlton, R.	Hunt	Peters[1]	
1966-67													
Ireland	2-0	Banks, G.	Cohen	Wilson	Stiles	Charlton, J.	Moore*	Ball	Hurst, G.	Charlton, R.	Hunt[1]	Peters[1]	
Czechoslovakia	0-0	Banks, G.	Cohen	Wilson	Stiles	Charlton, J.[1]	Moore*	Ball	Hurst, G.[2]	Charlton, R.	Hunt	Peters	†
Wales	5-1	Banks, G.	Cohen	Wilson	Stiles	Charlton, J.[1]	Moore*	Ball	Hurst, G.	Charlton, R.[1]	Hunt	Peters	
Scotland	2-3	Banks, G.	Cohen	Wilson	Stiles	Charlton, J.[1]	Moore*	Ball	Greaves	Charlton, R.	Hurst, G.[1]	Hollins	
Spain	2-0	Bonetti	Cohen	Newton, K.	Mullery	Labone	Moore*	Ball[1]	Greaves[1]	Hurst, G.	Hunt[1]	Hunter	
Austria	1-0	Bonetti	Newton, K.	Wilson	Mullery	Labone	Moore*	Ball[1]	Greaves	Hurst, G	Hunt	Hunter	
1967-68													
Wales	3-0	Banks, G.	Cohen	Newton, K.	Mullery	Charlton, J.	Moore*	Ball[1]	Hunt	Charlton, R.[1]	Hurst, G.[1]	Peters[1]	
Northern Ireland	2-0	Banks, G.	Cohen	Wilson	Mullery	Sadler	Moore*	Thompson, P.	Hunt	Charlton, R.[1]	Hurst, G.	Peters[1]	
USSR	2-2	Banks, G.	Knowles, C.	Wilson	Mullery	Sadler	Moore*	Ball[1]	Hunt	Charlton, R.	Hurst, G.	Peters[1]	
Scotland	1-1	Banks, G.	Knowles, C.	Wilson	Mullery	Labone	Moore*	Ball	Hurst, G.	Summerbee	Charlton, R.[1]	Peters[1]	
Spain	1-0	Bonetti	Newton, K.	Wilson	Mullery	Charlton, J.	Moore*	Ball	Hunt	Summerbee	Charlton, R.[1]	Peters	
Sweden	3-1	Stepney	Newton, K.	Knowles, C.	Mullery	Labone	Moore*	Bell	Peters[1]	Charlton, R.[1]	Hunt[1]	Hunter[1]	Hurst, G.(9)
West Germany	0-1	Banks, G.	Newton, K.	Knowles, C.	Hunter	Labone	Moore*	Ball	Bell	Summerbee	Hurst, G.	Thompson, P.	
Yugoslavia	0-1	Banks, G.	Newton, K.	Wilson	Mullery	Labone	Moore*	Peters	Peters	Charlton, R.	Hunt	Hunter	
USSR	2-0	Banks, G.	Wright, T.	Wilson	Stiles	Labone	Moore*	Hunter	Hunt	Charlton, R.[1]	Hurst, G.[1]	Peters	
1968-69													
Romania	0-0	Banks, G.	Wright, T.	Newton, K.	Mullery	Labone	Moore*	Ball	Hunt	Charlton, R.	Hurst, G.[1]	Peters	McNab(2)
Bulgaria	1-1	West	Newton, K.	McNab	Mullery	Labone	Moore*	Lee, F.	Bell	Charlton, R.	Hurst, G.	Peters	Reaney(2)
Romania	1-1	West	Wright, T.	McNab	Stiles	Charlton, J.[1]	Hunter	Radford	Bell	Charlton, R.*	Hurst, G.	Ball	
France	5-0	Banks, G.	Newton, K.	Cooper	Mullery	Charlton, J.	Moore*	Lee, F.[1]	Bell	Hurst, G.[3]	Peters	O'Grady[1]	
Northern Ireland	3-1	West	Newton, K.	McNab	Mullery	Labone	Moore*	Ball	Lee, F.[1]	Charlton, R.	Charlton, R.[1]	Peters[1]	
Wales	2-1	Banks, G.	Newton, K.	Cooper	Moore*	Charlton, J.	Hunter	Lee, F.[1]	Bell	Astle	Charlton, R.[1]	Ball	Wright, T.(2)
Scotland	4-1	West	Newton, K.	Cooper	Mullery	Labone	Moore*	Lee, F.[1]	Bell	Charlton, R.	Hurst, G.[2]	Peters[2]	
Mexico	0-0	Banks, G.	Newton, K.	Cooper	Mullery	Labone	Moore*	Lee, F.	Bell	Charlton, R.[1]	Hurst, G.	Peters	
Uruguay	2-1	Banks, G.	Wright, T.	Newton, K.	Mullery	Labone	Moore*	Lee, F.[1]	Bell	Hurst, G.[1]	Ball	Peters	
Brazil	1-2	Banks, G.	Wright, T.	Newton, K.	Mullery	Labone	Moore*	Ball	Bell[1]	Charlton, R.	Hurst, G.	Peters	

	Score	1	2	3	4	5	6	7	8	9	10	11	Substitutes
1969-70													
Holland	1-0	Bonetti	Wright, T.	Hughes, E.	Mullery	Charlton, J.	Moore*	Lee, F.	Bell	Charlton, R.	Hurst, G.	Peters	Thompson, P.(7)
Portugal	1-0	Bonetti	Reaney	Hughes, E.	Mullery	Charlton, J.	Moore*	Lee, F.	Bell	Astle	Hurst, G.	Peters	Peters(8)
Holland	0-0	Banks, G.	Newton, K.	Cooper	Moore*	Charlton, J.	Hunter	Lee, F.	Bell	Charlton, R.	Hurst, G.	Peters	Mullery(7) Hurst, G.(9)
Belgium	3-1	Banks, G.	Wright, T.	Cooper	Mullery	Labone	Hughes, E.	Lee, F.	Ball[2]	Osgood	Hurst, G.	Peters[1]	Bell(2)
Wales	1-1	Banks, G.	Wright, T.	Hughes, E.	Mullery	Labone	Moore*	Lee, F.	Ball	Charlton, R.[1]	Hurst, G.	Peters	Mullery(7)
Northern Ireland	3-1	Banks, G.	Newton, K.	Hughes, E.	Mullery	Labone	Moore*	Coates	Kidd	Astle	Hurst, G.	Peters[1]	Kidd(7)[1] Sadler(9)
Scotland	0-0	Banks, G.	Newton, K.	Hughes, E.	Stiles	Labone	Moore*	Thompson, P.	Ball	Charlton, R.[1]	Hurst, G.	Peters[2]	Wright, T.(2) Osgood(7)
Colombia	4-0	Banks, G.	Newton, K.	Cooper	Mullery	Labone	Moore*	Lee, F.	Ball[1]	Charlton, R.[1]	Hurst, G.	Peters[2]	Astle(7) Bell(9)
Ecuador	2-0	Banks, G.	Newton, K.	Cooper	Mullery	Labone	Moore*	Lee, F.	Ball[1]	Astle	Hurst, G.	Peters	Ball(7) Bell(9)
Romania	1-0	Banks, G.	Newton, K.	Cooper	Mullery	Labone	Moore*	Lee, F.	Ball	Charlton, R.	Hurst, G.	Peters	Ball(9) Osgood(9)
Brazil	0-1	Banks, G.	Wright, T.	Cooper	Mullery	Labone	Moore*	Lee, F.	Ball	Charlton, R.	Hurst, G.	Peters	
Czechoslovakia	1-0	Banks, G.	Newton, K.	Cooper	Mullery	Charlton, J.	Moore*	Lee, F.	Ball	Astle	Hurst, G.	Peters[1]	
West Germany	2-3	Bonetti	Newton, K.	Cooper	Mullery[1]	Labone	Moore*	Lee, F.	Ball	Charlton, R.	Hurst, G.	Peters[1]	Bell(9) Hunter(11)
1970-71													
East Germany	3-1	Shilton	Hughes, E.	Cooper	Mullery	Sadler	Moore*	Lee, F.[1]	Ball	Hurst, G.	Clarke, A.[1]	Peters[1]	Coates(8)
Malta	1-0	Banks, G.	Reaney	Hughes, E.	Mullery*	McFarland	Hunter	Ball	Chivers	Royle	Harvey	Peters	Ball(11)
Greece	3-0	Banks, G.	Storey	Hughes, E.	Mullery	McFarland	Moore*	Lee, F.[1]	Ball	Chivers[2]	Hurst, G.[1]	Peters	
Malta	5-0	Banks, G.	Lawler[1]	Cooper	Moore*	McFarland	Hughes, E.	Lee, F.	Coates	Chivers	Clarke, A.[1]	Peters	Clarke, A.(8)
Ireland	1-0	Banks, G.	Lawler	Cooper	Mullery	Lloyd	Hughes, E.	Lee, F.	Ball	Chivers	Clarke, A.[1]	Peters[1]	Clarke, A.(7)
Wales	0-0	Shilton	Madeley	Cooper	Storey	McFarland	Moore*	Lee, F.	Brown, A.	Hurst, G.[1]	Coates	Peters[1]	
Scotland	3-1	Banks, G.	Lawler	Cooper	Smith, T.	McFarland	Hughes, E.	Lee, F.	Ball	Chivers[2]	Hurst, G.	Peters[1]	
1971-72													
Switzerland	3-2	Banks, G.	Lawler	Cooper	Storey	McFarland	Moore*	Lee, F.	Madeley	Chivers[1]	Hurst, G.[1]	Peters	Radford(10)
Switzerland	1-1	Shilton	Madeley	Hughes, E.	Storey	Lloyd	Moore*	Summerbee	Ball	Hurst, G.	Lee, F.	Hughes, E.	Chivers(7) Marsh(10)
Greece	2-0	Banks, G.	Madeley	Hughes, E.	Bell	McFarland	Hunter	Lee, F.	Ball	Chivers[1]	Hurst, G.[1]	Peters	Marsh(10)
West Germany	1-3	Banks, G.	Madeley	Hughes, E.	Storey	McFarland	Moore*	Lee, F.[1]	Bell[1]	Chivers	Hurst, G.	Peters	Summerbee(10) Peters(11)
West Germany	0-0	Banks, G.	Madeley	Hughes, E.[1]	Storey	McFarland	Moore*	Ball	Bell*	Chivers	Marsh	Hunter	Peters(11) Chivers(9)
Wales	3-0	Banks, G.	Madeley	Hughes, E.	Storey	McFarland	Moore*	Summerbee	Bell	MacDonald	Marsh[1]	Hunter	MacDonald(10)
Northern Ireland	0-1	Shilton	Todd	Storey	Storey	Lloyd	Hunter	Ball[1]	Bell	MacDonald	Marsh	Hunter	
Scotland	1-0	Banks, G.	Madeley	Hughes, E.	Storey	McFarland	Moore*	Currie	Bell	Chivers	Marsh	Currie	
1972-73													
Yugoslavia	1-1	Shilton	Mills, M.	Lampard	Storey	Blockley	Moore*	Ball	Channon	Royle[1]	Bell	Marsh	MacDonald(10) Hunter(11)
Wales	1-0	Clemence	Storey	Hughes, E.	Hunter[1]	McFarland	Moore*	Keegan	Bell[1]	Chivers	Marsh	Ball	Summerbee(8)
Wales	1-1	Clemence	Storey	Hughes, E.	Bell	McFarland	Moore*	Keegan	Bell	Chivers	Marsh	Ball	
Scotland	5-0	Shilton	Storey	Nish	Bell	Madeley	Moore*	Ball	Channon[1]	Chivers[2]	Clarke, A.[2]	Peters	
Ireland	2-1	Shilton	Storey	Hughes, E.	Bell	McFarland	Moore*	Ball	Channon[1]	Chivers[1]	Richards	Peters[1]	
Wales	3-0	Shilton	Storey	Storey	Bell	McFarland	Moore*	Ball	Channon[1]	Chivers	Clarke, A.	Peters[1]	
Scotland	1-0	Shilton	Madeley	Hughes, E.	Storey	McFarland	Moore*	Ball	Channon	Chivers	Clarke, A.[1]	Peters	
Czechoslovakia	1-1	Shilton	Madeley	Hughes, E.	Bell[1]	McFarland	Moore*	Ball	Channon	Chivers	Clarke, A.	Peters[1]	
Poland	0-2	Shilton	Madeley	Hughes, E.	Bell	McFarland	Moore*	Currie	Channon	Chivers[1]	Clarke, A.	Peters	
USSR	2-1	Shilton	Madeley	Hughes, E.	Bell	McFarland	Moore*	Currie	Channon	Chivers	Clarke, A.	Peters†	
Italy	0-2	Shilton	Madeley	Hughes, E.	Bell	McFarland	Moore*	Currie	Channon	Osgood	Clarke, A.	Peters	
1973-74													
Austria	7-0	Shilton	Madeley	Hughes, E.	Bell[1]	McFarland	Hunter	Currie[1]	Channon[2]	Chivers[1]	Clarke, A.[2]	Peters*	Hector(9)
Poland	1-1	Shilton	Madeley	Hughes, E.	Bell	McFarland	Hunter	Currie	Channon	Chivers	Clarke, A.[1]	Peters*	Hector(10)
Italy	0-1	Shilton	Madeley	Hughes, E.	Bell	McFarland	Moore*	Currie	Channon	Osgood	Clarke, A.	Peters*	
Portugal	0-0	Parkes	Nish	Pejic	Dobson	Watson	Todd	Bowles	Channon	MacDonald	Brooking	Peters*	Ball(9)

ENGLAND'S FULL INTERNATIONAL TEAMS 1946-91 (cont'd)

versus	Result	1	2	3	4	5	6	7	8	9	10	11	Substitutes
1973-74 (cont'd)													
Wales	2-0	Shilton	Nish	Pejic	Hughes, E.*	McFarland	Todd	Keegan[1]	Bell	Channon	Weller[1]	Bowles[1]	Hunter(5) Worthington(11)
Northern Ireland	1-0	Shilton	Nish	Pejic	Hughes, E.*	McFarland	Todd	Keegan[1]	Bell	Channon	Weller[1]	Bowles[1]	Watson(5) MacDonald(9)
Scotland	0-2	Shilton	Nish	Pejic	Hughes, E.*	Hunter	Todd	Channon	Bell	Worthington	Weller	Peters	
Argentina	2-2	Shilton	Hughes, E.*	Lindsay	Todd	Watson	Dobson	Keegan	Channon[1]	Worthington[1]	Bell	Brooking	
East Germany	1-1	Clemence	Hughes, E.*	Lindsay	Todd	Watson	Dobson	Keegan	Channon[1]	Worthington[1]	Bell	Brooking	MacDonald(9)
Bulgaria	1-0	Clemence	Hughes, E.*	Lindsay	Todd	Watson	Dobson	Keegan	Channon[1]	Worthington[1]	Bell	Brooking	
Yugoslavia	2-2	Clemence	Hughes, E.*	Lindsay	Todd	Watson	Dobson	Keegan[1]	Channon[1]	Worthington[1]	Bell	Brooking	
1974-75													
Czechoslovakia	3-0	Clemence	Madeley	Hughes, E.*	Dobson	Watson	Hunter	Bell[2]	Channon[1]	Worthington	Keegan	Francis, G.	Brooking(4) Thomas(9)
Portugal	0-0	Clemence	Madeley	Cooper	Brooking	Watson	Hughes, E.*	Bell	Channon[1]	Francis, G.	Clarke, A.	Thomas	Todd(3) Worthington(10)
West Germany	2-0	Clemence	Whitworth	Gillard	Bell[1]	Watson	Todd	Ball*	Channon[1]	MacDonald	Hudson	Keegan	Thomas(8)
Cyprus	5-0	Shilton	Madeley	Beattie	Beattie	Watson	Todd	Ball*	Channon[1]	MacDonald[5]	Hudson	Keegan	Thomas(8)
Cyprus	1-0	Clemence	Whitworth	Beattie	Bell	Watson	Todd	Ball*	Channon[1]	MacDonald	Keegan[1]	Thomas	Hughes, E.(3) Tueart(11)
Northern Ireland	0-0	Clemence	Whitworth	Hughes, E.	Bell	Watson	Todd	Ball*	Channon[1]	MacDonald	Keegan	Tueart	Channon(9)
Wales	2-2	Clemence	Whitworth	Gillard	Francis, G.	Watson	Todd	Ball*	Channon[1]	Johnson[2]	Viljoen	Thomas	Little(8)
Scotland	5-1	Clemence	Whitworth	Beattie[1]	Bell[1]	Watson	Todd	Ball*	Channon[1]	Johnson[1]	Francis, G.[2]	Keegan	Thomas(.1)
1975-76													
Switzerland	2-1	Clemence	Whitworth	Beattie	Francis, G.*	Watson	Todd	Keegan[1]	Channon[1]	Johnson	Currie	Bell	MacDonald(9)
Czechoslovakia	1-2	Clemence	Whitworth	Gillard	Francis, G.*	McFarland	Todd	Keegan	Channon[1]	MacDonald	Clarke, A.	Bell	Watson(5) Thomas(8)
Portugal	1-1	Clemence	Whitworth	Beattie	Madeley	Watson	Todd	Keegan	Channon[1]	MacDonald	Francis, G.*	Brooking	Clarke, A.(9) Thomas(4)
Wales	2-1	Clemence	Cherry	Neal	Doyle	Thompson, P.	Mills, M.	Keegan*	Channon	Boyer	Kennedy, R.[1]	Brooking	Clement(2) Taylor, P.(8)
Wales	1-0	Clemence	Clement	Mills, M.	Thompson, P.	Greenhoff, B.	Kennedy, R.	Francis, G.*	Channon[1]	Pearson, S.	Towers	Taylor, P.[1]	Towers(11) Royle(7)
Northern Ireland	4-0	Clemence	Todd	Mills, M.	Thompson, P.	Greenhoff, B.	Kennedy, R.	Keegan	Channon[2]	Pearson, S.	Francis, G.*[1]	Taylor, P.	Cherry(9) Doyle(5)
Scotland	1-2	Clemence	Todd	Mills, M.	Thompson, P.	McFarland	Kennedy, R.	Keegan	Channon[1]	Pearson, S.	Francis, G.*[1]	Taylor, P.	
Italy	0-1	Rimmer	Clement	Neal	Thompson, P.[1]	Doyle	Cherry	Keegan	Channon	Royle	Brooking	Francis, G.*	
Finland	3-2	Clemence	Todd	Mills, M.	Thompson, P.	Madeley	Towers	Wilkins	Channon*[2]	Pearson, S.[1]	Brooking	Francis, G.*	Corrigan(1) Mills, M.(3)
1976-77													
Republic of Ireland	1-1	Clemence	Todd	Cherry	Greenhoff, B.	McFarland	Madeley	Keegan*	Wilkins	Pearson, S.[1]	Brooking	George	Hill, G.(11)
Finland	2-1	Clemence	Todd	Beattie	Thompson, P.	Greenhoff, B.	Wilkins	Keegan*	Channon	Royle[1]	Brooking	Tueart[1]	Mills, M.(10) Hill, G.(11)
Italy	0-2	Clemence	Clement	Mills, M.	Greenhoff, B.	McFarland	Hughes, E.	Keegan*	Channon	Bowles	Cherry	Brooking	Beattie(2)
Holland	0-2	Clemence	Gidman	Beattie	Doyle	Watson	Madeley	Keegan*[1]	Francis, T.[2]	Greenhoff, B.	Bowles	Brooking	Todd(9) Pearson, S.(6)
Luxembourg	5-0	Clemence	Cherry	Cherry	Kennedy, R.[1]	Watson	Hughes, E.	Keegan*[1]	Channon*[2]	Royle	Francis, T.[1]	Hill, G.	Mariner(9)
Northern Ireland	2-1	Shilton	Cherry	Mills, M.	Greenhoff, B.	Watson	Todd	Wilkins	Channon	Mariner	Brooking	Tueart[1]	Talbot(7)
Wales	0-1	Clemence	Neal	Mills, M.	Greenhoff, B.	Watson	Hughes, E.	Francis, T.	Channon	Pearson, S.	Brooking	Kennedy, R.	Tueart(10)
Scotland	1-2	Clemence	Neal	Cherry	Greenhoff, B.	Watson	Hughes, E.	Keegan*	Francis, T.	Pearson, S.	Talbot	Kennedy, R.	Cherry(4) Tueart(11)
Brazil	0-0	Clemence	Neal	Cherry	Greenhoff, B.	Watson	Hughes, E.	Keegan*	Channon	Pearson, S.	Wilkins	Talbot	Channon(9) Kennedy,R.(10)
Argentina	1-1	Clemence	Neal	Cherry	Greenhoff, B.	Watson	Hughes, E.	Keegan*	Channon	Pearson, S.[1]	Wilkins	Talbot	Kennedy, R.(4)
Uruguay	0-0	Clemence	Neal	Mills, M.	Greenhoff, B.	Watson	Currie	Keegan*[1]	Channon	Pearson, S.	Wilkins	Talbot	
1977-78													
Switzerland	0-0	Clemence	Neal	Cherry	McDermott	Watson	Hughes, E.*	Keegan	Channon	Francis, T.	Kennedy, R.	Callaghan	Hill, G. (8) Wilkins(11)
Luxembourg	2-0	Clemence	Cherry	Hughes, E.*	Watson	Kennedy, R.[1]	Callaghan	McDermott	Wilkins	Mariner[1]	Francis, T.[1]	Hill, G.	Whymark(7) Beattie(4)
Italy	2-0	Clemence	Neal	Cherry	Wilkins	Watson	Hughes, E.*	Keegan[1]	Coppell	Latchford, R.[1]	Brooking	Barnes	Pearson, S.(9) Francis, T.(7)
West Germany	1-2	Clemence	Neal	Mills, M.	Wilkins	Watson	Hughes, E.*	Keegan[1]	Coppell	Pearson, S.[1]	Brooking	Barnes	Francis, T.(7)
Brazil	1-1	Corrigan	Mills, M.	Cherry	Greenhoff, B.	Watson	Currie	Keegan*[1]	Coppell	Latchford, R.	Francis, T.	Barnes	

80

England international match line-ups, season by season:

Opponent	Score	1	2	3	4	5	6	7	8	9	10	11	Substitutes
Wales	3-1	Shilton	Neal	Mills, M.*	Greenhoff, B.	Watson	Wilkins	Coppell	Francis, T.	Latchford, R.	Brooking	Barnes	Currie(3) Mariner(9)
Northern Ireland	1-0	Clemence	Neal	Mills, M.	Greenhoff, B.	Watson	Hughes, E.*	Coppell	Wilkins	pearson, S.	Currie	Woodcock	Greenhoff, B.(6)
Scotland	1-0	Clemence	Neal	Mills, M.	Wilkins	Watson	Hughes, E.*	Coppell	Francis, T.	Mariner	Brooking	Barnes	Greenhoff, B.(5) Currie(8)
1978-79													
Hungary	4-1	Shilton	Neal	Mills, M.	Wilkins	Watson	Hughes, E.*	Keegan	Coppell	Latchford, R.	Brooking	Barnes	Brooking(9)
Denmark	4-3	Clemence	Neal	Mills, M.	Wilkins	Watson	Hughes, E.*	Keegan	Coppell	Latchford, R.	Brooking	Barnes	Greenhoff, B.(5) Currie(8)
Republic of Ireland	1-1	Clemence	Neal	Cherry	Wilkins	Watson	Hughes, E.*	Keegan	Currie	Latchford, R.	Brooking	Barnes	
Czechoslovakia	1-0	Shilton	Anderson	Mills, M.	Wilkins	Watson	Currie	Keegan	Coppell	Woodcock	Currie	Barnes	Thompson, P.(5) Woodcock(11)
Northern Ireland	4-0	Clemence	Neal	Mills, M.	Thompson, P.	Watson	Hughes, E.*	Keegan	Coppell	Latchford, R.	Brooking	Barnes	Latchford, R.(9)
Northern Ireland	2-0	Clemence	Neal	Mills, M.*	Currie	Watson	Currie	Keegan	Wilkins	Latchford, R.	McDermott	Barnes	
Wales	0-0	Corrigan	Cherry	Sansom	Thompson, P.	Watson	Hughes, E.*	Keegan*	Coppell	Latchford, R.	McDermott	Cunningham	Coppell(9) Brooking(4)
Scotland	3-1	Clemence	Neal	Mills, M.	Currie	Watson	Wilkins	Keegan*	Coppell	Latchford, R.	Brooking	Barnes	
Bulgaria	3-0	Clemence	Neal	Mills, M.	Thompson, P.	Watson	Wilkins	Keegan*	Coppell	Latchford, R.	Brooking	Barnes	Francis, T.(9) Woodcock(11) Wilkins, R.(4)
Sweden	0-0	Shilton	Anderson	Cherry	Thompson, P.	Watson	Hughes, E.*	Keegan	Coppell	Woodcock	Currie	Cunningham	
Austria	3-4	Shilton	Neal	Mills, M.	McDermott	Osman	Wilkins	Keegan*	Coppell	Latchford, R.	Brooking	Barnes	Thompson, P.(5) Brooking(10) Clemence(1) Francis, T.(9) Cunningham(11)
1979-80													
Denmark	1-0	Clemence	Neal	Mills, M.	Thompson, P.	Watson	Wilkins	Keegan*	Coppell	McDermott	Brooking	Barnes	
Northern Ireland	5-1	Shilton	Neal	Mills, M.	Thompson, P.	Watson	Wilkins	Keegan*	Coppell	Francis	Brooking	Woodcock	McDermott(10)
Bulgaria	2-0	Clemence	Anderson	Sansom	Thompson, P.*	Watson	Robson	Keegan*	Hoddle	Francis	Kennedy, R.	Woodcock	
Republic of Ireland	2-0	Clemence	Cherry	Cherry	Thompson, P.	Watson	Wilkins	Reeves	McDermott	Johnson	Kennedy, R.	Cunningham	Coppell(9)
Spain	2-0	Shilton	Neal	Mills, M.	Thompson, P.	Watson	Wilkins	Keegan*	Coppell	Francis	Kennedy, R.	Woodcock	Hughes(2) Cunningham(9)
Argentina	3-1	Corrigan	Neal	Cherry	Thompson, P.	Watson	Kennedy, R.	Keegan*	Coppell	Johnson	Woodcock	Kennedy, R.	Cherry(2) Birtles(9)
Wales	1-4	Clemence	Cherry	Sansom	Thompson, P.	Watson	Hughes*	Keegan*	Hoddle	Mariner	Brooking	Barnes	Sansom(2) Wilkins(5)
Northern Ireland	1-1	Corrigan	Cherry	Sansom	Brooking	Watson	Wilkins	Coppell	Wilkins	Johnson	Reeves	Devonshire	Mariner(11)
Scotland	2-0	Clemence	Cherry	Sansom	Thompson, P.*	Watson	Butcher	McDermott	McDermott	Johnson	Mariner	Brooking	Hughes(10)
Australia	2-1	Corrigan	Cherry*	Lampard	Talbot	Osman	Wilkins	Coppell	Hoddle	Mariner	Sunderland	Armstrong	Devonshire(7) Ward(10)
Belgium	1-1	Clemence	Neal	Sansom	Thompson, P.	Watson	Wilkins	Keegan*	Coppell	Johnson	Brooking	Woodcock	McDermott(8) Kennedy, R.(9)
Italy	0-1	Shilton	Neal	Sansom	Thompson, P.	Watson	Wilkins	Keegan*	Coppell	Birtles	Kennedy, R.	Woodcock	Mariner(9)
Spain	2-1	Clemence	Anderson	Mills, M.	Thompson, P.	Watson	Wilkins	Keegan*	Hoddle	McDermott	Brooking	Woodcock	Cherry(2) Mariner(8)
1980-81													
Norway	4-0	Shilton	Anderson	Sansom	Thompson*	Watson	Robson	Gates	McDermott	Mariner	Woodcock	Rix	
Romania	1-2	Clemence	Neal	Sansom	Thompson*	Watson	Robson	Rix	McDermott	Birtles	Woodcock	Gates	Cunningham(9) Coppell(11) Rix(10)
Switzerland	2-1	Shilton	Neal	Sansom	Robson	Watson	Mills*	Coppell	McDermott	Mariner	Brooking	Woodcock	Barnes(8) Wilkins(10)
Spain	1-2	Clemence	Neal	Sansom	Robson	Osman	Butcher	Keegan*	Francis	Mariner	Brooking	Woodcock	McDermott(10)
Romania	0-0	Corrigan	Anderson	Sansom	Robson	Osman	Osman	Coppell	Wilkins	Francis	Brooking	Woodcock	
Brazil	0-1	Shilton	Neal	Sansom	Robson	Watson*	Wilkins	Coppell	McDermott	Withe	Rix	Woodcock	Woodcock(9)
Wales	0-0	Corrigan	Anderson	Sansom	Robson	Watson*	Robson	Coppell	Hoddle	Withe	Rix	Barnes	Martin(5) Francis(11)
Scotland	0-1	Corrigan	Neal	Sansom	Robson	Watson	Robson	Keegan*	Hoddle	Mariner	Robson	Woodcock	McDermott(11) Barnes(5)
Switzerland	1-2	Clemence	Mills	Sansom	Wilkins	Thompson	Osman	Robson	Mariner	Mariner	Brooking	Francis	Wilkins(10)
Hungary	3-1	Clemence*	Neal	Mills	Thompson	Osman	Robson	Robson	Mariner	Mariner	Brooking	McDermott	Withe(9) Barnes(10)
1981-82													
Norway	1-2	Clemence	Neal	Mills	Thompson	Martin	Robson	Robson	Mariner	Mariner	Hoddle	McDermott	Morley(8)
Hungary	1-0	Shilton	Neal	Mills	Wilkins	Martin	Robson	Robson	Mariner	Mariner	Brooking	McDermott	
Northern Ireland	4-0	Clemence	Anderson	Sansom	Wilkins	Watson	Foster	Morley	Francis	Francis	Hoddle	Morley	Regis(9) Woodcock(11)

ENGLAND'S FULL INTERNATIONAL TEAMS 1946-91 *(cont'd)*

1981-82 *(cont'd)* versus	Result	1	2	3	4	5	6	7	8	9	10	11	Substitutes
Wales	1-0	Corrigan	Neal	Sansom	Thompson*	Butcher	Robson	Wilkins	Francis[1]	Withe	Hoddle	Morley	McDermott(8) Regis(10)
Holland	2-0	Shilton*	Neal	Sansom	Thompson	Foster	Robson	Wilkins	Devonshire	Mariner[1]	McDermott	Woodcock[1]	Rix(8) Barnes(9)
Scotland	1-0	Shilton	Mills	Sansom	Thompson	Butcher	Robson	Keegan*	Coppell	Mariner[1]	Brooking	Wilkins	McDermott(7) Francis(9)
Iceland	1-1	Corrigan	Anderson	Neal*	Watson	Osman	McDermott[2]	Hoddle	Devonshire	Withe	Regis	Morley	Perryman(8) Goddard(10)
Finland	4-1	Clemence	Mills	Sansom	Thompson	Martin	Robson[2]	Keegan*	Coppell	Mariner[2]	Brooking	Wilkins	Rix(6) Francis(8) Woodcock(10)
France	3-1	Shilton	Mills*	Sansom	Thompson	Butcher	Robson[2]	Coppell	Francis	Mariner[1]	Rix	Wilkins	Neal(3)
Czechoslovakia	2-0	Shilton	Mills*	Sansom	Thompson	Butcher	Robson	Coppell	Francis[1]	Mariner	Rix	Wilkins†	Hoddle(6)
Kuwait	1-0	Shilton	Neal*	Mills*	Thompson	Foster	Hoddle	Coppell	Francis[1]	Mariner	Rix	Wilkins	
West Germany	0-0	Shilton	Mills*	Sansom	Thompson	Butcher	Robson	Coppell	Francis	Mariner	Rix	Wilkins	Woodcock(8)
Spain	0-0	Shilton	Mills*	Sansom	Thompson	Butcher	Robson	Rix	Francis	Mariner	Woodcock	Wilkins	Brooking(7) Keegan(10)
1982-83													
Denmark	2-2	Shilton	Neal	Sansom	Wilkins*	Osman	Butcher	Morley	Robson	Mariner	Francis[2]	Rix	Hill(7)
West Germany	1-2	Shilton	Mabbutt	Sansom	Thompson	Butcher	Wilkins*	Hill	Regis	Mariner	Armstrong	Devonshire	Woodcock(8)[1] Blissett(9) Rix(10)
Greece	3-0	Shilton	Neal[1]	Sansom	Thompson	Martin	Robson*	Lee[1]	Mabbutt	Mariner	Woodcock[2]	Morley	Chamberlain(7)[1] Hoddle(11)[1]
Luxembourg	9-0	Clemence	Neal[1]	Sansom	Robson*	Martin	Butcher[1]	Coppell[1]	Lee	Woodcock[1]	Blissett[3]	Mabbutt†	
Wales	2-1	Shilton*	Neal[1]	Statham	Lee	Martin	Butcher[1]	Mabbutt	Blissett	Mariner	Cowans	Devonshire	Blissett(10) Rix(11)
Greece	0-0	Shilton*	Neal	Sansom	Lee	Martin	Butcher	Coppell	Mabbutt	Francis[1]	Woodcock	Devonshire	
Hungary	2-0	Shilton*	Neal	Sansom	Hoddle	Roberts	Butcher	Mabbutt	Francis[1]	Withe	Blissett	Cowans	Barnes, J.(10)
Northern Ireland	0-0	Shilton*	Neal	Sansom	Lee	Roberts	Butcher	Mabbutt	Francis	Withe	Blissett	Cowans	Mabbutt(7) Blissett(9)
Scotland	2-0	Shilton*	Neal	Sansom	Lee	Osman	Butcher	Robson*[1]	Francis	Withe	Hoddle	Cowans[1]	Barnes(3) Walsh(9)
Australia	0-0	Shilton*	Thomas	Statham	Williams	Osman	Butcher	Barham	Gregory	Blissett	Francis	Cowans	Williams(3)
Australia	1-0	Shilton*	Neal	Statham	Barham	Osman	Butcher	Gregory	Gregory	Walsh[1]	Francis	Barnes	Spink(1) Thomas(2) Blissett(9)
Australia	1-1	Shilton*	Neal	Pickering	Lee	Osman	Butcher	Gregory	Francis[1]	Walsh	Cowans	Barnes	
1983-84													
Denmark	0-1	Shilton	Neal	Sansom	Lee	Osman	Butcher	Wilkins*	Gregory	Mariner	Francis	Barnes	Blissett(4) Chamberlain(11)
Hungary	3-0	Shilton	Gregory	Sansom	Lee[1]	Martin	Butcher	Robson*	Hoddle[1]	Mariner[1]	Blissett	Mabbutt	Withe(10)
Luxembourg	4-0	Clemence	Duxbury	Sansom	Lee	Martin	Butcher	Robson*[2]	Hoddle	Mariner[1]	Woodcock	Devonshire	Barnes(10)
France	0-2	Shilton	Duxbury	Sansom	Lee	Roberts	Butcher	Robson*	Stein	Walsh	Woodcock	Williams	Barnes(4) Woodcock(8)
Northern Ireland	1-0	Shilton	Anderson	Kennedy	Lee	Martin	Butcher	Wilkins*	Wilkins	Woodcock[1]	Francis	Rix	
Wales	0-1	Shilton	Duxbury	Kennedy	Lee	Roberts	Wright	Chamberlain	Gregory	Walsh	Woodcock	Armstrong	Fenwick(5) Blissett(11)
Scotland	1-1	Shilton	Duxbury	Sansom	Wilkins	Roberts	Fenwick	Chamberlain	Robson*	Woodcock[1]	Blissett	Barnes	Hunt(7) Lineker(9)
USSR	0-2	Shilton	Duxbury	Sansom	Wilkins	Watson	Fenwick	Chamberlain	Robson*	Francis	Blissett	Barnes[1]	Hateley(9) Hunt(11)
Brazil	2-0	Shilton	Duxbury	Sansom	Wilkins	Watson	Fenwick	Robson*	Chamberlain	Hateley[1]	Woodcock	Barnes[1]	Allen(10)
Uruguay	0-2	Shilton	Duxbury	Sansom	Wilkins	Watson	Fenwick	Robson*	Chamberlain	Hateley	Allen	Barnes	Woodcock(10)
Chile	0-0	Shilton	Duxbury	Sansom	Wilkins	Watson	Fenwick	Robson*	Chamberlain	Hateley	Allen	Barnes	Lee(8)
1984-85													
East Germany	1-0	Shilton	Duxbury	Sansom	Williams	Wright	Butcher	Robson*[1]	Wilkins	Mariner[1]	Woodcock[2]	Barnes	Hateley(9) Francis(10)
Finland	5-0	Shilton	Duxbury[1]	Sansom	Williams	Wright	Butcher	Robson*[2]	Wilkins	Hateley[2]	Woodcock[1]	Barnes[2]	Stevens(2) Chamberlain(7)
Turkey	8-0	Shilton	Anderson[1]	Sansom	Williams	Wright	Butcher	Robson*[3]	Wilkins	Withe	Woodcock[1]	Barnes[2]	Stevens(4) Francis(10)
Northern Ireland	1-0	Shilton	Anderson	Sansom	Steven	Matin	Butcher	Steven	Wilkins*	Hateley[1]	Woodcock	Waddle	Francis(10)
Republic of Ireland	2-1	Bailey	Anderson	Sansom	Steven[1]	Wright	Butcher	Robson*	Wilkins	Hateley	Lineker[1]	Barnes	Hoddle(7) Davenport(9)
Romania	0-0	Shilton	Anderson	Sansom	Steven	Wright	Butcher	Robson*	Wilkins	Mariner	Francis	Barnes	Lineker(9) Waddle(11)
Finland	1-1	Shilton	Anderson	Sansom	Steven	Fenwick	Butcher	Robson*	Wilkins	Hateley[1]	Francis	Barnes	Waddle(4)

Opponent	Score	1	2	3	4	5	6	7	8	9	10	11	Substitutes
Scotland	0-1	Shilton	Anderson	Sansom	Hoddle	Fenwick	Butcher	Robson*	Wilkins	Hateley	Francis	Barnes	Lineker(4) Waddle(11)
Italy	1-2	Shilton	Stevens	Sansom	Steven	Wright	Butcher	Robson*	Wilkins	Hateley[1]	Francis	Waddle	Hoddle(4) Lineker(10) Barnes(11)
1985-86													
Mexico	0-1	Bailey	Anderson	Sansom	Hoddle	Fenwick	Watson	Robson*	Wilkins	Hateley	Francis	Barnes	Dixon(4) Reid(8) Waddle(11)
West Germany	3-0	Shilton	Stevens	Sansom	Hoddle	Wright	Butcher	Robson*[1]	Reid	Dixon[2]	Lineker	Waddle	Bracewell(7) Barnes(10)
USA	5-0	Woods	Anderson	Sansom	Hoddle	Fenwick	Butcher	Robson*[1]	Bracewell	Dixon[2]	Lineker[2]	Waddle	Watson(3) Steven(4) Reid(7) Barnes(11)
Romania	1-1	Shilton	Stevens	Sansom	Reid	Wright	Fenwick	Robson*[1]	Hoddle	Hateley	Lineker	Waddle	Woodcock(10) Barnes(11)
Turkey	5-0	Shilton	Stevens	Sansom	Hoddle	Wright	Fenwick	Robson*[1]	Wilkins	Hateley	Lineker[3]	Waddle[1]	Steven(7) Woodcock(9)
Northern Ireland	0-0	Shilton	Stevens	Sansom	Hoddle	Wright	Fenwick	Bracewell	Wilkins*	Dixon	Lineker	Waddle	Woods(1) Hill(7)
Egypt	4-0	Shilton	Stevens	Sansom	Cowans[1]	Wright	Fenwick	Steven[1]	Wilkins*	Hateley	Lineker	Wallace[1]†	Beardsley(10)
Israel	2-1	Shilton	Stevens	Sansom	Hoddle	Martin	Butcher	Robson*[2]	Wilkins	Dixon	Beardsley	Waddle	Woods(1) Woodcock(9) Barnes(11)
USSR	1-0	Shilton	Anderson	Sansom	Hoddle	Wright	Butcher	Cowans	Wilkins*	Hateley	Lineker	Waddle[1]	Hodge(7) Steven(11)
Scotland	2-1	Shilton	Stevens	Sansom	Hoddle[1]	Watson	Butcher	Wilkins*	Francis	Hateley[1]	Hodge	Waddle	Reid(7) Steven(10)
Mexico	3-0	Shilton	Anderson	Sansom	Hoddle	Fenwick	Butcher	Robson*	Wilkins	Hateley[2]	Beardsley[1]	Waddle	Stevens(7) Steven(8)
Canada	1-0	Shilton	Stevens	Sansom	Hoddle	Martin	Butcher	Hodge	Wilkins*	Hateley[1]	Lineker	Waddle	Dixon(9) Barnes(11) Woods(1) Reid(8)
Portugal	0-1	Shilton*	Stevens	Sansom	Hoddle	Fenwick	Butcher	Robson*	Wilkins	Hateley	Lineker	Waddle	Beardsley(10) Barnes(11)
Morocco	0-0	Shilton	Stevens	Sansom	Hoddle	Fenwick	Butcher	Robson*	Wilkins*	Hateley	Lineker	Waddle	Hodge(7) Beardsley(11)
Poland	3-0	Shilton*	Stevens	Sansom	Hoddle	Fenwick	Butcher	Hodge	Reid	Beardsley	Lineker[3]	Waddle	Hodge(7) Stevens(9)
Paraguay	3-0	Shilton*	Stevens	Sansom	Hoddle	Fenwick	Butcher	Hodge	Reid	Beardsley[1]	Lineker[2]	Waddle	Waddle(9) Dixon(10)
Argentina	1-2	Shilton*	Stevens	Sansom	Hoddle	Fenwick	Butcher	Hodge	Reid	Beardsley	Lineker[1]	Steven	Stevens(8) Hateley(9)
1986-87													
Sweden	0-1	Woods	Anderson	Sansom	Hoddle	Martin	Butcher	Steven	Wilkins	Dixon	Hodge	Steven	Waddle(8) Barnes(11)
Northern Ireland	3-0	Shilton	Anderson	Sansom	Hoddle	Wright	Butcher*	Robson*	Hodge	Beardsley	Lineker[2]	Waddle[1]	Cottee(7) Waddle(11)
Yugoslavia	2-0	Shilton	Anderson	Sansom	Hoddle	Watson	Butcher	Robson*	Hodge	Beardsley	Lineker	Waddle	Cottee(9)
Spain	4-2	Woods	Anderson	Sansom	Mabbutt	Adams	Butcher	Robson*[1]	Hodge	Beardsley[1]	Lineker[4]	Waddle[1]	Wilkins(8) Steven(11)
Northern Ireland	2-0	Woods	Anderson	Sansom	Hoddle	Wright	Mabbutt	Robson*[1]	Hodge	Beardsley	Lineker[2]	Waddle[1]	Woods(1)
Turkey	0-0	Shilton*	Stevens	Sansom	Reid	Adams	Butcher	Robson*	Barnes	Beardsley	Lineker[1]	Waddle	Barnes(8) Hateley(9)
Brazil	1-1	Shilton	Stevens	Sansom	Hoddle	Adams	Butcher	Robson*	Hodge	Beardsley	Lineker	Waddle	Hateley(10)
Scotland	0-0	Shilton	Stevens	Sansom	Hoddle	Wright	Butcher	Robson*	Hodge	Beardsley	Hateley	Waddle	
1987-88													
West Germany	1-3	Shilton*	Anderson	Sansom	Steven	Adams	Mabbutt	Reid	Barnes	Beardsley	Lineker	Waddle	Pearce(3) Webb(4) Hateley(11)
Turkey	8-0	Shilton	Stevens	Sansom	Webb	Adams	Butcher	Robson*[1]	Webb	Beardsley	Lineker[3]	Barnes[2]	Hoddle(4) Regis(9)
Yugoslavia	4-1	Shilton	Stevens	Pearce	Steven	Adams[1]	Butcher	Robson*[1]	Webb	Beardsley	Lineker	Barnes[1]	Reid(7) Hoddle(8)
Israel	0-0	Woods	Anderson	Sansom	Hoddle	Watson	Wright	Allen	McMahon	Allen	Lineker[1]	Barnes	Fenwick(6) Harford(7)
Holland	2-2	Shilton	Stevens	Sansom	Steven	Adams[1]	Watson	Robson*	Webb	Beardsley	Lineker	Barnes	Wright(6) Hoddle(8)
Hungary	0-0	Woods	Anderson	Pearce	Webb	Adams	Pallister	Robson*	McMahon	Beardsley	Lineker	Waddle	Hateley(9)
Scotland	1-0	Shilton	Stevens	Sansom	Steven	Watson	Adams	Robson*	Steven	Beardsley[1]	Lineker	Barnes	Stevens(3) Hateley(9)
Colombia	1-1	Shilton	Anderson	Sansom	Webb	Wright	Adams	Robson*	Waddle	Beardsley	Lineker[1]	Barnes	Cottee(10) Hoddle(11)
Switzerland	1-0	Shilton	Stevens	Sansom	Webb	Wright	Adams	Robson*	Steven	Beardsley	Lineker[1]	Barnes	Woods(1) Watson(6)
Republic of Ireland	0-1	Shilton	Stevens	Sansom	Waddle	Wright	Adams	Robson*	Waddle	Beardsley	Lineker	Barnes	Hoddle(4) Hateley(9)

ENGLAND'S FULL INTERNATIONAL TEAMS 1946-91 (cont'd)

versus	Result	1	2	3	4	5	6	7	8	9	10	11	Substitutes
1987-88 (cont'd)													
Holland	1-3	Shilton	Stevens	Sansom	Hoddle	Wright	Adams	Robson*[1]	Steven	Beardsley	Lineker	Barnes	Waddle(8) Hateley(9)
USSR	1-3	Woods	Stevens	Sansom	Hoddle	Watson	Adams[1]	Robson*	Steven	McMahon	Lineker	Barnes	Webb(9) Hateley(10)
1988-89													
Denmark	1-0	Shilton	Stevens	Pearce	Rocastle	Adams	Butcher	Robson*	Webb[1]	Harford	Beardsley	Hodge	Woods(1) Walker(5) Cottee(9) Gascoigne(10)
Sweden	0-0	Shilton	Stevens	Pearce	Webb	Adams[1]	Butcher	Robson*	Beardsley	Waddle	Lineker	Barnes	Walker(5) Cottee(11)
Saudi Arabia	1-1	Seaman	Sterland	Pearce	Thomas	Adams[1]	Pallister	Robson*	Rocastle	Beardsley	Lineker	Waddle	Gascoigne(4) Smith(9) Marwood(11)
Greece	2-1	Shilton	Stevens	Pearce	Webb	Walker	Butcher	Robson*[1]	Rocastle	Smith	Lineker	Barnes[1]	Beardsley(9)
Albania	2-0	Shilton	Stevens	Pearce	Webb	Walker	Butcher	Robson*[1]	Rocastle	Waddle	Lineker	Barnes[1]	Beardsley(9) Smith(10)
Albania	5-0	Shilton	Stevens	Pearce	Webb	Walker	Butcher	Robson*	Rocastle	Beardsley[2]	Lineker[1]	Waddle[1]	Parker(2) Gascoigne(8)[1]
Chile	0-0	Shilton	Parker	Pearce	Webb[1]	Walker	Butcher	Robson*	Gascoigne	Clough	Fashanu	Waddle[1]	Cottee(10)
Scotland	2-0	Shilton	Stevens	Pearce	Webb	Walker	Butcher	Robson*	Steven	Fashanu	Cottee	Waddle[1]	Bull(9)[1] Gascoigne(10)
Poland	3-0	Shilton	Stevens	Pearce	Webb[1]	Walker	Butcher	Robson*	Waddle	Beardsley	Lineker[1]	Barnes[1]	Rocastle(8) Smith(9)
Denmark	1-1	Shilton	Parker	Pearce	Webb	Walker	Butcher	Robson*	Rocastle	Beardsley	Lineker[1]	Barnes	Seaman(1) McMahon(4) Bull(9) Waddle(11)
1989-90													
Sweden	0-0	Shilton	Stevens	Pearce	Webb	Walker	Butcher*	Beardsley	McMahon	Waddle	Lineker	Barnes	Gascoigne(-) Rocastle(11)
Poland	0-0	Shilton	Stevens	Pearce	McMahon	Walker	Butcher	Robson*	Rocastle	Beardsley	Lineker	Waddle	Beasant(1) Winterburn(3) Hodge(4) Phelan(7) Platt(9)
Italy	0-0	Shilton	Stevens	Pearce	McMahon	Walker	Butcher	Robson*	Waddle	Beardsley	Lineker	Barnes	Beasant(1) Dorigo(3) Platt(4) McMahon(7) Hodge(8)
Yugoslavia	2-1	Shilton	Parker	Pearce	Thomas	Walker	Butcher	Robson*[2]	Rocastle	Bull	Lineker	Waddle	Woods(1) Gascoigne(9)
Brazil	1-0	Shilton	Stevens	Pearce[1]	McMahon	Walker	Butcher*	Platt	Waddle	Beardsley	Lineker[1]	Barnes	Seaman(1) Dorigo(3) Wright(5) McMahon(7)
Czechoslovakia	4-2	Shilton	Dixon	Pearce[1]	Steven	Walker	Butcher	Robson*	Gascoigne[1]	Bull[2]	Lineker	Hodge	Woods(1) Dorigo(3)
Denmark	1-0	Shilton	Stevens	Pearce	McMahon	Walker	Butcher*	Hodge	Gascoigne	Waddle	Lineker[1]	Barnes	Platt(4) Rocastle(9) Bull(10)
Uruguay	1-2	Shilton	Parker	Pearce	Hodge	Walker	Butcher	Robson*	Gascoigne	Waddle	Lineker	Barnes[1]	Beardsley(4) Bull(10)
Tunisia	1-1	Shilton	Stevens	Pearce	Hodge	Walker	Butcher	Robson*	Waddle	Gascoigne	Lineker	Barnes	Beardsley(4) Wright(6) Platt(8) Bull(10)[1]
1990-91													
Rep. of Ireland	1-1	Shilton	Stevens	Pearce	Gascoigne	Walker	Butcher	Robson*	Waddle	Beardsley	Lineker[1]	Barnes	McMahon(9) Bull(10)
Holland	0-0	Shilton	Parker	Pearce	Wright	Walker	Butcher	Robson*	Waddle	Gascoigne	Lineker	Barnes	Platt(7) Bull(8)
Egypt	1-0	Shilton*	Parker	Pearce	Gascoigne	Walker	Wright[1]	McMahon	Waddle	Bull	Lineker	Barnes	Platt(8) Beardsley(9)
Belgium	1-0	Shilton	Parker	Pearce	Wright	Walker	Butcher*	McMahon	Waddle	Gascoigne	Lineker[2]	Barnes	Platt(7)[1] Bull(11)
Cameroon	3-2	Shilton	Parker	Pearce	Wright	Walker	Butcher*	Platt[1]	Waddle	Gascoigne	Lineker[1]	Barnes	Steven(6) Beardsley(11)
West Germany	1-1	Shilton	Parker	Pearce	Wright	Walker	Wright	Platt[1]	Waddle	Gascoigne	Lineker[1]	Beardsley	Steven(6)
Italy	1-2	Shilton*	Stevens	Dorigo	Parker	Walker	Wright	Platt[1]	Steven	McMahon	Lineker	Beardsley	Waddle(6) Webb(9)
1990-91													
Hungary	1-0	Woods	Dixon	Pearce	Parker	Walker	Wright	Platt[1]	Gascoigne	Bull	Lineker*[1]	Barnes	Dorigo(3) Waddle(10)
Poland	2-0	Woods	Dixon	Pearce	Parker	Walker	Wright	Platt[1]	Gascoigne	Bull	Lineker*[1]	Barnes	Beardsley(9)[1] Waddle(10)
Rep. of Ireland	1-1	Woods	Dixon	Pearce	Adams	Walker	Wright	Platt[1]	Cowans	Beardsley	Lineker*	McMahon	

Opponent	Score												Substitutes
Cameroon	2-0	Seaman	Dixon[1]	Pearce	Steven	Walker	Wright	Robson*	Gascoigne	Wright I.	Lineker[2]	Barnes	Pallister(7) Hodge(8)
Rep. of Ireland	1-1	Seaman	Dixon[1]	Pearce	Adams	Walker	Wright	Robson*	Platt	Beardsley	Lineker	Barnes	Sharpe(4) Wright I.(10)
Turkey	1-0	Seaman	Dixon	Pearce	Wise[1]	Walker	Pallister	Platt	Thomas	Smith[1]	Lineker*	Barnes	Hodge(8)
USSR	3-1	Woods	Stevens	Dorigo	Wise	Parker	Wright*	Platt[1]	Thomas	Smith[1]	Wright I.	Barnes	Batty(4) Beardsley(10)
Argentina	2-2	Seaman	Dixon	Pearce	Batty	Walker	Wright	Platt[1]	Thomas	Smith	Lineker*[1]	Barnes	Clough(11)
Australia	1-0	Woods	Parker	Pearce	Batty	Walker	Barrett	Platt	Thomas	Clough	Lineker*[1]	Hirst	Wise(10) Salako(11)
New Zealand	1-0	Woods	Parker	Pearce*[1]	Wise	Walker	Wright	Platt	Thomas	Wise	Lineker*[1]	Walters	Deane(4) Salako(11)
New Zealand	2-0	Woods	Charles	Pearce	Wise	Walker	Wright	Platt	Thomas	Deane	Wright I.	Salako	Hirst(9)[1]
Malaysia	4-2	Woods	Charles	Pearce	Batty	Walker	Wright	Platt	Thomas	Clough	Lineker*[4]	Salako	

85

Gillette® Sensor®

AND

Gillette® Gel

The Ultimate Combination

International Matches 1872-1991

(Up to and including 12 June 1991)

WC World Cup   ENC European Nation's Cup   BJT Brazilian Jubilee Tournament
EC European Championship   SFAC Scottish F. A. Centenary   FAWC FA of Wales Centenary
USABCT United States of America Bi-Centenary Tournament   RC Rous Cup

Year   Date   Venue   Goals

ENGLAND v ALBANIA

			Eng	Alb
WC1989	Mar. 8	Tirana	2	0
WC1989	Apr. 26	Wembley	5	0

ENGLAND v ARGENTINA

			Eng	Arg
1951	May 9	Wembley	2	1
WC1962	June 2	Rancagua	3	1
BJT1964	June 6	Rio de Janeiro	0	1
WC1966	July 23	Wembley	1	0
1974	May 22	Wembley	2	2
1977	June 12	Buenos Aires	1	1
1980	May 13	Wembley	3	1
WC1986	June 22	Mexico City	1	2
1991	May 25	Wembley	2	2

ENGLAND v AUSTRALIA

			Eng	Aus
1980	May 31	Sydney	2	1
1983	June 12	Sydney	0	0
1983	June 15	Brisbane	1	0
1983	June 19	Melbourne	1	1
1991	June 1	Sydney	1	0

ENGLAND v AUSTRIA

			Eng	Aust
1908	June 6	Vienna	6	1
1908	June 8	Vienna	11	1
1909	June 1	Vienna	8	1
1930	May 14	Vienna	0	0
1932	Dec. 7	Chelsea	4	3
1936	May 6	Vienna	1	2
1951	Nov. 28	Wembley	2	2
1952	May 25	Vienna	3	2
WC1958	June 15	Boras	2	2
1961	May 27	Vienna	1	3
1962	Apr. 4	Wembley	3	1
1965	Oct. 20	Wembley	2	3
1967	May 27	Vienna	1	0
1973	Sept. 26	Wembley	7	0
1979	June 13	Vienna	3	4

ENGLAND v BELGIUM

			Eng	Belg
1921	May 21	Brussels	2	0
1923	Mar. 19	Highbury	6	1
1923	Nov. 1	Antwerp	2	2
1924	Dec. 8	West Bromwich	4	0
1926	May 24	Antwerp	5	3
1927	May 11	Brussels	9	1
1928	May 19	Antwerp	3	1
1929	May 11	Brussels	5	1
1931	May 16	Brussels	4	1
1936	May 9	Brussels	2	3
1947	Sept. 21	Brussels	5	2
1950	May 18	Brussels	4	1
1952	Nov. 26	Wembley	5	0
WC1954	June 17	Basle	4	4
1964	Oct. 21	Wembley	2	2
1970	Feb. 20	Brussels	3	1
EC1980	June 12	Turin	1	1
WC1990	June 26	Bologna	1	0

ENGLAND v BOHEMIA

			Eng	Boh
1908	June 13	Prague	4	0

ENGLAND v BRAZIL

			Eng	Brazil
1956	May 9	Wembley	4	2

ENGLAND v BRAZIL *(cont'd)*

			Eng	Brazil
WC1958	June 11	Gothenburg	0	0
1959	May 13	Rio de Janeiro	0	2
WC1962	June 10	Vina Del Mar	1	3
1963	May 8	Wembley	1	1
BJT1964	May 30	Rio de Janeiro	1	5
1969	June 12	Rio de Janeiro	1	2
WC1970	June 7	Guadalajara	0	1
USABCT1976	May 23	Los Angeles	0	1
1977	June 8	Rio de Janeiro	0	0
1978	Apr. 19	Wembley	1	1
1981	May 12	Wembley	0	1
1984	June 10	Rio de Janeiro	2	0
RC1987	May 19	Wembley	1	1
1990	Mar. 28	Wembley	1	0

ENGLAND v BULGARIA

			Eng	Bulg
WC1962	June 7	Rancagua	0	0
1968	Dec. 11	Wembley	1	1
1974	June 1	Sofia	1	0
EC1979	June 6	Sofia	3	0
EC1979	Nov. 22	Wembley	2	0

ENGLAND v CAMEROON

			Eng	Camer
WC1990	July 1	Naples	3	2
1991	Feb. 6	Wembley	2	0

ENGLAND v CANADA

			Eng	Can
1986	May 24	Vancouver	1	0

ENGLAND v CHILE

			Eng	Chile
WC1950	June 25	Rio de Janeiro	2	0
1953	May 24	Santiago	2	1
1984	June 17	Santiago	0	0
RC1989	May 23	Wembley	0	0

ENGLAND v COLOMBIA

			Eng	Col
1970	May 20	Bogota	4	0
RC1988	May 24	Wembley	1	1

ENGLAND v CYPRUS

			Eng	Cyp
EC1975	Apr. 16	Wembley	5	0
EC1975	May 11	Limassol	1	0

ENGLAND v CZECHOSLOVAKIA

			Eng	Czech
1934	May 16	Prague	1	2
1937	Dec. 1	Tottenham	5	4
1963	May 29	Bratislava	4	2
1966	Nov. 2	Wembley	0	0
WC1970	June 11	Guadalajara	1	0
1973	May 27	Prague	1	1
EC1974	Oct. 30	Wembley	3	0
EC1975	Oct. 30	Bratislava	1	2
1978	Nov. 29	Wembley	1	0
WC1982	June 20	Bilbao	2	0
1990	Apr. 25	Wembley	4	2

ENGLAND v DENMARK

			Eng	Den
1948	Sept. 26	Copenhagen	0	0
1955	Oct. 2	Copenhagen	5	1
WC1956	Dec. 5	Wolverhampton	5	2
WC1957	May 15	Copenhagen	4	1

Year	Date		Venue	Goals	

ENGLAND v DENMARK *(cont'd)*

Year	Date		Venue	Eng	Den
1966	July	3	Copenhagen	2	0
EC1978	Sept.	20	Copenhagen	4	3
EC1979	Sept.	12	Wembley	1	0
EC1982	Sept.	22	Copenhagen	2	2
EC1983	Sept.	21	Wembley	0	1
1988	Sept.	14	Wembley	1	0
1989	June	7	Copenhagen	1	1
1990	May	15	Wembley	1	0

ENGLAND v ECUADOR

Year	Date		Venue	Eng	Ecua
1970	May	24	Quito	2	0

ENGLAND v EGYPT

Year	Date		Venue	Eng	Egypt
1986	Jan.	29	Cairo	4	0
wc1990	June	21	Cagliari	1	0

ENGLAND v FIFA

Year	Date		Venue	Eng	FIFA
1953	Oct.	21	Wembley	4	4

ENGLAND v FINLAND

Year	Date		Venue	Eng	Fin
1937	May	20	Helsinki	8	0
1956	May	20	Helsinki	5	1
1966	June	26	Helsinki	3	0
wc1976	June	13	Helsinki	4	1
wc1976	Oct.	13	Wembley	2	1
1982	June	3	Helsinki	4	1
wc1984	Oct.	17	Wembley	5	0
wc1985	May	22	Helsinki	1	1

ENGLAND v FRANCE

Year	Date		Venue	Eng	France
1923	May	10	Paris	4	1
1924	May	17	Paris	3	1
1925	May	21	Paris	3	2
1927	May	26	Paris	6	0
1928	May	17	Paris	5	1
1929	May	9	Paris	4	1
1931	May	14	Paris	2	5
1933	Dec.	6	Tottenham	4	1
1938	May	26	Paris	4	2
1947	May	3	Highbury	3	0
1949	May	22	Paris	3	1
1951	Oct.	3	Highbury	2	2
1955	May	15	Paris	0	1
1957	Nov.	27	Wembley	4	0
ENC1962	Oct.	3	Sheffield	1	1
ENC1963	Feb.	27	Paris	2	5
wc1966	July	20	Wembley	2	0
1969	Mar.	12	Wembley	5	0
wc1982	June	16	Bilbao	3	1
1984	Feb.	29	Paris	0	2

ENGLAND v EAST GERMANY

Year	Date		Venue	Eng	EG
1963	June	2	Leipzig	2	1
1970	Nov.	25	Wembley	3	1
1974	May	29	Leipzig	1	1
1984	Sept.	12	Wembley	1	0

ENGLAND v WEST GERMANY

Year	Date		Venue	Eng	WG
1930	May	10	Berlin	3	3
1935	Dec.	4	Tottenham	3	0
1938	May	14	Berlin	6	3
1954	Dec.	1	Wembley	3	1
1956	May	26	Berlin	3	1
1965	May	12	Nuremberg	1	0
1966	Feb.	23	Wembley	1	0
wc1966	July	30	Wembley	4	2
1968	June	1	Hanover	0	1
wc1970	June	14	Leon	2	3
EC1972	Apr.	29	Wembley	1	3

ENGLAND v WEST GERMANY *(cont'd)*

Year	Date		Venue	Eng	WG
EC1972	May	13	Berlin	0	0
1975	Mar.	12	Wembley	2	0
1978	Feb.	22	Munich	1	2
wc1982	June	29	Madrid	0	0
1982	Oct.	13	Wembley	1	2
1985	June	12	Mexico City	3	0
1987	Sept.	9	Düsseldorf	1	3
wc1990	July	4	Turin	1	1

ENGLAND v GREECE

Year	Date		Venue	Eng	Greece
EC1971	Apr.	21	Wembley	3	0
EC1971	Dec.	1	Athens	2	0
EC1982	Nov.	17	Salonika	3	0
EC1983	Mar.	30	Wembley	0	0
1989	Feb.	8	Athens	2	1

ENGLAND v HOLLAND

Year	Date		Venue	Eng	Hol
1935	May	18	Amsterdam	1	0
1946	Nov.	27	Huddersfield	8	2
1964	Dec.	9	Amsterdam	1	1
1969	Nov.	5	Amsterdam	1	0
1970	Jan.	14	Wembley	0	0
1977	Feb.	9	Wembley	0	2
1982	May	25	Wembley	2	0
1988	Mar.	23	Wembley	2	2
EC1988	June	15	Düsseldorf	1	3
wc1990	June	16	Cagliari	0	0

ENGLAND v HUNGARY

Year	Date		Venue	Eng	Hung
1908	June	10	Budapest	7	0
1909	May	29	Budapest	4	2
1909	May	31	Budapest	8	2
1934	May	10	Budapest	1	2
1936	Dec.	2	Highbury	6	2
1953	Nov.	25	Wembley	3	6
1954	May	23	Budapest	1	7
1960	May	22	Budapest	0	2
wc1962	May	31	Rancagua	1	2
1965	May	5	Wembley	1	0
1978	May	24	Wembley	4	1
wc1981	June	6	Budapest	3	1
wc1981	Nov.	18	Wembley	1	0
EC1983	Apr.	27	Wembley	2	0
EC1983	Oct.	12	Budapest	3	0
1988	Apr.	27	Budapest	0	0
1990	Sept.	12	Wembley	1	0

ENGLAND v ICELAND

Year	Date		Venue	Eng	Ice
1982	June	2	Reykjavik	1	1

ENGLAND v IRELAND

Year	Date		Venue	Eng	Ire
1882	Feb.	18	Belfast	13	0
1883	Feb.	24	Liverpool	7	0
1884	Feb.	23	Belfast	8	1
1885	Feb.	28	Manchester	4	0
1886	Mar.	13	Belfast	6	1
1887	Feb.	5	Sheffield	7	0
1888	Mar.	31	Belfast	5	1
1889	Mar.	2	Everton	6	1
1890	Mar.	15	Belfast	9	1
1891	Mar.	7	Wolverhampton	6	1
1892	Mar.	5	Belfast	2	0
1893	Feb.	25	Birmingham	6	1
1894	Mar.	3	Belfast	2	2
1895	Mar.	9	Derby	9	0
1896	Mar.	7	Belfast	2	0
1897	Feb.	20	Nottingham	6	0
1898	Mar.	5	Belfast	3	2
1899	Feb.	18	Sunderland	13	2
1900	Mar.	17	Dublin	2	0
1901	Mar.	9	Southampton	3	0

Year	Date	Venue	Eng	Ire
		ENGLAND v IRELAND *(cont'd)*		
1902	Mar. 22	Belfast	1	0
1903	Feb. 14	Wolverhampton	4	0
1904	Mar. 12	Belfast	3	1
1905	Feb. 25	Middlesbrough	1	1
1906	Feb. 17	Belfast	5	0
1907	Feb. 16	Everton	1	0
1908	Feb. 15	Belfast	3	1
1909	Feb. 13	Bradford	4	0
1910	Feb. 12	Belfast	1	1
1911	Feb. 11	Derby	2	1
1912	Feb. 10	Dublin	6	1
1913	Feb. 15	Belfast	1	2
1914	Feb. 14	Middlesbrough	0	3
1919	Oct. 25	Belfast	1	1
1920	Oct. 23	Sunderland	2	0
1921	Oct. 22	Belfast	1	1
1922	Oct. 21	West Bromwich	2	0
1923	Oct. 20	Belfast	1	2
1924	Oct. 22	Everton	3	1
1925	Oct. 24	Belfast	0	0
1926	Oct. 20	Liverpool	3	3
1927	Oct. 22	Belfast	0	2
1928	Oct. 22	Everton	2	1
1929	Oct. 19	Belfast	3	0
1930	Oct. 20	Sheffield	5	1
1931	Oct. 17	Belfast	6	2
1932	Oct. 17	Blackpool	1	0
1933	Oct. 14	Belfast	3	0
1935	Feb. 6	Everton	2	1
1935	Oct. 19	Belfast	3	1
1936	Nov. 18	Stoke	3	1
1937	Oct. 23	Belfast	5	1
1938	Nov. 16	Manchester	7	0
1946	Sept. 28	Belfast	7	2
1947	Nov. 5	Everton	2	2
1949	Oct. 9	Belfast	6	2
wc1949	Nov. 16	Manchester	9	2
1950	Oct. 7	Belfast	4	1
1951	Nov. 14	Aston Villa	2	0
1952	Oct. 4	Belfast	2	2
wc1953	Nov. 11	Liverpool	3	1
1954	Oct. 2	Belfast	2	0
1955	Nov. 2	Wembley	3	0
1956	Oct. 6	Belfast	1	1
1957	Nov. 6	Wembley	2	3
1958	Oct. 4	Belfast	3	3
1959	Nov. 18	Wembley	2	1
1960	Oct. 8	Belfast	5	2
1961	Nov. 22	Wembley	1	1
1962	Oct. 20	Belfast	3	1
1963	Nov. 20	Wembley	8	3
1964	Oct. 3	Belfast	4	3
1965	Nov. 10	Wembley	2	1
ec1966	Oct. 22	Belfast	2	0
ec1967	Nov. 22	Wembley	2	0
1969	May 3	Belfast	3	1
1970	Apr. 21	Wembley	3	1
1971	May 15	Belfast	1	0
1972	May 23	Wembley	0	1
1973	May 12	Everton	2	1
1974	May 15	Wembley	1	0
1975	May 17	Belfast	0	0
1976	May 11	Wembley	4	0
1977	May 28	Belfast	2	1
1978	May 16	Wembley	1	0
ec1979	Feb. 7	Wembley	4	0
1979	May 19	Belfast	2	0
ec1979	Oct. 17	Belfast	5	1
1980	May 20	Wembley	1	1
1982	Feb. 23	Wembley	4	0
1983	May 28	Belfast	0	0
1984	Apr. 4	Wembley	1	0
wc1985	Feb. 27	Belfast	1	0
wc1985	Nov. 13	Wembley	0	0
ec1986	Oct. 15	Wembley	3	0
ec1987	Apr. 1	Belfast	2	0

Year	Date	Venue	Eng	Israel
		ENGLAND v ISRAEL		
1986	Feb. 26	Tel Aviv	2	1
1988	Feb. 17	Tel Aviv	0	0

Year	Date	Venue	Eng	Italy
		ENGLAND v ITALY		
1933	May 13	Rome	1	1
1934	Nov. 14	Highbury	3	2
1939	May 13	Milan	2	2
1948	May 16	Turin	4	0
1949	Nov. 30	Tottenham	2	0
1952	May 18	Florence	1	1
1959	May 6	Wembley	2	2
1961	May 24	Rome	3	2
1973	June 14	Turin	0	2
1973	Nov. 14	Wembley	0	1
USABCT1976	May 28	New York	3	2
wc1976	Nov. 17	Rome	0	2
wc1977	Nov. 16	Wembley	2	0
ec1980	June 15	Turin	0	1
1985	June 6	Mexico City	1	2
1989	Nov. 15	Wembley	0	0
wc1990	July 7	Bari	1	2

Year	Date	Venue	Eng	Kuw
		ENGLAND v KUWAIT		
wc1982	June 25	Bilbao	1	0

Year	Date	Venue	Eng	Lux
		ENGLAND v LUXEMBOURG		
1927	May 21	Luxembourg	5	2
wc1960	Oct. 19	Luxembourg	9	0
wc1961	Sept. 28	Highbury	4	1
wc1977	Mar. 30	Luxembourg	5	0
wc1977	Oct. 12	Luxembourg	2	0
ec1982	Dec. 15	Wembley	9	0
ec1983	Nov. 16	Luxembourg	4	0

Year	Date	Venue	Eng	Mal
		ENGLAND v MALAYSIA		
1991	June 12	Kuala Lumpur	4	2

Year	Date	Venue	Eng	Malta
		ENGLAND v MALTA		
ec1971	Feb. 3	Valletta	1	0
ec1971	May 12	Wembley	5	0

Year	Date	Venue	Eng	Mex
		ENGLAND v MEXICO		
1959	May 24	Mexico City	1	2
1961	May 10	Wembley	8	0
wc1966	July 16	Wembley	2	0
1969	June 1	Mexico City	0	0
1985	June 9	Mexico City	0	1
1986	May 17	Los Angeles	3	0

Year	Date	Venue	Eng	Mor
		ENGLAND v MOROCCO		
wc1986	June 6	Monterrey	0	0

Year	Date	Venue	Eng	NZ
		ENGLAND v NEW ZEALAND		
1991	June 3	Auckland	1	0
1991	June 8	Wellington	2	0

Year	Date	Venue	Eng	Nor
		ENGLAND v NORWAY		
1937	May 14	Oslo	6	0
1938	Nov. 9	Newcastle	4	0
1949	May 18	Oslo	4	1
1966	June 29	Oslo	6	1
wc1980	Sept. 10	Wembley	4	0
wc1981	Sept. 9	Oslo	1	2

Year	Date	Venue	Eng	Para
		ENGLAND v PARAGUAY		
wc1986	June 18	Mexico City	3	0

Year	Date	Venue	Goals	
		ENGLAND v PERU	Eng	Peru
1939	May 17	Lima	1	4
1962	May 20	Lima	4	0

ENGLAND v POLAND

Year	Date	Venue	Eng	Pol
1966	Jan. 5	Everton	1	1
1966	July 5	Chorzow	1	0
wc1973	June 6	Chorzow	0	2
wc1973	Oct. 17	Wembley	1	1
wc1986	June 11	Monterrey	3	0
wc1989	June 3	Wembley	3	0
wc1989	Oct. 11	Katowice	0	0
EC1990	Oct. 17	Wembley	2	0

ENGLAND v PORTUGAL

Year	Date	Venue	Eng	Port
1947	May 25	Lisbon	10	0
1950	May 14	Lisbon	5	3
1951	May 19	Everton	5	2
1955	May 22	Oporto	1	3
1958	May 7	Wembley	2	1
wc1961	May 21	Lisbon	1	1
wc1961	Oct. 25	Wembley	2	0
1964	May 17	Lisbon	4	3
BJT1964	June 4	Sao Paulo	1	1
wc1966	July 26	Wembley	2	1
1969	Dec. 10	Wembley	1	0
1974	Apr. 3	Lisbon	0	0
EC1974	Nov. 20	Wembley	0	0
EC1975	Nov. 19	Lisbon	1	1
wc1986	June 3	Monterrey	0	1

ENGLAND v REPUBLIC OF IRELAND

Year	Date	Venue	Eng	Rep of Ire
1946	Sept. 30	Dublin	1	0
1949	Sept. 21	Everton	0	2
wc1957	May 8	Wembley	5	1
wc1957	May 19	Dublin	1	1
1964	May 24	Dublin	3	1
1976	Sept. 8	Wembley	1	1
EC1978	Oct. 25	Dublin	1	1
EC1980	Feb. 6	Wembley	2	0
1985	Mar. 26	Wembley	2	1
EC1988	June 12	Stuttgart	0	1
wc1990	June 11	Cagliari	1	1
EC1990	Nov. 14	Dublin	1	1
EC1991	Mar. 27	Wembley	1	1

ENGLAND v REST OF EUROPE

Year	Date	Venue	Eng	RoE
1938	Oct. 26	Highbury	3	0

ENGLAND v REST OF THE WORLD

Year	Date	Venue	Eng	RoW
1963	Oct. 23	Wembley	2	1

ENGLAND v ROMANIA

Year	Date	Venue	Eng	Rom
1939	May 24	Bucharest	2	0
1968	Nov. 6	Bucharest	0	0
1969	Jan. 15	Wembley	1	1
wc1970	June 2	Guadalajara	1	0
wc1980	Oct. 15	Bucharest	1	2
wc1981	Apr. 29	Wembley	0	0
wc1985	May 1	Bucharest	0	0
wc1985	Sept. 11	Wembley	1	1

ENGLAND v SAUDI ARABIA

Year	Date	Venue	Eng	Saud
1988	Nov. 16	Riyadh	1	1

ENGLAND v SCOTLAND

Year	Date	Venue	Eng	Scot
1872	Nov. 30	Glasgow	0	0

ENGLAND v SCOTLAND *(cont'd)*

Year	Date	Venue	Eng	Scot
1873	Mar. 8	Kennington Oval	4	2
1874	Mar. 7	Glasgow	1	2
1875	Mar. 6	Kennington Oval	2	2
1876	Mar. 4	Glasgow	0	3
1877	Mar. 3	Kennington Oval	1	3
1878	Mar. 2	Glasgow	2	7
1879	Apr. 5	Kennington Oval	5	4
1880	Mar. 13	Glasgow	4	5
1881	Mar. 12	Kennington Oval	1	6
1882	Mar. 11	Glasgow	1	5
1883	Mar. 10	Sheffield	2	3
1884	Mar. 15	Glasgow	0	1
1885	Mar. 21	Kennington Oval	1	1
1886	Mar. 31	Glasgow	1	1
1887	Mar. 19	Blackburn	2	3
1888	Mar. 17	Glasgow	5	0
1889	Apr. 13	Kennington Oval	2	3
1890	Apr. 5	Glasgow	1	1
1891	Apr. 6	Blackburn	2	1
1892	Apr. 2	Glasgow	4	1
1893	Apr. 1	Richmond	5	2
1894	Apr. 7	Glasgow	2	2
1895	Apr. 6	Everton	3	0
1896	Apr. 4	Glasgow	1	2
1897	Apr. 3	Crystal Palace	1	2
1898	Apr. 2	Glasgow	3	1
1899	Apr. 8	Birmingham	2	1
1900	Apr. 7	Glasgow	1	4
1901	Mar. 30	Crystal Palace	2	2
1902	Mar. 3	Birmingham	2	2
1903	Apr. 4	Sheffield	1	2
1904	Apr. 9	Glasgow	1	0
1905	Apr. 1	Crystal Palace	1	0
1906	Apr. 7	Glasgow	1	2
1907	Apr. 6	Newcastle	1	1
1908	Apr. 4	Glasgow	1	1
1909	Apr. 3	Crystal Palace	2	0
1910	Apr. 2	Glasgow	0	2
1911	Apr. 1	Everton	1	1
1912	Mar. 23	Glasgow	1	1
1913	Apr. 5	Chelsea	1	0
1914	Apr. 14	Glasgow	1	3
1920	Apr. 10	Sheffield	5	4
1921	Apr. 9	Glasgow	0	3
1922	Apr. 8	Aston Villa	0	1
1923	Apr. 14	Glasgow	2	2
1924	Apr. 12	Wembley	1	1
1925	Apr. 4	Glasgow	0	2
1926	Apr. 17	Manchester	0	1
1927	Apr. 2	Glasgow	2	1
1928	Mar. 31	Wembley	1	5
1929	Apr. 13	Glasgow	0	1
1930	Apr. 5	Wembley	5	2
1931	Mar. 28	Glasgow	0	2
1932	Apr. 9	Wembley	3	0
1933	Apr. 1	Glasgow	1	2
1934	Apr. 14	Wembley	3	0
1935	Apr. 6	Glasgow	0	2
1936	Apr. 4	Wembley	1	1
1937	Apr. 17	Glasgow	1	3
1938	Apr. 9	Wembley	0	1
1939	Apr. 15	Glasgow	2	1
1947	Apr. 12	Wembley	1	1
1948	Apr. 10	Glasgow	2	0
1949	Apr. 9	Wembley	1	3
wc1950	Apr. 15	Glasgow	1	0
1951	Apr. 14	Wembley	2	3
1952	Apr. 5	Glasgow	2	1
1953	Apr. 18	Wembley	2	2
wc1954	Apr. 3	Glasgow	4	2
1955	Apr. 2	Wembley	7	2
1956	Apr. 14	Glasgow	1	1
1957	Apr. 6	Wembley	2	1
1958	Apr. 19	Glasgow	4	0
1959	Apr. 11	Wembley	1	0
1960	Apr. 9	Glasgow	1	1

ENGLAND v SCOTLAND (cont'd)

Year	Date		Venue	EngScot	
1961	Apr.	15	Wembley	9	3
1962	Apr.	14	Glasgow	0	2
1963	Apr.	6	Wembley	1	2
1964	Apr.	11	Glasgow	0	1
1965	Apr.	10	Wembley	2	2
1966	Apr.	2	Glasgow	4	3
EC1967	Apr.	15	Wembley	2	3
EC1968	Feb.	24	Glasgow	1	1
1969	May	10	Wembley	4	1
1970	Apr.	25	Glasgow	0	0
1971	May	22	Wembley	3	1
1972	May	27	Glasgow	1	0
SFAC1973	Feb.	14	Glasgow	5	0
1973	May	19	Wembley	1	0
1974	May	18	Glasgow	0	2
1975	May	24	Wembley	5	1
1976	May	15	Glasgow	1	2
1977	June	4	Wembley	1	2
1978	May	20	Glasgow	1	0
1979	May	26	Wembley	3	1
1980	May	24	Glasgow	2	0
1981	May	23	Wembley	0	1
1982	May	29	Glasgow	1	0
1983	June	1	Wembley	2	0
1984	May	26	Glasgow	1	1
RC1985	May	25	Glasgow	0	1
RC1986	Apr.	23	Wembley	2	1
RC1987	May	23	Glasgow	0	0
RC1988	May	21	Wembley	1	0
RC1989	May	27	Glasgow	2	0

ENGLAND v SPAIN

Year	Date		Venue	EngSpain	
1929	May	15	Madrid	3	4
1931	Dec.	9	Highbury	7	1
WC1950	July	2	Rio de Janeiro	0	1
1955	May	18	Madrid	1	1
1955	Nov.	30	Wembley	4	1
1960	May	15	Madrid	0	3
1960	Oct.	26	Wembley	4	2
1965	Dec.	8	Madrid	2	0
1967	May	24	Wembley	2	0
EC1968	Apr.	3	Wembley	1	0
EC1968	May	8	Madrid	2	1
1980	Mar.	26	Barcelona	2	0
EC1980	June	18	Naples	2	1
1981	Mar.	25	Wembley	1	2
WC1982	July	5	Madrid	0	0
1987	Feb.	18	Madrid	4	2

ENGLAND v SWEDEN

Year	Date		Venue	Eng Swe	
1923	May	21	Stockholm	4	2
1923	May	24	Stockholm	3	1
1937	May	17	Stockholm	4	0
1947	Nov.	19	Highbury	4	2
1949	May	13	Stockholm	1	3
1956	May	16	Stockholm	0	0
1959	Oct.	28	Wembley	2	3
1965	May	16	Gothenburg	2	1
1968	May	22	Wembley	3	1
1979	June	10	Stockholm	0	0
1986	Sept.	10	Stockholm	0	1
WC1988	Oct.	19	Wembley	0	0
WC1989	Sept.	6	Stockholm	0	0

ENGLAND v SWITZERLAND

Year	Date		Venue	EngSwit	
1933	May	29	Berne	4	0
1938	May	21	Zurich	1	2
1947	May	18	Zurich	0	1
1948	Dec.	2	Highbury	6	0
1952	May	28	Zurich	3	0
WC1954	June	20	Berne	2	0
1962	May	9	Wembley	3	1
1963	June	5	Basle	8	1

ENGLAND v SWITZERLAND (cont'd)

Year	Date		Venue	EngSwit	
EC1971	Oct.	13	Basle	3	2
EC1971	Nov.	10	Wembley	1	1
1975	Sept.	3	Basle	2	1
1977	Sept.	7	Wembley	0	0
WC1980	Nov.	19	Wembley	2	1
WC1981	May	30	Basle	1	2
1988	May	28	Lausanne	1	0

ENGLAND v TUNISIA

Year	Date		Venue	Eng Tun	
1990	June	2	Tunis	1	1

ENGLAND v TURKEY

Year	Date		Venue	EngTurk	
WC1984	Nov.	14	Istanbul	8	0
WC1985	Oct.	16	Wembley	5	0
EC1987	Apr.	29	Izmir	0	0
EC1987	Oct.	14	Wembley	8	0
EC1991	May	1	Izmir	1	0

ENGLAND v USA

Year	Date		Venue	EngUSA	
WC1950	June	20	Belo Horizonte	0	1
1953	June	8	New York	6	3
1959	May	28	Los Angeles	8	1
1964	May	27	New York	10	0
1985	June	16	Los Angeles	5	0

ENGLAND v USSR

Year	Date		Venue	EngUSSR	
1958	May	18	Moscow	1	1
WC1958	June	8	Gothenburg	2	2
WC1958	June	17	Gothenburg	0	1
1958	Oct.	22	Wembley	5	0
1967	Dec.	6	Wembley	2	2
EC1968	June	8	Rome	2	0
1973	June	10	Moscow	2	1
1984	June	2	Wembley	0	2
1986	Mar.	26	Tbilisi	1	0
EC1988	June	18	Frankfurt	1	3
1991	May	21	Wembley	3	1

ENGLAND v URUGUAY

Year	Date		Venue	Eng Uru	
1953	May	31	Montevideo	1	2
WC1954	June	26	Basle	2	4
1964	May	6	Wembley	2	1
WC1966	July	11	Wembley	0	0
1969	June	8	Montevideo	2	1
1977	June	15	Montevideo	0	0
1984	June	13	Montevideo	0	2
1990	May	22	Wembley	1	2

ENGLAND v WALES

Year	Date		Venue	EngWales	
1879	Jan.	18	Kennington Oval	2	1
1880	Mar.	15	Wrexham	3	2
1881	Feb.	26	Blackburn	0	1
1882	Mar.	13	Wrexham	3	5
1883	Feb.	3	Kennington Oval	5	0
1884	Mar.	17	Wrexham	4	0
1885	Mar.	14	Blackburn	1	1
1886	Mar.	29	Wrexham	3	1
1887	Feb.	26	Kennington Oval	4	0
1888	Feb.	4	Crewe	5	1
1889	Feb.	23	Stoke	4	1
1890	Mar.	15	Wrexham	3	1
1891	Mar.	7	Sunderland	4	1
1892	Mar.	5	Wrexham	2	0
1893	Mar.	13	Stoke	6	0
1894	Mar.	12	Wrexham	5	1
1895	Mar.	18	Queen's Club, Kensington	1	1
1896	Mar.	16	Cardiff	9	1
1897	Mar.	29	Sheffield	4	0
1898	Mar.	28	Wrexham	3	0

ENGLAND *v* WALES *(cont'd)*

Year	Date	Venue	Eng	Wales
1899	Mar. 20	Bristol	4	0
1900	Mar. 26	Cardiff	1	1
1901	Mar. 18	Newcastle	6	0
1902	Mar. 3	Wrexham	0	0
1903	Mar. 2	Portsmouth	2	1
1904	Feb. 29	Wrexham	2	2
1905	Mar. 27	Liverpool	3	1
1906	Mar. 19	Cardiff	1	0
1907	Mar. 18	Fulham	1	1
1908	Mar. 16	Wrexham	7	1
1909	Mar. 15	Nottingham	2	0
1910	Mar. 14	Cardiff	1	0
1911	Mar. 13	Millwall	3	0
1912	Mar. 11	Wrexham	2	0
1913	Mar. 17	Bristol	4	3
1914	Mar. 16	Cardiff	2	0
1920	Mar. 15	Highbury	1	2
1921	Mar. 14	Cardiff	0	0
1922	Mar. 13	Liverpool	1	0
1923	Mar. 5	Cardiff	2	2
1924	Mar. 3	Blackburn	1	2
1925	Feb. 28	Swansea	2	1
1926	Mar. 1	Crystal Palace	1	3
1927	Feb. 12	Wrexham	3	3
1927	Nov. 28	Burnley	1	2
1928	Nov. 17	Swansea	3	2
1929	Nov. 20	Chelsea	6	0
1930	Nov. 22	Wrexham	4	0
1931	Nov. 18	Liverpool	3	1
1932	Nov. 16	Wrexham	0	0
1933	Nov. 15	Newcastle	1	2
1934	Sept. 29	Cardiff	4	0
1936	Feb. 5	Wolverhampton	1	2
1936	Oct. 17	Cardiff	1	2
1937	Nov. 17	Middlesbrough	2	1
1938	Oct. 22	Cardiff	2	4
1946	Nov. 13	Manchester	3	0
1947	Oct. 18	Cardiff	3	0
1948	Nov. 10	Aston Villa	1	0
wc1949	Oct. 15	Cardiff	4	1
1950	Nov. 15	Sunderland	4	2
1951	Oct. 20	Cardiff	1	1
1952	Nov. 12	Wembley	5	2
wc1953	Oct. 10	Cardiff	4	1
1954	Nov. 10	Wembley	3	2
1955	Oct. 22	Cardiff	1	2
1956	Nov. 14	Wembley	3	1

ENGLAND *v* WALES *(cont'd)*

Year	Date	Venue	Eng	Wales
1957	Oct. 19	Cardiff	4	0
1958	Nov. 26	Aston Villa	2	2
1959	Oct. 17	Cardiff	1	1
1960	Nov. 23	Wembley	5	1
1961	Oct. 14	Cardiff	1	1
1962	Nov. 21	Wembley	4	0
1963	Oct. 12	Cardiff	4	0
1964	Nov. 18	Wembley	2	1
1965	Oct. 2	Cardiff	0	0
EC1966	Nov. 16	Wembley	5	1
EC1967	Oct. 21	Cardiff	3	0
1969	May 7	Wembley	2	1
1970	Apr. 18	Cardiff	1	1
1971	May 19	Wembley	0	0
1972	May 20	Cardiff	3	0
wc1972	Nov. 15	Cardiff	1	0
wc1973	Jan. 24	Wembley	1	1
1973	May 15	Wembley	3	0
1974	May 11	Cardiff	2	0
1975	May 21	Wembley	2	2
FAWC1976	Mar. 24	Wrexham	2	1
1976	May 8	Cardiff	1	0
1977	May 31	Wembley	0	1
1978	May 13	Cardiff	3	1
1979	May 23	Wembley	0	0
1980	May 17	Wrexham	1	4
1981	May 20	Wembley	0	0
1982	Apr. 27	Cardiff	1	0
1983	Feb. 23	Wembley	2	1
1984	May 2	Wrexham	0	1

ENGLAND *v* YUGOSLAVIA

Year	Date	Venue	Eng	Yugo
1939	May 18	Belgrade	1	2
1950	May 22	Highbury	2	2
1954	May 16	Belgrade	0	1
1956	Nov. 28	Wembley	3	0
1958	May 11	Belgrade	0	5
1960	May 11	Wembley	3	3
1965	May 9	Belgrade	1	1
1966	May 4	Wembley	2	0
EC1968	June 5	Florence	0	1
1972	Oct. 11	Wembley	1	1
1974	June 5	Belgrade	2	2
EC1986	Nov. 12	Wembley	2	0
EC1987	Nov. 11	Belgrade	4	1
1989	Dec. 13	Wembley	2	1

England Semi-Professional Matches 1990-91

England 0   Italy 0
5th March 1991 at Kettering Town FC

Italian defences are notoriously difficult to break down, whatever the level of international, and England could feel reasonably satisfied with this result. There were several new faces in the England line-up but pre-match preparation at Lilleshall had ensured that the team functioned well as a unit. England came close to scoring on many occasions in the second period, particularly following corner-kicks, but a draw was probably fair on balance. Paul Rogers and Kenny Lowe, the latter having just switched from Barrow to Barnet, were outstanding in midfield for the home side.

England: McKenna (Boston United), Lee (Witton Albion), Watts (Redbridge Forest), Skivington (Barrow), Nicol (Kettering Town), Conner (Redbridge Forest), Lowe (Barnet), Rogers (Sutton United), Carter (Runcorn), Furlong (Enfield), Showler (Altrincham).

Substitutes: Ashford (Redbridge Forest) for Showler, Willis (Barnet) for Furlong.

Team Manager: Tony Jennings.

Assistant: Ron Reid.

Referee: D. Elleray (England).

Attendance: 1,910.

England 1   Wales 2
17th May 1991 at Stafford Rangers FC

The standard of England's performance fell well below that achieved against the Italians and Manager Jennings felt it was most possibly the most disappointing display by an England team that he had worked with. With the domestic league season over, the flair ingredient was missing and the pitch

The England team line up for the National Anthem at Kettering.

The England squad at Stafford.

too inevitably had an end-of-season look to it. In a match short on quality football, England created few chances. The only one to count was substitute Mark Carter's tap-in a minute after Colville had made it 2-0 to Wales (75 minutes). Wales had gone ahead with Giles's penalty on 58 minutes after the winger himself had been fouled.

England: McKenna, Lee, Bancroft (Kettering Town), Skivington, Nicol, Conner, Lowe, Todd (Berwick Rangers), Rogers, Furlong, West (Wycombe Wanderers).

Substitutes: Showler for Nicol, Humphreys (Kidderminster Harriers) for Todd, Carter (now Barnet) for West.

Scorer: Carter.

Team Manager: Tony Jennings.

Assistant: Ron Reid.

Referee: L. Dilkes (England).

Attendance: 683.

F.A. Representative Matches 1990-91

F.A. XI 3 British Students 1
6th November 1990 at Willenhall Town FC

FA: Jones (Kidderminster Harriers), Buckland and Willetts (Cheltenham Town), Weir (Kidderminster Harriers), Brindley (Telford United), Forsyth (Kidderminster Harriers), Stein and Poole (Barnet), Cavel (Boston United), Davies (Kidderminster Harriers), Brain (Cheltenham Town).

Substitutes: Price (Stafford Rangers) for Jones, Simpson (Stafford Rangers) for Buckland, Brogan (Cheltenham Town) for Brindley, Beech (Boston United) for Poole, Collymore (Stafford Rangers) for Davies.

Scorers: Forsyth, Cavell, Simpson.

Team Manager: Graham Allner.

F.A. XI 7 Combined Services 1
27th November 1990 at Frickley Athletic FC

FA: Smith S. (Gateshead), Kitchen (Frickley Athletic), O'Brien (Gateshead), Skivington (Barrow), Scott (Whitley Bay), Simpson (Altrincham), Robinson (Spennymoor United), Chandler (Whitley Bay), Todd (Berwick Rangers), Lowe (Barrow), Peattie (Spennymoor United).

Substitutes: Chilton (Barrow) for O'Brien, Woodhead (Frickley Athletic) for Peattie, Elliott (Spennymoor United) for Robinson, Ingham (Bridlington Town) for Smith.

Scorers: Simpson 2, Todd 2 Woodhead, Chandler, Peattie.

Team Manager: Ray Wilkie.

F.A. XI 2 Northern Premier League 1
18th December 1990 at Witton Albion FC

FA: Wealands (Altrincham), Young (Northwich Victoria), Chilton and Messenger (Barrow), Carroll (Runcorn), Hanlon (Macclesfield Town), Daws and Anderson (Altrincham), Hanchard (Northwich Victoria), Carter (Runcorn), Doherty (Barrow).

Substitutes: McDonnell (Barrow) for Wealands, Edwards (Runcorn) for Young, Rudge (Runcorn) for Daws, Askey (Macclesfield Town) for Hanchard.

Scorers: Carter 2.

Team Manager: Cliff Roberts.

F.A. XI 4 Isthmian League 0
23rd January 1991 at Kingstonian FC

FA: Phillips and Wilson (Barnet), Horton and Hone (Welling United), Conner (Redbridge Forest), Rogers (Sutton United), Carroll (Wycombe Wanderers), Clarke (Barnet), West and Evans (Wycombe Wanderers), Handford (Welling United).

Substitutes: Pape (Enfield) for Phillips, Kerr (Wycombe Wanderers) for Conner, Nugent (Barnet) for Hone, Thompson (Slough Town) for Carroll, Robbins (Welling United) for Evans.

Scorers: West, Robbins, Clarke + 1 OG

Team Manager: Barry Fry.

F.A. Challenge Cup Winners 1872-1991

1872 & 1874-92	Kennington Oval
1873	Lillie Bridge
1893	Fallowfield, Manchester
1894	Everton
1895-1914	Crystal Palace
1915	Old Trafford, Manchester
1920-22	Stamford Bridge
1923 to date	Wembley

Year	Winners	Runners-up	Score
1872	Wanderers	Royal Engineers	1-0
1873	Wanderers	Oxford University	2-0
1874	Oxford University	Royal Engineers	2-0
1875	Royal Engineers	Old Etonians	2-0 after 1-1 draw
1876	Wanderers	Old Etonians	3-0 after 0-0 draw
1877	Wanderers	Oxford University	2-0 after extra time
1878 *	Wanderers	Royal Engineers	3-1
1879	Old Etonians	Clapham Rovers	1-0
1880	Clapham Rovers	Oxford University	1-0
1881	Old Carthusians	Old Etonians	3-0
1882	Old Etonians	Blackburn Rovers	1-0
1883	Blackburn Olympic	Old Etonians	2-1 after extra time
1884	Blackburn Rovers	Queen's Park, Glasgow	2-1
1885	Blackburn Rovers	Queen's Park, Glasgow	2-0
1886 †	Blackburn Rovers	West Bromwich Albion	2-0 after 0-0 draw
1887	Aston Villa	West Bromwich Albion	2-0
1888	West Bromwich Albion	Preston North End	2-1
1889	Preston North End	Wolverhampton Wanderers	3-0
1890	Blackburn Rovers	Sheffield Wednesday	6-1
1891	Blackburn Rovers	Notts. County	3-1
1892	West Bromwich Albion	Aston Villa	3-0
1893	Wolverhampton Wanderers	Everton	1-0
1894	Notts. County	Bolton Wanderers	4-1
1895	Aston Villa	West Bromwich Albion	1-0
1896	Sheffield Wednesday	Wolverhampton Wanderers	2-1
1897	Aston Villa	Everton	3-2
1898	Nottingham Forest	Derby County	3-1
1899	Sheffield United	Derby County	4-1
1900	Bury	Southampton	4-0
1901	Tottenham Hotspur	Sheffield United	3-1 after 2-2 draw
1902	Sheffield United	Southampton	2-1 after 1-1 draw
1903	Bury	Derby County	6-0
1904	Manchester City	Bolton Wanderers	1-0
1905	Aston Villa	Newcastle United	2-0
1906	Everton	Newcastle United	1-0
1907	Sheffield Wednesday	Everton	2-1
1908	Wolverhampton Wanderers	Newcastle United	3-1
1909	Manchester United	Bristol City	1-0
1910	Newcastle United	Barnsley	2-0 after 1-1 draw
1911	Bradford City	Newcastle United	1-0 after 0-0 draw
1912	Barnsley	West Bromwich Albion	1-0 after 0-0 draw
1913	Aston Villa	Sunderland	1-0
1914	Burnley	Liverpool	1-0
1915	Sheffield United	Chelsea	3-0
1920	Aston Villa	Huddersfield Town	1-0 after extra time
1921	Tottenham Hotspur	Wolverhampton Wanderers	1-0
1922	Huddersfield Town	Preston North End	1-0
1923	Bolton Wanderers	West Ham United	2-0
1924	Newcastle United	Aston Villa	2-0
1925	Sheffield United	Cardiff City	1-0
1926	Bolton Wanderers	Manchester City	1-0
1927	Cardiff City	Arsenal	1-0
1928	Blackburn Rovers	Huddersfield Town	3-1
1929	Bolton Wanderers	Portsmouth	2-0
1930	Arsenal	Huddersfield Town	2-0
1931	West Bromwich Albion	Birmingham	2-1
1932	Newcastle United	Arsenal	2-1
1933	Everton	Manchester City	3-0
1934	Manchester City	Portsmouth	2-1
1935	Sheffield Wednesday	West Bromwich Albion	4-2
1936	Arsenal	Sheffield United	1-0
1937	Sunderland	Preston North End	3-1
1938	Preston North End	Huddersfield Town	1-0 after extra time
1939	Portsmouth	Wolverhampton Wanderers	4-1

Year	Winners	Runners-up	Score
1946	Derby County	Charlton Athletic	4-1 after extra time
1947	Charlton Athletic	Burnley	1-0 after extra time
1948	Manchester United	Blackpool	4-2
1949	Wolverhampton Wanderers	Leicester City	3-1
1950	Arsenal	Liverpool	2-0
1951	Newcastle United	Blackpool	2-0
1952	Newcastle United	Arsenal	1-0
1953	Blackpool	Bolton Wanderers	4-3
1954	West Bromwich Albion	Preston North End	3-2
1955	Newcastle United	Manchester City	3-1
1956	Manchester City	Birmingham City	3-1
1957	Aston Villa	Manchester United	2-1
1958	Bolton Wanderers	Manchester United	2-0
1959	Nottingham Forest	Luton Town	2-1
1960	Wolverhampton Wanderers	Blackburn Rovers	3-0
1961	Tottenham Hotspur	Leicester City	2-0
1962	Tottenham Hotspur	Burnley	3-1
1963	Manchester United	Leicester City	3-1
1964	West Ham United	Preston North End	3-2
1965	Liverpool	Leeds United	2-1 after extra time
1966	Everton	Sheffield Wednesday	3-2
1967	Tottenham Hotspur	Chelsea	2-1
1968	West Bromwich Albion	Everton	1-0 after extra time
1969	Manchester City	Leicester City	1-0
1970	Chelsea	Leeds United	2-1 after 2-2 draw both games extra time
1971	Arsenal	Liverpool	2-1 after extra time
1972	Leeds United	Arsenal	1-0
1973	Sunderland	Leeds United	1-0
1974	Liverpool	Newcastle United	3-0
1975	West Ham United	Fulham	2-0
1976	Southampton	Manchester United	1-0
1977	Manchester United	Liverpool	2-1
1978	Ipswich Town	Arsenal	1-0
1979	Arsenal	Manchester United	3-2
1980	West Ham United	Arsenal	1-0
1981	Tottenham Hotspur	Manchester City	3-2 after 1-1 draw after extra time
1982	Tottenham Hotspur	Queens Park Rangers	1-0 after 1-1 draw after extra time
1983	Manchester United	Brighton & Hove Albion	4-0 after 2-2 draw after extra time
1984	Everton	Watford	2-0
1985	Manchester United	Everton	1-0 after extra time
1986	Liverpool	Everton	3-1
1987	Coventry City	Tottenham Hotspur	3-2 after extra time
1988	Wimbledon	Liverpool	1-0
1989	Liverpool	Everton	3-2 after extra time
1990	Manchester United	Crystal Palace	1-0 after 3-3 draw after extra time
1991	Tottenham Hotspur	Nottingham Forest	2-1 after extra time

* Won outright but restored to the Association
† A special trophy was awarded for third consecutive win

F.A. Challenge Cup – Final Tie 1991

Tottenham Hotspur 2   Nottingham Forest 1

Prior to the 110th Challenge Cup Final, played out on the mostly dull afternoon of 18 May, Tottenham had shared the record with Aston Villa and Manchester United for the most Final wins (seven). Now there was daylight between the North London club and the others as Gary Mabbutt received the famous trophy from HRH The Duchess of Kent after Spurs' exciting extra-time victory.

It had been a neat change of fortune for the Tottenham captain. Four years earlier, in his club's last Final appearance, he had deflected McGrath's centre into his own net to give Coventry City the Cup in the extra period. Now he was showing the trophy to the massed ranks of Tottenham fans to his right after England star Des Walker's attempt at a headed clearance had given Forest's opponents

a winning 2-1 lead.

The Cup Final brought together two larger-than-life personalities in Brian Clough and Paul Gascoigne. Clough, Forest's controversial manager for 16 years, had won the European Cup, the League Championship and the League Cup – but never the FA Cup. Gascoigne, the hugely-talented England midfielder who won the nation's hearts at Italia '90, could have been playing his last match in Tottenham's colours before a multi-million pound transfer to Italy. As it happened, neither had an afternoon that he would want to remember. The FA Cup still eludes the Forest supremo and the unfortunate 'Gazza' was carted off to hospital less than 20 minutes into the game.

A 'fired-up' Gascoigne jarred his knee as he lunged at Gary Charles a couple of yards outside the Spurs

Walker blocks this short centre from Walsh.

penalty area and was clearly in some distress. Referee Milford, the oldest in Cup Final history at 50, awarded a free-kick to Forest and Stuart Pearce, lethal from that range, rammed the ball high into the net before the 'Viking' could move. So it was 1-0 to Forest, the slight favourites, with 15 minutes and 20 seconds gone.

Then things went from bad to worse for Spurs in that grim first half. Gary Lineker, striving for his first winners' medal in domestic soccer, converted Paul Allen's short centre from the right on 23 minutes but was ruled marginally offside. Ten minutes later Crossley sent him sprawling in the box and the resulting spot-kick, though the England striker struck it firmly towards the right-hand corner, was pushed away by the young Forest goalkeeper. Only Liverpool's Aldridge in 1988 had missed before in an FA Cup Final at Wembley.

Tottenham, with the Moroccan Nayim having so far proved an able deputy for the stricken Gascoigne, sprinted out to start the second half and fairly bristled with determination. Within ten minutes they had achieved equality. Allen, in space, controlled Nayim's waist-high pass and pushed quickly forward before sliding the ball out to Paul Stewart veering in from the right flank. The Final's 'Man of the Match' took his time before planting a measured shot along the ground and into the far corner of the goal.

Spurs kept driving forward for the winner, only to be denied repeatedly by the excellence of Walker and the 21-year-old Charles, the latter having recently been named by Graham Taylor in the England squad for the summer tour to Australasia. But in extra time Spurs really turned the screw. Paul

Parker tries to keep possession as Stewart and Sedgley move in to challenge.

Walsh, on for Samways, rose above Charles to loop a header against the bar and Crossley's back connected with a post as he scrambled back to try and tip the ball over.

Then, almost immediately, came the goal that won the Cup. Nayim swung a right-wing corner into the near-post area, Stewart nudged it on and Walker beat Mabbutt by inches to the ball at the far post but headed it over Charles, standing on the line, and into the top corner. It was the cruellest blow for a player who had performed to perfection until that moment. So Spurs, despite all their first-half tribulations, had done it.

Tottenham Hotspur: Thorstvedt, Edinburgh, Van den Hauwe, Sedgley, Howells, Mabbutt, Stewart, Gascoigne (Nayim), Samways (Walsh), Lineker, Allen.

Nottingham Forest: Crossley, Charles, Pearce, Walker, Chettle, Keane, Crosby, Parker, Clough, Glover (Laws), Woan (Hodge).

Referee: R. Milford (Bristol).

F.A. Challenge Cup Competition 1990-91

Preliminary Round	Result				Attendance			
Saturday 1st September 1990	*1st Tie*	*1st Rep*	*2nd Rep*	*3rd Rep*	*1st Tie*	*1st Rep*	*2nd Rep*	*3rd Rep*
Willington *v* Cleator Moor Athletic	0-1				48			
Ashington *v* Prudhoe East End	1-4				22			
Shildon *v* Garforth Town	3-1				129			
North Shields *v* Whickham	2-0				132			
West Auckland Town *v* Annfield Plain...................	4-2				57			
Bedlington Terriers *v* Norton & Stockton Ancients ...	0-4				60			
Blackpool (Wren) Rovers *v* Accrington Stanley ...	2-4				104			
Billingham Town *v* Brandon United.......................	1-0				80			
Netherfield *v* Murton	0-3				160			
Chester-le-Street Town *v* Easington Colliery	0-2				69			
Penrith *v* Harrogate Railway	0-5				75			
Langley Park *v* Washington....................................	2-0				47			
Ferryhill Athletic *v* Blackpool Mechanics.............	3-1				63			
Shotton Comrades *v* Esh Winning	1-2				12			
Crook Town *v* Horden CW	1-2				39			
Great Harwood Town *v* Harrogate Town	2-2				121			
Harrogate Town *v* Great Harwood Town		2-1				352		
Northallerton Town *v* Clitheroe	4-2				120			
Darwen *v* Peterlee Newtown	2-0				94			
Darlington CB *v* Evenwood Town	0-1				17			
Lancaster City *v* Thackley	2-0				129			
Hebburn *v* Ryhope CA	0-2				52			
Whitby Town *v* Leyland DAF	2-0				213			
Irlam Town *v* Formby	2-0				38			
Ashton United *v* Denaby United.............................	0-2				160			
Bridgnorth Town *v* Vauxhall GM	1-1				125			
Vauxhall GM *v* Bridgnorth Town		4-1				80		
Knowsley United *v* Ossett Town	1-1				75			
Ossett Town *v* Knowsley United.......................		2-3				190		
Glossop *v* Skelmersdale United	1-1				290			
Skelmersdale United *v* Glossop		0-2				190		
Atherton LR *v* Rossendale United	3-1				208			
Burscough *v* Maine Road	0-3				92			
Farsley Celtic *v* Ossett Albion	1-1				196			
Ossett Albion *v* Farsley Celtic		0-2				146		
Prescot AFC *v* Emley	1-1				237			
Emley *v* Prescot AFC		2-1				417		
Bootle *v* Winsford United	1-0				60			
Chadderton *v* Radcliffe Borough	1-2				91			
Armthorpe Welfare *v* Sheffield	3-0				45			
Hednesford Town *v* Guiseley	2-0				338			
Salford City *v* Warrington Town	0-3				121			
Newtown *v* Eastwood Town	1-1				230			
Eastwood Town *v* Newtown		2-1				241		
Belper Town *v* St Helens Town	2-3				158			
Oakham United *v* Long Eaton United	1-1				48			
Long Eaton United *v* Oakham United		0-1				61		
Sutton Town *v* Rocester	2-2				154			
Rocester *v* Sutton Town		1-0				223		
Borrowash Victoria *v* Gresley Rovers	1-2				176			
North Ferriby United *v* Leicester United	1-2				136			
Willenhall Town *v* Brigg Town	1-1				119			
Brigg Town *v* Willenhall Town		1-1				150		
Brigg Town *v* Willenhall Town			1-3				240	
Louth United *v* Princes End United	1-1				61			
Princes End United *v* Louth United		1-0				54		
Alfreton Town *v* Rushall Olympic	2-2				96			
Rushall Olympic *v* Alfreton Town		3-0				243		

Match							
Paget Rangers v Boldmere St Michaels	2-0				95		
Nuneaton Borough v Hinckley Town	4-1				834		
Wellingborough Town v Tividale	1-0				65		
Arnold Town v Wednesfield	1-1				180		
Wednesfield v Arnold Town		1-0				65	
Alvechurch v Desborough Town	2-1				154		
Stratford Town v Highgate United	3-1				80		
Solihull Borough v Banbury United	0-0				147		
Banbury United v Solihull Borough		1-1				229	
Solihull Borough v Banbury United			2-2				155
Banbury United v Solihull Borough				3-4				263
Heanor Town v Halesowen Harriers	0-4				134		
Dudley Town v Corby Town	1-1				201		
Corby Town v Dudley Town		1-0				254	
Hinckley Athletic v Friar Lane OB	3-1				183		
Eastwood Hanley v West Midlands Police	0-2				65		
Irthlingborough Diamonds v Buckingham Town	3-4				51		
Chasetown v Evesham United	0-2				84		
Brackley Town v Walsall-Wood	1-0				102		
Oldbury United v Wolverton	0-0				87		
Wolverton v Oldbury United		2-1				31	
Mile Oak Rovers v Stourbridge	0-5				51		
Sandwell Borough v Northampton Spencer	4-1				25		
Holbeach United v Potton United	1-2				105		
Boston v Kings Lynn	2-0				332		
Malvern Town v Soham Town Rangers	3-0				83		
Rothwell Town v Stamford	7-2				65		
Welwyn GC v Chalfont St Peter	1-2				33		
Wisbech Town v Barton Rovers	1-1				358		
Barton Rovers v Wisbech Town		2-1				156	
Baker Perkins v Letchworth GC	5-2				57		
Lowestoft Town v Mirrless Blackstone	1-0				187		
Boreham Wood v Gorleston	2-0				85		
Haverhill Rovers v Eynesbury Rovers	1-1				101		
Eynesbury Rovers v Haverhill Rovers		0-2				200	
Leighton Town v Spalding United	0-1				160		
Bourne Town v Ely City	3-0				137		
Great Yarmouth Town v Langford	2-2				160		
Langford v Great Yarmouth Town		0-1				230	
Wembley v Bury Town	1-0				73		
Newmarket Town v Cheshunt	2-1				66		
Tiptree United v Harlow Town	0-1				75		
Braintree Town v Collier Row	1-0				212		
Rayners Lane v Hoddesdon Town	2-1				43		
Clapton v Felixstowe Town	5-2				54		
Ford United v Kingsbury Town	3-1				13		
Ruislip Manor v Northwood	2-1				197		
Halstead Town v Canvey Island	1-1				247		
Canvey Island v Halstead Town		1-7				147	
Cray Wanderers v Waltham Abbey	3-1				86		
Stowmarket Town v Saffron Walden Town	1-1				120		
Saffron Walden Town v Stowmarket Town		2-1				120	
Hemel Hempstead v Metropolitan Police	1-2				110		
Clacton Town v Hertford Town	0-1				156		
Burnham Ramblers v Hornchurch	0-2				94		
Chesham United v Baldock Town	4-1				195		
Arlesey Town v Walthamstow Pennant	0-4				89		
Witham Town v Basildon United	2-3				137		
Harwich & Parkeston v Berkhamsted Town	4-1				221		
Wootton Blue Cross v Hounslow	1-3				52		
Barkingside v Aveley	2-1				55		
East Thurrock United v Stevenage Borough	0-1				225		
Molesey v Vauxhall Motors	1-1				60		
Vauxhall Motors v Molesey		0-5				75	
Flackwell Heath v Tring Town	5-0				45		
Banstead Athletic v Malden Vale	1-0				51		
Ware v Corinthian Casuals	0-0				70		
Corinthian Casuals v Ware		1-0				85	

Alma Swanley v Purfleet	1-2		40
Billericay Town v Hanwell Town	4-0		228
Croydon v Egham Town	0-4		71
Eton Manor v Edgware Town	0-2		80
Tilbury v Southall	0-0		77
Southall v Tilbury		1-3	86
Horsham YMCA v Darenth Heathside	3-2		36
Harefield United v Merstham	0-1		41
Croydon Athletic v Andover	2-2		47
Andover v Croydon Athletic		7-1	292
Royston Town v Rainham Town	1-1		71
Rainham Town v Royston Town		1-2	75
Chertsey Town v Walton & Hersham	0-3		207
Horsham v Epsom & Ewell	2-0		88
Slade Green v Ringmer	2-0		36
Tooting & Mitcham United v Hastings Town	1-1		230
Hastings Town v Tooting & Mitcham United		0-2	338
Tonbridge AFC v Shoreham	2-1		311
Chipstead v Littlehampton Town	2-3		70
Southwick v Corinthians	1-0		104
Steyning Town v Whitehawk	1-2		66
Peacehaven & Telscombe v Selsey	8-1		126
Ramsgate v Margate	0-1		560
Camberley Town v Oakwood	0-5		26
Ashford Town v Leatherhead	3-1		345
Sheppey United v Pagham	0-2		102
Sittingbourne v Burgess Hill Town	2-0		434
Cove v Haywards Heath Town	4-0		52
Canterbury City v Dorking	0-0		127
Dorking v Canterbury City		4-1	280
Arundel v Chatham Town	2-3		61
Three Bridges v Wick	1-3		121
Eastbourne United v Tunbridge Wells	6-5		97
Langney Sports v Portfield	3-0		130
Lancing v Lewes	0-3		125
Havant Town v Horndean	3-0		203
Bracknell Town v Hampton	2-3		70
Hungerford Town v Fareham Town	1-0		105
Feltham v Thame United	2-0		30
Salisbury v Uxbridge	1-1		199
Uxbridge v Salisbury		1-2	134
Sholing Sports v Abingdon United	1-3		47
Bournemouth v Thatcham Town	1-0		39
Newbury Town v Eastleigh	2-1		74
Chichester City v Lymington AFC	1-5		55
Trowbridge Town v Clandown	7-1		326
Totton AFC v Warminster Town	2-3		35
Calne Town v Paulton Rovers	2-0		86
Romsey Town v Frome Town	1-0		67
Melksham Town v Keynsham Town	2-1		80
Westbury United v Stroud	1-1		92
Stroud v Westbury United		3-0	90
Clevedon Town v Dawlish Town	3-3		72
Dawlish Town v Clevedon Town		2-3	80
Swanage Town & Herston v Devizes Town	4-0		95
Barry Town v Minehead	2-1		276
Shortwood United v St Blazey	1-2		128
Cwmbran Town v Mangotsfield United	0-4		152
Maesteg Park v Sharpness (walkover for Maesteg Park – Sharpness withdrew)			
Bridgend Town v Ton Pentre	2-1		61
Radstock Town v Weston-Super-Mare	0-3		120
Yate Town v Glastonbury	4-0		164
Ilfracombe Town v Barnstaple Town	4-0		220
Wimborne Town v Bideford	3-2		120
Tiverton Town v Welton Rovers	4-1		217
St Austell v Falmouth Town	0-4		210
Saltash United v Torrington	1-1		147
Torrington v Saltash United		2-5	87

102

COSSACK

THE HAIRCARE RANGE
FOR TODAY'S HAIR FASHIONS!

Saturday 15th September 1990	1st Tie	1st Rep	2nd Rep	3rd Rep	1st Tie	1st Rep	2nd Rep	3rd Rep
Shildon *v* Cleator Moor Celtic	2-1				91			
Alnwick Town *v* Fleetwood Town	0-5				80			
North Shields *v* Gateshead	1-1				423			
Gateshead *v* North Shields		0-1				441		
Durham City *v* Prudhoe East End	0-3				40			
Accrington Stanley *v* West Auckland Town	3-0				537			
Blyth Spartans *v* Bridlington Town	2-0				368			
Billingham Town *v* Guisborough Town	1-2				150			
Gretna *v* Norton & Stockton Ancients	5-1				169			
Harrogate Railway *v* Murton	2-0				110			
Ferryhill Athletic *v* South Bank	1-1				125			
South Bank *v* Ferryhill Athletic		1-0				105		
Langley Park *v* Tow Law Town	2-1				144			
Colne Dynamoes *v* Easington Colliery								
(walkover for Easington Colliery – Colne Dynamoes disbanded)								
Harrogate Town *v* Esh Winning	1-3				170			
Stockton *v* Spennymoor United	0-2				145			
Northallerton Town *v* Billingham Synthonia	2-0				83			
Workington *v* Horden CW	1-1				201			
Horden CW *v* Workington		2-1				159		
Lancaster City *v* Darwen	1-0				194			
Whitby Town *v* Newcastle Blue Star	4-7				275			
Ryhope CA *v* Consett	1-2				33			
Seaham Red Star *v* Evenwood Town	1-1				111			
Evenwood Town *v* Seaham Red Star		0-1				52		
Vauxhall GM *v* Irlam Town	0-2				58			
Morecambe *v* Horwich RMI	2-2				285			
Horwich RMI *v* Morecambe		3-0				249		
Knowsley United *v* Colwyn Bay	0-0				313			
Colwyn Bay *v* Knowsley United		3-0				529		
Caernarfon Town *v* Denaby United								
(tie awarded to Caernarfon Town as Denaby United unable to fulfil fixture)								
Maine Road *v* Glossop	1-0				108			
Altrincham *v* Rhyl	3-2				817			
Farsley Celtic *v* Bangor City	0-0				157			
Bangor City *v* Farsley Celtic		3-0				298		
Harworth CI *v* Atherton LR	1-2				30			
Radcliffe Borough *v* Emley	0-0				280			
Emley *v* Radcliffe Borough		1-0				478		
Chorley *v* Mossley	4-0				470			
Armthorpe Welfare *v* Southport	1-2				168			
Ilkeston Town *v* Bootle	2-3				296			
Eastwood Town *v* Hednesford Town	1-1				236			
Hednesford Town *v* Eastwood Town		1-1				470		
Eastwood Town *v* Hednesford Town			2-3				316	
Oakham United *v* Hyde United	1-2				158			
St Helens Town *v* Curzon Ashton	0-3				202			
South Liverpool *v* Warrington Town	2-0				237			
Leicester United *v* Rocester	1-0				248			
Droylsden *v* Stalybridge Celtic	1-1				530			
Stalybridge Celtic *v* Droylsden		1-2				549		
Willenhall Town *v* Marine	0-0				164			
Marine *v* Willenhall Town		2-2				245		
Marine *v* Willenhall Town			4-1				202	
Worksop Town *v* Gresley Rovers	2-1				161			
Paget Rangers *v* Princes End United	1-2				59			
Frickley Athletic *v* Gainsborough Trinity	4-3				317			
Nuneaton Borough *v* Goole Town	1-0				872			
Blakenall *v* Rushall Olympic	3-2				319			
Alvechurch *v* Wellingborough Town	4-1				129			
Witton Albion *v* Congleton Town	2-0				611			
Stratford Town *v* Buxton	1-4				164			
Bilston Town *v* Wednesfield	6-0				145			

Match	Score			Att		
Corby Town *v* Solihull Borough	3-0			295		
West Midlands Police *v* Matlock Town	0-6			85		
Hinckley Athletic *v* Grantham Town	2-1			219		
Burton Albion *v* Halesowen Harriers	2-0			767		
Brackley Town *v* Buckingham Town	1-1			303		
Buckingham Town *v* Brackley Town		1-1			376	
Buckingham Town *v* Brackley Town			2-0			401
Shepshed Charterhouse *v* Lye Town	3-1			362		
Wolverton AFC *v* Atherstone United	2-2			200		
Atherstone United *v* Wolverton AFC		4-1			377	
Racing Club Warwick *v* Evesham United	0-0			128		
Evesham United *v* Racing Club Warwick		5-1			486	
Potton United *v* Stourbridge	1-1			106		
Stourbridge *v* Potton United		7-0			401	
Bedworth United *v* Sutton Coldfield Town	1-5			131		
Boston *v* Bromsgrove Rovers	0-3			95		
March Town United *v* Sandwell Borough	1-1			154		
Sandwell Borough *v* March Town United		2-2			137	
Sandwell Borough *v* March Town United			1-0			125
Chalfont St Peter *v* Malvern Town	2-6			125		
Moor Green *v* Tamworth	1-2			865		
Barton Rovers *v* Redditch United	0-2			138		
Histon *v* Rothwell Town	2-1			101		
Boreham Wood *v* Baker Perkins	0-0			112		
Baker Perkins *v* Boreham Wood		1-2			120	
Spalding United *v* Rushden Town	0-3			302		
Haverhill Rovers *v* VS Rugby	1-1			214		
VS Rugby *v* Haverhill Rovers		5-0			475	
Boston United *v* Lowestoft Town	7-0			1135		
Wembley *v* Bourne Town	4-1			77		
Sudbury Town *v* Heybridge Swifts	1-3			665		
Newmarket Town *v* Cambridge City	1-2			437		
Finchley *v* Great Yarmouth Town	1-2			60		
Rayners Lane *v* Harlow Town	0-3			80		
Ford United *v* St Albans City	3-1			116		
Clapton *v* Barnet	0-2			764		
Hitchin Town *v* Braintree Town	0-1			410		
Cray Wanderers *v* Ruislip Manor	2-3			117		
Metropolitan Police *v* Hendon	1-3			90		
Saffron Walden Town *v* Wealdstone	0-4			270		
Wivenhoe Town *v* Halstead Town	3-1			309		
Chesham United *v* Hertford Town	0-0			265		
Hertford Town *v* Chesham United		1-5			210	
Enfield *v* Barking	4-1			579		
Walthamstow Pennant *v* Chelmsford City	0-3			240		
Biggleswade Town *v* Hornchurch	2-2			53		
Hornchurch *v* Biggleswade Town		3-1			122	
Hounslow *v* Basildon United	4-3			78		
Stevenage Borough *v* Bishops Stortford	2-3			476		
Barkingside *v* Redbridge Forest	1-3			174		
Fisher Athletic *v* Harwich & Parkeston	0-0			157		
Harwich & Parkeston *v* Fisher Athletic		2-1			550	
Banstead Athletic *v* Molesey	3-3			67		
Molesey *v* Banstead Athletic		2-0			76	
Dagenham *v* Burnham	1-1			413		
Burnham *v* Dagenham		1-2			155	
Corinthian Casuals *v* Grays Athletic	1-5			114		
Beckenham Town *v* Flackwell Heath	0-2			110		
Egham Town *v* Purfleet	2-1			93		
Tilbury *v* Witney Town	1-1			76		
Witney Town *v* Tilbury		2-1			202	
Edgware Town *v* Harrow Borough	1-0			401		
Leyton Wingate *v* Billericay Town	0-0			176		
Billericay Town *v* Leyton Wingate		1-0			404	
Andover *v* Horsham YMCA	3-0			251		
Walton & Hersham *v* Bromley	2-3			376		
Royston Town *v* Yeading	3-2			110		
Marlow *v* Merstham	3-0			215		

	1st Tie	1st Rep	2nd Rep	3rd Rep	1st Tie	1st Rep	2nd Rep	3rd Rep
Tooting & Mitcham United v Horsham	0-0				180			
Horsham v Tooting & Mitcham United		1-2				368		
Littlehampton Town v Dulwich Hamlet	2-0				264			
Tonbridge v Hythe Town	3-1				429			
Whyteleafe v Slade Green	2-1				139			
Peacehaven & Telscombe v Southwick	4-1				338			
Folkestone v Bognor Regis Town	1-2				260			
Margate v Gravesend & Northfleet	2-2				651			
Gravesend & Northfleet v Margate		1-4				465		
Redhill v Whitehawk	2-3				114			
Pagham v Oakwood	4-0				103			
Cove v Windsor & Eton	1-3				210			
Sittingbourne v Whitstable Town	1-1				385			
Whitstable Town v Sittingbourne		1-4				435		
Dover Athletic v Ashford Town	1-0				1210			
Wick v Dorking	0-3				111			
Carshalton Athletic v Erith & Belvedere	3-0				204			
Eastbourne United v Crawley Town	0-2				180			
Worthing v Chatham Town	3-0				206			
Havant Town v Langney Sports	4-0				167			
Kingstonian v Staines Town	2-1				571			
Hampton v Hailsham Town	0-1				195			
Herne Bay v Lewes	0-1				121			
Salisbury v Hungerford Town	2-0				264			
Bournemouth v Abingdon Town	2-1				50			
Abingdon United v Farnborough Town	0-1				214			
Slough Town v Feltham	8-0				436			
Trowbridge Town v Newbury Town	3-0				398			
Wycombe Wanderers v Maidenhead United	3-0				1910			
Warminster Town v Wokingham Town	0-1				233			
Chippenham Town v Lymington AFC	1-1				126			
Lymington AFC v Chippenham Town		1-0				100		
Melksham Town v Calne Town	2-1				110			
Waterlooville v Newport (IOW)	1-1				323			
Newport (IOW) v Waterlooville		3-0				758		
Stroud v Gosport Borough	4-1				117			
Chard Town v Romsey Town	4-4				107			
Romsey Town v Chard Town		3-0				117		
Barry Town v Clevedon Town	0-0				263			
Clevedon Town v Barry Town		0-3				142		
Mangotsfield United v Bashley	2-2				304			
Bashley v Mangotsfield United		6-3				323		
St Blazey v Weymouth	0-2				249			
Taunton Town v Swanage Town & Herston	1-2				302			
Weston-Super-Mare v Maesteg Park	2-2				189			
Maesteg Park v Weston-Super-Mare		0-4				78		
Cheltenham Town v Exmouth Town	2-2				736			
Exmouth Town v Cheltenham Town		3-3				288		
Cheltenham Town v Exmouth Town			3-0				653	
Yate Town v Worcester City	1-3				464			
Bristol Manor Farm v Bridgend Town	1-1				47			
Bridgend Town v Bristol Manor Farm		3-0				82		
Tiverton Town v Ilfracombe Town	5-1				266			
Saltash United v Poole Town	1-1				215			
Poole Town v Saltash United		2-2				234		
Saltash United v Poole Town			3-1				243	
Falmouth Town v Dorchester Town	2-4				362			
Liskeard Athletic v Wimborne Town	5-2				92			

| **Second Round Qualifying** | Result | | | | Attendance | | | |
Saturday 29th September 1990	1st Tie	1st Rep	2nd Rep	3rd Rep	1st Tie	1st Rep	2nd Rep	3rd Rep
Shildon v Fleetwood Town	0-4				182			
Prudhoe East End v North Shields	0-1				203			
Accrington Stanley v Blyth Spartans	2-1				805			

Match			Att		
Gretna v Guisborough Town	2-2			176		
Guisborough Town v Gretna		1-3			413	
Harrogate Railway v South Bank	1-0			135		
Easington Colliery v Langley Park	1-1			38		
Langley Park v Easington Colliery		0-1			56	
Esh Winning v Spennymoor United	1-3			100		
Horden CW v Northallerton Town	0-3			77		
Lancaster City v Newcastle Blue Star	0-2			245		
Seaham Red Star v Consett	1-1			140		
Consett v Seaham Red Star		2-0			190	
Irlam Town v Horwich RMI	1-3			91		
Caernarfon Town v Colwyn Bay	2-6			273		
Maine Road v Altrincham	0-1			875		
Atherton LR v Bangor City	0-0			300		
Bangor City v Atherton LR		4-0			240	
Emley v Chorley	0-1			502		
Bootle v Southport	2-0			400		
Hednesford Town v Hyde United	2-2			447		
Hyde United v Hednesford Town		5-2			621	
South Liverpool v Curzon Ashton	1-0			192		
Leicester United v Droylsden	0-0			244		
Droylsden v Leicester United		2-2			410	
Leicester United v Droylsden			4-3			375
Worksop Town v Marine	1-3			142		
Princes End United v Frickley Athletic	0-4			102		
Blakenall v Nuneaton Borough	3-3			402		
Nuneaton Borough v Blakenall		3-0			1021	
Alvechurch v Witton Albion	2-7			229		
Bilston Town v Buxton	2-1			160		
Corby Town v Matlock Town	2-0			324		
Burton Albion v Hinckley Athletic	4-0			823		
Buckingham Town v Shepshed Charterhouse	2-4			183		
Evesham United v Atherstone United	1-2			397		
Stourbridge v Sutton Coldfield Town	1-2			258		
Sandwell Borough v Bromsgrove Rovers	0-2			253		
Malvern Town v Tamworth	3-3			429		
Tamworth v Malvern Town		5-1			1525	
Histon v Redditch United	1-1			142		
Redditch United v Histon		1-0			265	
Boreham Wood v Rushden Town	1-0			172		
Boston United v VS Rugby	3-1			1245		
Wembley v Heybridge Swifts	2-2			118		
Heybridge Swifts v Wembley		3-1			280	
Great Yarmouth Town v Cambridge City	0-4			223		
Harlow Town v Ford United	1-0			147		
Braintree Town v Barnet	0-2			1411		
Ruislip Manor v Hendon	2-1			301		
Wivenhoe Town v Wealdstone	0-0			403		
Wealdstone v Wivenhoe Town		2-1			539	
Chesham United v Enfield	0-3			588		
Hornchurch v Chelmsford City	1-2			354		
Hounslow v Bishops Stortford	1-5			179		
Harwich & Parkeston v Redbridge Forest	1-3			573		
Molesey v Dagenham	1-2					
Flackwell Heath v Grays Athletic	2-2			155		
Grays Athletic v Flackwell Heath		2-0			336	
Egham Town v Witney Town	1-0			119		
Billericay Town v Edgware Town	1-0			433		
Andover v Bromley	2-0			377		
Marlow v Royston Town	2-2			280		
Royston Town v Marlow		0-2			251	
Tooting & Mitcham United v Littlehampton Town	1-2			220		
Whyteleafe v Tonbridge	0-2			261		
Peacehaven & Telscombe v Bognor Regis Town	3-1			397		
Whitehawk v Margate	0-1			216		
Pagham v Windsor & Eton	0-3			210		
Dover Athletic v Sittingbourne	2-0			1121		
Dorking v Carshalton Athletic	2-0			438		

	Result				Attendance			
Worthing v Crawley Town	3-2				372			
Havant Town v Kingstonian	0-4				367			
Lewes v Hailsham Town	0-3				152			
Salisbury v Bournemouth	4-0				501			
Slough Town v Farnborough Town	2-3				925			
Trowbridge Town v Wycombe Wanderers	0-0				839			
Wycombe Wanderers v Trowbridge Town		2-1				1850		
Lymington AFC v Wokingham Town	1-1				223			
Wokingham Town v Lymington AFC		2-1				266		
Melksham Town v Newport (IOW)	0-2				150			
Romsey Town v Stroud	1-0				176			
Barry Town v Bashley	0-2				309			
Swanage Town & Herston v Weymouth	1-1				295			
Weymouth v Swanage Town & Herston		2-1				746		
Weston-Super-Mare v Cheltenham Town	0-2				454			
Bridgend Town v Worcester City	1-7				150			
Tiverton Town v Saltash United	4-2				189			
Liskeard Athletic v Dorchester Town	5-1				181			

Third Round Qualifying	Result				Attendance			
Saturday 13th October 1990	*1st Tie*	*1st Rep*	*2nd Rep*	*3rd Rep*	*1st Tie*	*1st Rep*	*2nd Rep*	*3rd Rep*
Fleetwood Town v North Shields	2-0				371			
Accrington Stanley v Gretna	2-1				1121			
Harrogate Railway v Easington Colliery	2-0				355			
Spennymoor United v Northallerton Town	2-0				241			
Newcastle Blue Star v Consett	3-0				180			
Horwich RMI v Colwyn Bay	1-3				288			
Altrincham v Bangor City	3-0				1033			
Chorley v Bootle	6-2				452			
Hyde United v South Liverpool	1-1				688			
South Liverpool v Hyde United		3-1				325		
Leicester United v Marine	0-2				410			
Frickley Athletic v Nuneaton Borough	1-0				654			
Witton Albion v Bilston Town	4-0				841			
Corby Town v Burton Albion	0-1				736			
Shepshed Charterhouse v Atherstone United	2-3				664			
Sutton Coldfield Town v Bromsgrove Rovers	0-0				512			
Bromsgrove Rovers v Sutton Coldfield Town		4-2				1081		
Tamworth v Redditch United	2-0				1682			
Boreham Wood v Boston United	1-1				564			
Boston United v Boreham Wood		4-0				1456		
Heybridge Swifts v Cambridge City	1-0				369			
Harlow Town v Barnet	1-3				1937			
Ruislip Manor v Wealdstone	1-0				854			
Enfield v Chelmsford City	1-1				879			
Chelmsford City v Enfield		1-0				1442		
Bishops Stortford v Redbridge Forest	2-1				485			
Dagenham v Grays Athletic	3-1				1114			
Egham Town v Billericay Town	1-1				318			
Billericay Town v Egham Town		1-2				771		
Andover v Marlow	0-1				701			
Littlehampton Town v Tonbridge	0-0				525			
Tonbridge v Littlehampton Town		2-3				778		
Peacehaven & Telscombe v Margate	1-0				612			
Windsor & Eton v Dover Athletic	1-1				710			
Dover Athletic v Windsor & Eton		3-0				1415		
Dorking v Worthing	1-1				460			
Worthing v Dorking		2-4				560		
Kingstonian v Hailsham Town	4-0				1032			
Salisbury v Farnborough Town	0-3				937			
Wycombe Wanderers v Wokingham Town	4-1				2319			
Newport (IOW) v Romsey Town	0-1				919			
Bashley v Weymouth	2-2				884			
Weymouth v Bashley		2-3				1043		

	Result				Attendance			
Cheltenham Town v Worcester City	4-2				2007			
Tiverton Town v Liskeard Athletic	1-0				306			

Fourth Round Qualifying

	Result				Attendance			
Saturday 27th October 1990	*1st Tie*	*1st Rep*	*2nd Rep*	*3rd Rep*	*1st Tie*	*1st Rep*	*2nd Rep*	*3rd Rep*
Accrington Stanley v Fleetwood Town	0-2				2096			
Marine v Stafford Rangers	1-1				620			
Stafford Rangers v Marine		2-1				1217		
Frickley Athletic v Witton Albion	0-2				636			
Macclesfield Town v Altrincham	2-2				1843			
Altrincham v Macclesfield Town		3-0				2306		
Chorley v Harrogate Railway	3-1				530			
Northwich Victoria v Spennymoor United	1-1				740			
Spennymoor United v Northwich Victoria		2-1				769		
Bishop Auckland v South Liverpool	1-0				496			
Colwyn Bay v Whitley Bay	1-4				742			
Runcorn v Newcastle Blue Star	1-0				693			
Dagenham v Aylesbury United	0-2				805			
Burton Albion v Tamworth	0-0				2913			
Tamworth v Burton Albion		3-2				2545		
Telford United v Egham Town	2-0				1137			
Barnet v Heybridge Swifts	3-1				1813			
Halesowen Town v Ruislip Manor	5-2				1406			
Bishops Stortford v Atherstone United	0-1				626			
Chelmsford City v Kettering Town	0-0				2265			
Kettering Town v Chelmsford City		1-2				3292		
Bromsgrove Rovers v Kidderminster Harriers	1-2				2372			
Dartford v Boston United	1-1				805			
Boston United v Dartford		2-1				1774		
Yeovil Town v Marlow	3-1				2560			
Farnborough Town v Gloucester City	4-1				838			
Romsey Town v Littlehampton Town	1-2				586			
Tiverton Town v Peacehaven & Telscombe	3-2				802			
Woking v Bath City	2-1				2029			
Wycombe Wanderers v Basingstoke Town	6-0				2203			
Hayes v Kingstonian	2-0				759			
Welling United v Bashley	1-0				1177			
Dover Athletic v Merthyr Tydfil	0-0				1801			
Merthyr Tydfil v Dover Athletic		2-0				1050		
Dorking v Cheltenham Town	2-3				903			

First Round Proper

	Result				Attendance			
Saturday 17th November 1990	*1st Tie*	*1st Rep*	*2nd Rep*	*3rd Rep*	*1st Tie*	*1st Rep*	*2nd Rep*	*3rd Rep*
Lincoln City v Crewe Alexandra	1-4				3596			
Preston North End v Mansfield Town	0-1				5230			
Chorley v Bury	2-1				2834			
Witton Albion v Bolton Wanderers	1-2				3790			
Bishop Auckland v Barrow	0-1				1645			
Stafford Rangers v Burnley	1-3				4117			
Halesowen Town v Tranmere Rovers	1-2				3699			
Atherstone United v Fleetwood Town	3-1				1422			
Darlington v York City	1-1				4638			
York City v Darlington		1-0				4035		
Rochdale v Scunthorpe United	1-1				3259			
Scunthorpe United v Rochdale		2-1				3761		
Runcorn v Hartlepool United	0-3				1675			
Bradford City v Shrewsbury Town	0-0				6629			
Shrewsbury Town v Bradford City		2-1				3708		
Chester City v Doncaster Rovers	2-2				1749			
Doncaster Rovers v Chester City		1-2				3543		
Tamworth v Whitley Bay	4-6				2600			

	1st Tie	1st Rep	2nd Rep	3rd Rep	1st Tie	1st Rep	2nd Rep	3rd Rep
Scarborough v Leek Town	0-2				1589			
Halifax Town v Wrexham	3-2				2002			
Blackpool v Grimsby Town	2-0				4175			
Telford United v Stoke City	0-0				3709			
Stoke City v Telford United		1-0				11985		
Chesterfield v Spennymoor United	3-2				4142			
Altrincham v Huddersfield Town	1-2				3000			
Rotherham United v Stockport County	1-0				4471			
Wigan Athletic v Carlisle United	5-0				3947			
AFC Bournemouth v Gillingham	2-1				6113			
Birmingham City v Cheltenham Town	1-0				7942			
Fulham v Farnborough Town	2-1				4990			
Swansea City v Welling United	5-2				3156			
Barnet v Chelmsford City	2-2				3217			
Chelmsford City v Barnet		0-2				2612		
Brentford v Yeovil Town	5-0				4893			
Colchester United v Reading	2-1				3761			
Littlehampton Town v Northampton Town	0-4				3540			
Hereford United v Peterborough United	1-1				4209			
Peterborough United v Hereford United		2-1				4179		
Aldershot v Tiverton Town	6-2				2706			
Aylesbury United v Walsall	0-1				3366			
Maidstone United v Torquay United	4-1				2303			
Leyton Orient v Southend United	3-2				6095			
Boston United v Wycombe Wanderers	1-1				2755			
Wycombe Wanderers v Boston United		4-0				4954		
Merthyr Tydfil v Sutton United	1-1				1279			
Sutton United v Merthyr Tydfil		0-1				1934		
Exeter City v Cambridge United	1-2				4714			
Woking v Kidderminster Harriers	0-0				3249			
Kidderminster Harriers v Woking		1-1				2827		
Kidderminster Harriers v Woking			1-2				3015	
Cardiff City v Hayes	0-0				1844			
Hayes v Cardiff City		1-0				4312		

Second Round Proper

Saturday 8th December 1990

	Result				Attendance			
	1st Tie	1st Rep	2nd Rep	3rd Rep	1st Tie	1st Rep	2nd Rep	3rd Rep
Shrewsbury Town v Chorley	1-0				3380			
Rotherham United v Halifax Town	1-1				2986			
Halifax Town v Rotherham United		1-2				2132		
Mansfield Town v York City	2-1				3800			
Scunthorpe United v Tranmere Rovers	3-2				3576			
Burnley v Stoke City	2-0				12954			
Leek Town v Chester City	1-1				3048			
Chester City v Leek Town		4-0				2420		
Wigan Athletic v Hartlepool United	2-0				2492			
Chesterfield v Bolton Wanderers	3-4				4836			
Crewe Alexandra v Atherstone United	1-0				4113			
Huddersfield Town v Blackpool	0-2				6329			
Whitley Bay v Barrow	0-1				2522			
Woking v Merthyr Tydfil	5-1				4188			
Birmingham City v Brentford	1-3				5072			
Wycombe Wanderers v Peterborough United	1-1				5695			
Peterborough United v Wycombe Wanderers		2-0				5692		
Aldershot v Maidstone United	2-1				3404			
Swansea City v Walsall	2-1				3744			
Colchester United v Leyton Orient	0-0				6150			
Leyton Orient v Colchester United		4-1				4623		
Barnet v Northampton Town	0-0				5022			
Northampton Town v Barnet		0-1				5837		
AFC Bournemouth v Hayes	1-0				6510			
Fulham v Cambridge United	0-0				5929			
Cambridge United v Fulham		2-1				4996		

Third Round Proper

Saturday 5th January 1991	Result				Attendance			
	1st Tie	*1st Rep*	*2nd Rep*	*3rd Rep*	*1st Tie*	*1st Rep*	*2nd Rep*	*3rd Rep*
Oldham Athletic v Brentford	3-1				12588			
Wolverhampton Wanderers v Cambridge United	0-1				15100			
Chelsea v Oxford United	1-3				14586			
Sheffield United v Luton Town	1-3				13958			
Shrewsbury Town v Watford	4-1				5327			
Bristol Rovers v Crewe Alexandra	0-2				6242			
Charlton Athletic v Everton	1-2				12234			
Crystal Palace v Nottingham Forest	0-0				15396			
Nottingham Forest v Crystal Palace		2-2				23201		
Nottingham Forest v Crystal Palace			3-0					22164
Aston Villa v Wimbledon	1-1				19305			
Wimbledon v Aston Villa		1-0				7496		
Mansfield Town v Sheffield Wednesday	0-2				9076			
Brighton & Hove Albion v Scunthorpe United	3-2				7785			
Manchester United v Queens Park Rangers	2-1				35065			
Port Vale v Peterborough United	2-1				7490			
Aldershot v West Ham United	0-0				22929			
West Ham United v Aldershot		6-1				21484		
Blackpool v Tottenham Hotspur	0-1				9151			
Chester City v AFC Bournemouth	2-3				1833			
Blackburn Rovers v Liverpool	1-1				18584			
Liverpool v Blackburn Rovers		3-0				34175		
Arsenal v Sunderland	2-1				35128			
Millwall v Leicester City	2-1				10766			
Barnet v Portsmouth	0-5				6209			
Southampton v Ipswich Town	3-2				15101			
Barnsley v Leeds United	1-1				22424			
Leeds United v Barnsley		4-0				21377		
Leyton Orient v Swindon Town	1-1				6697			
Swindon Town v Leyton Orient		1-0				7395		
West Bromwich Albion v Woking	2-4				14516			
Hull City v Notts County	2-5				6655			
Middlesbrough v Plymouth Argyle	0-0				13042			
Plymouth Argyle v Middlesbrough		1-2				6956		
Norwich City v Bristol City	2-1				12630			
Coventry City v Wigan Athletic	1-1				10777			
Wigan Athletic v Coventry City		0-1				7429		
Bolton Wanderers v Barrow	1-0				11475			
Burnley v Manchester City	0-1				20331			
Newcastle United v Derby County	2-0				19714			
Swansea City v Rotherham United	0-0				6478			
Rotherham United v Swansea City		4-0				4233		

Fourth Round Proper

Saturday 26th January 1991	Result				Attendance			
	1st Tie	*1st Rep*	*2nd Rep*	*3rd Rep*	*1st Tie*	*1st Rep*	*2nd Rep*	*3rd Rep*
Woking v Everton	0-1				34705			
Newcastle United v Nottingham Forest	2-2				29231			
Nottingham Forest v Newcastle United		3-0				28962		
Luton Town v West Ham United	1-1				16283			
West Ham United v Luton Town		5-0				25659		
Shrewsbury Town v Wimbledon	1-0				8269			
Arsenal v Leeds United	0-0				30900			
Leeds United v Arsenal		1-1				27753		
Arsenal v Leeds United			0-0				30433	
Leeds United v Arsenal				1-2				27170
Liverpool v Brighton & Hove Albion	2-2				32670			
Brighton & Hove Albion v Liverpool		2-3				14440		
Norwich City v Swindon Town	3-1				14408			
Cambridge United v Middlesbrough	2-0				9531			
Notts County v Oldham Athletic	2-0				14002			

	Result				Attendance			
	1st Tie	1st Rep	2nd Rep	3rd Rep	1st Tie	1st Rep	2nd Rep	3rd Rep
Tottenham Hotspur v Oxford United	4-2				31665			
Manchester United v Bolton Wanderers	1-0				43293			
Port Vale v Manchester City	1-2				19132			
Millwall v Sheffield Wednesday	4-4				13663			
Sheffield Wednesday v Millwall		2-0				25140		
Portsmouth v AFC Bournemouth	5-1				15800			
Crewe Alexandra v Rotherham United	1-0				6057			
Coventry City v Southampton	1-1				14112			
Southampton v Coventry City		2-0				17001		

Fifth Round Proper

Saturday 16th February 1991

	Result				Attendance			
	1st Tie	1st Rep	2nd Rep	3rd Rep	1st Tie	1st Rep	2nd Rep	3rd Rep
Southampton v Nottingham Forest	1-1				18512			
Nottingham Forest v Southampton		3-1				26633		
Norwich City v Manchester United	2-1				22936			
Notts County v Manchester City	1-0				18979			
West Ham United v Crewe Alexandra	1-0				25298			
Portsmouth v Tottenham Hotspur	1-2				26049			
Liverpool v Everton	0-0				38023			
Everton v Liverpool		4-4					37648	
Everton v Liverpool			1-0					40054
Cambridge United v Sheffield Wednesday	4-0				9624			
Shrewsbury Town v Arsenal	0-1				12356			

Sixth Round Proper

Saturday 9th March 1991

	Result				Attendance			
	1st Tie	1st Rep	2nd Rep	3rd Rep	1st Tie	1st Rep	2nd Rep	3rd Rep
Norwich City v Nottingham Forest	0-1				24018			
Tottenham Hotspur v Notts County	2-1				29686			
West Ham United v Everton	2-1				28162			
Arsenal v Cambridge United	2-1				42960			

Semi-Final

	Result	Attendance
Sunday 14th April 1991		
Tottenham Hotspur v Arsenal	3-1	77893
at Wembley Stadium		
Nottingham Forest v West Ham United	4-0	40041
at Villa Park		

Final

	Result	Attendance
Saturday 18th May 1991		
Tottenham Hotspur v Nottingham Forest	2-1	78500
at Wembley Stadium		

F.A. Challenge Cup Competition 1991-92

Exemptions

44 Clubs to the Third Round Proper

Arsenal
Aston Villa
Barnsley
Blackburn Rovers
Brighton & Hove Albion
Bristol City
Bristol Rovers
Cambridge United
Charlton Athletic
Chelsea
Coventry City
Crystal Palce
Derby County
Everton
Ipswich Town

Leeds United
Leicester City
Liverpool
Luton Town
Manchester City
Manchester United
Middlesbrough
Millwall
Newcastle United
Norwich City
Nottingham Forest
Notts County
Oldham Athletic
Oxford United
Plymouth Argyle

Portsmouth
Port Vale
Queens Park Rangers
Sheffield United
Sheffield Wednesday
Southampton
Southend United
Sunderland
Swindon Town
Tottenham Hotspur
Watford
West Ham United
Wimbledon
Wolverhampton Wanderers

52 Clubs to the First Round Proper

Aldershot
Barnet
Birmingham City
Blackpool
Bolton Wanderers
AFC Bournemouth
Bradford City
Brentford
Burnley
Bury
Cardiff City
Carlisle United
Chester City
Chesterfield
Crewe Alexandra
Darlington
Doncaster Rovers
Exeter City

Fulham
Gillingham
Grimsby Town
Halifax Town
Hartlepool United
Hereford United
Huddersfield Town
Hull City
Kidderminster Harriers+
Leyton Orient
Lincoln City
Maidstone United
Mansfield Town
Northampton Town
Peterborough United
Preston North End
Reading
Rochdale

Rotherham United
Scarborough
Scunthorpe United
Shrewsbury Town
Stockport County
Stoke City
Swansea City
Torquay United
Tranmere Rovers
Walsall
West Bromwich Albion
Wigan Athletic
Woking*
Wrexham
Wycombe Wanderers+
York City

20 Clubs to the Fourth Round Qualifying

Atherstone United
Altrincham
Aylesbury United
Barrow
Bishop Auckland
Chorley
Colchester United

Farnborough Town
Halesowen Town
Hayes
Leek Town
Merthyr Tydfil
Runcorn
Stafford Rangers

Sutton United
Telford United
Welling United
Whitley Bay
Witton Albion
Yeovil Town

+ Trophy Finalists
* Club outside The Football League considered most appropriate

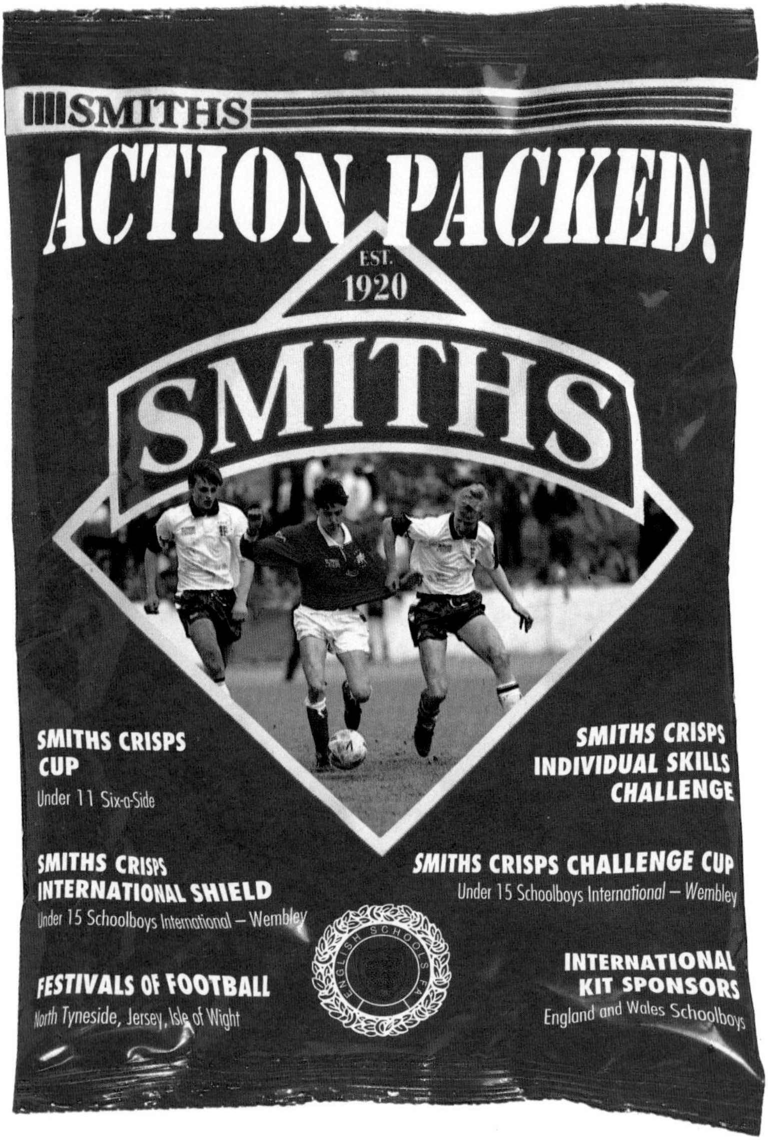
SMITHS
ACTION PACKED!
EST. 1920
SMITHS
SMITHS CRISPS CUP
Under 11 Six-a-Side
SMITHS CRISPS INDIVIDUAL SKILLS CHALLENGE
SMITHS CRISPS INTERNATIONAL SHIELD
Under 15 Schoolboys International – Wembley
SMITHS CRISPS CHALLENGE CUP
Under 15 Schoolboys International – Wembley
ENGLISH SCHOOLS F.A.
FESTIVALS OF FOOTBALL
North Tyneside, Jersey, Isle of Wight
INTERNATIONAL KIT SPONSORS
England and Wales Schoolboys

F.A. Cup Final Dates 1872-1991

1872	16th March
1873	29th March
1874	14th March
1875	13th (16th) March
1876	11th (18th) March
1877	24th March
1878	23rd March
1879	29th March
1880	10th April
1881	9th April
1882	25th March
1883	31st March
1884	29th March
1885	4th April
1886	3rd (10th) April
1887	2nd April
1888	24th March
1889	30th March
1890	29th March
1891	25th March
1892	19th March
1893	26th March
1894	31st March
1895	20th April
1896	18th April
1897	10th April
1898	16th April
1899	15th April
1900	21st April
1901	20th (27th) April
1902	19th (26th) April
1903	18th April
1904	23rd April
1905	15th April
1906	21st April
1907	20th April
1908	25th April

1909	26th April
1910	23rd (28th) April
1911	22nd(26th) April
1912	20th (24th) April
1913	19th April
1914	25th April
1915	24th April
1920	24th April
1921	23rd April
1922	29th April
1923	28th April
1924	26th April
1925	25th April
1926	24th April
1927	23rd April
1928	21st April
1929	27th April
1930	26th April
1931	25th April
1932	23rd April
1933	29th April
1934	28th April
1935	27th April
1936	25th April
1937	1st May
1938	30th April
1939	29th April
1946	27th April
1947	26th April
1948	24th April
1949	30th April
1950	29th April
1951	28th April
1952	3rd May
1953	2nd May
1954	1st May
1955	7th May

1956	5th May
1957	4th May
1958	3rd May
1959	2nd May
1960	7th May
1961	6th May
1962	5th May
1963	25th May
1964	2nd May
1965	1st May
1966	14th May
1967	20th May
1968	18th May
1969	26th April
1970	11th (29th) April
1971	8th May
1972	6th May
1973	5th May
1974	4th May
1975	3rd May
1976	1st May
1977	21st May
1978	6th May
1979	12th May
1980	10th May
1981	9th (14th) May
1982	22nd (27th) May
1983	21st (26th) May
1984	19th May
1985	18th May
1986	10th May
1987	16th May
1988	14th May
1989	20th May
1990	12th (17th) May
1991	18th May

Replay dates in brackets

F.A. Challenge Trophy – Final Tie 1991

Wycombe Wanderers 2   Kidderminster Harriers 1

On a dull afternoon at the national stadium Wycombe Wanderers of the GM Vauxhall Conference won the Trophy for the first time against another Conference club, Kidderminster Harriers. The attendance of 34,842 established a record for the competition and, in the Barclays League, only Arsenal, Liverpool and Manchester City managed better on the day.

Reaching the Trophy final, an appearance in an FA Cup second round tie featured on national television, and a top five place in the Conference would have been enough to make it a season to remember for any club. However, when you add the move to a superb new £3 million stadium, then it is obvious why 1990-91 has been a major milestone in the history of Wycombe Wanderers FC. The Wanderers had been to Wembley before,

losing in the old FA Amateur Cup to Bishop Auckland in 1957, and their overdue return visit was masterminded by Manager Martin O'Neill, a 39-year-old with an undisputed playing pedigree – 64 Northern Ireland caps and all manner of winners' medals with Nottingham Forest.

Wycombe were the more inventive side in the first half and were ahead on 16 minutes through Keith Scott, the striker signed from Lincoln City for a £10,000 fee in March. The goal itself was an untidy one. There was a suspicion of offside in the build-up down the left and Scott needed two stabs at the ball to squeeze it past Kidderminster goalkeeper Paul Jones and into the net. With defender Barnett also sliding in to challenge, three players finished in a heap near the goal-line.

Jones was a little unlucky then but

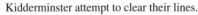
Kidderminster attempt to clear their lines.

Scott scrambles the ball in for Wycombe's opening goal.

his performance throughout must have impressed former England keeper Ray Clemence, who was guest of honour and presented the trophy at the finish to Wycombe skipper Glyn Creaser. Jones kept his side in the game by getting solidly behind a number of worthy Wycombe efforts in the first period and making an acrobatic leap to his left to tip a Scott shot around the post.

A five-minute period in the second half had the massive crowd on the edge of their seats as both teams scored. Kidderminster forward David Hadley's long-range attempt on the hour seemed to be covered by Wycombe goalkeeper John Granville (ex-Millwall, 35 caps for Trinidad and Tobago) but the ball slipped under his body and into the corner of the goal. Then, just four minutes later, Scott was racing away down the right to set up Mark West for the Trophy winner. Wycombe's leading marksman for the fifth consecutive season, who had scored at Wembley ten years earlier for England Schoolboys, diverted Scott's centre into the net with a brave header close to the ground.

Wycombe Wanderers: Granville, Crossley, Cash, Kerr, Creaser, Carroll, Ryan, Stapleton, West, Scott, Guppy (Hutchinson).

Kidderminster Harriers: Jones, Kurila, McGrath, Weir, Barnett, Forsyth, Joseph (Wilcox), Howell (White-house), Hadley, Lilwall, Humphreys.

Referee: J. Watson (Whitley Bay).

117

F.A. Challenge Trophy Competition 1990-91

First Round Qualifying	Result				Attendance			
Saturday 22nd September 1990	1st Tie	1st Rep	2nd Rep	3rd Rep	1st Tie	1st Rep	2nd Rep	3rd Rep
Easington Colliery v Durham City	4-1				40			
Accrington Stanley v Whitley Bay	3-2				402			
Ferryhill Athletic v North Shields	0-0				91			
North Shields v Ferryhill Athletic		0-2				125		
Stockton v Fleetwood Town	1-4				73			
Emley v Southport	2-1				302			
Consett v Whitby Town	2-1				105			
South Liverpool v Brandon United	3-1				109			
Whickham v Alnwick Town	0-1				58			
Morecambe v Workington	3-0				236			
Horwich RMI v Alfreton Town	1-0				136			
Congleton Town v Newtown	3-1				98			
Moor Green v Hednesford Town	1-0				304			
Winsford United v Droylsden	1-4				150			
Alvechurch v Mossley	0-1				140			
Halesowen Town v Colwyn Bay	1-3				1157			
Gainsborough Trinity v Worksop Town	2-0				453			
Rhyl v Goole Town	1-0				249			
Stalybridge Celtic v Shepshed Charterhouse	1-0				308			
Grantham Town v Atherstone United	0-1				325			
Redditch United v Eastwood Town	1-0				163			
Bedworth United v Willenhall Town	4-0				141			
Matlock Town v Buxton	3-2				458			
Caernarfon Town v Leicester United	0-1				150			
Cambridge City v Chalfont St Peter	3-0				283			
Sutton Coldfield Town v Boreham Wood	2-2				170			
Boreham Wood v Sutton Coldfield Town		1-1				175		
Boreham Wood v Sutton Coldfield Town			1-1				217	
Sutton Coldfield Town v Boreham Wood				1-0				192
Burnham v Wembley	2-2				134			
Wembley v Burnham		3-1				76		
Bishops Stortford v Rushden Town	2-1				414			
Chelmsford City v Tamworth	0-1				724			
Uxbridge v Stourbridge	1-1				139			
Stourbridge v Uxbridge		0-2				403		
Marlow v Aveley	2-1				175			
Yeading v Bury Town	3-1				140			
Barking v Witney Town	4-1				67			
St Albans City v Chesham United	0-4				304			
Banbury United v VS Rugby	1-5				343			
Grays Athletc v Heybridge Swifts	1-0				339			
Staines Town v Harlow Town	0-3				204			
Corby Town v Hayes	0-1				243			
Whyteleafe v Tooting & Mitcham United	0-1				209			
Fareham Town v Worthing	3-0				157			
Basingstoke Town v Molesey	1-1				271			
Molesey v Basingstoke Town		1-0				120		
Crawley Town v Hampton	0-0				343			
Hampton v Crawley Town		2-2				208		
Crawley Town v Hampton			4-2				402	
Walton & Hersham v Lewes	2-0				140			
Andover v Canterbury City	1-1				196			
Canterbury City v Andover		2-3				166		
Dulwich Hamlet v Bromley	0-0				348			
Bromley v Dulwich Hamlet		4-1				581		
Gosport Borough v Bashley	2-1				312			
Bognor Regis Town v Erith & Belvedere	5-2				255			
Dorking v Waterlooville	2-1				257			

	Result 1st Tie	1st Rep	Attendance 1st Tie	1st Rep
Ashford Town v Southwick	1-1		287	
Southwick v Ashford Town		1-0		193
Croydon v Folkestone	5-3		86	
Bridgend Town v Bideford	2-2		25	
Bideford v Bridgend Town		0-2		185
Dorchester Town v Taunton Town	3-0		663	
Barry Town v Saltash United	5-0		224	
Cwmbran Town v Maesteg Park	1-0		66	
Weston-Super-Mare v Newport AFC	0-0		494	
Newport AFC v Weston-Super-Mare		3-1		1011
Gloucester City v Ton Pentre	2-2		551	
Ton Pentre v Gloucester City		0-2		381
Stroud v Poole Town	3-0		124	

Second Round Qualifying

Saturday 20th October 1990

	Result 1st Tie	1st Rep	2nd Rep	3rd Rep	Attendance 1st Tie	1st Rep	2nd Rep	3rd Rep
Accrington Stanley v Easington Colliery	2-1				602			
Consett v Alnwick Town	1-1				97			
Alnwick Town v Consett		1-0				121		
Shildon v Morecambe	0-3				159			
Ferryhill Athletic v Emley	0-0				145			
Emley v Ferryhill Athletic		4-1				438		
South Liverpool v Fleetwood Town	0-1				175			
Congleton Town v Radcliffe Borough	1-0				157			
Redditch United v Bedworth United	1-2				142			
Stalybridge Celtic v Colwyn Bay	0-1				321			
Droylsden v Matlock Town	3-3				210			
Matlock Town v Droylsden		0-2				555		
Gainsborough Trinity v Moor Green	1-3				319			
Horwich RMI v Rhyl	3-2				136			
Leicester United v Dudley Town	5-2				254			
Mossley v Atherstone United	1-3				272			
Sutton Coldfield Town v Baldock Town	2-1				217			
VS Rugby v Grays Athletic	1-1				588			
Grays Athletic v VS Rugby		0-2				407		
Barking v Uxbridge	1-2				95			
Bishops Stortford v Harlow Town	2-3				585			
Marlow v Wembley	5-0				309			
Cambridge City v Yeading	1-1				277			
Yeading v Cambridge City		2-1				180		
Hayes v Hitchin Town	1-1				304			
Hitchin Town v Hayes		1-2				482		
Tamworth v Chesham United	1-2				1188			
Gosport Borough v Crawley Town	1-1				234			
Crawley Town v Gosport Borough		0-1				449		
Andover v Salisbury	1-2				593			
Dorking v Tooting & Mitcham United	2-2				306			
Tooting & Mitcham United v Dorking		0-1				324		
Fareham Town v Bognor Regis Town	0-2				254			
Walton & Hersham v Croydon	6-0				172			
Margate v Bromley	2-1				462			
Southwick v Molesey	0-3				150			
Gloucester City v Llanelli	3-0				638			
Cwmbran Town v Dorchester Town	1-1				125			
Dorchester Town v Cwmbran Town		4-1				616		
Barry Town v Bridgend Town	4-0				294			
Newport AFC v Stroud	0-3				886			

Third Round Qualifying

Saturday 1st December 1990

	Result				Attendance			
	1st Tie	1st Rep	2nd Rep	3rd Rep	1st Tie	1st Rep	2nd Rep	3rd Rep
Emley v Morecambe	2-1				367			
Spennymoor United v Chorley	0-0				239			
Chorley v Spennymoor United		1-0				343		
Frickley Athletic v Seaham Red Star	2-0				230			
South Bank v Blyth Spartans	2-2				103			
Blyth Spartans v South Bank		1-1				420		
South Bank v Blyth Spartans			2-0				175	
Bishop Auckland v Newcastle Blue Star	3-1				281			
Tow Law Town v Alnwick Town	2-1				119			
Fleetwood Town v Marine	2-0				339			
Guisborough Town v Accrington Stanley	4-1				245			
Colwyn Bay v Witton Albion	1-3				603			
Boston United v Leicester United	3-2				1054			
Droylsden v Bromsgrove Rovers	3-3				390			
Bromsgrove Rovers v Droylsden		1-3				762		
Nuneaton Borough v Burton Albion	1-2				1261			
Sutton Coldfield Town v Horwich RMI	1-3				154			
Congleton Town v Moor Green	0-3				210			
Bedworth United v Bangor City	1-1				139			
Bangor City v Bedworth United		1-2				275		
Dagenham v Enfield	0-1				556			
Margate v VS Rugby	1-1				483			
VS Rugby v Margate		5-0				543		
Leyton-Wingate v Wealdstone	0-1				363			
Harrow Borough v Fisher Athletic	0-2				211			
Hayes v Kingstonian	3-2				401			
Metropolitan Police v Harlow Town	3-2				82			
Yeading v Molesey	0-1				125			
Atherstone United v Wivenhoe Town	0-2				577			
Gravesend & Northfleet v Hendon	3-0				311			
Marlow v Chesham United	1-2				475			
Bognor Regis Town v Worcester City	3-0				280			
Stroud v Uxbridge	3-1				122			
Walton & Hersham v Windsor & Eton	0-1				326			
Weymouth v Gloucester City	1-1				684			
Gloucester City v Weymouth		3-0				682		
Dorking v Gosport Borough	2-1				219			
Carshalton Athletic v Dorchester Town	5-0				335			
Barry Town v Salisbury	0-0				337			
Salisbury v Barry Town	1-0				342			

First Round Proper

Saturday 12th January 1991

	Result				Attendance			
	1st Tie	1st Rep	2nd Rep	3rd Rep	1st Tie	1st Rep	2nd Rep	3rd Rep
Northwich Victoria v Tow Law Town	2-1				561			
South Bank v Bishop Auckland	1-0				300			
Horwich RMI v Bedworth United	2-0				164			
Guisborough Town v Witton Albion	2-2				414			
Witton Albion v Guisborough Town		2-1				965		
Runcorn v Boston United	2-0				853			
Droylsden v Fleetwood Town	2-1				384			
Hyde United v Stafford Rangers	1-2				680			
Burton Albion v Moor Green	3-0				1300			
Barrow v Chorley	2-0				1523			
Macclesfield Town v Gretna	0-2				1060			
Gateshead v Billingham Synthonia	2-2				487			
Billingham Synthonia v Gateshead		0-3				585		
Leek Town v Altrincham	0-4				1054			
Telford United v Emley	0-0				1240			
Emley v Telford United		1-0				1331		

120

	Result					Attendance			
Barnet v Farnborough Town	2-3					1016			
Slough Town v Bath City	2-4					860			
Wokingham Town v Wivenhoe Town	1-2					542			
Kidderminster Harriers v Sutton United	4-2					1201			
Carshalton Athletic v Dartford	0-0					552			
Dartford v Carshalton Athletic		1-1					572		
Carshalton Athletic v Dartford			2-3					411	
Enfield v Chesham United	1-0					618			
Dover Athletic v Dorking	1-0					1125			
Gloucester City v Yeovil Town	1-0					1368			
Gravesend & Northfleet v Cheltenham Town	2-2					523			
Cheltenham Town v Gravesend & Northfleet ...		5-1					610		
Fisher Athletic v Redbridge Forest	1-2					420			
Salisbury v VS Rugby	1-4					542			
Wycombe Wanderers v Wealdstone	1-0					2692			
Windsor & Eton v Colchester United	0-1					727			
Bognor Regis Town v Aylesbury United	2-4					503			
Molesey v Merthyr Tydfil	1-1					378			
Merthyr Tydfil v Molesey		1-0					684		
Welling United v Hayes	3-1					1004			
Kettering Town v Woking	2-0					4021			
Stroud v Metropolitan Police	2-2					113			
Metropolitan Police v Stroud		0-2					183		

Bye for Frickley Athletic

Second Round Proper

Saturday 2nd February 1991	Result				Attendance			
	1st Tie	1st Rep	2nd Rep	3rd Rep	1st Tie	1st Rep	2nd Rep	3rd Rep
Dartford v Cheltenham Town	0-2				559			
Colchester United v Runcorn	2-0				2348			
Kidderminster Harriers v Dover Athletic	1-0				1455			
Merthyr Tydfil v Gloucester City	1-3				752			
Hyde United v Emley	0-0				1041			
Emley v Hyde United		3-2				1348		
Welling United v Aylesbury United	2-1				1117			
Farnborough Town v Bath City	1-3				621			
Barrow v Kettering Town	0-0				3033			
Kettering Town v Barrow		2-1				2522		
VS Rugby v Wycombe Wanderers	0-1				1835			
Northwich Victoria v Droylsden	4-1				737			
Horwich RMI v Gretna	2-1				313			
Enfield v Wivenhoe Town	0-2				608			
Witton Albion v South Bank	3-2				843			
Redbridge Forest v Frickley Athletic	2-1				326			
Altrincham v Gateshead	3-1				1191			
Stroud v Burton Albion	3-2				680			

Third Round Proper

Saturday 23rd February 1991	Result				Attendance			
	1st Tie	1st Rep	2nd Rep	3rd Rep	1st Tie	1st Rep	2nd Rep	3rd Rep
Horwich RMI v Redbridge Forest	2-1				409			
Witton Albion v Gloucester City	3-0				1162			
Welling United v Altrincham	1-2				1344			
Colchester United v Wivenhoe Town	3-0				4923			
Emley v Kettering Town	3-2				2726			
Kidderminster Harriers v Bath City	3-1				1412			
Northwich Victoria v Stroud	2-0				683			
Wycombe Wanderers v Cheltenham Town	2-1				3143			

Fourth Round Proper	Result				Attendance			
Saturday 16th March 1991	*1st Tie*	*1st Rep*	*2nd Rep*	*3rd Rep*	*1st Tie*	*1st Rep*	*2nd Rep*	*3rd Rep*
Colchester United *v* Witton Albion	0-2				3079			
Kidderminster Harriers *v* Emley	3-0				2408			
Altrincham *v* Horwich RMI	5-0				1486			
Northwich Victoria *v* Wycombe Wanderers	2-3				1968			

Semi-Final	Result	Attendance
First Leg – Saturday 6th April 1991		
Kidderminster Harriers *v* Witton Albion	1-0	2865
Wycombe Wanderers *v* Altrincham	2-1	5248

Second Leg – Saturday 13th April 1991

	Result	Attendance
Witton Albion *v* Kidderminster Harriers	4-3	3800
Altrincham *v* Wycombe Wanderers	0-2	3500

Wycombe Wanderers beat Altrincham 4-1 on aggregate
Witton Albion drew with Kidderminster Harriers 4-4 on aggregate

Replay – Tuesday 16th April 1991

	Result	Attendance
Kidderminster Harriers *v* Witton Albion	2-1	3277
at Stafford Rangers FC		

Final	Result	Attendance
Saturday 11th May 1991		
Wycombe Wanderers *v* Kidderminster Harriers	2-1	34842
at Wembley Stadium		

F.A. Challenge Trophy Winners 1970-91

Year		Winners		Runners-up		Venue
1970		Macclesfield Town	2	Telford United	0	Wembley
1971		Telford United	3	Hillingdon Borough	2	Wembley
1972		Stafford Rangers	3	Barnet	0	Wembley
1973	*	Scarborough	2	Wigan Athletic	1	Wembley
1974		Morecambe	2	Dartford	1	Wembley
1975		Matlock Town	4	Scarborough	0	Wembley
1976	*	Scarborough	3	Stafford Rangers	2	Wembley
1977		Scarborough	2	Dagenham	1	Wembley
1978		Altrincham	3	Leatherhead	1	Wembley
1979		Stafford Rangers	2	Kettering Town	0	Wembley
1980		Dagenham	2	Mossley	1	Wembley
1981		Bishop's Stortford	1	Sutton United	0	Wembley
1982	*	Enfield	1	Altrincham	0	Wembley
1983		Telford United	2	Northwich Victoria	1	Wembley
1984	†	Northwich Victoria	2	Bangor City	1	Stoke
1985		Wealdstone	2	Boston United	1	Wembley
1986		Altrincham	1	Runcorn	0	Wembley
1987	§	Kidderminster Harriers	2	Burton Albion	1	West Bromwich
1988	§	Enfield	3	Telford United	2	West Bromwich
1989	*	Telford United	1	Macclesfield Town	0	Wembley
1990		Barrow	3	Leek Town	0	Wembley
1991		Wycombe Wanderers	2	Kidderminster Harriers	1	Wembley

* After extra time   † After 1-1 draw at Wembley   § After 0-0 draw at Wembley

F.A. Challenge Trophy Competition 1991-92

Exemptions

32 Clubs to the First Round Proper

Altrincham	Gloucester City	Runcorn
Aylesbury United	Gretna	Stalybridge Celtic
Barrow	Guisborough Town	Stafford Rangers
Bath City	Hyde United	Telford United
Cheltenham Town	Kettering Town	Welling United
Colchester United	Kidderminster Harriers	Witton Albion
Dartford	Leek Town	Wivenhoe Town
Dover Athletic	Macclesfield Town	Woking
Enfield	Merthyr Tydfil	Wycombe Wanderers
Farnborough Town	Northwich Victoria	Yeovil Town
Gateshead	Redbridge Forest	

32 Clubs to the Third Round Qualifying

Bangor City	Fisher Athletic	South Bank
Billingham Synthonia	Fleetwood Town	Stroud
Bishop Auckland	Frickley Athletic	Sutton United
Blyth Spartans	Gravesend & Northfleet	Tow Law Town
Boston United	Harrow Borough	VS Rugby
Burton Albion	Hendon	Wealdstone
Cambridge City	Horwich RMI	Weymouth
Carshalton Athletic	Kingstonian	Windsor & Eton
Chorley	Morecambe	Wokingham Town
Dagenham Town	Seaham Red Star	Worcester City
Emley	Slough Town	

F.A. Challenge Vase – Final Tie 1991

Guiseley 3   Gresley Rovers 1
(After a 4-4 draw)

The Vase final at Wembley on 4 May promised an interesting contest between teams which had dominated their leagues in outstanding fashion during the season. Gresley Rovers, the Banks's Brewery League champions, and Guiseley, who swept away with the Weekly Wynner League, drew a crowd of close on 12,000 to the national stadium and provided an eight-goal thriller. Three days later, at Sheffield United's Bramall-lane ground, Guiseley won the Vase for the first time with a 3-1 replay victory.

Guiseley, near Bradford, is best known for Harry Ramsden's, the world's biggest fish and chip shop, which had duly invited the players for a pre-Wembley treat. Gordon Rayner, Guiseley's Manager, had enjoyed a very successful first season in charge, with his team losing only two of their 50 matches. The club, which was eliminated at the semi-final stage last season, were striving to become the first of six Yorkshire finalists in the Vase to actually win it.

Gresley, from Burton-on-Trent, had lost in the first round of this season's competition to Mile Oak Rovers but had gone through to the next round after it had been discovered that their opponents had fielded ineligible players. In as exciting a game as Wembley could have produced – with more goals than any previous Cup, Trophy or Vase final in history – the teams were locked at 4-4 after two hours' play.

Guiseley built a three-goal lead in 30 minutes, top scorer Mark Tennison netting twice and Dean Walling once. Gresley responded quickly through Carl Rathbone and, three minutes into

Guiseley's Hogarth slides in to tackle Smith.

Atkinson of Guiseley moves smartly away with Lovell in hot pursuit.

the second half, Kieron Smith scored with a 20-yarder. Guiseley held onto their 3-2 lead until Smith equalised in the last seconds to force extra time. Stuart Stokes converted a 94th-minute penalty after Morgan's challenge on Rathbone and Alan Roberts levelled for Guiseley with just two minutes remaining.

Nobody who saw the original match wanted to miss the replay and the kick-off was delayed slightly to allow Gresley supporters to enter the ground safely (7,585 watched in total). Memories of the early blitz that had taken Guiseley into such a commanding lead at Wembley seemed to contribute to a nervous start by their opponents' defence. Play was more even once they had settled down and there was a burst of goals before half-time, Steve Astley hammering in a free-kick for Gresley and Tennison curling in a clever shot two minutes later.

Guiseley's powerful attack finally swayed the match their way in the second period. Walling's leaping header put them ahead on 48 minutes and Peter Atkinson increased the advantage by forcing Tennison's cross home in the 68th minute.

Guiseley: Maxted, Bottomley (Annan in replay), Hogarth, Tetley, Morgan, McKenzie (sub Bottomley in replay), Atkinson (sub Adams at Wembley), Tennison (sub Noteman in replay), Walling, Roberts A., Roberts B. (sub Annan at Wembley).

Gresley Rovers: Aston, Barry, Elliott (sub Adcock at Wembley), Denby, Land, Astley, Stokes (sub Weston in replay), Smith K., Acklam, Rathbone, Lovell (sub Weston at Wembley and Adcock in replay).

Referee: C. Trussell (Liverpool).

F.A. Challenge Vase Competition 1990-91

	Result				Attendance			
First Round	*1st Tie*	*1st Rep*	*2nd Rep*	*3rd Rep*	*1st Tie*	*1st Rep*	*2nd Rep*	*3rd Rep*
Saturday 3rd November 1990								
Darlington CB *v* Horden CW	1-2				35			
Billingham Town *v* Netherfield	2-0				40			
Chester-le-Street Town *v* Peterlee Newtown	1-0				63			
Murton *v* Shotton Comrades	2-0				45			
Ashington *v* Hebburn	3-0				100			
Langley Park *v* Prudhoe East End	1-0				39			
Eppleton CW *v* West Allotment Celtic	5-1				97			
Dunston FB *v* Newton Aycliffe	3-1				61			
Blackpool (Wren) Rovers *v* Ashton United	3-0				74			
Maine Road *v* Warrington Town	0-2				132			
Great Harwood Town *v* Vauxhall GM	2-0				63			
Prescot AFC *v* Nantwich Town	4-5				103			
Leyland Motors *v* Skelmersdale United	0-2				82			
Glossop *v* Curzon Ashton	6-1				404			
Clitheroe *v* Newcastle Town	3-2				142			
Knowsley United *v* Knypersley Victoria	5-0				100			
St Helens Town *v* Cammell Laird	1-2				92			
Lancaster City *v* Blackpool Mechanics	1-0				102			
Selby Town *v* Harrogate Town	0-2				284			
Belper Town *v* Harworth CI	3-1				182			
Garforth Town *v* Ossett Albion	3-1				130			
Yorkshire Main *v* Sheffield	1-2				40			
Denaby United *v* Worsboro Bridge MW	0-4				131			
Winterton Rangers *v* Arnold Town	1-0				92			
Rainworth MW *v* Armthorpe Welfare	2-1				210			
Eccleshill United *v* Priory (Eastwood)	1-2				90			
Borrowash Victoria *v* Maltby MW	2-0				58			
Stratford Town *v* Hamlet S & L	0-3				65			
Boldmere St Michaels *v* Bridgnorth Town	1-2				91			
Rothwell Town *v* Wednesfield	2-0				62			
Racing Club Warwick *v* Tividale	6-1				81			
Hinckley Athletic *v* Desborough Town	3-1				209			
Chasetown *v* Walsall Wood	1-1				140			
Walsall Wood *v* Chasetown		1-0				107		
Raunds Town *v* Irthlingborough Diamonds	2-0				120			
Brackley Town *v* Northfield	1-2				58			
Hinckley Town *v* Holwell Sports	0-1				228			
Melton Town *v* Rushall Olympic	0-2				48			
Boston *v* Lincoln United	1-6				108			
Baker Perkins *v* Evesham United	4-3				67			
Mile Oak Rovers *v* Gresley Rovers	2-1				146			
(tie awarded to Gresley Rovers, as Mile Oak Rovers played an ineligible player)								
Gorleston *v* Saffron Walden Town	2-4				122			
Histon *v* Bourne Town	5-0				93			
Halstead Town *v* St Ives Town	3-1				148			
Royston Town *v* Thetford Town	1-2				124			
Kings Lynn *v* Mirrless Blackstone	2-0				422			
Watton United *v* Felixstowe Town	0-1				80			
Tilbury *v* Harwich & Parkeston	4-6				91			
RamseyTown *v* Witham Town	2-2				80			
Witham Town *v* Ramsey Town		3-2				110		
Berkhamsted Town *v* Lowestoft Town	3-5				142			
March Town United *v* Brightlingsea United	3-0				100			
Mount Grace (Potters Bar) *v* Wootton Blue Cross	1-0				125			
Purfleet *v* Stotfold	2-0				75			
Barkingside *v* Collier Row	2-1				106			
Edgware Town *v* Letchworth GC	1-0				123			
Hemel Hempstead *v* Stevenage Borough	1-0				195			
Buckingham Town *v* Bracknell Town	4-1				143			

	1st Tie	1st Rep	2nd Rep	3rd Rep	1st Tie	1st Rep	2nd Rep	3rd Rep
Ruislip Manor v Leighton Town	4-3				148			
Brimsdown Rovers v Hounslow	3-0				21			
Elliott Star v Hertford Town	5-4				122			
Vauxhall Motors v Finchley	3-2				28			
Walthamstow Pennant v Langford	1-0				47			
Flackwell Heath v Northwood	0-2				67			
Epsom & Ewell v Shoreham	2-3				84			
Littlehampton Town v Godalming Town	5-0				203			
Faversham Town v Ringmer	1-0				134			
Alma Swanley v Tunbridge Wells	1-2				41			
Farnham Town v Egham Town	4-0				200			
Darenth Heathside v Hailsham Town	1-0				48			
Sittingbourne v Pagham	1-2				255			
Horsham v Whitehawk	2-1				102			
(tie awarded to Whitehawk, as Horsham played an ineligible player)								
Crockenhill v Haywards Heath Town	0-3				22			
Eastbourne United v Burgess Hill Town	1-2				157			
Langney Sports v Beckenham Town	3-1				128			
Slade Green v Whitstable Town	2-0				45			
Camberley Town v Malden Vale	1-1				38			
(abandoned in extra time – floodlight failure)								
Malden Vale v Camberley Town		3-0				110		
Greenwich Borough v Croydon Athletic	2-1				40			
Corinthian v Banstead Athletic	2-2				35			
Banstead Athletic v Corinthian		2-1				40		
Ramsgate v Merstham	1-1				99			
Merstham v Ramsgate		1-1				102		
Ramsgate v Merstham			0-2				141	
Wimborne Town v Newport (IOW)	1-0				140			
AFC Totton v Trowbridge Town	1-4				195			
Abingdon United v Didcot Town	0-3				120			
Havant Town v Bishops Cleeve	4-0				139			
Sholing Sports v First Tower United	2-1				71			
Thame United v Bournemouth	0-1				68			
Eastleigh v Westbury United	1-0				94			
Frome Town v Yate Town	2-2				175			
Yate Town v Frome Town		3-0				210		
Wotton Rovers v Almondsbury Picksons	0-2				113			
Chard Town v Shortwood United	1-2				102			
Hallen v Old Georgians	1-2				60			
Melksham Town v Wellington	0-1				65			
Clevedon Town v Chippenham Town	3-1				80			
Cinderford Town v Mangotsfield United	1-3				124			
Welton Rovers v Keynsham Town	2-0				78			
Newquay v Torrington	2-1				207			
Tiverton Town v Dawlish Town	3-4				285			
Barnstaple Town v Exmouth Town	5-1				155			

Second Round	Result				Attendance			
Saturday 24th November 1990	1st Tie	1st Rep	2nd Rep	3rd Rep	1st Tie	1st Rep	2nd Rep	3rd Rep
Bridlington Town v Blackpool (Wren) Rovers	1-0				173			
Horden CW v Great Harwood Town	1-2				49			
Harrogate RA v Chester-le-Street Town	2-1				82			
Rossendale United v Ossett Town	0-2				163			
Lancaster City v Eppleton CW	1-2				113			
North Ferriby United v Murton	5-3				62			
Langley Park v Ashington	0-1				54			
Farsley Celtic v Clitheroe	1-0				90			
Dunston FB v Billingham Town	2-3				83			
Rainworth MW v Harrogate Town	2-1				226			
Knowsley United v Eastwood Hanley	5-3				71			
Glossop v Winterton Rangers	4-0				350			
Cammell Laird v Sheffield	4-1				177			
Borrowash Victoria v Belper Town	5-3				83			

Match	1st Tie	1st Rep	2nd Rep	3rd Rep	1st Tie	1st Rep	2nd Rep	3rd Rep
Warrington Town v Guiseley	2-2				163			
Guiseley v Warrington Town		1-1				503		
Warrington Town v Guiseley			1-3				278	
Skelmersdale United v Garforth Town	1-4				85			
Lincoln United v Priory (Eastwood)	1-2				137			
Worsboro Bridge MW v Heanor Town	4-1				115			
Hucknall Town v Nantwich Town	2-2				190			
Nantwich Town v Hucknall Town		1-2				275		
Holbeach United v Raunds Town	2-2				121			
Raunds Town v Holbeach United		3-0				130		
Hinckley Athletic v March Town United	3-0				208			
Racing Club Warwick v Gresley Rovers	1-3				157			
Walsall Wood v Rushall Olympic	1-2				149			
Spalding United v Northfield	1-0				158			
Hamlet S & L v Wisbech Town	1-3				219			
Rothwell Town v Holwell Sports	3-2				95			
Potton United v Paget Rangers	1-3				140			
Baker Perkins v Histon	1-3				71			
Kings Lynn v Bridgnorth Town	4-0				469			
Sudbury Town v Ruislip Manor	0-0				650			
Ruislip Manor v Sudbury Town		0-2				270		
Harwich & Parkeston v Burnham Ramblers	6-1				168			
Braintree Town v Barkingside	2-2				138			
Barkingside v Braintree Town		3-2				103		
Northwood v Felixstowe Town	2-1				93			
Elliott Star v Mount Grace (Potters Bar)	1-3				150			
Halstead Town v Great Yarmouth Town	5-1				208			
Thetford Town v Billericay Town	4-1				198			
Vauxhall Motors v Purfleet	0-1				30			
Walthamstow Pennant v Edgware Town	2-1				70			
Saffron Walden Town v Witham Town	5-2				132			
Brimsdown Rovers v East Thurrock United	0-1				42			
Buckingham Town v Lowestoft Town	2-1				124			
Haverhill Rovers v Hemel Hempstead	1-0				67			
Pagham v Hythe Town	3-4				140			
Slade Green v Faversham Town	1-0				84			
Littlehampton Town v Abingdon Town	2-0				250			
Eastleigh v Langney Sports	1-0				65			
Didcot Town v Banstead Athletic	2-0				65			
Haywards Heath Town v Farnham Town	3-1				95			
Burgess Hill Town v Shoreham	2-0				140			
Havant Town v Merstham	2-0				102			
Hungerford Town v Chertsey Town	1-0				123			
Whitehawk v Malden Vale	1-2				66			
Thatcham Town v Tunbridge Wells	4-5				137			
Harefield United v Greenwich Borough	2-0				54			
Darenth Heathside v Hastings Town	2-3				140			
Old Georgians v Almondsbury Picksons	0-2				102			
Bridport v Shortwood United	2-0				230			
Clevedon Town v Paulton Rovers	0-0				93			
Paulton Rovers v Clevedon Town		3-0				142		
Dawlish Town v Barnstaple Town	3-3				83			
Barnstaple Town v Dawlish Town		0-1				154		
Newquay v Bournemouth	1-0				223			
Mangotsfield United v Wimborne Town	1-4				186			
Sholing Sports v Trowbridge Town	1-2				134			
Wellington v Welton Rovers	3-1				75			
Yate Town v Falmouth Town	2-1				204			

Third Round

Saturday 15th December 1990

	Result				Attendance			
	1st Tie	1st Rep	2nd Rep	3rd Rep	1st Tie	1st Rep	2nd Rep	3rd Rep
Glossop v North Ferriby United	1-0				250			
Cammell Laird v Ashington	1-1				201			
Ashington v Cammell Laird		0-3				405		

128

Match	Result 1st Tie	1st Rep	2nd Rep	3rd Rep	Att 1st Tie	1st Rep	2nd Rep	3rd Rep
Garforth Town v Borrowash Victoria	2-6				126			
Farsley Celtic v Guiseley	0-1				430			
Bridlington Town v Eppleton CW	4-0				218			
Knowsley United v Ossett Town	4-2				86			
Billingham Town v Harrogate RA	3-1				120			
Worsboro Bridge MW v Great Harwood Town	1-2				240			
Kings Lynn v Rushall Olympic	2-1				577			
Paget Rangers v Hinckley Athletic	0-4				86			
Rainworth MW v Hucknall Town	1-2				651			
Gresley Rovers v Raunds Town	2-1				329			
Spalding United v Wisbech Town	1-0				653			
Rothwell Town v Priory (Eastwood)	2-2				115			
Priory (Eastwood) v Rothwell Town		0-1				180		
East Thurrock United v Eastleigh	1-2				173			
Saffron Walden Town v Burgess Hill Town	4-3				202			
Haywards Heath Town v Thetford Town	1-2				140			
Hythe Town v Haverhill Rovers	4-0				214			
Halstead Town v Histon	0-1				180			
Harefield United v Havant Town	3-1				82			
Hastings Town v Tunbridge Wells	5-0				384			
Buckingham Town v Mount Grace (Potters Bar)	2-1				199			
Sudbury Town v Harwich & Parkeston	3-3				620			
Harwich & Parkeston v Sudbury Town		2-1				800		
Walthamstow Pennant v Barkingside	5-2				80			
Littlehampton Town v Slade Green	5-0				220			
Malden Vale v Didcot Town	1-1				82			
Didcot Town v Malden Vale		2-1				167		
Northwood v Purfleet	0-1				84			
Almondsbury Picksons v Trowbridge Town	1-2				193			
Hungerford Town v Newquay	0-2				149			
Dawlish Town v Wellington	4-1				65			
Paulton Rovers v Bridport	0-1				98			
Yate Town v Wimborne Town	5-3				184			

Fourth Round

Saturday 19th January 1991

Match	Result 1st Tie	1st Rep	2nd Rep	3rd Rep	Att 1st Tie	1st Rep	2nd Rep	3rd Rep
Bridlington Town v Borrowash Victoria	3-1				292			
Knowsley United v Spalding United	3-0				153			
Glossop v Cammell Laird	2-2				542			
Cammell Laird v Glossop		2-1				456		
Gresley Rovers v Billingham Town	2-1				722			
Great Harwood Town v Rothwell Town	1-1				602			
Rothwell Town v Great Harwood Town		0-1				383		
Kings Lynn v Guiseley	1-4				997			
Hinckley Athletic v Hucknall Town	2-1				502			
Harefield United v Hythe Town	0-5				141			
Trowbridge Town v Yate Town	5-0				673			
Eastleigh v Littlehampton Town	0-1				243			
Didcot Town v Dawlish Town	0-1				222			
Harwich & Parkeston v Purfleet	2-1				343			
Hastings Town v Histon	4-0				432			
Buckingham Town v Bridport	0-0				232			
Bridport v Buckingham Town		0-2				472		
Newquay v Saffron Walden Town	2-2				440			
Saffron Walden Town v Newquay		1-0				722		
Walthamstow Pennant v Thetford Town	5-1				170			

Fifth Round

Saturday 9th February 1991

Match	Result 1st Tie	1st Rep	2nd Rep	3rd Rep	Att 1st Tie	1st Rep	2nd Rep	3rd Rep
Cammell Laird v Harwich & Parkeston	2-3				415			
Great Harwood Town v Bridlington Town	1-1				730			

129

Bridlington Town *v* Great Harwood Town 0-1   462

	Result	Attendance
Bridlington Town *v* Great Harwood Town	0-1	462
Hinckley Athletic *v* Guiseley	1-4	
Knowsley United *v* Gresley Rovers	4-5	522
Littlehampton Town *v* Walthamstow Pennant	3-2	780
Hastings Town *v* Hythe Town	0-0	1189
Hythe Town *v* Hastings Town	3-1	857
Saffron Walden Town *v* Buckingham Town	1-2	
Trowbridge Town *v* Dawlish Town	1-0	846

Sixth Round	Result				Attendance			
Saturday 2nd March 1991	1st Tie	1st Rep	2nd Rep	3rd Rep	1st Tie	1st Rep	2nd Rep	3rd Rep
Buckingham Town *v* Guiseley	0-1				550			
Hythe Town *v* Trowbridge Town	0-0				794			
Trowbridge Town *v* Hythe Town		1-1				1656		
Trowbridge Town *v* Hythe Town			3-1				2468	
Littlehampton Town *v* Great Harwood Town	2-1				1015			
Harwich & Parkeston *v* Gresley Rovers	0-2				961			

Semi-Final	Result	Attendance

First Leg – Saturday 23rd March 1991

Gresley Rovers *v* Littlehampton Town	3-1	1982
Trowbridge Town *v* Guiseley	1-2	2358

Second Leg – Saturday 30th March 1991

Littlehampton Town *v* Gresley Rovers	1-2	2000
Guiseley *v* Trowbridge Town	1-1	2014

Gresley Rovers beat Littlehampton Town 5-2 on aggregate
Guiseley beat Trowbridge Town 3-2 on aggregate

Final	Result	Attendance

Saturday 4th May 1991

Gresley Rovers *v* Guiseley	4-4	11314

at Wembley Stadium

Replay – Tuesday 7th May 1991

Guiseley *v* Gresley Rovers	3-1	7585

at Sheffield United FC

F.A. Challenge Vase Winners 1975-91

Year	Winners		Runners-up		Venue
1975	Hoddesdon Town	2	Epsom & Ewell	1	Wembley
1976	* Billericay Town	1	Stamford	0	Wembley
1977	† Billericay Town	2	Sheffield	1	Nottingham
1978	Blue Star	2	Barton Rovers	1	Wembley
1979	Billericay Town	4	Almondsbury Greenway	1	Wembley
1980	Stamford	2	Guisborough Town	0	Wembley
1981	* Whickham	3	Willenhall Town	2	Wembley
1982	Forest Green Rovers	3	Rainworth Miners' Welfare	0	Wembley
1983	V.S. Rugby	1	Halesowen Town	0	Wembley
1984	Stansted	3	Stamford.	2	Wembley
1985	Halesowen Town	3	Fleetwood Town	1	Wembley
1986	Halesowen Town	3	Southall	0	Wembley
1987	St Helens Town	3	Warrington Town	2	Wembley
1988	* Colne Dynamoes	1	Emley	0	Wembley
1989	† Tamworth	3	Sudbury Town	0	Peterborough
1990	§ Yeading	1	Bridlington Town	0	Leeds
1991	¥ Guiseley	3	Gresley Rovers	1	Sheffield

*After extra time
†After 1-1 draw at Wembley
§After 0-0 draw at Wembley
¥After 4-4 draw at Wembley

F.A. Challenge Vase Competition 1991-92

Exemptions

32 Clubs Exempt to the Second Round

Billericay Town
Bridlington Town
Bridport
Buckingham Town
Cammell Laird
Dawlish Town
East Thurrock United
Farsley Celtic
Great Harwood Town
Great Yarmouth Town
Gresley Rovers

Guiseley
Harefield United
Harrogate RA
Harwich & Parkeston
Hastings Town
Haverhill Rovers
Hinckley Athletic
Hucknall Town
Hungerford Town
Hythe Town
Knowsley United

Littlehampton Town
North Ferriby United
Paulton Rovers
Potton United
Saffron Walden Town
Spalding United
Sudbury Town
Walthamstow Pennant
Wisbech Town
Yate Town

32 Clubs Exempt to the First Round

Billingham Town
Borrowash Victoria
Braintree Town
Burnham Ramblers
Chertsey Town
Didcot Town
Eastleigh
Eastwood Hanley
Eppleton CW
Falmouth Town
Garforth Town

Glossop
Greenwich Borough
Harrogate Town
Havant Town
Heanor Town
Histon
Holbeach United
Kings Lynn
Merstham
Newquay
Ossett Town

Paget Rangers
Purfleet
Rainworth MW
Raunds Town
Rossendale United
Rothwell Town
Thatcham Town
Thetford Town
Wellington Town
Wimborne Town

G.M. Vauxhall F.A. National School International Youth Caps 1990-91

Under-16	Iceland	Denmark	Norway	Finland	Sweden	Spain	France	Austria
N. Rust (Arsenal)	1		1	*1	1	1		1
L. Cotterell (Ipswich Town)	2	2	2	2	2	2	6	6
A. Gray (Charlton Athletic)	3	3					3	*8
S. Binks (Tottenham Hotspur)	4	5	4			5	4	4
I. Blyth	5		*4	4	4		2	3
K. Sharp (Auxerre)	6	6	5	5	5	6	5	5
S. Campbell (Tottenham Hotspur)	7		7	8	7	7		*3
D. Hill (Tottenham Hotspur)	8	4	6	6	8	4	7	7
D. McDougald (Tottenham Hotspur)	9	9	9	9	9	9	9	9
J. Forrester (Auxerre)	10	8	*10	*10	10	10	10	10
A. Turner (Tottenham Hotspur)	11	7	11	11	*11	11	11	11
S. Cousin (Norwich City)	*1	1	*1	1			1	*1
C. Dean (Manchester United)	*8	10	8	7	6	8	*7	8
J. Darkoh (Millwall)	*10	*9	10	10	*10	*10	*10	*10
S. Daly	*11	11	*11	*7	11	*4	8	
S. Campbell		*3	3	3	3	3		2

* Substitute

G.M. Vauxhall F.A. National School International Matches 1990-91

Under-16

28.7.90	England	4	Iceland	0	Maalahti
29.7.90	England	1	Denmark	2	Kauhajoki
31.7.90	England	4	Norway	0	Pietarsaari
1.8.90	England	3	Finland	0	Seinajoki
3.8.90	England	1	Sweden	2	Narpio
9.10.90	England	0	Spain	3	Chiavari
10.10.90	England	1	France	3	Sestri
11.10.90	England	0	Austria	1	Chiavari

F.A. Youth Challenge Cup Winners 1953-91

(AGGREGATE SCORES)

Year	Winners		Runners-up	
1953	Manchester United	9	Wolverhampton W	3
1954	Manchester United	5	Wolverhampton W	4
1955	Manchester United	7	West Bromwich Albion	1
1956	Manchester United	4	Chesterfield	3
1957	Manchester United	8	West Ham United	2
1958	Wolverhampton Wanderers	7	Chelsea	6
1959	Blackburn Rovers	2	West Ham United	1
1960	Chelsea	5	Preston North End	2
1961	Chelsea	5	Everton	3
1962	Newcastle United	2	Wolverhampton W	1
1963	West Ham United	6	Liverpool	5
1964	Manchester United	5	Swindon Town	2
1965	Everton	3	Arsenal	2
1966	Arsenal	5	Sunderland	3
1967	Sunderland	2	Birmingham City	0
1968	Burnley	3	Coventry City	2
1969	Sunderland	6	West Bromwich Albion	3
1970	Tottenham Hotspur	4	Coventry City	3
1971	Arsenal	2	Cardiff City	0
1972	Aston Villa	5	Liverpool	2
1973	Ipswich Town	4	Bristol City	1
1974	Tottenham Hotspur	2	Huddersfield Town	1
1975	Ipswich Town	5	West Ham United	1
1976	West Bromwich Albion	5	Wolverhampton W	0
1977	Crystal Palace	1	Everton	0
1978*	Crystal Palace	1	Aston Villa	0
1979	Millwall	2	Manchester City	0
1980	Aston Villa	3	Manchester City	2
1981	West Ham United	2	Tottenham Hotspur	1
1982	Watford	7	Manchester United	6
1983†	Norwich City	6	Everton	5
1984	Everton	4	Stoke City	2
1985	Newcastle United	4	Watford	1
1986	Manchester City	3	Manchester United	1
1987	Coventry City	2	Charlton Athletic	1
1988	Arsenal	6	Doncaster Rovers	1
1989	Watford	2	Manchester City	1
1990	Tottenham Hotspur	3	Middlesbrough	2
1991	Millwall	3	Sheffield Wednesday	0

*One leg only †After a replay

Does your foot odour strike quicker than Ian Rush?

Maybe you need OdorEaters!

OdorEaters – the winning team against foot odour.

Ultra Comfort for everyday shoes.

Super Tuff for work shoes and boots.

Trainer Tamers for trainers.

Foot Powder stops wetness and odour all day.

OdorEaters
REGISTERED TRADE MARK
ODOUR–DESTROYING COMFORT INSOLES

F.A. County Youth Challenge Cup
Winners 1945-91

(AGGREGATE SCORES)

Year	Winners		Runners-up	
1945	Staffordshire	3	Wiltshire	2
1946	Berks. & Bucks	4	Durham	3
1947	Durham	4	Essex	2
1948	Essex	5	Liverpool	3
1949	Liverpool	4	Middlesex	3
1950	Essex	4	Middlesex	3
1951	Middlesex	3	Leics. & Rutland	1
1952	Sussex	3	Liverpool	1
1953	Sheffield & Hallam	5	Hampshire	3
1954	Liverpool	4	Gloucestershire	1
1955	Bedfordshire	2	Sheffield & Hallam	0
1956	Middlesex	3	Staffordshire	2
1957	Hampshire	4	Cheshire	3
1958	Staffordshire	8	London	0
1959	Birmingham	7	London	5
1960	London	6	Birmingham	4
1961	Lancashire	6	Nottinghamshire	3
1962	Middlesex	6	Nottinghamshire	3
1963	Durham	3	Essex	2
1964	Sheffield & Hallam	1	Birmingham	0
1965	Northumberland	7	Middlesex	4
1966	Leics. & Rutland	6	London	5
1967	Northamptonshire	5	Hertfordshire	4
1968	North Riding	7	Devon	4
1969	Northumberland	1	Sussex	0
1970*	Hertfordshire	2	Cheshire	1
1971*	Lancashire	2	Gloucestershire	0
1972*	Middlesex	2	Liverpool	0
1973*	Hertfordshire	3	Northumberland	0
1974*	Nottinghamshire	2	London	0
1975*	Durham	2	Bedfordshire	1
1976*	Northamptonshire	7	Surrey	1
1977*	Liverpool	3	Surrey	0
1978*	Liverpool	3	Kent	1
1979*	Hertfordshire	4	Liverpool	1
1980*	Liverpool	2	Lancashire	0
1981*	Lancashire	3	East Riding	2
1982*†	Devon	3	Kent	2
1983*	London	3	Gloucestershire	0
1984*	Cheshire	2	Manchester	1
1985*	East Riding	2	Middlesex	1
1986*	Hertfordshire	4	Manchester	0
1987*	North Riding	3	Gloucestershire	1
1988*§	East Riding	5	Middlesex	3
1989*	Liverpool	2	Hertfordshire	1
1990*§	Staffordshire	2	Hampshire	1
1991*	Lancashire	6	Surrey	0

*One leg only †After extra time §After a 1-1 draw

135

F.A. Youth Challenge Cup Competition 1990-91

First Round Qualifying	Result		
	1st *Tie*	*1st* *Rep*	*2nd* *Rep*
Stockton *v* Billingham Synthonia	2-0		
Guisborough Town *v* Murton	4-1		
Rotherham United *v* Huddersfield Town	2-1		
York City *v* Scarborough	1-0		
Accrington Stanley *v* Blackpool Mechanics	3-1		
Bolton Wanderers *v* Marine	5-1		
Bury *v* Shrewsbury Town	2-0		
Rochdale *v* Chester City	2-2		
Chester City *v* Rochdale		1-2	
Lye Town *v* Willenhall Town	1-2		
Leek Town *v* Telford United	0-3		
Alvechurch *v* Burton Albion	4-0		
Moor Green *v* Kidderminster Harriers	0-3		
Cambridge City *v* Rothwell Town	9-1		
Norwich City *v* Nuneaton Borough	9-0		
Bishops Stortford *v* Witham Town	5-1		
Canvey Island *v* Basildon United	3-4		
East Thurrock United *v* St Albans City	0-5		
Enfield *v* Boreham Wood	5-0		
Fisher Athletic *v* Kingsbury Town	1-1		
Kingsbury Town *v* Fisher Athletic		0-5	
Finchley *v* Clapton	0-1		
Slough Town *v* Wycombe Wanderers	2-6		
Bedfont *v* Hillingdon Borough	2-1		
Northwood *v* Maidenhead United	3-5		
Uxbridge *v* Egham Town	0-3		
Ringmer *v* Chatham Town	0-6		
Herne Bay *v* Dover Athletic	0-2		
Three Bridges *v* Worthing	1-3		
Shoreham *v* Horsham YMCA	4-2		
Malden Vale *v* Walton & Hersham	1-10		
Feltham *v* Carshalton Athletic	1-2		
Bicester Town *v* Hungerford Town	1-1		
Hungerford Town *v* Bicester Town		1-5	
Basingstoke Town *v* Aldershot	0-7		
Frome Town *v* Torquay United	0-7		
Romsey Town *v* Exeter City	0-3		
Gloucester City *v* Bristol Rovers	2-4		
Trowbridge Town *v* Worcester City	3-3		
Worcester City *v* Trowbridge Town		3-0	

Second Round Qualifying	Result		
	1st *Tie*	*1st* *Rep*	*2nd* *Rep*
Stockton *v* Guisborough Town	1-5		
Rotherham United *v* York City	1-2		
Accrington Stanley *v* Bolton Wanderers	0-3		
Bury *v* Rochdale	4-1		
Willenhall Town *v* Telford United	1-2		
Alvechurch *v* Kidderminster Harriers	4-3		
Cambridge City *v* Norwich City	3-3		
Norwich City *v* Cambridge City		2-1	
Bishops Stortford *v* Basildon United	1-2		
St Albans City *v* Enfield	0-3		
Fisher Athletic *v* Clapton	0-1		
Wycombe Wanderers *v* Bedfont	3-1		
Maidenhead United *v* Egham Town	2-6		

Chatham Town *v* Dover Athletic	0-1		
Worthing *v* Shoreham	2-2		
Shoreham *v* Worthing		4-0	
Walton & Hersham *v* Carshalton Athletic	2-2		
Carshalton Athletic *v* Walton & Hersham		6-0	
Bicester Town *v* Aldershot	1-3		
Torquay United *v* Exeter City	1-1		
Exeter City *v* Torquay United		2-1	
Bristol Rovers *v* Worcester City	11-0		

First Round Proper   Result

	1st Tie	1st Rep	2nd Rep
Bolton Wanderers *v* Oldham Athletic	3-3		
Oldham Athletic *v* Bolton Wanderers	2-0		
Wigan Athletic *v* Burnley	0-3		
Darlington *v* Harlepool United	1-1		
Hartlepool United *v* Darlington		1-3	
Mansfield Town *v* Blackburn Rovers	2-4		
Hull City *v* Carlisle United	2-0		
Bradford City *v* Guisborough Town	7-0		
Blackpool *v* Barnsley	0-1		
Tranmere Rovers *v* Bury	1-1		
Bury *v* Tranmere Rovers		3-0	
Sunderland *v* York City	0-0		
York City *v* Sunderland		3-0	
Alvechurch *v* Northampton Town	2-1		
Scunthorpe United *v* Telford United	3-2		
Wolverhampton Wanderers *v* Port Vale	2-2		
Port Vale *v* Wolverhampton Wanderers		0-1	
Crewe Alexandra *v* Nottingham Forest	1-0		
Cambridge United *v* Derby County	0-1		
Walsall *v* Norwich City	1-0		
Hednesford Town *v* Notts County	0-8		
Oxford United *v* Hendon	3-0		
Shoreham *v* Wimbledon	0-12		
West Ham United *v* Horndean	21-1		
Wokingham Town *v* Egham Town	1-1		
Egham Town *v* Wokingham Town		3-1	
Fulham *v* Colchester United	0-2		
Millwall *v* Sutton United	4-0		
Dover Athletic *v* Epsom & Ewell	2-2		
Epsom & Ewell *v* Dover Athletic		4-0	
Basildon United *v* Carshalton Athletic	0-0		
Carshalton Athletic *v* Basildon United		5-2	
Peterborough United *v* Brighton & Hove Albion	3-0		
Wycombe Wanderers *v* Aldershot	0-4		
Whyteleafe *v* Enfield	3-3		
Enfield *v* Whyteleafe		1-2	
Clapton *v* Gillingham	1-4		
Bristol City *v* Exeter City	1-2		
Southampton *v* AFC Bournemouth	4-1		
Cardiff City *v* Hereford United	0-1		
Newbury Town *v* Swansea City	1-9		
Swindon Town *v* Bristol Rovers	3-0		

Bye for Aston Villa

Second Round Proper   Result

	1st Tie	1st Rep	2nd Rep
Bradford City *v* Sheffield United	3-0		
Everton *v* Scunthorpe United	1-0		
Hull City *v* York City	1-1		
York City *v* Hull City		1-2	

Liverpool v Middlesbrough	3-0		
Sheffield Wednesday v Bury	4-1		
Newcastle United v Oldham Athletic	2-0		
Darlington v Manchester United	0-6		
Manchester City v Barnsley	0-1		
Doncaster Rovers v Burnley	4-0		
Blackburn Rovers v Leeds United	1-1		
Leeds United v Blackburn Rovers		3-1	
Leyton Orient v Ipswich Town	2-1		
West Bromwich Albion v Peterborough United	3-2		
Wolverhampton Wanderers v Walsall	0-2		
Notts County v Arsenal	0-0		
Arsenal v Notts County		1-1	
Notts County v Arsenal			2-1
Leicester City v Coventry City	2-3		
Birmingham City v Tottenham Hotspur	1-0		
Alvechurch v Crewe Alexandra	0-4		
Watford v Luton Town	1-0		
Southend United v Stoke City	0-0		
Stoke City v Southend United		2-3	
Derby County v Aston Villa	0-3		
Colchester United v Carshalton Athletic	3-2		
Whyteleafe v Epsom & Ewell	2-3		
Egham Town v Exeter City	0-0		
Exeter City v Egham Town		2-0	
Charlton Athletic v Plymouth Argyle	1-2		
Portsmouth v Hereford United	2-1		
Wimbledon v Oxford United	3-0		
Reading v Swansea City	1-1		
Swansea City v Reading		2-1	
Brentford v Chelsea	2-2		
Chelsea v Brentford		1-1	
Brentford v Chelsea			4-7
Swindon Town v Millwall	0-1		
Aldershot v West Ham United	1-1		
West Ham United v Aldershot		4-0	
Crystal Palace v Queens Park Rangers	3-3		
Queens Park Rangers v Crystal Palace		0-1	
Gillingham v Southampton	2-3		

Third Round Proper   Result

	1st Tie	1st Rep	2nd Rep
Bradford City v Barnsley	2-1		
Aston Villa v Sheffield Wednesday	2-3		
Doncaster Rovers v Leeds United	0-3		
Walsall v Liverpool	2-2		
Liverpool v Walsall		4-1	
Manchester United v Everton	1-1		
Everton v Manchester United		1-2	
Newcastle United v West Bromwich Albion	1-2		
Crewe Alexandra v Hull City	0-2		
Millwall v Portsmouth	3-1		
Leyton Orient v Birmingham City	1-2		
Swansea City v Colchester United	1-3		
Plymouth Argyle v Epsom & Ewell	2-0		
Wimbledon v Coventry City	2-0		
Watford v Notts County	0-0		
Notts County v Watford		2-1	
Southend United v West Ham United	1-5		
Southampton v Exeter City	6-0		
Chelsea v Crystal Palace	4-0		

Fourth Round Proper

	1st Tie	1st Rep	2nd Rep
	Result		
Plymouth Argyle *v* Millwall	0-1		
Liverpool *v* Manchester United	1-3		
Chelsea *v* Wimbledon	2-2		
Wimbledon *v* Chelsea		2-0	
Sheffield Wednesday *v* West Bromwich Albion	2-1		
West Ham United *v* Birmingham City	2-0		
Southampton *v* Bradford City	4-0		
Leeds United *v* Hull City	1-2		
Notts County *v* Colchester United	2-0		

Fifth Round Proper

	1st Tie	1st Rep	2nd Rep
	Result		
Sheffield Wednesday *v* Hull City	1-1		
Hull City *v* Sheffield Wednesday		1-1	
Sheffield Wednesday *v* Hull City			5-1
Southampton *v* Manchester United	0-2		
West Ham United *v* Notts County	3-1		
Millwall *v* Wimbledon	1-1		
Wimbledon *v* Millwall		2-3	

Semi-Final

Result

First Leg

West Ham United *v* Millwall	1-2
Sheffield Wednesday *v* Manchester United	1-1

Second Leg

Millwall *v* West Ham United	2-0
Manchester United *v* Sheffield Wednesday	0-1

Millwall beat West Ham United 4-1 on aggregate
Sheffield Wednesday beat Manchester United 2-1 on aggregate

Final

Result

First Leg

Sheffield Wednesday *v* Millwall	0-3

Second Leg

Millwall *v* Sheffield Wednesday	0-0

Millwall won 3-0 on aggregate

F.A. County Youth Challenge Cup Competition
1990-91

First Round

	1st Tie	1st Rep
Northumberland v Westmorland	10-0	
Cumberland v North Riding	3-1	
West Riding v Derbyshire	4-1	
Liverpool v Shropshire	2-3	
Cheshire v Leicestershire & Rutland	2-3	
Birmingham v Oxfordshire	6-3	
Norfolk v Suffolk	4-2	
Huntingdonshire v Essex	3-2	
London v Middlesex	2-0	
Kent v Sussex	2-1	
Army v Dorset	1-4	
Devon v Herefordshire	5-2	
Somerset & Avon (South) v Wiltshire	0-5	

Second Round

	1st Tie	1st Rep
Northumberland v Durham	1-2	
Cumberland v Lancashire	0-2	
West Riding v East Riding	4-2	
Shropshire v Manchester	2-0	
Leicestershire & Rutland v Nottinghamshire	1-0	
Staffordshire v Sheffield & Hallamshire	2-3	
Lincolnshire v Northamptonshire	1-3	
Birmingham v Worcestershire	4-4	
Worcestershire v Birmingham		5-3
Norfolk v Cambridgeshire	1-2	
Huntingdonshire v Bedfordshire	3-1	
London v Hertfordshire	4-2	
Kent v Surrey	2-4	
Berks & Bucks v Hampshire	2-3	
Dorset v Royal Navy	1-1	
Royal Navy v Dorset		3-2
Devon v Gloucestershire	4-2	
Wiltshire v Cornwall	3-5	

Third Round

	1st Tie	!st Rep
Durham v Lancashire	1-2	
Shropshire v Leicestershire & Rutland	1-1	
Leicestershire & Rutland v Shropshire		1-2
West Riding v Sheffield & Hallamshire	4-1	
Worcestershire v Cambridgeshire	3-1	
Northamptonshire v Huntingdonshire	3-1	
Surrey v Hampshire	8-3	
London v Royal Navy	2-0	
Devon v Cornwall	2-0	

Fourth Round

West Riding v Northamptonshire	2-1	Lancashire v Shropshire	3-2
Worcestershire v Devon	5-2	Surrey v London	2-0

Semi-Final

Lancashire v West Riding	2-0	Surrey v Worcestershire	3-2

Final

Lancashire v Surrey	6-0

at Bolton Wanderers FC

FIFA World Youth Championship
14th–30th June 1991, Portugal

Final Competition
1st Phase

GROUP A

14.6.91	Portugal	2	Republic of Ireland	0
15.6.91	Argentina	0	Korea	1
17.6.91	Republic of Ireland	1	Korea	1
17.6.91	Portugal	3	Argentina	0
20.6.91	Republic of Ireland	2	Argentina	2
20.6.91	Portugal	1	Korea	0

	P	W	D	L	F	A	Pts
Portugal	3	3	0	0	6	0	6
Korea	3	1	1	1	2	2	3
Ireland	3	0	2	1	3	5	2
Argentina	3	0	1	2	2	6	1

GROUP B

15.6.91	Mexico	3	Sweden	0
15.6.91	Brazil	2	Ivory Coast	1
17.6.91	Brazil	2	Mexico	2
18.6.91	Ivory Coast	1	Sweden	4
20.6.91	Ivory Coast	1	Mexico	1
20.6.91	Brazil	2	Sweden	0

	P	W	D	L	F	A	Pts
Brazil	3	2	1	0	6	3	5
Mexico	3	1	2	0	6	3	4
Sweden	3	1	0	2	4	6	2
Ivory Coast	3	0	1	2	3	7	1

GROUP C

15.6.91	Trinidad & Tobago	0	Australia	2
16.6.91	Egypt	0	USSR	1
18.6.91	Trinidad & Tobago	0	Egypt	6
18.6.91	Australia	1	USSR	0
20.6.91	Australia	1	Egypt	0
20.6.91	Trinidad & Tobago	0	USSR	4

	P	W	D	L	F	A	Pts
Australia	3	3	0	0	4	0	6
USSR	3	2	0	1	5	1	4
Egypt	3	1	0	2	6	2	2
Trinidad & Tobago	3	0	0	3	0	12	0

GROUP D

15.6.91	England	0	Spain	1
16.6.91	Syria	1	Uruguay	0
18.6.91	Spain	6	Uruguay	0
18.6.91	England	3	Syria	3
20.6.91	Spain	0	Syria	0
20.6.91	England	0	Uruguay	0

	P	W	D	L	F	A	Pts
Spain	3	2	1	0	7	0	5
Syria	3	1	2	0	4	3	4
England	3	0	2	1	3	4	2
Uruguay	3	0	1	2	0	7	1

2nd Phase

QUARTER-FINAL

22.6.91	Portugal	2	Mexico	1
22.6.91	Brazil	5	Korea	1
23.6.91	Australia	1*	Syria	1
23.6.91	Spain	1	USSR	3

SEMI-FINAL

26.6.91	Brazil	3	USSR	0
26.6.91	Portugal	1	Australia	0

3RD/4TH PLACE

29.6.91	USSR	1*	Australia	1

FINAL

30.6.91	Portugal	0*	Brazil	0

* Won on penalty-kicks

Summary of previous World Youth Championships

Year	Venue	Winner	Runner-Up	Third	Fourth
1977	Tunisia	USSR	Mexico	Brazil	Uruguay
1979	Japan	Argentina	USSR	Uruguay	Poland
1981	Australia	W. Germany	Qatar	Romania	England
1983	Mexico	Brazil	Argentina	Poland	S. Korea
1985	USSR	Brazil	Spain	Nigeria	USSR
1987	Chile	Yugoslavia	W. Germany	E. Germany	Chile
1989	Saudi Arabia	Portugal	Nigeria	Brazil	USA

England Youth Caps 1990-91

	Belgium	USSR	Spain	Iceland	Belgium	Denmark	Trinidad & Tobago	Mexico	Wales	Wales	Spain	Spain	Syria	Uruguay
. Walker (Tottenham Hotspur)	1	1				1					1	1	1	1
. Kavanagh (Derby County)	2					7	5	5			*2		*10	4
A. Wright (Blackpool)	3	3	3				3	3				3	3	3
. Hayward (Derby County)	4	4	4				7	7			7	7	7	
D. Tuttle (Tottenham Hotspur)	5	5	5			5					4	4	4	
A. Awford (Portsmouth)	6	6	6				6	6			6	6	6	6
. Harkness (Liverpool)	7	7	7			*11	11	11			11	11		
. Rouse (Rangers)	8	8	8				8	8			8	8	8	8
A. Cole (Arsenal)	9	9	9			8	9	9			9	9	9	*9
A. Newhouse (Wimbledon)	10	10	10			10	10	10						
. Houghton (Tottenham Hotspur)	11		*7				*9	*4			*10	*7	*7	7
B. Small (Aston Villa)	*7		*11			11								
. Allen (Queens Park Rangers)	*10	11											10	10	10
. Hendon (Tottenham Hotspur)		2	2			4	2	2			5	5	5	5
... Clark (Newcastle United)		*10	11				*10							*10
. Livingstone (Aston Villa)			1								*1			
. Thomson (Derby County)				1	1									
A. Marlowe (Tottenham Hotspur)				2	2									
A. Hughes (Crewe Alexandra)				3	3				6	6				
M. Harriott (West Ham United)				4	4				4	4				
D. Hall (Oldham Athletic)				5	5									
D. Unsworth (Everton)				6	6				3	3				
. Howe (Nottingham Forest)				7					11	11				
D. Caskey (Tottenham Hotspur)				8	8				7	8				
J. Barmby (Tottenham Hotspur)				9	9				9	9				
... Hodges (Tottenham Hotspur)				10	10					*11				
. Lee (Arsenal)				11	11									
A. Myers (Chelsea)				*7	7				10	10	*11			
. Nguyen (Charlton Athletic)					*11									
D. Sutch (Norwich City)						2								
. Minto (Charlton Athletic)						3	4	4			3	*2	11	11
J. Whitworth (Manchester United) ...						6	*5	*5						
. McManaman (Liverpool)						9					*9			
. Taylor (Wolves)						*9								
. Peake (Leicester City)						*10								
. Winters (Chelsea)							1	1						
A. Smith (Sunderland)							*3	*2						
. Redknapp (Liverpool)							*11							
A. Bayes (Brentford)								*1						
J. Heaney (Arsenal)								*11						
. Sheppard (Watford)									1	1				
. Watson (Newcastle United)									2	2	2	2	2	2
M. Basham (West Ham United)									5					
. Bart-Williams (Leyton Orient)									8	7	10			
M. Jackson (Crewe Alexandra)										5				
. Phillips (Derby County)												*5		
D. Anderton (Portsmouth)												**10		
. Mills (Port Vale)														9

Substitute

143

Youth International Matches 1947-91

WYC World Youth Championship
IYT International Youth Tournament
*Qualifying Competition †Professionals §Abandoned

ENGLAND v ALGERIA

Year	Date	Venue	Eng	Alg
†1984	Apr. 22	Cannes	3	0

ENGLAND v ARGENTINA

Year	Date	Venue	Eng	Arg
†WYC1981	Oct. 5	Sydney	1	1

ENGLAND v AUSTRALIA

Year	Date	Venue	Eng	Aus
†WYC1981	Oct. 8	Sydney	1	1

ENGLAND v AUSTRIA

Year	Date	Venue	Eng	Aust
IYT1949	Apr. 19	Zeist	4	2
IYT1952	Apr. 17	Barcelona	5	5
IYT1957	Apr. 16	Barcelona	0	3
1958	Mar. 4	Highbury	3	2
1958	June 1	Graz	4	3
IYT1960	Apr. 20	Vienna	0	1
†IYT1964	Apr. 1	Rotterdam	2	1
†1980	Sept. 6	Pazin	0	1
†IYT1981	May 29	Bonn	7	0
†1981	Sept. 3	Umag	3	0
†1984	Sept. 6	Izola	2	2

ENGLAND v BELGIUM

Year	Date	Venue	Eng	Belg
IYT1948	Apr. 16	West Ham	3	1
IYT1951	Mar. 22	Cannes	1	1
IYT1953	Mar. 31	Brussels	2	0
§1956	Nov. 7	Brussels	3	2
1957	Nov. 3	Sheffield	2	0
†IYT1965	Apr. 15	Ludwigshafen	3	0
*IYT1969	Mar. 11	West Ham	1	0
*IYT1972	May 13	Palma	0	0
†IYT1973	June 4	Viareggio	0	0
†IYT1977	May 19	Lokeren	1	0
†1979	Jan. 17	Brussels	4	0
†1980	Sept. 8	Labin	6	1
†1983	Apr. 13	Birmingham	1	1
†1988	May 20	Chatel	0	0
†IYT1990	July 24	Nyiregyhaza	1	1
*†IYT1990	Oct. 16	Sunderland	0	0

ENGLAND v BRAZIL

Year	Date	Venue	Eng	Brazil
†1986	Mar. 29	Cannes	0	0
†1986	May 13	Peking	1	2
†1987	June 2	Niteroi	0	2

ENGLAND v BULGARIA

Year	Date	Venue	Eng	Bulg
IYT1956	Mar. 28	Salgotarjan	1	2
IYT1960	Apr. 16	Graz	0	1
IYT1962	Apr. 24	Ploesti	0	0
†IYT1968	Apr. 7	Nimes	0	0
†IYT1969	Mar. 26	Waregem	2	0
†IYT1972	May 13	Palma	0	0
†IYT1979	May 31	Vienna	0	1

ENGLAND v CAMEROON

Year	Date	Venue	Eng	Cam
†WYC1981	Oct. 3	Sydney	2	0
†1985	June 1	Toulon	1	0

ENGLAND v CHINA

Year	Date	Venue	Eng	China
†1983	Mar. 31	Cannes	5	1

ENGLAND v CHINA

Year	Date	Venue	Eng	China
†WYC1985	Aug. 26	Baku	0	2
†1986	May 5	Peking	1	0

ENGLAND v CZECHOSLOVAKIA

Year	Date	Venue	Eng	Czech
IYT1955	Apr. 7	Lucca	0	1
†IYT1966	May 21	Rijeka	2	3
†IYT1969	May 20	Leipzig	3	1
IYT1979	May 24	Bischofshofen	3	0
†1979	Sept. 8	Pula	1	2
†1982	Apr. 11	Cannes	0	1
†IYT1983	May 20	Highbury	1	1
*†IYT1989	Apr. 26	Bystrica	0	1
*†IYT1989	Nov. 14	Portsmouth	1	0
†1990	Apr. 25	Wembley	1	1

ENGLAND v DENMARK

Year	Date	Venue	Eng	Den
†1955	Oct. 1	Plymouth	9	2
1956	May 20	Esbjerg	2	1
*†IYT1979	Oct. 31	Esbjerg	3	1
*IYT1980	Mar. 26	Coventry	4	0
†1982	July 15	Stjordal	5	2
†1983	July 16	Holbeck	0	1
†1987	Feb. 16	Manchester	2	1
†1990	Mar. 28	Wembley	0	0
†1991	Feb. 6	Oxford	1	5

ENGLAND v EGYPT

Year	Date	Venue	Eng	Egypt
†WYC1981	Oct. 11	Sydney	4	2

ENGLAND v FINLAND

Year	Date	Venue	Eng	Fin
†IYT1975	May 19	Berne	1	0

ENGLAND v FRANCE

Year	Date	Venue	Eng	France
1957	Mar. 24	Fontainbleau	1	0
1958	Mar. 22	Eastbourne	0	1
†IYT1966	May 23	Rijeka	1	2
†IYT1967	May 11	Istanbul	2	0
†1968	Jan. 25	Paris	0	1
*IYT1978	Feb. 8	Crystal Palace	3	1
*IYT1978	Mar. 1	Paris	0	0
†IYT1979	June 2	Vienna	0	0
†1982	Apr. 12	Cannes	0	1
†1983	Apr. 2	Cannes	0	2
†1984	Apr. 23	Cannes	1	2
†1985	June 7	Toulon	1	3
†1986	Mar. 31	Cannes	1	2
†1986	May 11	Peking	1	1
†1988	May 22	Monthey	1	2
*†IYT1988	Nov. 15	Bradford	1	1
*†IYT1989	Oct. 11	Martigues	0	0
†1990	May 22	Wembley	1	3

ENGLAND v EAST GERMANY

Year	Date	Venue	Eng	EG
IYT1958	Apr. 7	Neunkirchen	1	0
1959	Mar. 8	Zwickau	3	4
1960	Apr. 2	Portsmouth	1	1
†IYT1965	Apr. 25	Essen	2	3
†IYT1969	May 22	Magdeburg	0	4
†IYT1973	June 10	Florence	3	2
†IYT1984	May 25	Moscow	1	1
†1988	May 21	Monthey	1	0

ENGLAND v WEST GERMANY

			Eng	WG
IYT1953	Apr. 4	Boom	3	1
IYT1954	Apr. 15	Gelsenkirchen	2	2
IYT1956	Apr. 1	Sztalinvaros	2	1
1957	Mar. 31	Oberhausen	4	1
1958	Mar. 12	Bolton	1	2
1961	Mar. 12	Flensberg	0	2
†1962	Mar. 31	Northampton	1	0
†1967	Feb. 14	Moenchengladbach	1	0
†IYT1972	May 22	Barcelona	2	0
†1975	Jan. 25	Las Palmas	4	2
†1976	Nov. 14	Monte Carlo	1	1
†IYT1979	May 28	Salzburg	2	0
†1979	Sept. 1	Pula	1	1
†1983	Sept. 5	Pazin	2	0

ENGLAND v GREECE

			Eng	Greece
IYT1957	Apr. 18	Barcelona	2	3
IYT1959	Apr. 2	Dimitrovo	4	0
†IYT1977	May 23	Beveren	1	1
†1983	May 23	Puspokladany	1	0
*†IYT1988	Oct. 26	Birkenhead	5	0
*†IYT1989	Mar. 8	Xanthi	3	0

ENGLAND v HOLLAND

			Eng	Hol
IYT1948	Apr. 17	Tottenham	3	2
IYT1951	Mar. 26	Cannes	2	1
†1954	Nov. 21	Arnhem	2	3
†1955	Nov. 5	Norwich	3	1
1957	Mar. 2	Brentford	5	5
IYT1957	Apr. 14	Barcelona	1	2
1957	Oct. 2	Amsterdam	3	2
1961	Mar. 9	Utrecht	0	1
†1962	Jan. 31	Brighton	4	3
IYT1962	Apr. 22	Ploesti	0	3
†IYT1963	Apr. 13	Wimbledon	5	0
IYT1968	Apr. 9	Nimes	1	0
*†IYT1974	Feb. 13	West Bromwich	1	1
*†IYT1974	Feb. 27	The Hague	1	0
†IYT1980	May 23	Halle	1	0
†1982	Apr. 9	Cannes	1	0
†1985	Apr. 7	Cannes	1	3
†1987	Aug. 1	Wembley	3	1

ENGLAND v HUNGARY

			Eng	Hung
IYT1954	Apr. 11	Dusseldorf	1	3
IYT1956	Mar. 31	Tatabanya	2	4
†1956	Oct. 23	Tottenham	2	1
†1956	Oct. 25	Sunderland	2	1
†IYT1965	Apr. 21	Wuppertal	5	0
†IYT1975	May 16	Olten	3	1
†1977	Oct. 16	Las Palmas	3	0
†1979	Sept. 5	Pula	2	0
†1980	Sept. 11	Pula	1	2
†1981	Sept. 7	Porec	4	0
†1983	July 29	Debrecen	1	2
†1983	Sept. 3	Umag	3	2
†1986	Mar. 30	Cannes	2	0

ENGLAND v ICELAND

			Eng	Ice
†IYT1973	May 31	Viareggio	2	0
†IYT1977	May 21	Turnhout	0	0
*†IYT1983	Oct. 12	Reykjavik	3	0
*†IYT1983	Nov. 1	Crystal Palace	3	0
*†IYT1984	Oct. 16	Manchester	5	3
*†IYT1985	Sept. 11	Reykjavik	5	0
*†IYT1990	Sept. 12	Reykjavik	3	2

ENGLAND v IRELAND

			Eng	Ire
1948	May 15	Belfast	2	2
IYT1949	Apr. 18	Haarlem	3	3
1949	May 14	Hull	4	2

Year	Date	Venue	Goals Eng	Ire
1950	May 6	Belfast	0	1
1951	May 5	Liverpool	5	2
1952	Apr. 19	Belfast	0	2
1953	Apr. 11	Wolverhampton	0	0
IYT1954	Apr. 10	Bruehl	5	0
1954	May 8	Newtonards	2	2
1955	May 14	Watford	3	0
1956	May 12	Belfast	0	1
1957	May 11	Leyton	6	2
1958	May 10	Bangor	2	4
1959	May 9	Liverpool	5	0
1960	May 14	Belfast	5	2
1961	May 13	Manchester	2	0
1962	May 12	Londonderry	1	2
†IYT1963	Apr. 23	Wembley	4	0
1963	May 11	Oldham	1	1
1964	Jan. 25	Belfast	3	1
1965	Jan. 22	Birkenhead	2	3
1966	Feb. 26	Belfast	4	0
1967	Feb. 25	Stockport	3	0
1968	Feb. 23	Belfast	0	2
1969	Feb. 28	Birkenhead	0	2
1970	Feb. 28	Lurgan	1	3
1971	Mar. 6	Blackpool	1	1
1972	Mar. 11	Chester	1	1
1973	Mar. 24	Wellington	3	0
1974	Apr. 19	Birkenhead	1	2
†IYT1975	May 13	Kriens	3	0
†IYT1980	May 16	Arnstadt	1	0
*†IYT1981	Feb. 11	Walsall	1	0
*†IYT1981	Mar. 11	Belfast	3	0

ENGLAND v ISRAEL

			Eng	Israel
†1962	May 20	Tel Aviv	3	1
†1962	May 22	Haifa	1	2

ENGLAND v ITALY

			Eng	Italy
IYT1958	Apr. 13	Luxembourg	0	1
IYT1959	Mar. 25	Sofia	1	3
IYT1961	Apr. 4	Braga	2	3
†IYT1965	Apr. 23	Marl-Huels	3	1
†IYT1966	May 25	Rijeka	1	1
†IYT1967	May 5	Izmir	1	0
†1973	Feb. 14	Cava Dei Tirreni	0	1
†1973	Mar. 14	Highbury	1	0
†IYT1973	June 7	Viareggio	1	0
†1978	Nov. 19	Monte Carlo	1	2
*†1979	Feb. 28	Rome	1	0
*†IYT1979	Apr. 4	Birmingham	2	0
†IYT1983	May 22	Watford	1	1
†1984	Apr. 20	Cannes	1	0
†1985	Apr. 5	Cannes	2	2

ENGLAND v LUXEMBOURG

			Eng	Lux
IYT1950	May 25	Vienna	1	2
IYT1954	Apr. 17	Bad Neuenahr	0	2
1957	Feb. 2	West Ham	7	1
1957	Nov. 17	Luxembourg	1	0
IYT1958	Apr. 9	Eschsalzett	5	0
†IYT1984	May 29	Moscow	2	0

ENGLAND v MALTA

			Eng	Malta
†IYT1969	May 18	Wolfen	6	0
†IYT1979	May 26	Salzburg	3	0

ENGLAND v MEXICO

			Eng	Mex
†1984	Apr. 18	Cannes	4	0
†1985	June 5	Toulon	2	0
†WYC1985	Aug. 29	Baku	0	1
†1991	Mar. 27	Port of Spain	1	3

ENGLAND v NORWAY

Year	Date	Venue	Eng	Nor
†1982	July 13	Levanger	1	4
†1983	July 14	Korsor	1	0

ENGLAND v PARAGUAY

Year	Date	Venue	Eng	Para
†WYC1985	Aug. 24	Baku	2	2

ENGLAND v POLAND

Year	Date	Venue	Eng	Pol
IYT1960	Apr. 18	Graz	4	2
†IYT1964	Mar. 26	Breda	1	1
†IYT1971	May 26	Presnov	0	0
†IYT1972	May 20	Valencia	1	0
†1975	Jan. 21	Las Palmas	1	1
IYT1978	May 9	Chorzow	0	2
†1979	Sept. 3	Porec	0	1
†IYT1980	May 25	Leipzig	2	1
†1982	July 17	Steinkjer	3	2
†1983	July 12	Siagelse	1	0
†1990	May 15	Wembley	3	0

ENGLAND v PORTUGAL

Year	Date	Venue	Eng	Port
IYT1954	Apr. 18	Bonn	0	2
IYT1961	Apr. 2	Lisbon	0	4
†IYT1964	Apr. 3	The Hague	4	0
†IYT1971	May 30	Prague	3	0
†1978	Nov. 13	Monte Carlo	2	0
†IYT1980	May 18	Rosslau	1	1
†1982	Apr. 7	Cannes	3	0

ENGLAND v QATAR

Year	Date	Venue	Eng	Qat
†WYC1981	Oct. 14	Sydney	1	2
†1983	Apr. 4	Cannes	1	1

ENGLAND v REP. OF IRELAND

Year	Date	Venue	Eng	Rep of Ire
IYT1953	Apr. 5	Leuven	2	0
†IYT1964	Mar. 30	Middleburg	6	0
*†IYT1968	Feb. 7	Dublin	0	0
*†IYT1968	Feb. 28	Portsmouth	4	1
*†IYT1970	Jan. 14	Dublin	4	1
*†IYT1970	Feb. 4	Luton	10	0
†IYT1972	May 15	Sabadell	4	0
†IYT1975	May 9	Brunnen	1	0
*†IYT1985	Feb. 26	Dublin	0	1
*†IYT1986	Feb. 25	Leeds	2	0
†1988	Feb. 17	Stoke	2	0
†1988	Sept. 20	Dublin	2	0

ENGLAND v ROMANIA

Year	Date	Venue	Eng	Rom
1957	Oct. 15	Tottenham	4	2
IYT1958	Apr. 11	Luxembourg	1	0
IYT1959	Mar. 31	Pazardjic	1	2
†IYT1963	Apr. 15	Highbury	3	0
†WYC1981	Oct. 17	Adelaide	0	1

ENGLAND v SAAR

Year	Date	Venue	Eng	Saar
IYT1954	Apr. 13	Dortmund	1	1
IYT1955	Apr. 9	Prato	3	1

ENGLAND v SCOTLAND

Year	Date	Venue	Eng	Scot
1947	Oct. 25	Doncaster	4	2
1948	Oct. 30	Aberdeen	1	3
IYT1949	Apr. 21	Utrecht	0	1
1950	Feb. 4	Carlisle	7	1
1951	Feb. 3	Kilmarnock	6	1
1952	Mar. 15	Sunderland	3	1
1953	Feb. 7	Glasgow	4	3
1954	Feb. 6	Middlesbrough	2	1
1955	Mar. 5	Kilmarnock	3	4
1956	Mar. 3	Preston	2	2
1957	Mar. 9	Aberdeen	3	1
1958	Mar. 1	Hull	2	0
1959	Feb. 28	Aberdeen	1	1
1960	Feb. 27	Newcastle	1	1
1961	Feb. 25	Elgin	3	2
1962	Feb. 24	Peterborough	4	2
†IYT1963	Apr. 19	White City	1	0
1963	May 18	Dumfries	3	1
1964	Feb. 22	Middlesbrough	1	1
1965	Feb. 27	Inverness	1	2
1966	Feb. 5	Hereford	5	3
1967	Feb. 4	Aberdeen	0	1
*†IYT1967	Mar. 1	Southampton	1	0
*†IYT1967	Mar. 15	Dundee	0	0
1968	Feb. 3	Walsall	0	5
1969	Feb. 1	Stranraer	1	1
1970	Jan. 31	Derby	1	2
1971	Jan. 30	Greenock	1	2
1972	Jan. 29	Bournemouth	2	0
1973	Jan. 20	Kilmarnock	3	2
1974	Jan. 26	Brighton	2	2
†IYT1981	May 27	Aachen	0	1
*†IYT1982	Feb. 23	Glasgow	0	1
*†IYT1982	Mar. 23	Coventry	2	2
†IYT1983	May 15	Birmingham	3	0
*†IYT1984	Nov. 27	Fulham	1	2
*1985	Apr. 8	Cannes	1	0
*†IYT1986	Mar. 25	Aberdeen	1	4

ENGLAND v SPAIN

Year	Date	Venue	Eng	Spain
IYT1952	Apr. 15	Barcelona	1	4
1957	Sept. 26	Birmingham	4	4
IYT1958	Apr. 5	Saarbruecken	2	2
†1958	Oct. 8	Madrid	4	2
IYT1961	Mar. 30	Lisbon	0	0
†1964	Feb. 27	Murcia	2	1
†IYT1964	Apr. 5	Amsterdam	4	0
†IYT1965	Apr. 17	Heilbronn	0	0
†1966	Mar. 30	Swindon	3	0
†IYT1967	May 7	Manisa	2	1
†1971	Mar. 31	Pamplona	2	3
†1971	Apr. 20	Luton	1	1
†1972	Feb. 9	Alicante	0	0
*†IYT1972	Mar. 15	Sheffield	4	1
*†IYT1975	Feb. 25	Bristol	1	1
*†IYT1975	Mar. 18	Madrid	1	0
†1976	Nov. 12	Monte Carlo	3	0
†IYT1978	May 7	Bukowas	1	0
†1978	Nov. 17	Monte Carlo	1	1
†IYT1981	May 25	Siegen	1	2
†IYT1983	May 13	Stoke	1	0
†IYT1990	July 29	Gyula	0	1
†1991	May 25	Wembley	1	1
†WYC1991	June 15	Faro	0	1

ENGLAND v SWEDEN

Year	Date	Venue	Eng	Swe
†IYT1971	May 24	Poprad	1	0
†1981	Sept. 5	Pazin	3	2
†1984	Sept. 10	Rovinj	1	1
†1986	Nov. 10	West Bromwich	3	3
†1988	May 19	Sion	2	0

ENGLAND v SWITZERLAND

Year	Date	Venue	Eng	Swit
IYT1950	May 26	Stockerau	2	1
IYT1951	Mar. 27	Nice	3	1
IYT1952	Apr. 13	Barcelona	4	0
IYT1955	Apr. 11	Florence	0	1
1956	Mar. 11	Schaffhausen	2	0
1956	Oct. 13	Brighton	2	2
1958	May 26	Zurich	3	0
†1960	Oct. 8	Leyton	4	3
*1962	Nov. 22	Coventry	1	0
†1963	Mar. 21	Bienne	7	1

			Eng	Swit
†IYT1973	June 2	Forte Dei Marmi	2	0
†IYT1975	May 11	Buochs	4	0
†1980	Sept. 4	Rovinj	3	0
†1982	Sept. 6	Porec	2	0
†1983	July 26	Hajduboszormeny	4	0
†1983	Sept. 1	Porec	4	2

ENGLAND v SYRIA

			Eng	Syria
†WYC1991	June 18	Faro	3	3

ENGLAND v THAILAND

			Eng	Thai
†1986	May 7	Peking	1	2

ENGLAND v TRINIDAD & TOBAGO

			Eng	Trin
†1991	Mar. 25	Port of Spain	4	0

ENGLAND v TURKEY

			Eng	Turk
IYT1959	Mar. 29	Dimitrovo	1	1
†IYT1978	May 5	Wodzislaw	1	1

ENGLAND v URUGUAY

			Eng	Uru
†1977	Oct. 9	Las Palmas	1	1
†1987	June 10	Montevideo	2	2
†WYC1991	June 20	Faro	0	0

ENGLAND v USSR

			Eng	USSR
†IYT1963	Apr. 17	Tottenham	2	0
†IYT1967	May 13	Istanbul	0	1
†IYT1968	Apr. 11	Nimes	1	1
†IYT1971	May 28	Prague	1	1
†1978	Oct. 10	Las Palmas	1	0
†1982	Sept. 4	Umag	1	0
†1983	Mar. 29	Cannes	0	0
†IYT1983	May 17	Aston Villa	0	2
†IYT1984	May 27	Moscow	1	1
†1984	Sept. 8	Porec	1	0
†1985	Apr. 3	Cannes	2	1
†1985	June 3	Toulon	0	2
†IYT1990	July 26	Debrecen	1	3

ENGLAND v WALES

			Eng	Wales
1948	Feb. 28	High Wycombe	4	3
IYT1948	Apr. 15	London	4	0
1949	Feb. 26	Swansea	0	0

Year	Date	Venue	Goals	
			Eng	Wales
1950	Feb. 25	Worcester	1	0
1951	Feb. 17	Wrexham	1	1
1952	Feb. 23	Plymouth	6	0
1953	Feb. 21	Swansea	4	2
1954	Feb. 20	Derby	2	1
1955	Feb. 19	Milford Haven	7	2
1956	Feb. 18	Shrewsbury	5	1
1957	Feb. 9	Cardiff	7	1
1958	Feb. 15	Reading	8	2
1959	Feb. 14	Portmadoc	3	0
1960	Mar. 19	Canterbury	1	1
1961	Mar. 18	Newtown	4	0
1962	Mar. 17	Swindon	4	0
1963	Mar. 16	Haverfordwest	1	0
1964	Mar. 14	Leeds	2	1
1965	Mar. 20	Newport	2	2
1966	Mar. 19	Northampton	4	1
1967	Mar. 18	Cwmbran	3	3
1968	Mar. 16	Watford	2	3
1969	Mar. 15	Haverfordwest	3	1
*†IYT1970	Feb. 25	Newport	0	0
*†IYT1970	Mar. 18	Leyton	1	2
1970	Apr. 20	Reading	0	0
1971	Feb. 20	Aberystwyth	1	2
1972	Feb. 19	Swindon	4	0
1973	Feb. 24	Portmadoc	4	1
*†IYT1974	Jan. 9	West Bromwich	1	0
1974	Mar. 2	Shrewsbury	2	1
*†IYT1974	Mar. 13	Cardiff	0	1
*†IYT1976	Feb. 11	Cardiff	1	0
*†IYT1976	Mar. 3	Manchester	2	3
*†IYT1977	Mar. 9	West Bromwich	1	0
•†IYT1977	Mar. 23	Cardiff	1	1
*†IYT1991	Apr. 30	Wrexham	1	0
*†IYT1991	May 22	Yeovil	3	0

ENGLAND v YUGOSLAVIA

			Eng	Yugo
IYT1953	Apr. 2	Liege	1	1
1958	Feb. 4	Chelsea	2	2
IYT1962	Apr. 20	Ploesti	0	5
†IYT1967	May 9	Izmir	1	1
†IYT1971	May 22	Bardejov	1	0
†IYT1972	May 17	Barcelona	1	0
†1976	Nov. 16	Monte Carlo	0	3
†1978	May 20	Altenberg	2	0
†1981	Sept. 10	Pula	5	0
†1982	Sept. 9	Pula	1	0
†1983	July 25	Debrechen	4	4
†1983	Sept. 8	Pula	2	2
†1984	Sept. 12	Buje	1	4

Football League Champions 1888-1991

FIRST DIVISION 1888-1991

Season	Winners	Pts	Max	Season	Winners	Pts	Max
1888-89	Preston North End	40		1938-39	Everton	59	
1889-90	Preston North End	33	} 44	1946-47	Liverpool	57	
1890-91	Everton	29		1947-48	Arsenal	59	
1891-92	Sunderland	42	52	1948-49	Portsmouth	58	
1892-93	Sunderland	48		1949-50 *	Portsmouth	53	} 84
1893-94	Aston Villa	44		1950-51	Tottenham Hotspur	60	
1894-95	Sunderland	47		1951-52	Manchester United	57	
1895-96	Aston Villa	45	} 60	1952-53 *	Arsenal	54	
1896-97	Aston Villa	47		1953-54	Wolverhampton Wanderers	57	
1897-98	Sheffield United	42		1954-55	Chelsea	52	
1898-99	Aston Villa	45		1955-56	Manchester United	60	
1899-1900	Aston Villa	50		1956-57	Manchester United	64	
1900-01	Liverpool	45		1957-58	Wolverhampton Wanderers	64	
1901-02	Sunderland	44	} 68	1958-59	Wolverhampton Wanderers	61	} 84
1902-03	Sheffield Wednesday	42		1959-60	Burnley	55	
1903-04	Sheffield Wednesday	47		1960-61	Tottenham Hotspur	66	
1904-05	Newcastle United	48		1961-62	Ipswich Town	56	
1905-06	Liverpool	51		1962-63	Everton	61	
1906-07	Newcastle United	51		1963-64	Liverpool	57	
1907-08	Manchester United	52		1964-65 *	Manchester United	61	
1908-09	Newcastle United	53		1965-66	Liverpool	61	
1909-10	Aston Villa	53	} 76	1966-67	Manchester United	60	
1910-11	Manchester United	52		1967-68	Manchester City	58	} 84
1911-12	Blackburn Rovers	49		1968-69	Leeds United	67	
1912-13	Sunderland	54		1969-70	Everton	66	
1913-14	Blackburn Rovers	51		1970-71	Arsenal	65	
1914-15	Everton	46		1971-72	Derby County	53	
1919-20	West Bromwich Albion	60		1972-73	Liverpool	60	
1920-21	Burnley	59		1973-74	Leeds United	62	
1921-22	Liverpool	57		1974-75	Derby County	58	
1922-23	Liverpool	60		1975-76	Liverpool	60	
1923-24 *	Huddersfield Town	57	} 84	1976-77	Liverpool	57	} 84
1924-25	Huddersfield Town	58		1977-78	Nottingham Forest	64	
1925-26	Huddersfield Town	57		1978-79	Liverpool	68	
1926-27	Newcastle United	56		1979-80	Liverpool	60	
1927-28	Everton	53		1980-81	Aston Villa	60	
1928-29	Sheffield Wednesday	52		1981-82	Liverpool	87	
1929-30	Sheffield Wednesday	60		1982-83	Liverpool	82	
1930-31	Arsenal	66		1983-84	Liverpool	80	
1931-32	Everton	56		1984-85	Everton	90	} 126
1932-33	Arsenal	58		1985-86	Liverpool	88	
1933-34	Arsenal	59	} 84	1986-87	Everton	86	
1934-35	Arsenal	58		1987-88	Liverpool	90	120
1935-36	Sunderland	56		1988-89 *	Arsenal	76	
1936-37	Manchester City	57		1989-90	Liverpool	79	} 114
1937-38	Arsenal	52		1990-91	Arsenal	83	

SECOND DIVISION 1892-1991

Season	Winners	Pts	Max	Season	Winners	Pts	Max
1892-93	Small Heath	36	44	1913-14	Notts County	53	
1893-94	Liverpool	50	56	1914-15	Derby County	53	
1894-95	Bury	48		1919-20	Tottenham Hotspur	70	
1895-96 *	Liverpool	46	} 60	1920-21	Birmingham	58	
1896-97	Notts. County	42		1921-22	Nottingham Forrest	56	
1897-98	Burnley	48		1922-23	Notts County	53	} 76
1898-99	Manchester City	52		1923-24	Leeds United	54	
1899-1900	Sheffield Wednesday	54		1924-25	Leicester City	59	
1900-01	Grimsby Town	49		1925-26	Sheffield Wednesday	60	
1901-02	West Bromwich Albion	55	} 68	1926-27	Middlesborough	62	
1902-03	Manchester City	54		1927-28	Manchester City	59	
1903-04	Preston North End	50		1928-29	Middlesborough	55	
1904-05	Liverpool	58		1929-30	Blackpool	58	
1905-06	Bristol City	66		1930-31	Everton	61	
1906-07	Nottingham Forest	60		1931-32	Wolverhampton Wanderers	56	
1907-08	Bradford City	54		1932-33	Stoke City	56	} 76
1908-09	Bolton Wanderers	52	} 76	1933-34	Grimsby Town	59	
1909-10	Manchester City	54		1934-35	Brentford	61	
1910-11	West Bromwich Albion	53		1935-36	Manchester United	56	
1911-12	Derby County	54		1936-37	Leicester City	56	
1912-13	Preston North End	53		1937-38	Aston Villa	57	

*Won on goal average/difference

No competition 1915-19 and 1939-46

SECOND DIVISION 1892-1991 *(cont'd)*

Season	Winners	Pts	Max	Season	Winners	Pts	Max
1938-39	Blackburn Rovers	55		1968-69	Derby County	63	
1946-47	Manchester City	62		1969-70	Huddersfield Town	60	
1947-48	Birmingham City	59		1970-71	Leicester City	59	
1948-49	Fulham	57		1971-72	Norwich City	57	84
1949-50	Tottenham Hotspur	61		1972-73	Burnley	62	
1950-51	Preston North End	57	84	1973-74	Middlesbrough	65	
1951-52	Sheffield Wednesday	53		1974-75	Manchester City	61	
1952-53	Sheffield United	60		1975-76	Sunderland	56	
1953-54	* Leicester City	56		1976-77	Wolverhampton Wanderers	57	
1954-55	* Birmingham City	54		1977-78	Bolton Wanderers	58	84
1955-56	Sheffield Wednesday	55		1978-79	Crystal Palace	57	
1956-57	Leicester City	61		1979-80	Leicester City	55	
1957-58	West Ham United	57		1980-81	West Ham United	66	
1958-59	Sheffield Wednesday	62		1981-82	Luton Town	88	
1959-60	Aston Villa	59		1982-83	Queens Park Rangers	85	
1960-61	Ipswich Town	59		1983-84	* Chelsea	88	126
1961-62	Liverpool	62		1984-85	Oxford United	84	
1962-63	Stoke City	53	84	1985-86	Norwich City	84	
1963-64	Leeds United	63		1986-87	Derby County	84	
1964-65	Newcastle United	57		1987-88	Millwall	82	132
1965-66	Manchester City	59		1988-89	Chelsea	99	
1966-67	Coventry City	59		1989-90	Leeds United	85	138
1967-68	Ipswich Town	59		1990-91	Oldham Athletic	88	

THIRD DIVISION (S) 1920-58

Season	Winners	Pts	Max	Season	Winners	Pts	Max
1920-21	Crystal Palace	59		1936-37	Luton Town	58	
1921-22	* Southampton	61		1937-38	Millwall	56	
1922-23	Bristol City	59		1938-39	Newport County	55	
1923-24	Portsmouth	59	84	1946-47	Cardiff City	66	84
1924-25	Swansea Town	57		1947-48	Queens Park Rangers	61	
1925-26	Reading	57		1948-49	Swansea Town	62	
1926-27	Bristol City	62		1949-50	Notts County	58	
1927-28	Millwall	65		1950-51	Nottingham Forest	70	
1928-29	* Charlton Athletic	54		1951-52	Plymouth Argyle	66	
1929-30	Plymouth Argyle	68		1952-53	Bristol Rovers	64	
1930-31	Notts County	59		1953-54	Ipswich Town	64	
1931-32	Fulham	57		1954-55	Bristol City	70	92
1932-33	Brentford	62	84	1955-56	Leyton Orient	66	
1933-34	Norwich City	61		1956-57	* Ipswich Town	59	
1934-35	Charlton Athletic	61		1957-58	Brighton and Hove Albion	60	
1935-36	Coventry City	57					

THIRD DIVISION (N) 1921-58

Season	Winners	Pts	Max	Season	Winners	Pts	Max
1921-22	Stockport County	56	76	1936-37	Stockport County	60	
1922-23	Nelson	51		1937-38	Tranmere Rovers	56	
1923-24	Wolverhampton Wanderers	63		1938-39	Barnsley	67	
1924-25	Darlington	58		1946-47	Doncaster Rovers	72	84
1925-26	Grimsby Town	61		1947-48	Lincoln City	60	
1926-27	Stoke City	63		1948-49	Hull City	65	
1927-28	Bradford	63	84	1949-50	Doncaster Rovers	55	
1928-29	Bradford City	63		1950-51	Rotherham United	71	
1929-30	Port Vale	67		1951-52	Lincoln City	69	
1930-31	Chesterfield	58		1952-53	Oldham Athletic	59	
1931-32	* Lincoln City	57	80	1953-54	Port Vale	69	
1932-33	Hull City	59		1954-55	Barnsley	65	92
1933-34	Barnsley	62		1955-56	Grimsby Town	68	
1934-35	Doncaster Rovers	57	84	1956-57	Derby County	63	
1935-36	Chesterfield	60		1957-58	Scunthorpe United	66	

THIRD DIVISION 1958-91

Season	Winners	Pts	Max	Season	Winners	Pts	Max
1958-59	Plymouth Argyle	62		1962-63	Northampton Town	62	
1959-60	Southampton	61	92	1963-64	* Coventry City	60	92
1960-61	Bury	68		1964-65	Carlisle United	60	
1961-62	Portsmouth	65		1965-66	Hull City	69	

*Won on goal average

No competition 1939-46

THIRD DIVISION 1958-91 (cont'd)

Season	Winners	Pts	Max	Season	Winners	Pts	Max
1966-67	Queens Park Rangers	67		1979-80	Grimsby Town	62	
1967-68	Oxford United	57		1980-81	Rotherham United	61	92
1968-69	* Watford	64		1981-82	Burnley	80	
1969-70	Orient	62	92	1982-83	Portsmouth	91	
1970-71	Preston North End	61		1983-84	Oxford United	95	
1971-72	Aston Villa	70		1984-85	Bradford City	94	
1972-73	Bolton Wanderers	61		1985-86	Reading	94	
1973-74	Oldham Athletic	62		1986-87	AFC Bournemouth	97	138
1974-75	Blackburn Rovers	60		1987-88	Sunderland	93	
1975-76	Hereford United	63	92	1988-89	Wolverhampton Wanderers	92	
1976-77	Mansfield Town	64		1989-90	Bristol Rovers	93	
1977-78	Wrexham	61		1990-91	Cambridge United	86	
1978-79	Shrewsbury Town	61					

FOURTH DIVISION 1958-91

Season	Winners	Pts	Max	Season	Winners	Pts	Max
1958-59	Port Vale	64		1975-76	Lincoln City	74	
1959-60	Walsall	65	92	1976-77	Cambridge United	65	
1960-61	Peterborough United	66		1977-78	Watford	71	92
1961-62	Millwall	56	88	1978-79	Reading	65	
1962-63	Brentford	62		1979-80	Huddersfield Town	66	
1963-64	* Gillingham	60		1980-81	Southend United	67	
1964-65	Brighton and Hove Albion	63	92	1981-82	Sheffield United	96	
1965-66	Doncaster Rovers	59		1982-83	Wimbledon	98	
1966-67	Stockport County	64		1983-84	York City	101	
1967-68	Luton Town	66		1984-85	Chesterfield	91	
1968-69	Doncaster Rovers	59		1985-86	Swindon Town	102	138
1969-70	Chesterfield	64		1986-87	Northampton Town	99	
1970-71	Notts. County	69		1987-88	Wolverhampton Wanderers	90	
1971-72	Grimsby Town	63	92	1988-89	Rotherham United	82	
1972-73	Southport	62		1989-90	Exeter City	89	
1973-74	Peterborough United	65		1990-91	Darlington	83	
1974-75	Mansfield Town	68					

HEY
we're not selling you a
DUMMY

Review of the Barclays League Season 1990-91

George Graham's Arsenal won their second League championship in three years and tenth overall. They also became the first club this century to lose just one First Division match throughout the season, mid-table Chelsea edging them 2-1 at Stamford Bridge in February. When Liverpool, now managed by former midfield star Graeme Souness, failed to win the 'live' game at Nottingham Forest on Bank Holiday Monday (6 May), Arsenal knew the title was theirs. The champions still had two fixtures to fulfil and they finished the campaign in style with conclusive home victories against Manchester United (3-1) and Coventry City (6-1). So the 'Gunners' now compete in the European Cup for the first time for twenty years and Liverpool are back in Europe themselves (UEFA Cup) after a six-year exile.

Only two clubs were going to be relegated from the First Division this season and Sheffield United, with a mere four League points gained by Christmas, had looked certainties for a quick return to the Second. But they got their act together sufficiently to finish thirteenth. It was not until the last Saturday (11 May) that Sunderland knew they would be going down with hapless Derby County. Dennis Smith's team had achieved promotion in 1989-90 by a somewhat unusual route – finishing sixth in the Second Division and losing the play-off final to Swindon Town (later demoted) – and they had to win their last fixture at Maine Road to have any chance of staying in the top flight. City won 3-2 with David White's last-minute goal and Luton Town, 2-0 winners, had retained their First Division status on

the final day of the season for the third year in succession and the second time in a row against Derby. Luton fans reportedly celebrated by digging up the plastic pitch.

Three clubs with great First Division potential had forced the pace in the Second – West Ham United, Oldham Athletic and Sheffield Wednesday – and all three knew of their promotion before the last Saturday arrived. It was just a question of who would go on to clinch the championship. And that wasn't settled until the final *minute* of the season. The 'Hammers' came off the field at Upton Park on 11 May, 2-1 losers against Notts County but convinced that Oldham had only drawn at home. After the players had congratulated each other in the dressing room they heard the cruel news that Neil Redfearn had converted a spot-kick in the dying seconds. Oldham had frustratingly missed promotion in 1989-90 when distracted by unexpected success in the Littlewoods Cup (finalists) and the FA Cup (semi-finalists). Wednesday were back in the First Division just twelve months after traumatic relegation and, in a marvellous season for Ron Atkinson, his team lifted the Rumbelows Cup at Wembley too.

As in the First, only two clubs would go down from the Second this time. Hull City's home defeat against Brighton on 27 April consigned them to the drop and several clubs found themselves dangerously close to accompanying them. Watford and Swindon pulled clear and left two 'big' clubs on the same points, Leicester City and West Bromwich Albion, to fight it out on the last Saturday. Leicester achieved arguably the most important result in the 107-year history by beating Oxford United 1-0 at Filbert Street to remain in Division 2. Albion got a draw at Bristol Rovers with Tony Ford's last-minute effort but it wasn't enough.

Southend United and Grimsby Town looked automatic promotion candidates for much of the season and in the end they both made it up into the Second Division, although the latter managed it only on goal difference from Bolton Wanderers. But Cambridge United were a revelation. Heavily involved in the FA Cup once again (quarter-finalists for the second year running) they were a long way behind the leading group but had a significant number of games in hand. Southend lost their chance of the championship when Brentford won at Roots Hall on 11 May and Cambridge, two promotions in two years under John Beck, took it with a 2-0 home victory against Swansea City in front of a season's best crowd of over 9,000. Going into the last Saturday, any one of five clubs could have joined Bolton, Tranmere Rovers and Brentford in the play-offs. Bury's 2-1 win at Tranmere proved decisive.

The Fourth Division champions were Darlington, the GM Vauxhall Conference's top team from the previous season. It had been very close in the final weeks and five clubs were in with a chance of the title as they started their matches on 11 May. Darlington (2-0 v Rochdale), Stockport County (5-0 v Scunthorpe United) and Hartlepool United (3-1 v Northampton Town) all won at home to confirm their top three positions. Peterborough United drew at Chesterfield after being 2-0 down and that was enough to hold off Blackpool's challenge for fourth spot.

Barclays League Play-Offs

Division 2
Semi-Finals: Middlesbrough v Notts County 1-1, 0-1
Brighton & Hove Albion v Millwall 4-1, 2-1
Final: Notts County v Brighton & Hove Albion 3-1 (at Wembley)

Division 3
Semi-Finals: Bury v Bolton Wanderers 1-1, 0-1
Brentford v Tranmere Rovers 2-2, 0-1
Final: Bolton Wanderers v Tranmere Rovers 0-1 (at Wembley)

Division 4
Semi-Finals: Scunthorpe United v Blackpool 1-1, 1-2
Torquay United v Burnley 2-0, 0-1
Final: Blackpool v Torquay United 2-2* (at Wembley)

*Torquay won on penalty-kicks

First Division Results 1990-91

(Home \ Away)	Arsenal	Aston Villa	Chelsea	Coventry City	Crystal Palace	Derby County	Everton	Leeds United	Liverpool	Luton Town	Manchester City	Manchester United	Norwich City	Nottingham Forest	Queens Park Rangers	Sheffield United	Southampton	Sunderland	Tottenham Hotspur	Wimbledon
Arsenal	—	5-0	4-1	6-1	4-0	3-0	1-0	2-0	3-0	2-1	2-2	3-1	2-0	1-1	2-0	4-1	4-0	1-0	0-0	2-2
Aston Villa	1-0	—	2-2	2-1	2-0	3-2	2-2	0-0	0-0	1-2	1-5	1-1	2-1	1-1	2-2	2-1	1-1	3-0	3-2	1-2
Chelsea	2-1	1-0	—	2-1	2-1	2-1	2-1	1-2	4-2	3-3	1-1	3-2	1-1	0-0	2-0	2-2	0-2	3-2	3-2	0-0
Coventry City	0-2	2-1	2-3	—	2-1	0-1	0-1	1-0	3-0	2-2	2-0	0-1	1-1	2-3	1-0	0-0	1-2	0-0	2-0	0-0
Crystal Palace	0-0	1-2	0-0	0-3	—	1-0	2-0	1-0	1-0	3-0	0-2	2-0	0-0	1-2	0-0	0-2	3-1	2-1	1-0	4-3
Derby County	0-2	0-2	0-1	1-0	0-2	—	0-1	2-3	1-7	2-2	1-1	0-0	1-1	1-2	1-0	1-1	6-2	3-3	0-1	1-1
Everton	1-1	1-0	2-1	1-1	0-0	1-0	—	0-2	2-3	2-1	0-0	0-2	0-1	1-0	0-0	2-1	3-0	2-0	2-2	1-0
Leeds United	2-2	2-0	4-1	2-0	1-2	1-0	3-1	—	1-0	1-0	3-2	0-0	2-0	0-0	3-0	2-0	2-0	0-0	2-0	1-1
Liverpool	3-0	2-0	2-1	1-0	3-0	1-1	3-1	4-5	—	4-0	3-0	3-1	3-0	2-0	3-1	2-0	3-1	2-1	2-0	3-0
Luton Town	1-1	2-0	1-1	1-3	2-1	1-0	1-0	1-0	1-1	—	2-0	1-0	1-0	1-0	2-1	4-0	3-3	1-2	2-1	1-1
Manchester City	2-2	1-5	1-1	3-1	1-3	1-1	2-0	1-2	2-2	1-0	—	1-0	1-2	1-3	1-0	1-1	2-1	3-2	2-1	1-1
Manchester United	0-1	1-1	2-3	1-0	1-0	0-0	2-0	1-1	1-1	1-0	1-0	—	3-0	1-0	2-1	2-0	2-0	3-1	1-1	1-1
Norwich City	0-2	2-1	1-1	1-0	0-0	1-1	0-1	2-0	0-0	1-0	1-2	3-0	—	1-3	0-0	2-1	2-0	2-0	1-2	2-1
Nottingham Forest	1-3	1-1	0-0	2-2	2-2	2-1	0-1	3-1	2-0	1-0	3-1	0-1	3-1	—	1-2	3-2	1-1	1-0	1-2	0-1
Queens Park Rangers	2-0	2-2	2-0	3-1	0-0	1-1	3-0	2-3	1-3	1-2	2-1	3-1	1-0	3-1	—	1-1	3-4	1-2	2-1	3-0
Sheffield United	2-0	2-1	0-1	1-0	2-0	1-1	2-1	2-0	1-1	0-1	1-1	2-1	1-1	3-2	1-1	—	2-0	0-0	1-1	0-1
Southampton	1-1	1-1	1-0	3-0	2-0	3-1	3-1	3-4	1-1	0-0	3-1	1-1	2-0	1-1	3-0	2-0	—	3-1	0-0	1-0
Sunderland	1-0	3-0	3-2	0-0	2-1	3-3	2-0	5-0	1-2	3-2	3-0	3-2	2-0	0-2	1-1	2-0	3-1	—	3-3	2-2
Tottenham Hotspur	0-0	2-2	3-2	2-0	1-0	3-3	1-1	0-2	2-0	0-0	2-1	1-1	1-2	1-2	2-1	1-2	2-2	3-0	—	5-1
Wimbledon	0-3	0-0	1-1	0-2	2-1	3-1	2-1	0-1	1-3	4-0	1-1	1-2	0-1	3-1	3-1	1-1	2-0	3-3	4-2	—

First Division Final Positions 1990-91

		Home					Away					Total			
	P	W	D	L	F	A	W	D	L	F	A	F	A	GD	Pts
1. Arsenal	38	15	4	0	51	10	9	9	1	23	8	74	18	+56	83
2. Liverpool	38	14	3	2	42	13	9	4	6	35	27	77	40	+37	76
3. Crystal Palace	38	11	6	2	26	17	9	3	7	24	24	50	41	+9	69
4. Leeds United	38	12	2	5	46	23	7	5	7	19	24	65	47	+18	64
5. Manchester City	38	12	3	4	35	25	5	8	6	29	28	64	53	+11	62
6. Manchester United	38	11	4	4	34	17	5	8	6	24	28	58	45	+13	59
7. Wimbledon	38	8	6	5	28	22	6	8	5	25	24	53	46	+7	56
8. Nottingham Forest	38	11	4	4	42	21	3	8	8	23	29	65	50	+15	54
9. Everton	38	9	5	5	26	15	4	7	8	24	31	50	46	+4	51
10. Tottenham Hotspur	38	8	9	2	35	22	3	7	9	16	28	51	50	+1	49
11. Chelsea	38	10	6	3	33	25	3	4	12	25	44	58	69	−11	49
12. Queen's Park Rangers	38	8	5	6	27	22	4	5	10	17	31	44	53	−9	46
13. Sheffield United	38	9	3	7	23	23	4	4	11	13	32	36	55	−19	46
14. Southampton	38	9	6	4	33	22	3	3	13	25	47	58	69	−11	45
15. Norwich City	38	9	3	7	27	32	4	3	12	14	32	41	64	−23	45
16. Coventry City	38	10	6	3	30	16	1	5	13	12	33	42	49	−7	44
17. Aston Villa	38	7	9	3	29	25	2	5	12	17	33	46	58	−12	41
18. Luton Town	38	7	5	7	22	18	3	2	14	20	43	42	61	−19	37
19. Sunderland	38	6	6	7	15	16	2	4	13	23	44	38	60	−22	34
20. Derby County	38	3	8	8	25	36	2	1	16	12	39	37	75	−38	24

Arsenal 2pts deducted; Manchester United 1pt deducted

Arsenal – First Division Champions.

Second Division Results 1990-91

	Barnsley	Blackburn Rovers	Brighton & Hove Albion	Bristol City	Bristol Rovers	Charlton Athletic	Hull City	Ipswich Town	Leicester City	Middlesbrough	Millwall	Newcastle United	Notts County	Oldham Athletic	Oxford United	Plymouth Argyle	Portsmouth	Port Vale	Sheffield Wednesday	Swindon Town	Watford	West Bromwich Albion	West Ham United	Wolverhampton Wanderers
Barnsley	—	1-2	1-0	2-0	1-0	1-1	3-1	5-1	0-0	1-0	1-2	1-0	1-0	0-1	3-0	1-0	4-0	1-1	1-1	5-1	2-1	1-1	1-0	1-1
Blackburn Rovers	0-1	—	1-0	0-1	2-2	2-2	3-1	0-1	4-1	1-0	1-0	0-1	0-1	3-1	1-3	0-0	1-1	1-1	1-0	2-1	0-2	0-3	3-1	1-1
Brighton & Hove Albion	1-0	1-0	—	0-1	0-1	3-2	3-1	2-1	3-0	2-4	0-0	4-2	0-0	1-2	0-3	3-2	3-2	1-2	0-4	3-3	3-0	2-0	1-0	1-1
Bristol City	2-0	4-2	3-1	—	1-0	0-1	4-1	4-2	1-0	3-0	1-4	1-0	3-2	2-0	1-0	1-1	4-1	2-0	0-1	0-4	3-2	2-0	1-1	1-1
Bristol Rovers	1-0	1-2	1-3	2-2	—	2-2	1-1	1-0	0-0	2-0	1-0	1-0	1-1	1-1	3-3	0-0	2-1	0-0	0-1	2-1	3-1	2-0	0-1	0-0
Charlton Athletic	2-1	0-0	1-2	2-1	2-2	—	2-1	1-1	1-2	0-1	0-0	2-1	3-1	2-2	3-3	0-1	0-2	3-2	0-1	1-2	1-2	1-0	1-1	1-2
Hull City	1-2	3-1	0-1	1-2	2-0	2-2	—	3-3	5-2	0-0	0-1	1-0	1-2	2-1	1-1	2-0	2-2	3-0	0-2	1-1	1-1	2-0	0-0	0-0
Ipswich Town	2-0	2-1	1-3	1-2	2-1	4-4	2-0	—	3-2	4-3	0-3	5-4	0-0	0-0	1-0	3-1	2-2	1-1	2-4	1-1	1-1	1-1	0-1	1-0
Leicester City	2-1	1-3	3-0	0-3	3-2	1-2	1-1	1-2	—	6-0	1-2	3-0	2-1	0-1	0-0	3-1	1-2	4-0	0-2	2-2	0-0	2-1	1-2	2-1
Middlesbrough	1-0	0-1	2-0	2-1	1-2	1-2	3-0	1-1	6-0	—	2-1	0-1	1-0	2-2	1-2	0-0	2-0	1-2	4-2	2-0	1-2	3-2	0-0	0-0
Millwall	4-1	2-1	3-0	1-2	1-1	3-1	3-3	2-2	2-1	2-1	—	3-0	1-2	0-0	3-2	4-1	2-1	2-0	2-2	1-0	0-2	4-1	1-1	1-1
Newcastle United	0-0	1-0	1-0	0-0	0-2	1-3	1-2	3-1	0-2	0-1	1-2	—	0-2	0-1	3-1	2-0	3-1	1-1	1-1	1-0	1-0	2-1	1-1	4-1
Notts County	2-3	4-1	2-1	3-2	3-2	2-2	2-1	2-0	2-2	3-2	0-1	1-1	—	2-1	3-3	4-0	1-0	2-0	3-2	0-0	1-0	1-2	2-1	1-1
Oldham Athletic	2-0	1-1	6-1	2-1	2-1	1-1	1-0	2-1	2-2	1-1	1-1	0-0	2-1	—	5-1	5-3	1-1	5-2	3-2	3-2	1-0	2-0	0-1	1-0
Oxford United	2-0	0-0	3-0	3-1	3-1	2-0	4-1	0-0	3-1	0-3	3-2	0-1	3-3	5-1	—	0-0	2-1	2-0	2-2	2-4	4-1	1-1	2-1	0-0
Plymouth Argyle	1-1	4-1	1-0	2-0	2-2	0-1	5-1	1-1	0-0	3-1	0-0	0-1	0-0	1-2	2-1	—	3-1	2-4	2-1	3-1	1-1	1-2	0-1	1-2
Portsmouth	0-0	0-0	0-1	4-1	3-1	1-1	0-0	1-2	5-2	2-0	2-1	2-2	2-1	1-4	0-0	3-1	—	2-4	2-0	3-1	0-1	1-3	1-1	2-2
Port Vale	0-1	3-0	1-3	3-2	4-1	2-0	5-1	2-2	1-0	2-5	0-2	3-2	2-2	1-0	2-0	5-1	2-4	—	2-4	3-1	0-0	2-1	0-1	3-1
Sheffield Wednesday	3-1	3-1	0-1	3-1	3-2	1-1	3-1	1-0	2-0	2-0	0-2	1-2	1-2	2-2	0-0	3-0	2-1	1-1	—	3-1	0-0	1-1	1-1	1-1
Swindon Town	1-2	1-1	1-1	0-1	2-1	0-0	0-1	1-1	0-0	1-3	1-2	1-1	1-3	2-2	2-0	1-1	2-1	1-2	2-1	—	2-0	2-1	0-1	1-1
Watford	0-0	0-3	0-1	2-3	0-2	2-1	1-1	1-2	2-1	0-1	0-1	1-1	2-2	1-1	2-0	2-0	0-1	2-1	0-0	2-2	—	1-1	1-0	0-0
West Bromwich Albion	1-1	2-0	1-1	2-1	3-1	1-0	1-1	3-1	1-0	0-1	0-1	1-1	1-2	0-0	3-3	1-2	0-0	1-0	1-3	2-1	1-1	—	0-0	2-2
West Ham United	3-2	1-0	2-1	1-0	1-0	1-0	7-1	3-1	2-1	0-0	3-1	2-1	0-2	0-0	2-0	2-2	0-1	3-1	1-1	2-0	1-0	0-0	—	2-1
Wolverhampton Wanderers	0-5	2-3	2-3	4-0	1-1	3-0	0-0	2-2	2-1	1-0	4-1	2-1	0-2	2-3	3-3	3-1	1-1	3-1	3-2	1-2	0-0	2-2	2-1	—

Second Division Final Positions 1990-91

		Home					Away					Total			
	P	W	D	L	F	A	W	D	L	F	A	F	A	GD	Pts
1. Oldham Athletic	46	17	5	1	55	21	8	8	7	28	32	83	53	+30	88
2. West Ham United	46	15	6	2	41	18	9	9	5	19	16	60	34	+26	87
3. Sheffield Wednesday	46	12	10	1	43	23	10	6	7	37	28	80	51	+29	82
4. Notts County	46	14	4	5	45	28	9	7	7	31	27	76	55	+21	80*
5. Millwall	46	11	6	6	43	28	9	7	7	27	23	70	51	+19	73
6. Brighton & Hove Albion	46	12	4	7	37	31	9	3	11	26	38	63	69	−6	70
7. Middlesbrough	46	12	4	7	36	17	8	5	10	30	30	66	47	+19	69
8. Barnsley	46	13	7	3	39	16	6	5	12	24	32	63	48	+15	69
9. Bristol City	46	14	5	4	44	28	6	2	15	24	43	68	71	−3	67
10. Oxford United	46	10	9	4	41	29	4	10	9	28	37	69	66	+3	61
11. Newcastle United	46	8	10	5	24	22	6	7	10	25	34	49	56	−7	59
12. Wolverhampton Wanderers	46	11	6	6	45	35	2	13	8	18	28	63	63	−	58
13. Bristol Rovers	46	11	7	5	29	20	4	6	13	27	39	56	59	−3	58
14. Ipswich Town	46	9	8	6	32	28	4	10	9	28	40	60	68	−8	57
15. Port Vale	46	10	4	9	32	24	5	8	10	24	40	56	64	−8	57
16. Charlton Athletic	46	8	7	8	27	25	5	10	8	30	36	57	61	−4	56
17. Portsmouth	46	10	6	7	34	27	4	5	14	24	43	58	70	−12	53
18. Plymouth Argyle	46	10	10	3	36	20	2	7	14	18	48	54	68	−14	53
19. Blackburn Rovers	46	8	6	9	26	27	6	4	13	25	39	51	66	−15	52
20. Watford	46	5	8	10	24	32	7	7	9	21	27	45	59	−14	51
21. Swindon Town	46	8	6	9	31	30	4	8	11	34	43	65	73	−8	50
22. Leicester City	46	12	4	7	41	33	2	4	17	19	50	60	83	−23	50
23. West Bromwich Albion	46	7	11	5	26	21	3	7	13	26	40	52	61	−9	48
24. Hull City	46	6	10	7	35	32	4	5	14	22	53	57	85	−28	45

* Promoted via the play-offs

Oldham Athletic – Second Division Champions.

Third Division Results 1990-91

	Birmingham City	Bolton Wanderers	A.F.C. Bournemouth	Bradford City	Brentford	Bury	Cambridge United	Chester City	Crewe Alexandra	Exeter City	Fulham	Grimsby Town	Huddersfield Town	Leyton Orient	Mansfield Town	Preston North End	Reading	Rotherham United	Shrewsbury Town	Southend United	Stoke City	Swansea City	Tranmere Rovers	Wigan Athletic
Birmingham City	—	1-3	1-2	1-1	0-2	1-0	0-3	1-0	0-2	1-1	2-0	0-0	1-2	3-1	0-0	1-2	1-1	2-1	0-1	1-0	2-1	2-0	1-0	0-0
Bolton Wanderers	3-1	—	1-0	1-0	1-0	1-3	2-2	2-0	3-2	1-0	3-0	1-3	1-1	1-0	1-1	1-2	3-1	0-0	3-2	3-1	1-1	1-0	2-1	2-1
A.F.C. Bournemouth	1-2	1-0	—	3-1	2-0	1-1	0-1	1-0	1-1	2-1	3-0	2-1	3-1	2-2	0-0	0-0	2-0	4-2	2-4	2-1	1-1	1-0	1-0	0-3
Bradford City	2-0	1-1	3-0	—	0-1	3-1	0-1	2-1	2-0	3-0	0-0	0-2	2-2	4-0	0-0	2-1	2-1	1-0	3-0	0-1	0-4	0-1	1-2	2-1
Brentford	2-2	4-2	0-0	6-1	—	3-2	0-1	0-1	1-3	3-1	1-2	1-2	1-0	1-0	0-0	3-1	1-0	1-2	2-1	1-4	1-1	1-0	0-2	1-0
Bury	0-1	2-2	2-4	0-0	1-1	—	3-1	0-1	3-4	1-0	1-0	1-2	2-1	1-0	1-0	1-1	3-0	3-1	2-1	1-0	3-0	2-0	3-0	2-2
Cambridge United	0-1	2-1	4-0	2-1	0-0	2-2	—	2-1	3-1	1-2	1-0	1-0	0-0	1-0	2-1	2-2	1-0	4-1	3-2	0-2	1-1	2-1	3-1	2-3
Chester City	1-1	0-2	0-0	4-2	1-2	1-0	3-1	—	3-1	1-1	1-0	1-2	1-2	1-0	1-0	4-0	0-1	1-2	3-0	1-2	1-1	3-0	0-2	1-2
Crewe Alexandra	0-2	1-3	1-3	0-0	3-3	2-2	0-1	1-1	—	3-2	0-1	1-2	1-1	2-0	3-0	1-0	1-1	3-1	4-0	0-3	2-0	2-0	2-3	1-0
Exeter City	2-2	2-1	2-0	2-2	1-1	2-0	0-2	1-1	2-1	—	3-0	0-0	2-2	3-3	2-0	4-1	3-0	2-0	1-0	1-0	0-1	1-1	0-0	1-2
Fulham	0-0	0-1	3-0	0-0	0-1	2-0	1-0	4-1	0-1	1-0	—	1-1	0-0	1-1	2-0	1-0	0-2	2-0	2-1	1-2	3-0	1-0	2-1	4-3
Grimsby Town	0-1	0-1	2-1	1-1	2-0	0-1	3-1	2-0	3-1	1-0	3-0	—	4-0	3-3	2-2	0-1	4-0	4-0	2-1	0-1	0-2	3-0	0-1	1-0
Huddersfield Town	1-1	4-0	3-1	1-2	1-2	1-0	0-3	0-0	3-2	1-0	1-0	1-3	—	2-1	2-1	3-3	2-0	3-0	3-2	0-1	1-0	2-0	4-0	1-1
Leyton Orient	1-2	0-1	2-2	2-1	1-2	0-1	2-2	2-2	1-3	1-0	1-1	1-1	0-0	—	3-1	1-0	1-2	1-2	2-1	0-1	2-0	0-0	0-2	2-1
Mansfield Town	2-0	1-2	0-0	0-1	0-1	1-0	0-2	2-1	5-1	1-0	1-0	0-0	1-2	2-2	—	0-1	0-2	1-2	4-3	2-4	0-0	2-3	0-4	3-1
Preston North End	2-2	4-0	0-0	0-3	1-2	1-0	2-2	1-1	2-1	2-4	3-1	2-0	1-3	0-0	1-1	—	5-1	2-0	1-2	0-1	2-0	1-2	1-0	5-1
Reading	1-1	0-1	2-0	1-2	2-2	0-3	3-2	2-2	1-0	2-1	2-1	1-1	0-0	3-0	0-3	0-1	—	0-0	2-1	4-0	1-0	4-1	0-1	0-0
Rotherham United	4-1	1-2	4-2	0-2	1-1	1-1	1-2	2-3	3-2	2-1	2-1	0-2	0-1	3-0	2-1	3-2	3-1	—	1-3	1-4	2-1	2-2	1-0	0-2
Shrewsbury Town	2-1	2-2	3-2	1-0	0-1	1-1	0-0	1-0	1-0	2-1	2-1	2-0	2-0	0-0	3-1	2-1	0-0	0-0	—	3-1	1-2	4-1	1-1	2-0
Southend United	0-1	0-1	3-1	1-0	2-2	1-1	1-1	1-2	3-2	2-1	2-2	0-0	1-0	3-0	2-1	2-1	5-1	2-1	2-2	—	0-0	2-3	0-1	1-6
Stoke City	2-0	1-1	1-1	2-1	2-1	2-2	2-0	1-1	1-0	2-1	1-1	1-2	2-0	1-2	3-1	3-1	1-2	3-1	1-3	4-0	—	1-2	1-0	1-1
Swansea City	1-0	2-2	1-2	0-2	1-2	1-2	2-0	2-3	3-1	0-3	2-0	2-0	1-0	0-0	1-2	2-1	3-1	5-0	0-1	1-3	2-1	—	1-1	2-0
Tranmere Rovers	1-0	1-1	1-0	2-1	1-0	1-2	2-0	1-0	2-0	1-0	1-1	1-2	2-0	3-0	6-2	2-1	0-0	1-2	1-1	3-1	1-1	2-4	—	1-1
Wigan Athletic	1-1	2-1	2-0	3-0	1-0	1-2	0-1	2-0	1-0	4-1	2-0	2-0	1-1	1-2	0-2	2-1	1-0	2-0	2-2	4-1	1-1	2-4	0-1	—

158

Third Division Final Positions 1990-91

	P	W	D	L	F	A	W	D	L	F	A	F	A	GD	Pts
			Home						Away				Total		
1. Cambridge United	46	14	5	4	42	22	11	6	6	33	23	75	45	+30	86
2. Southend United	46	13	6	4	34	23	13	1	9	33	28	67	51	+16	85
3. Grimsby Town	46	16	3	4	42	13	8	8	7	24	21	66	34	+32	83
4. Bolton Wanderers	46	14	5	4	33	18	10	6	7	31	32	64	50	+14	83
5. Tranmere Rovers	46	13	5	5	38	21	10	4	9	26	25	64	46	+18	78*
6. Brentford	46	12	4	7	30	22	9	9	5	29	25	59	47	+12	76
7. Bury	46	13	6	4	39	26	7	7	9	28	30	67	56	+11	73
8. Bradford City	46	13	3	7	36	22	7	7	9	26	32	62	54	+8	70
9. AFC Bournemouth	46	14	6	3	37	20	5	7	11	21	38	58	58	–	70
10. Wigan Athletic	46	14	3	6	40	20	6	6	11	31	34	71	54	+17	69
11. Huddersfield Town	46	13	3	7	37	23	5	10	8	20	28	57	51	+6	67
12. Birmingham City	46	8	9	6	21	21	8	8	7	24	28	45	49	–4	65
13. Leyton Orient	46	15	2	6	35	19	3	8	12	20	39	55	58	–3	64
14. Stoke City	46	9	7	7	36	29	7	5	11	19	30	55	59	–4	60
15. Reading	46	11	5	7	34	28	6	3	14	19	38	53	66	–13	59
16. Exeter City	46	12	6	5	35	16	4	3	16	23	36	58	52	+6	57
17. Preston North End	46	11	5	7	33	29	4	6	13	21	38	54	67	–13	56
18. Shrewsbury Town	46	8	7	8	29	22	6	3	14	32	46	61	68	–7	52
19. Chester City	46	10	3	10	27	27	4	6	13	19	31	46	58	–12	51
20. Swansea City	46	8	6	9	31	33	5	3	15	18	39	49	72	–23	48
21. Fulham	46	8	8	7	27	22	2	8	13	14	34	41	56	–15	46
22. Crewe Alexandra	46	6	9	8	35	35	5	2	16	27	45	62	80	–18	44
23. Rotherham United	46	5	10	8	31	38	5	2	16	19	49	50	87	–37	42
24. Mansfield Town	46	5	8	10	23	27	3	6	14	19	36	42	63	–21	38

* Promoted via the play-offs

Cambridge United – Third Division Champions.

Fourth Division Results 1990-91

	Aldershot	Blackpool	Burnley	Cardiff City	Carlisle United	Chesterfield	Darlington	Doncaster Rovers	Gillingham	Halifax Town	Hartlepool United	Hereford United	Lincoln City	Maidstone United	Northampton Town	Peterborough United	Rochdale	Scarborough	Scunthorpe United	Stockport County	Torquay United	Walsall	Wrexham	York City
Aldershot	—	1-4	1-2	0-0	3-0	1-0	0-2	1-1	1-0	2-2	1-5	1-0	0-3	4-3	3-3	5-0	2-2	2-2	3-2	2-2	2-3	0-4	3-2	0-1
Blackpool	4-2	—	1-2	3-0	6-0	2-2	1-2	1-0	2-2	5-3	1-2	3-0	1-1	1-0	0-0	1-1	2-1	0-1	2-0	0-0	2-1	2-0	0-1	0-1
Burnley	3-0	2-0	—	2-0	2-1	2-1	3-1	3-2	1-2	0-0	3-0	1-0	2-2	1-0	0-0	4-1	0-1	0-1	1-1	2-0	1-0	2-0	2-0	2-0
Cardiff City	1-3	1-1	3-0	—	3-1	0-0	3-1	1-1	4-0	1-2	1-0	1-1	0-1	3-0	0-0	1-1	0-0	1-2	1-0	3-3	3-3	0-2	2-0	2-1
Carlisle United	1-2	1-0	1-1	3-2	—	2-1	0-2	2-1	2-1	1-1	1-0	0-1	0-0	1-2	0-1	3-2	3-0	0-1	0-0	1-1	3-1	0-3	2-1	1-0
Chesterfield	1-0	2-2	2-1	0-0	2-1	—	1-0	0-1	2-1	2-0	2-3	1-0	1-1	1-2	1-0	2-2	2-0	1-1	1-1	1-0	1-1	2-2	2-1	2-2
Darlington	3-1	1-1	3-1	4-1	3-1	2-2	—	1-1	3-0	3-0	0-1	3-1	1-1	1-1	4-1	0-1	1-1	1-0	1-1	1-0	3-0	2-0	3-1	0-0
Doncaster Rovers	3-0	1-0	3-2	1-1	4-0	0-1	0-1	—	1-0	2-0	2-3	3-1	2-2	3-0	2-1	2-3	1-1	0-2	3-0	1-3	1-1	2-0	2-3	2-2
Gillingham	1-1	2-2	1-2	4-0	2-1	2-1	3-0	1-0	—	1-0	3-0	0-4	1-1	0-2	2-1	1-1	2-1	1-1	2-2	0-0	2-2	5-2	2-0	0-0
Halifax Town	3-0	5-3	0-0	1-2	1-1	2-0	3-0	2-0	1-0	—	1-2	2-1	0-1	3-2	2-0	2-0	1-0	1-2	1-0	0-0	0-1	2-1	2-1	2-1
Hartlepool United	1-0	1-2	3-0	0-1	4-1	2-3	1-2	0-1	1-1	1-2	—	2-1	0-1	1-0	1-0	0-0	2-0	3-3	0-1	3-1	0-0	2-2	1-0	0-1
Hereford United	1-0	3-0	1-0	1-1	6-2	1-0	0-1	2-0	1-1	2-1	1-3	—	0-1	4-0	3-0	0-2	1-2	2-0	0-4	0-0	0-0	2-1	0-0	2-0
Lincoln City	2-2	1-1	1-0	0-0	0-0	1-1	1-0	2-2	1-1	0-1	1-4	0-1	—	2-1	1-1	2-0	0-1	0-1	2-2	0-3	3-2	1-3	0-2	2-0
Maidstone United	1-1	1-0	1-0	3-0	1-1	1-2	1-0	3-0	0-0	3-2	3-2	4-0	4-1	—	2-0	1-2	3-2	0-2	3-2	2-3	2-2	5-0	1-0	5-4
Northampton Town	2-1	0-0	0-0	0-0	0-1	0-0	4-1	2-1	2-1	2-0	1-0	3-0	1-1	2-0	—	0-0	1-0	2-0	1-0	0-0	1-4	2-1	2-2	2-1
Peterborough United	3-2	3-2	4-1	3-0	3-2	2-2	0-1	2-3	1-1	2-0	2-0	2-1	2-0	1-1	1-0	—	1-2	1-1	0-2	0-2	1-2	1-0	1-0	2-0
Rochdale	4-0	2-1	0-1	0-0	3-0	2-0	1-1	1-1	2-1	1-0	1-3	3-0	0-0	3-2	1-1	0-3	—	0-0	0-3	0-3	0-0	1-0	2-2	2-1
Scarborough	2-0	0-1	0-1	1-2	1-1	3-0	2-3	1-1	1-1	1-2	0-1	4-2	3-0	0-2	3-0	1-1	0-0	—	2-3	2-3	3-2	3-2	2-0	2-2
Scunthorpe United	6-2	2-0	1-3	0-2	0-1	1-1	1-1	3-0	2-2	1-0	2-0	0-4	2-1	3-2	2-0	0-2	0-3	3-0	—	0-0	2-2	1-0	4-2	2-1
Stockport County	3-2	0-0	2-0	2-1	3-1	1-0	1-0	1-3	0-0	0-0	1-3	0-0	4-0	2-3	0-0	0-2	3-0	2-2	0-2	—	3-0	1-0	2-0	2-0
Torquay United	5-0	2-1	1-0	0-0	3-0	1-1	3-0	1-1	2-2	0-1	0-1	1-0	0-1	2-2	3-3	1-2	0-0	3-2	3-0	1-1	—	0-0	1-0	2-1
Walsall	2-2	2-0	2-0	1-0	1-1	2-2	2-0	2-0	5-2	2-1	2-2	2-1	0-0	5-0	0-2	1-0	1-0	3-2	1-1	0-2	2-1	—	1-0	1-1
Wrexham	4-2	0-1	2-4	1-2	3-0	2-1	3-1	2-3	2-0	2-1	0-0	0-0	2-2	1-0	2-2	0-4	2-1	2-0	0-2	1-3	0-1	1-1	—	0-4
York City	2-0	0-1	2-0	1-2	2-0	2-2	0-0	2-2	0-0	2-1	0-1	2-0	1-0	5-4	2-1	2-0	2-1	2-2	0-2	0-2	0-0	1-0	0-0	—

Fourth Division Final Positions 1990-91

	P	Home					Away					Total			
	P	W	D	L	F	A	W	D	L	F	A	F	A	GD	Pts
1. Darlington	46	13	8	2	36	14	9	9	5	32	24	68	38	+30	83
2. Stockport County	46	16	6	1	54	19	7	7	9	30	28	84	47	+37	82
3. Hartlepool United	46	15	5	3	35	15	9	5	9	32	33	67	48	+19	82
4. Peterborough United	46	13	9	1	38	15	8	8	7	29	30	67	45	+22	80
5. Blackpool	46	17	3	3	55	17	6	7	10	23	30	78	47	+31	79
6. Burnley	46	17	5	1	46	16	6	5	12	24	35	70	51	+19	79
7. Torquay United	46	14	7	2	37	13	4	11	8	27	34	64	47	+17	72*
8. Scunthorpe United	46	17	4	2	51	20	3	7	13	20	42	71	62	+9	71
9. Scarborough	46	13	5	5	36	21	6	7	10	23	35	59	56	+3	69
10. Northampton Town	46	14	5	4	34	21	4	8	11	23	37	57	58	−1	67
11. Doncaster Rovers	46	12	5	6	36	22	5	9	9	20	24	56	46	+10	65
12. Rochdale	46	10	9	4	29	22	5	8	10	21	31	50	53	−3	62
13. Cardiff City	46	10	6	7	26	23	5	9	9	17	31	43	54	−11	60
14. Lincoln City	46	10	7	6	32	27	4	10	9	18	34	50	61	−11	59
15. Gillingham	46	9	9	5	35	27	3	9	11	22	33	57	60	−3	54
16. Walsall	46	7	12	4	25	17	5	5	13	23	34	48	51	−3	53
17. Hereford United	46	9	10	4	32	19	4	4	15	21	39	53	58	−5	53
18. Chesterfield	46	8	12	3	33	26	5	2	16	14	36	47	62	−15	53
19. Maidstone United	46	9	5	9	42	34	4	7	12	24	37	66	71	−5	51
20. Carlisle United	46	12	3	8	30	30	1	6	16	17	59	47	89	−42	48
21. York City	46	8	6	9	21	23	3	7	13	24	34	45	57	−12	46
22. Halifax Town	46	9	6	8	34	29	3	4	16	25	50	59	79	−20	46
23. Aldershot	46	8	7	8	38	43	2	4	17	23	58	61	101	−40	41
24. Wrexham	46	8	7	8	33	34	2	3	18	15	40	48	74	−26	40

* Promoted via the play-offs

Darlington – Fourth Division Champions.

Football League/Milk/Littlewoods/Rumbelows Cup Winners 1961-91

Year		Winners	Runners-up	Score	Venue
1961	*	Aston Villa	Rotherham United	3-2	
1962	*	Norwich City	Rochdale	4-0	
1963	*	Birmingham City	Aston Villa	3-1	
1964	*	Leicester City	Stoke City	4-3	
1965	*	Chelsea	Leicester City	3-2	
1966	*	West Bromwich Albion	West Ham United	5-3	
1967		Queens Park Rangers	West Bromwich Albion	3-2	Wembley
1968		Leeds United	Arsenal	1-0	Wembley
1969	†	Swindon Town	Arsenal	3-1	Wembley
1970	†	Manchester City	West Bromwich Albion	2-1	Wembley
1971		Tottenham Hotspur	Aston Villa	2-0	Wembley
1972		Stoke City	Chelsea	2-1	Wembley
1973		Tottenham Hotspur	Norwich City	1-0	Wembley
1974		Wolverhampton Wanderers	Manchester City	2-1	Wembley
1975		Aston Villa	Norwich City	1-0	Wembley
1976		Manchester City	Newcastle United	2-1	Wembley
1977	§	Aston Villa	Everton	3-2	Wembley
1978	¶	Nottingham Forest	Liverpool	1-0	Manchester
1979		Nottingham Forest	Southampton	3-2	Wembley
1980		Wolverhampton Wanderers	Nottingham Forest	1-0	Wembley
1981	∫	Liverpool	West Ham United	2-1	Birmingham
1982	†	Liverpool	Tottenham Hotspur	3-1	Wembley
1983	†	Liverpool	Manchester United	2-1	Wembley
1984	¶	Liverpool	Everton	1-0	Manchester
1985		Norwich City	Sunderland	1-0	Wembley
1986		Oxford United	Queens Park Rangers	3-0	Wembley
1987		Arsenal	Liverpool	2-1	Wembley
1988		Luton Town	Arsenal	3-2	Wembley
1989		Nottingham Forest	Luton Town	3-1	Wembley
1990		Nottingham Forest	Oldham Athletic	1-0	Wembley
1991		Sheffield Wednesday	Manchester United	1-0	Wembley

*Aggregate score †After extra time §After 0-0 and 1-1 draws at Wembley and Sheffield
¶After 0-0 draw at Wembley ∫ After 1-1 draw at Wembley

Rumbelows League Cup 1990-91

First Round (Two Legs)

Birmingham City	0:1	AFC Bournemouth	1:1
Bradford City	2:2	Bury	0:3
Brentford	2:0	Hereford United	0:1
Brighton & Hove Albion	0:1	Northampton Town	2:1
Bristol Rovers	1:1	Torquay United	2:1
Carlisle United	1:1	Scunthorpe United	0:1
Chesterfield	1:2	Hartlepool United	2:2
Darlington	0:1†	Blackpool	0-1
Doncaster Rovers	2:1	Rotherham United	6:2
Exeter City	1:0	Notts County	1:1
Fulham	1:0	Peterborough United	2:2
Gillingham	1:0	Shrewsbury Town	0:2
Grimsby Town	2:0	Crewe Alexandra	1:1†
Halifax Town	2:0	Lincoln City	0:1
Huddersfield Town	0:1	Bolton Wanderers	3:2
Maidstone United	2:1	Leyton Orient	2:4
Mansfield Town	1:0	Cardiff City	1:3
Middlesbrough	1:2	Tranmere Rovers	1:1
Preston North End	2:1	Chester City	0:5
Reading	0:1	Oxford United	1:2
Rochdale	4:3	Scarborough	0:3
Southend United	2:2	Aldershot	1:2
Stockport County	0:1	Burnley	2:0
Stoke City	0:1	Swansea City	0:0
Walsall	4:1	Cambridge United	2:2
West Bromwich Albion	2:0	Bristol City	2:1
Wigan Athletic	0:1	Barnsley	1:0§
York City	0:0	Wrexham	1:2

Rumbelows League Cup Competition 1990-91

```
Sheffield Wednesday  2:2 ┐
Brentford            1:1 ┘ *Sheffield Weds    0:1 ┐
Darlington           3:0 ┐                        ├ *Sheffield Weds  1:2 ┐
Swindon Town         0:4 ┘  Swindon Town     0:0 ┘                      ├ Sheffield Weds  1 ┐
Carlisle United      1:0 ┐                                              │                   │
Derby County         1:1 ┘ *Derby County      6  ┐                      │                   │
Sunderland           0:6 ┐                        ├ Derby County  1:1 ──┘                    │
Bristol City         1:1 ┘  Sunderland       0    ┘                                          ├ Sheff. Weds  2:3 ┐
Coventry City        4:3 ┐                                                                   │                  │
Bolton Wanderers     2:2 ┘ *Coventry City     3  ┐                                           │                  │
Hull City            0:1† ┐                       ├ *Coventry City  5  ┐                      │                  │
Wolves               0:1 ┘  Hull City        0    ┘                    ├ *Coventry City  0 ──┘                  │
Plymouth Argyle      1:2 ┐                                             │                                        │
Wimbledon            0:0 ┘ *Plymouth Argyle   1  ┐                     │                                        │
Nottingham Forest    4:1 ┐                        ├ Nottm Forest  4 ───┘             First leg at              │
Burnley              1:0 ┘  Nottingham Forest 2   ┘                                 Chelsea                     │
Port Vale            0:0 ┐                                                          Second leg at              │
Oxford United        2:0 ┘ *Oxford United     2  ┐                                  Sheffield                   ├─ Sheffield Wednesday 1
West Ham United      3:2 ┐                        ├ *Oxford United  1  ┐                                         │
Stoke City           0:1 ┘  West Ham United   1   ┘                    ├ *Chelsea     0:3 ┐                      │
Walsall              0:1 ┐                                             │                  │                      │
Chelsea              5:4 ┘ *Chelsea           0:3 ┐                    │                  │                      │
Cardiff City         1:1 ┐                        ├ Chelsea       2 ──┘                  ├ Chelsea      0:1 ─────┘
Portsmouth           1:3 ┘  Portsmouth        0:2 ┘                                       │
Northampton Town     0:1 ┐                                                                │
Sheffield United     1:2 ┘ *Sheffield United  2  ┐                                        │
Wrexham              0:0 ┐                        ├ *Sheffield Utd  0  ┐                   │
Everton              5:6 ┘  Everton           1   ┘                    ├ Tottenham    0:0 ┘
Tottenham Hotspur    5:2 ┐                                             │
Hartlepool United    0:1 ┘ *Tottenham Hotspur 2  ┐                     │
Luton Town           1:1 ┐                        ├ Tottenham     2 ───┘
Bradford City        1:1§ ┘  Bradford City     1   ┘
Queens Park Rangers  3:1 ┐
Peterborough United  1:1 ┘ *Queens Park Rangers 2 ┐
Rotherham United     1:0 ┐                         ├ *QPR          0  ┐
Blackburn Rovers     1:1 ┘  Blackburn Rovers  1    ┘                  ├ *Leeds United  4 ┐
Leicester City       1:0 ┐                                           │                  │
Leeds United         1:3 ┘ *Leeds United      2  ┐                    │                  │
Notts County         1:2 ┐                        ├ Leeds United  3 ──┘                  ├ Leeds Utd    1:0 ┐
Oldham Athletic      0:5 ┘  Oldham Athletic   0   ┘                                       │                 │
Aston Villa          1:1 ┐                                                                │                 │
Barnsley             0:0 ┘ *Aston Villa        2  ┐                                        │                 │
A.F.C. Bournemouth   0:1 ┐                         ├ *Aston Villa  3  ┐                     │                 │
Millwall             0:2 ┘  Millwall          0    ┘                  ├ Aston Villa   1 ──┘                  │
Middlesbrough        2:0 ┐                                            │            First leg at             │
Newcastle United     0:1 ┘ *Middlesbrough      2  ┐                    │            Manchester                │
Norwich City         2:3 ┐                         ├ Middlesbrough 2 ──┘            Second leg                │
Watford              0:0 ┘  Norwich City      0    ┘                               at Leeds                   ├─ Manchester United 0
Shrewsbury Town      1:0 ┐                                                                                     │
Ipswich Town         1:3 ┘ *Ipswich Town      0  ┐                                                             │
Rochdale             0:0 ┐                         ├ *Southampton  2  ┐                                         │
Southampton          5:3 ┘  Southampton       2    ┘                  ├ *Southampton  1:2 ┐                    │
Crystal Palace       8:2 ┐                                            │                   │                    │
Southend United      0:1 ┘ *Crystal Palace     0:1 ┐                   │                   │                    │
Charlton Athletic    2:0 ┐                          ├ Crystal Palace 0 ┘                   ├ Man. United  2:1 ──┘
Leyton Orient        2:1 ┘  Leyton Orient     0:0  ┘                                       │
Torquay United       0:0 ┐                                                                 │
Manchester City      4:0 ┘ *Manchester City    1  ┐                                         │
Chester City         0:0 ┐                         ├ *Arsenal      2  ┐                      │
Arsenal              1:5 ┘  Arsenal           2    ┘                  ├ Man. United   1:3 ──┘
Liverpool            5:4 ┐                                            │
Crewe Alexandra      1:1 ┘  Liverpool          1  ┐                   │
Halifax Town         1:1 ┐                         ├ Man. United   6 ─┘
Manchester United    3:2 ┘ *Manchester United  3  ┘
```

At Wembley

* Denotes home team in first match †Won on away goals §Won on penalty-kicks

163

Leyland Daf Cup Competition 1990-91

Preliminary Round

Northern Section

Bolton Wanderers	1	Tranmere Rovers	0
Tranmere Rovers	4	Blackpool	0
Blackpool	3	Bolton Wanderers	0
Burnley	2	Crewe Alexandra	1
Crewe Alexandra	1	Stockport County	1
Stockport County	1	Burnley	1
Carlisle United	1	Preston North End	1
Preston North End	3	Rochdale	1
Rochdale	1	Carlisle United	0
Wigan Athletic	4	Chester City	0
Chester City	2	Bury	0
Bury	2	Wigan Athletic	1
Bradford City	1	Huddersfield Town	1
Huddersfield Town	1	Hartlepool United	4
Hartlepool United	0	Bradford City	4
Halifax Town	1	Rotherham United	1
Rotherham United	1	Scarborough	1
Scarborough	1	Halifax Town	2
Grimsby Town	1	York City	3
York City	3	Darlington	2
Darlington	3	Grimsby Town	1
Chesterfield	1	Doncaster Rovers	1
Doncaster Rovers	1	Scunthorpe United	0
Scunthorpe United	3	Chesterfield	1

Southern Section

Stoke City	1	Northampton Town	1
Northampton Town	1	Mansfield Town	2
Mansfield Town	3	Stoke City	0
Cambridge United	1	Wrexham	0
Wrexham	3	Peterborough United	3
Peterborough United	0	Cambridge United	2
Walsall	0	Birmingham City	1
Birmingham City	2	Lincoln City	0
Lincoln City	1	Walsall	1
Torquay United	1	Swansea City	1
Swansea City	1	Shrewsbury Town	1
Shrewsbury Town	1	Torquay United	1*
Torquay United	2	Swansea City	0
Swansea City	4	Shrewsbury Town	2
Shrewsbury Town	2	Torquay United	6
Cardiff City	0	Exeter City	1
Exeter City	2	Hereford United	2
Hereford United	1	Cardiff City	1
Southend United	10	Aldershot	1
Aldershot	3	Reading	1
Reading	1	Southend United	4
AFC Bournemouth	0	Gillingham	0
Gillingham	4	Maidsone United	1
Maidstone United	3	AFC Bournemouth	1
Leyton Orient	0	Fulham	2
Fulham	1	Brentford	1
Brentford	2	Leyton Orient	0

First Round

Northern Section

Preston North End	2	Darlington	1
Doncaster Rovers	0	Scunthorpe United	0†
Tranmere Rovers	3	Rotherham United	0
Bradford City	3	Hartlepool United	2

Burnley	3	Stockport County	2
Halifax Town	0	Blackpool	1
Wigan Athletic	2	Rochdale	0
York City	1	Bury	2

Southern Section

Gillingham	0	Hereford United	1
Southend United	2	Maidstone United	0
Exeter City	1	Aldershot	0
Cambridge United	1	Walsall	0
Birmingham City	0†	Swansea City	0
Mansfield Town	2	Fulham	1
Torquay United	2	Northampton Town	0
Brentford	0†	Wrexham	0

Quarter-Final

Northern Section

Bradford City	0	Burnley	1
Scunthorpe United	1	Preston North End	4
Tranmere Rovers	2	Blackpool	0
Wigan Athletic	2	Bury	0

Southern Section

Exeter City	0	Cambridge United	1
Birmingham City	2	Mansfield Town	0
Southend United	7	Torquay United	0
Hereford United	0	Brentford	2

Semi-Final

Northern Section

Preston North End	6	Burnley	1
Wigan Athletic	0	Tranmere Rovers	3

Southern Section

Birmingham City	3	Cambridge United	1
Southend United	0	Brentford	3

Final

Northern Section
First Leg:

Tranmere Rovers	4	Preston North End	0

Second Leg:

Preston North End	1	Tranmere Rovers	0

Southern Section
First Leg:

Birmingham City	2	Brentford	1

Second Leg:

Brentford	0	Birmingham City	1

Play-Off Final (at Wembley Stadium)

Birmingham City	3	Tranmere Rovers	2

*Group replayed after all teams finished level
†Won on penalty-kicks

Zenith Data Systems Cup Competition 1990-91

First Round

Leicester City	0	Wolverhampton Wanderers	1
Middlesbrough	3	Hull City	1
Notts County	1	Port Vale	0
Oxford United	2*	Bristol City	2
Plymouth Argyle	0	Brighton & Hove Albion	0*
Watford	1	Bristol Rovers	2
West Bromwich Albion	3	Barnsley	5

Second Round

Barnsley	3*	Sheffield Wednesday	3
Blackburn Rovers	1	Everton	4
Brighton & Hove Albion	3	Charlton Athletic	1
Chelsea	1	Swindon Town	0
Crystal Palace	2	Bristol Rovers	1
Derby County	1	Coventry City	0
Luton Town	5	West Ham United	1
Manchester City	2	Middlesbrough	1
Norwich City	1*	Millwall	1
Nottingham Forest	2	Newcastle United	1
Notts County	2	Sunderland	2*
Oxford United	1	Portsmouth	0
Sheffield United	7	Oldham Athletic	2
Southampton	4	Queens Park Rangers	0
Wimbledon	0	Ipswich Town	2
Wolverhampton Wanderers	1	Leeds United	2

Area Quarter-Finals

Barnsley	2	Nottingham Forest	1
Brighton & Hove Albion	0	Crystal Palace	2
Chelsea	1	Luton Town	1*
Everton	4	Sunderland	1
Ipswich Town	2	Oxford United	1
Leeds United	2	Derby County	1
Norwich City	2	Southampton	1
Sheffield United	0	Manchester City	2

Area Semi-Finals

Barnsley	0	Everton	1
Crystal Palace	3	Luton Town	1
Leeds United	2	Manchester City	0
Norwich City	2	Ipswich Town	0

Area Finals (2 Legs)

Leeds United	3	Everton	3
Everton	3	Leeds United	1
Norwich City	1	Crystal Palace	1
Crystal Palace	2	Norwich City	0

Final

Crystal Palace	4	Everton	1
at Wembley Stadium			

* Won on penalty-kicks

Birmingham City – Leyland Daf Cup Winners.

Freight Rover/Sherpa Van Trophy/Leyland Daf CupWinners 1985-91

Year	Winners		Runners-up		Venue
1985	Wigan Athletic	3	Brentford	1	Wembley
1986	Bristol City	3	Bolton Wanderers	0	Wembley
1987	* Mansfield Town	1	Bristol City	1	Wembley
1988	Wolverhampton Wanderers	2	Burnley	0	Wembley
1989	Bolton Wanderers	4	Torquay United	1	Wembley
1990	Tranmere Rovers	2	Bristol Rovers	1	Wembley
1991	Birmingham City	3	Tranmere Rovers	2	Wembley

*Won on penalty-kicks

Full Members'/Simod/Zenith Data Systems Cup Winners 1986-91

Year	Winners		Runners-up		Venue
1986	Chelsea	5	Manchester City	4	Wembley
1987	Blackburn Rovers	1	Charlton Athletic	0	Wembley
1988	Reading	4	Luton Town	1	Wembley
1989	Nottingham Forest	4	Everton	3	Wembley
1990	Chelsea	1	Middlesbrough	0	Wembley
1991	* Crystal Palace	4	Everton	1	Wembley

* After extra time

F.A. Sunday Cup Winners 1965-91

Year	Winners		Runners-up		Venue
1965	* London	6	Staffordshire	2	
1966	Unique United	1	Aldridge Fabrications	0	Dudley
1967	Carlton United	2	Stoke Works	0	Hendon
1968	Drovers	2	Brook United	0	Cambridge
1969	Leigh Park	3	Loke United	1	Romford
1970	Vention United	1	Unique United	0	Corby
1971	Beacontree Rovers	2	Saltley United	0	Leamington
1972	Newtown Unity	4	Springfield Colts	0	Dudley
1973	† Carlton United	2	Wear Valley	1	Spennymoor
1974	Newtown Unity	3	Brentford East	0	Birmingham
1975	Fareham Town Centipedes	1	Players Ath Engineers	0	High Wycombe
1976	Brandon United	2	Evergreen	1	Spennymoor
1977	Langley Park R.H.	2	Newtown Unity	0	Spennymoor
1978	Arras	2	Lion Rangers	1	Bishop's Stortford
			(After 2-2 draw at Nuneaton)		
1979	Lobster	3	Carlton United	2	Southport
1980	Fantail	1	Twin Foxes	0	Letchworth
1981	Fantail	1	Mackintosh	0	Birkenhead
1982	Dingle Rail	2	Twin Foxes	1	Hitchin
1983	Eagle	2	Lee Chapel North	1	Walthamstow
1984	† Lee Chapel North	4	Eagle	3	Dagenham
			(After 1-1 draw at Runcorn)		
1985	Hobbies	2	Avenue	1	Nuneaton
			(After 1-1 draw at Norwich and 2-2 draw at Birkenhead)		
1986	Avenue	1	Glenn Sports	0	Birkenhead
1987	† Lodge Cottrell	1	Avenue	0	Birmingham
1988	Nexday	2	Sunderland Humb Plains	0	Newcastle
1989	Almethak	3	East Levenshulme	1	Stockport
1990	Humbledon Plains Farm	2	Marston Sports	1	West Bromwich
1991	† Nicosia	3	Ouzavich	2	Wigan

* Aggregate score
† After extra time

F.A. Sunday Cup Competition 1990-91

First Round

Result

Sunday 14th October 1990

	1st Tie	1st Rep	2nd Rep

Baildon Athletic v Croxteth & Gilmoss RBL	1-0
Royal Oak v Toshiba Sharples	3-0
Woodlands Hotel 84 v A3	1-3
Blyth Waterloo SC v Western Approaches	3-2
Dudley & Weetslade v Carnforth	2-3
Blue Union v Chesterfield Park	2-5
East Bowling Unity v Hartlepool Lion Hotel	2-0
Iron Bridge v Airedale Magnet	0-2
AC Sparks v Kebroyd Rovers	6-3
Dock v Carlisle United Supporters	2-1
Green Man 88 v Lynemouth Inn	2-3
Hope Farm Metro v West Wideopen	0-4
Netherley RBL v Framwellgate Moor & Pity Me	3-1
Eagle-Knowsley v Oakenshaw	2-1
Nenthead v Littlewoods AFC	3-0
Deborah United v Clubmoor Nalgo	1-2
Railway Hotel v Stanton Dale	3-1
Whetley Lane v St Josephs (Wallasey)	2-0
Overpool United v Queens Arms	0-4
FC Coachman v Radford Park Rangers	1-1
Radford Park Rangers v FC Coachman	0-1

Ansells Stockland Star *v* Altone Steels 1-3
Kenwick Dynamo *v* Brookvale Athletic 2-1
Hanham Sunday *v* Inter Volante 1-4
Birmingham Celtic *v* Kettering Odyssey 0-0
    Kettering Odyssey *v* Birmingham Celtic 1-0
St Josephs (Luton) v Chequers 5-0
Rolls Royce *v* Olympic Star 3-2
Cork & Bottle *v* Beaufort 4-1
Elliott Star *v* St Josephs (South Oxey) 1-2
Grosvenor Park *v* Phoenix 2-1
Chequers (Hunts) *v* Dereham Hobbies 4-1
Fryerns Community *v* Trinity 2-1
Watford Labour Club *v* Shouldham Sunday 1-3
Ely City *v* Ouzavich 0-3
Trax *v* Sawston Keys 4-3
Merton Admiral *v* Oxford Road Social 3-2
Shakespeare *v* St Clements Hospital 2-7
Whittingham *v* Chapel United (walkover for Chapel United, Whittingham withdrew)
Concord Rangers *v* Inter Royalle 2-0
Priory Sports *v* Essex Sports 2-0
Collier Row Supporters *v* Santogee 66 1-5
Ranelagh Sports *v* Theale 1-0
Biddestone *v* Broad Plain House 2-4
Lebeq Tavern *v* Bishopstoke AFC 3-0
Brimsdown Rovers *v* Old Paludians 3-0
Bye: Hallen Sunday (withdrew)

Second Round

Result

	1st Tie	1st Rep	2nd Rep
AC Sparks *v* Baildon Athletic	1-3		
Almithak *v* A3	1-2		
West Wideopen *v* Nenthead	1-2		
Dock *v* East Bowling Unity	3-2		
Railway Hotel *v* East Levenshulme	1-4		
Royal Oak *v* Humbledon Plains Farm	0-3		
Blyth Waterloo Social Club *v* East & West Toxteth	3-1		
Morrison Sports *v* Eagle-Knowsley	2-5		
Lynemouth Inn *v* Netherley RBL	1-4		
Nicosia *v* Whetley Lane	3-2		
Queens Arms *v* Airedale Magnet	0-0		
Airedale Magnet *v* Queens Arms		2-3	
Chesterfield Park *v* Northwood	2-3		
Avenue Victoria Lodge *v* Carnforth	2-1		
Concord Rangers *v* Slade Celtic	1-1		
Slade Celtic *v* Concord Rangers		2-1	
Brereton Town *v* Newey Goodman	3-0		
Priory Sports *v* Poringland Wanderers	0-1		
FC Coachman *v* Chequers (Hunts)	0-1		
Lodge Cottrell *v* Brimsdown Rovers	2-1		
Marston Sports *v* St Clements Hospital	2-0		
Rolls Royce *v* Fryerns Community	0-1		
Shouldham Sunday *v* Ford Basildon	2-5		
Chapel United *v* Altone Steels	2-2		
Altone Steels *v* Chapel United		0-0	
Altone Steels *v* Chapel United			4-2
Grosvenor Park *v* Ouzavich	1-3		
St Josephs (South Oxhey) v Trax	0-1		
Cork & Bottle *v* Santogee 66	1-2		
Lee Chapel North *v* Merton Admiral	3-1		
Ranelagh Sports *v* Inter Volante	2-1		
Broad Plain House *v* St Josephs (Luton)	2-0		
Leyton Argyle *v* Sandwell	4-3		
Lebeq Tavern *v* Kenwick Dynamo	0-2		

Byes: Clubmoor Nalgo, Kettering Odyssey

Third Round	Result		
	1st Tie	1st Rep	2nd Rep

Sunday 9th December 1990

	1st Tie	1st Rep	2nd Rep
Brereton Town v Netherley RBL	2-3		
Nenthead v East Levenshulme	1-2		
Dock v A3	0-1		
Clubmoor Nalgo v Nicosia	0-1		
Baildon Athletic v Northwood	3-0		
Eagle-Knowsley v Queens Arms	2-0		
Blyth Waterloo SC v Avenue Victoria Lodge	2-1		
Humbledon Plains Farm v Marston Sports	0-3		
Kenwick Dynamo v Kettering Odyssey	3-0		
Chequers (Hunts) v Slade Athletic	0-2		
Leyton Argyle v Altone Steels	3-2		
Ranelagh Sports v Santogee 66	5-0		
Ouzavich v Fryerns Community	0-0		
Fryerns Community v Ouzavich		2-3	
Lodge Cottrell v Lee Chapel North	1-0		
Ford Basildon v Trax	6-4		
Broad Plain House v Poringland Wanderers	0-4		

Fourth Round	Result		

Sunday 20th January 1991

	1st Tie	1st Rep	2nd Rep
A3 v Baildon Athletic	4-0		
Netherley RBL v Nicosia	0-1		
East Levenshulme v Blyth Waterloo SC	3-2		
Marston Sports v Eagle-Knowsley	2-3		
Leyton Argyle v Ouzavich	0-1		
Kenwick Dynamo v Ranelagh Sports	1-2		
Slade Athletic v Ford Basildon	1-0		
Poringland Wanderers v Lodge Cottrell	0-3		

Fifth Round	Result		

Sunday 17th February 1991

	1st Tie	1st Rep	2nd Rep
Nicosia v East Levenshulme	2-1		
Eagle-Knowsley v A3	3-1		
Ranelagh Sports v Lodge Cottrell	0-0		
Lodge Cottrell v Ranelagh Sports		0-3	
Slade Celtic v Ouzavich	0-2		

Semi-Final — Result

Sunday 24th March 1991

	Result
Nicosia v Eagle-Knowsley	1-0
(at Marine FC)	
Ranelagh Sports v Ouzavich	0-2
(at Carshalton Athletic FC)	

Final — Result

Sunday 5th May 1991

	Result
Nicosia v Ouzavich	3-2
(at Wigan Athletic FC)	

171

Other Leagues' Tables 1990-91

GM VAUXHALL CONFERENCE

	P	W	D	L	Goals F	A	Pts
Barnet	42	26	9	7	103	52	87
Colchester United	42	25	10	7	68	35	85
Altrincham	42	23	13	6	87	46	82
Kettering Town	42	23	11	8	67	45	80
Wycombe Wanderers	42	21	11	10	75	46	74
Telford United	42	20	7	15	62	52	67
Macclesfield Town	42	17	12	13	63	52	63
Runcorn	42	16	10	16	69	67	58
Merthyr Tydfil	42	16	9	17	62	61	57
Barrow	42	15	12	15	59	65	57
Welling United	42	13	15	14	55	57	54
Northwich Victoria	42	13	13	16	65	75	52
Kidderminster Harriers	42	14	10	18	56	67	52
Yeovil Town	42	13	11	18	58	58	50
Stafford Rangers	42	12	14	16	48	51	50
Cheltenham Town	42	12	12	18	54	72	48
Gateshead	42	14	6	22	52	92	48
Boston United	42	12	11	19	55	69	47
Slough Town	42	13	6	23	51	80	45
Bath City	42	10	12	20	55	61	42
Sutton United	42	10	9	23	62	82	39
Fisher Athletic	42	5	15	22	38	79	30

HFS LOANS LEAGUE

Premier Division

	P	W	D	L	Goals F	A	Pts
Witton Albion	40	28	9	3	81	31	93
Stalybridge Celtic	40	22	11	7	44	26	77
Morecombe	40	19	16	5	72	44	73
Fleetwood Town	40	20	9	11	69	44	69
Southport	40	18	14	8	66	48	68
Marine	40	18	11	11	56	39	65
Bishop Auckland	40	17	10	13	62	56	61
Buxton	40	17	11	12	66	61	59
Leek Town	40	15	11	14	48	44	56
Frickley Athletic	40	16	6	18	64	62	54
Hyde United	40	14	11	15	73	63	53
Goole Town	40	14	10	16	68	74	52
Droylsden	40	12	11	17	67	70	47
Chorley	40	12	10	18	55	55	46
Mossley	40	13	10	17	55	68	45
Horwich	40	13	6	21	62	81	45
Matlock Town	40	12	7	21	52	70	43
Bangor City	40	9	12	19	52	70	39
South Liverpool	40	10	9	21	58	92	39
Gainsborough Trinity	40	9	11	20	57	84	38
Shepshed Chouse	40	6	7	27	38	83	25

BEAZER HOMES LEAGUE

Premier Division

	P	W	D	L	Goals F	A	Pts
Farnborough Town	42	26	7	9	79	43	85
Gloucester City	42	23	14	5	86	49	83
Cambridge City	42	21	14	7	63	43	77
Dover Athletic	42	21	11	10	56	37	74
Bromsgrove Rovers	42	20	11	11	68	49	71
Worcester City	42	18	12	12	55	42	66
Burton Albion	42	15	15	12	59	48	60
Halesowen Town	42	17	9	16	73	67	60
V.S. Rugby	42	16	11	15	56	46	59
Bashley	42	15	12	15	56	52	57
Dorchester Town	42	15	12	15	47	54	57
Wealdstone	42	16	8	18	57	58	56
Dartford	42	15	9	18	61	64	54
Rushden Town	42	14	11	17	64	66	53
Atherstone United	42	14	10	18	55	58	52
Moor Green	42	15	6	21	64	75	51
Poole Town	42	12	13	17	56	69	49
Chelmsford City	42	11	15	16	57	68	48
Crawley Town	42	12	12	18	45	67	48
Waterlooville	42	11	13	18	51	70	46
Gravesend & Northfleet	42	9	7	26	46	91	34
Weymouth	42	4	12	26	50	88	24

Midland Division

	P	W	D	L	Goals F	A	Pts
Stourbridge	42	28	6	8	80	48	90
Corby Town	42	27	4	11	99	48	85
Hednesford Town	42	25	7	10	79	47	82
Tamworth	42	25	5	12	84	45	80
Nuneaton Borough	42	21	11	10	74	51	*70
Barry Town	42	20	7	15	61	48	67
Newport A.F.C.	42	19	6	17	54	46	63
King's Lynn	42	17	9	16	53	62	60
Grantham Town	42	17	7	18	62	56	58
Redditch United	42	16	10	16	66	75	58
Hinckley Town	42	16	9	17	72	68	57
Sutton Coldfield Town	42	15	11	16	56	65	56
Bedworth United	42	15	9	18	57	73	54
Bilston Town	42	14	9	19	69	79	51
Leicester United	42	14	10	18	65	77	*51
Racing Club Warwick	42	12	13	17	56	65	49
Bridgnorth Town	42	13	9	20	62	74	48
Stroud	42	11	14	17	51	64	47
Dudley Town	42	11	13	18	48	73	46
Alvechurch	42	10	8	24	54	92	38
Willenhall Town	42	10	10	22	58	69	*37
Spalding United	42	8	9	25	35	70	33

* Points deducted

Southern Division

	P	W	D	L	Goals F	A	Pts
Buckingham Town	40	25	8	7	73	38	83
Trowbridge Town	40	22	12	6	67	31	78
Salisbury	40	22	11	7	63	39	77
Baldock Town	40	21	9	10	66	52	72
Ashford Town	40	22	5	13	82	52	71
Yate Town	40	21	8	11	76	48	71
Hastings Town	40	18	11	11	66	46	65
Hythe Town	40	17	9	14	55	44	*59
Andover	40	16	6	18	69	76	54
Margate	40	14	11	15	52	55	53
Burnham	40	12	16	12	57	49	52
Bury Town	40	15	5	20	58	74	50
Sudbury Town	40	13	10	17	60	68	49
Newport I.O.W.	40	13	9	18	56	62	48
Gosport Borough	40	12	11	17	47	58	47
Witney Town	40	12	11	17	57	75	47
Dunstable	40	9	15	16	48	63	42
Canterbury City	40	12	6	22	60	83	42
Erith & Belvedere	40	10	6	24	46	73	36
Fareham Town	40	9	9	22	46	74	36
Corinthian	40	5	12	23	34	78	27

* Point deducted

172

VAUXHALL LEAGUE

Premier Division

	P	W	D	L	Goals F	A	Pts
Redbridge Forest	42	29	6	7	74	43	93
Enfield	42	26	11	5	83	30	89
Aylesbury United	42	25	10	7	91	47	85
Woking	42	24	10	8	84	39	82
Kingstonian	42	21	12	9	86	57	75
Grays Athletic	42	20	8	14	66	53	68
Marlow	42	18	13	11	72	49	67
Carshalton Athletic	42	19	7	16	80	67	64
Hayes	42	20	4	18	60	58	64
Wivenhoe Town	42	16	11	15	69	66	59
Wokingham Town	42	15	13	14	58	54	58
Windsor & Eton	42	15	10	17	48	63	55
Bishop's Stortford	42	14	12	16	54	49	54
Dagenham	42	13	11	18	62	68	50
Hendon	42	12	10	20	48	62	46
St. Albans City	42	11	12	19	60	74	45
Bognor Regis Town	42	12	8	22	44	71	44
Basingstoke Town	42	12	7	23	57	95	43
Staines Town	42	10	10	22	46	79	*39
Harrow Borough	42	10	8	24	57	84	38
Barking	42	8	10	24	41	85	34
Leyton-Wingate	42	7	7	28	44	91	28

* Point deducted

Division One

	P	W	D	L	Goals F	A	Pts
Chesham United	42	27	8	7	102	37	89
Bromley	42	22	14	6	62	37	80
Yeading	42	23	8	11	75	45	77
Aveley	42	21	9	12	76	43	72
Hitchin Town	42	21	9	12	78	50	72
Tooting & Mitcham United	42	20	12	10	71	48	72
Walton & Hersham	42	21	8	13	73	48	71
Molesey	42	22	5	15	65	46	71
Whyteleafe	42	21	6	15	62	53	69
Dorking	42	20	5	17	78	67	65
Chalfont St. Peter	42	19	5	18	56	63	62
Dulwich Hamlet	42	16	11	15	67	54	59
Harlow Town	42	17	8	17	73	64	59
Boreham Wood	42	15	8	19	46	53	53
Wembley	42	13	12	17	62	59	51
Uxbridge	42	15	5	22	45	61	50
Croydon	42	15	5	22	44	85	50
Heybridge Swifts	42	13	10	19	46	59	49
Southwick	42	13	8	21	49	75	47
Lewes	42	10	8	24	49	82	38
Metropolitan Police	42	9	6	27	55	76	33
Worthing	42	2	4	36	28	157	10

Division Two North

	P	W	D	L	Goals F	A	Pts
Stevenage Borough	42	34	5	3	122	29	107
Vauxhall Motors	42	24	10	8	82	50	82
Billericay Town	42	22	8	12	70	41	74
Ware	42	22	8	12	78	51	74
Berkhamsted Town	42	19	11	12	60	51	68
Witham Town	42	19	10	13	70	59	67
Purfleet	42	17	14	11	68	57	65
Rainham Town	42	19	7	16	57	46	64
Hemel Hempstead	42	16	14	12	62	56	62
Barton Rovers	42	17	10	15	61	58	61
Saffron Walden Town	42	16	13	13	72	77	61
Collier Row	42	16	11	15	63	63	59
Kingsbury Town	42	17	8	17	64	72	59
Edgware Town	42	17	7	18	73	65	58
Hertford Town	42	16	10	16	69	70	58
Royston Town	42	14	15	13	78	62	57
Tilbury	42	14	6	22	70	79	48
Basildon United	42	11	10	21	61	90	43
Hornchurch	42	10	9	23	53	87	39
Clapton	42	9	10	23	54	93	*34
Finchley	42	6	7	29	50	112	25
Tring Town	42	1	9	32	30	99	12

* Points deducted

Division Two South

	P	W	D	L	Goals F	A	Pts
Abingdon Town	42	29	7	6	95	28	94
Maidenhead United	42	28	8	6	85	33	92
Egham Town	42	27	6	9	100	46	87
Malden Vale	42	26	5	11	72	44	83
Ruislip Manor	42	25	5	12	93	44	80
Southall	42	23	10	9	84	43	79
Harefield United	42	23	10	9	81	56	79
Newbury Town	42	23	8	11	71	45	77
Hungerford Town	42	16	13	13	84	69	61
Leatherhead	42	17	9	16	82	55	60
Banstead Athletic	42	15	13	14	58	62	58
Hampton	42	14	15	13	62	43	57
Epsom & Ewell	42	15	12	15	49	50	57
Chertsey Town	42	15	9	18	76	72	54
Horsham	42	14	7	21	58	67	49
Flackwell Heath	42	11	11	20	56	78	44
Bracknell Town	42	11	7	24	60	97	40
Feltham	42	10	8	24	45	80	38
Cove	42	10	7	25	51	94	37
Eastbourne United	42	10	7	25	53	109	37
Petersfield United	42	6	3	33	35	119	21
Camberley Town	42	1	6	35	27	143	9

F.A. Charity Shield Winners 1908-90

Year	Winners	Runners-up	Score
1908	Manchester United	Queens Park Rangers	4-0 after 1-1 draw
1909	Newcastle United	Northampton Town	2-0
1910	Brighton and Hove Albion	Aston Villa	1-0
1911	Manchester United	Swindon Town	8-4
1912	Blackburn Rovers	Queens Park Rangers	2-1
1913	Professionals	Amateurs	7-2
1920	West Bromwich Albion	Tottenham Hotspur	2-0
1921	Tottenham Hotspur	Burnley	2-0
1922	Huddersfield Town	Liverpool	1-0
1923	Professionals	Amateurs	2-0
1924	Professionals	Amateurs	3-1
1925	Amateurs	Professionals	6-1
1926	Amateurs	Professionals	6-3
1927	Cardiff City	Corinthians	2-1
1928	Everton	Blackburn Rovers	2-1
1929	Professionals	Amateurs	3-0
1930	Arsenal	Sheffield Wednesday	2-1
1931	Arsenal	West Bromwich Albion	1-0
1932	Everton	Newcastle United	5-3
1933	Arsenal	Everton	3-0
1934	Arsenal	Manchester City	4-0
1935	Sheffield Wednesday	Arsenal	1-0
1936	Sunderland	Arsenal	2-1
1937	Manchester City	Sunderland	2-0
1938	Arsenal	Preston North End	2-1
1948	Arsenal	Manchester United	4-3
1949	Portsmouth	Wolverhampton Wanderers	1-1*
1950	World Cup Team	Canadian Touring Team	4-2
1951	Tottenham Hotspur	Newcastle United	2-1
1952	Manchester United	Newcastle United	4-2
1953	Arsenal	Blackpool	3-1
1954	Wolverhampton Wanderers	West Bromwich Albion	4-4*
1955	Chelsea	Newcastle United	3-0
1956	Manchester United	Manchester City	1-0
1957	Manchester United	Aston Villa	4-0
1958	Bolton Wanderers	Wolverhampton Wanderers	4-1
1959	Wolverhampton Wanderers	Nottingham Forest	3-1
1960	Burnley	Wolverhampton Wanderers	2-2*
1961	Tottenham Hotspur	F.A. XI	3-2
1962	Tottenham Hotspur	Ipswich Town	5-1
1963	Everton	Manchester United	4-0
1964	Liverpool	West Ham United	2-2*
1965	Manchester United	Liverpool	2-2*
1966	Liverpool	Everton	1-0
1967	Manchester United	Tottenham Hotspur	3-3*
1968	Manchester City	West Bromwich Albion	6-1
1969	Leeds United	Manchester City	2-1
1970	Everton	Chelsea	2-1
1971	Leicester City	Liverpool	1-0
1972	Manchester City	Aston Villa	1-0
1973	Burnley	Manchester City	1-0
1974	Liverpool	Leeds United	1-1†
1975	Derby County	West Ham United	2-0
1976	Liverpool	Southampton	1-0
1977	Liverpool	Manchester United	0-0*
1978	Nottingham Forest	Ipswich Town	5-0
1979	Liverpool	Arsenal	3-1
1980	Liverpool	West Ham United	1-0
1981	Aston Villa	Tottenham Hotspur	2-2*
1982	Liverpool	Tottenham Hotspur	1-0
1983	Manchester United	Liverpool	2-0
1984	Everton	Liverpool	1-0
1985	Everton	Manchester United	2-0
1986	Everton	Liverpool	1-1*
1987	Everton	Coventry City	1-0
1988	Liverpool	Wimbledon	2-1
1989	Liverpool	Arsenal	1-0
1990	Liverpool	Manchester United	1-1*

* Each Club retained Shield for six months
† Liverpool won 6-5 on penalty-kicks

Attendances at Football League Matches

Season	Matches Played	Total (Millions)	Div. 1	Div. 2	Div. 3(S)	Div. 3 (N)
1946-47	1848	35.6	15.0	11.1	5.7	3.9
1947-48	1848	40.3	16.7	12.3	6.7	4.6
1948-49	1848	41.3	17.9	11.4	7.0	5.0
1949-50	1848	40.5	17.3	11.7	7.1	4.4
1950-51	2028	39.6	16.7	10.8	7.4	4.8
1951-52	2028	39.0	16.1	11.1	7.0	4.9
1952-53	2028	37.1	16.1	9.7	6.7	4.7
1953-54	2028	36.2	16.2	9.5	6.3	4.2
1954-55	2028	34.1	15.1	9.0	6.0	4.1
1955-56	2028	33.2	14.1	9.1	5.7	4.3
1956-57	2028	32.7	13.8	8.7	5.6	4.6
1957-58	2028	33.6	14.5	8.7	6.1	4.3
1958-59	2028	33.6	14.7	8.6	5.9	4.3
1959-60	2028	32.5	14.4	8.4	5.7	4.0
1960-61	2028	28.6	12.9	7.0	4.8	3.9
1961-62	2015	28.0	12.1	7.5	5.2	3.3
1962-63	2028	28.9	12.5	7.8	5.3	3.3
1963-64	2028	28.5	12.5	7.6	5.4	3.0
1964-65	2028	27.6	12.7	7.0	4.4	3.5
1965-66	2028	27.2	12.5	6.9	4.8	3.0
1966-67	2028	28.9	14.2	7.3	4.4	3.0
1967-68	2028	30.1	15.3	7.5	4.0	3.4
1968-69	2028	29.4	14.6	7.4	4.3	3.1
1969-70	2028	29.6	14.9	7.6	4.2	2.9
1970-71	2028	28.2	14.0	7.1	4.4	2.8
1971-72	2028	28.7	14.5	6.8	4.7	2.7
1972-73	2028	25.4	14.0	5.6	3.7	2.1
1973-74	2027	25.0	13.1	6.3	3.4	2.2
1974-75	2028	25.6	12.6	7.0	4.1	2.0
1975-76	2028	24.9	13.1	5.8	3.9	2.1
1976-77	2028	26.2	13.6	6.3	4.2	2.1
1977-78	2028	25.4	13.3	6.5	3.3	2.3
1978-79	2028	24.5	12.7	6.2	3.4	2.3
1979-80	2028	24.6	12.2	6.1	4.0	2.3
1980-81	2028	21.9	11.4	5.2	3.6	1.7
1981-82	2028	20.0	10.4	4.8	2.8	2.0
1982-83	2028	18.8	9.3	5.0	2.9	1.6
1983-84	2028	18.3	8.7	5.3	2.7	1.5
1984-85	2028	17.8	9.8	4.0	2.7	1.4
1985-86	2028	16.5	9.0	3.6	2.5	1.4
1986-87	2028	17.4	9.1	4.2	2.4	1.7
1987-88	2030	18.0	8.1	5.3	2.8	1.8
1988-89	2036	18.5	7.8	5.8	3.0	1.8
1989-90	2036	19.5	7.9	6.9	2.8	1.9
1990-91	2036	19.5	8.6	6.3	2.8	1.8

NOTE: From Season 1958-1959 onwards for Div. 3(S) read Div. 3 and for Div. 3(N) read Div. 4.

FA Cup Attendances 1967-91

	1st Round	2nd Round	3rd Round	4th Round	5th Round
1990-91	194,915	121,450	594,502	530,279	276,122
1989-90	209,542	133,483	683,047	412,483	351,423
1988-89	212,775	121,326	690,199	421,255	206,781
1987-88	204,411	104,561	720,121	443,133	281,461
1986-87	209,290	146,761	593,520	349,342	263,550
1985-86	171,142	130,034	486,838	495,526	311,833
1984-85	174,604	137,078	616,229	320,772	269,232
1983-84	192,276	151,647	625,965	417,298	181,832
1982-83	191,312	150,046	670,503	452,688	260,069
1981-82	236,220	127,300	513,185	356,987	203,334
1980-81	246,824	194,502	832,578	534,402	320,530
1979-80	267,121	204,759	804,701	507,725	364,039
1978-79	243,773	185,343	880,345	537,748	243,683
1977-78	258,248	178,930	881,406	540,164	400,751
1976-77	379,230	192,159	942,523	631,265	373,330
1975-76	255,533	178,099	867,880	573,843	471,925
1974-75	283,956	170,466	914,994	646,434	393,323
1973-74	214,236	125,295	840,142	747,909	346,012
1972-73	259,432	169,114	938,741	735,825	357,386
1971-72	277,726	236,127	986,094	711,399	486,378
1970-71	329,687	230,942	956,683	757,852	360,687
1969-70	345,229	195,102	925,930	651,374	319,893
1968-69	331,858	252,710	1,094,043	883,675	464,915
1967-68	322,121	236,195	1,229,519	771,284	563,779

	6th Round	Semi-Finals & Final	Total	No. of matches	Average per match
1990-91	124,826	196,434	2,038,528	162	12,584
1989-90	123,065	277,420	2,190,463	170	12,885
1988-89	176,629	167,353	1,966,318	164	12,173
1987-88	119,313	177,585	2,050,585	155	13,229
1986-87	119,396	195,533	1,877,400	165	11,378
1985-86	184,262	192,316	1,971,951	168	11,738
1984-85	148,690	242,754	1,909,359	157	12,162
1983-84	185,382	187,000	1,941,400	166	11,695
1982-83	193,845	291,162	2,209,625	154	14,348
1981-82	124,308	279,621	1,840,955	160	11,506
1980-81	288,714	339,250	2,756,800	169	16,312
1979-80	157,530	355,541	2,661,416	163	16,328
1978-79	263,213	249,897	2,604,002	166	15,687
1977-78	137,059	198,020	2,594,578	160	16,216
1976-77	205,379	258,216	2,982,102	174	17,139
1975-76	206,851	205,810	2,759,941	161	17,142
1974-75	268,361	291,369	2,968,903	172	17,261
1973-74	233,307	273,051	2,779,952	167	16,646
1972-73	241,934	226,543	2,928,975	160	18,306
1971-72	230,292	248,546	3,158,562	160	19,741
1970-71	304,937	279,644	3,220,432	162	19,879
1969-70	198,537	390,700	3,026,765	170	17,805
1968-69	188,121	216,232	3,431,554	157	21,857
1967-68	240,095	223,831	3,586,824	160	22,418

The Football Association Fixture Programme 1991-92

AUGUST 1991

Sat 3	Official Opening of Season
Sat 10	Tennent's F.A. Charity Shield
Sat 17	Football League Season starts
Wed 21	Rumbelows Cup 1st Round (1st Leg)
Wed 28	Rumbelows Cup 1st Round (2nd Leg)
Sat 31	F.A. Challenge Cup Preliminary Round

SEPTEMBER 1991

Sat 7	F.A. Challenge Vase Extra Preliminary Round
	F.A. Youth Challenge Cup Preliminary Round*
Tue 10	England *v* Germany (Under-21) at Scunthorpe United FC
Wed 11	England *v* Germany (F)
Thur 12	England *v* Iceland (EYC)
Sat 14	F.A. Challenge Cup 1st Round Qualifying
Wed 18	EC/ECWC/UEFA 1st Round (1st Leg)
Sat 21	F.A. Challenge Trophy 1st Round Qualifying
Wed 25	Rumbelows Cup 2nd Round (1st Leg)
Sat 28	F.A. Challenge Cup 2nd Round Qualifying
	F.A. Youth Challenge Cup 1st Round Qualifying*

OCTOBER 1991

Wed 2	EC/ECWC/UEFA 1st Round (2nd Leg)
Sat 5	F.A. Challenge Vase Preliminary Round
Wed 9	Rumbelows Cup 2nd Round (2nd Leg)
Sat 12	F.A. Challenge Cup 3rd Round Qualifying
	F.A. Youth Challenge Cup 2nd Round Qualifying*
Sun 13	F.A. Sunday Cup 1st Round
Tue 15	England *v* Turkey (Under-21) at Reading FC
Wed 16	England *v* Turkey (EC)
	Belgium *v* England (EYC)
Sat 19	F.A. Challenge Trophy 2nd Round Qualifying
	F.A. County Youth Challenge Cup 1st Round*
Wed 23	EC/ECWC/UEFA 2nd Round (1st Leg)
Sat 26	F.A. Challenge Cup 4th Round Qualifying
Wed 30	Rumbelows Cup 3rd Round

NOVEMBER 1991

Sat 2	F.A. Challenge Vase 1st Round
Wed 6	EC/ECWC/UEFA 2nd Round (2nd Leg)
Sat 9	F.A. Youth Challenge Cup 1st Round Proper*
Sun 10	F.A. Sunday Cup 2nd Round

Tue 12	Poland *v* England (Under-21)
Wed 13	Poland *v* England (EC)
Sat 16	F.A. Challenge Cup 1st Round Proper
Sat 23	F.A. Challenge Vase 2nd Round
Wed 27	EC Quarter-Final Group UEFA Cup 3rd Round (1st Leg)
Sat 30	F.A. Challenge Trophy 3rd Round Qualifying
	F.A. County Youth Challenge Cup 2nd Round*

DECEMBER 1991

Wed 4	Rumbelows Cup 4th Round
Sat 7	F.A. Challenge Cup 2nd Round Proper
	F.A. Youth Challenge Cup 2nd Round Proper*
Sun 8	F.A. Sunday Cup 3rd Round
Wed 11	EC Quarter-Final Group UEFA Cup 3rd Round (2nd Leg)
Sat 14	F.A. Challenge Vase 3rd Round

JANUARY 1992

Sat 4	F.A. Challenge Cup 3rd Round Proper
Wed 8	Rumbelows Cup 5th Round
Sat 11	F.A. Challenge Trophy 1st Round Proper
	F.A. Youth Challenge Cup 3rd Round Proper*
Sat 18	F.A. Challenge Vase 4th Round
	F.A. County Youth Challenge Cup 3rd Round*
Sun 19	F.A. Sunday Cup 4th Round
Sat 25	F.A. Challenge Cup 4th Round Proper

FEBRUARY 1992

Sat 1	F.A. Challenge Trophy 2nd Round Proper
Sat 8	F.A. Challenge Vase 5th Round
	F.A. Youth Challenge Cup 4th Round Proper*
Sun 9	Rumbelows Cup Semi-Final (1st Leg)
Sat 15	F.A. Challenge Cup 5th Round Proper
Sun 16	F.A. Sunday Cup 5th Round
Wed 19	England *v* France (F)
Sat 22	F.A. Challenge Trophy 3rd Round Proper
	F.A. County Youth Challenge Cup 4th Round*
Sat 29	F.A. Challenge Vase 6th Round

MARCH 1992

Sun 1	Rumbelows Cup Semi-Final (2nd Leg)
Wed 4	EC/ECWC/UEFA Quarter-Final (1st Leg or Group)
Sat 7	F.A. Challenge Cup 6th Round Proper

F.A. Youth Challenge Cup 5th Round Proper*

Sat 14	F.A. Challenge Trophy 4th Round Proper
Wed 18	EC/ECWC/UEFA Quarter-Final (2nd Leg or Group)
21 Sat	F.A. Challenge Vase Semi-Final (1st Leg)
	F.A. County Youth Challenge Cup Semi-Final*
Sun 22	F.A. Sunday Cup Semi-Final
Wed 25	Czechoslovakia *v* England (F)
Sat 28	F.A. Challenge Vase Semi-Final (2nd Leg)

APRIL 1992

Wed 1	EC Quarter-Final Group/ECWC/UEFA Semi-Final (1st Leg)
Sat 4	F.A. Challenge Trophy Semi-Final (1st Leg)
	F.A. Youth Challenge Cup Semi-Final*
Sun 5	F.A. Challenge Cup Semi-Final
Sat 11	F.A. Challenge Trophy Semi-Final 2nd Leg
Sun 12	Rumbelows Cup Final
Wed 15	EC Quarter-Final Group/ECWC/UEFA

Semi-Final (2nd Leg)

Sat 25	FA CHALLENGE VASE FINAL *(Wembley Stadium)*
Wed 29	USSR *v* England (F)
	UEFA CUP FINAL (1st Leg)

MAY 1992

Sat 2	F.A. COUNTY YOUTH CHALLENGE CUP FINAL (fixed date)
Sun 3	F.A. SUNDAY CUP FINAL
Wed 6	ECWC FINAL
Sat 9	F.A. CHALLENGE CUP FINAL *(Wembley Stadium)*
	F.A. Youth Challenge Cup Final*
Sun 10	FA CHALLENGE TROPHY FINAL *(Wembley Stadium)*
Tue 12	International Date
Wed 13	UEFA CUP FINAL (2nd Leg)
Fri 15	International Date
Sun 17	International Date
Wed 20	EC FINAL

JUNE 1992

Wed 3	Finland *v* England (F)
Mon 15	Termination of Season
10-26	European Championship Finals

* = Closing date   F = Friendly   EC = European Championship
EC/ECWC/UEFA = European Champion Clubs' Cup/ European Winners' Cup/ UEFA Cup
EYC = European Youth Championship

Tennent's F.A. Charity Shield 1990

Liverpool 1   Manchester United 1

Liverpool: Grobbelaar, Hysen, Burrows, Venison, Whelan, Ablett, Beardsley (Rosenthal), Houghton, Rush, Barnes, McMahon.

Manchester United: Sealey, Irwin, Donaghy, Bruce, Phelan, Pallister, Blackmore, Ince, McClair, Hughes, Wallace (Robins).

Referee: G. Courtney (Spennymoor).

Attendance: 66,558.

THE FOOTBALL ASSOCIATION
AMATEUR
CUP COMPETITION
FINAL TIE
SATURDAY, APRIL 21st, 1951   Kick-Off 3 pm

BISHOP AUCKLAND A.F.C.

PEGASUS A.F.C.

BISHOP AUCKLAND v PEGASUS

EMPIRE STADIUM
WEMBLEY
Chairman and Managing Director: SIR ARTHUR J. ELVIN, MBE

OFFICIAL PROGRAMME · ONE SHILLING

The Romance of Pegasus

When Oxford and Cambridge met in the annual inter-university football match in 1945, there was programme comment regretting the fact that such a small crowd would be attending (it was played at Dulwich Hamlet FC). The hope was expressed that the universities might one day draw a 100,000 capacity crowd to Wembley Stadium. On the face of it, an absurd thought. But it actually happened!

The meteoric rise of the 'Pegasus' club is undoubtedly one of the most romantic stories in football history. The club came into existence through the efforts of a few enthusiasts at Oxford, headed by Dr 'Tommy' Thompson. They had realised for some time that the flow from Association to the Rugby

code in the schools and universities had begun to reach alarming proportions. If unchecked, they thought, this could well have proved harmful to English football even in the international sphere – for the highest professional skill needed a sound body of amateurs to support it.

'Pegasus FC' was an entirely new club, strictly amateur, formed from members of Oxford and Cambridge Universities. If the club could prove itself strong enough to compete successfully, not only in 'friendlies' against the best amateur clubs but also in the FA Amateur Cup competition, it would surely strike a telling blow in the cause of Association Football. They began, on 8 December 1948, with a

Action from Pegasus's Amateur Cup Final win in 1951.

'friendly' against an Arsenal XI.

Pegasus played comparatively few matches in a season, were not a member of any league and had no recognised supporters' club or wealthy patron. Its members were widely scattered, with little opportunity of meeting each other off the field. Even the most optimistic Pegasus fan could hardly have expected the team to reach the last eight of the Amateur Cup in their very first season. But they did.

They went out to Walthamstow Avenue in the second round in the following season but then, in season 1950-51, the unbelievable happened. In slightly less than three years after its formation, Pegasus reached the Final of the FA Amateur Cup. But their Wembley triumph was something more than a victory for an individual club. It was a triumph for amateur football as a whole, an encouragement to Association Football in the schools and a blow against the rising tide of semi-professionalism. It was a return to the legendary 'Corinthian spirit' and 100,000 fans were in the national stadium to witness it – a British record for an amateur match that still stands today.

Pegasus reached the Final after beating Gosport Borough Athletic,

Slough Town, Brentwood & Warley, Oxford City and Hendon (after a replay in the semi-final). On 21 April 1951 they faced their greatest trial against an experienced and skilful side with the most distinguished cup traditions – the mighty Bishop Auckland. They began the match nervously – not an unusual thing for a team making its first appearance at Wembley – and 'Bishops' had more of the game in the first twenty minutes. But Pegasus employed the better tactics. Instead of keeping to short, square passes, they played the ball in old-fashioned swinging style.

After half an hour it was becoming clear that they had the measure of the Bishop Auckland attack and, after the interval, Pegasus really got into their stride. Dutchman turned over a perfect centre six minutes into the second half and Potts rushed in to score with a tremendous diving header. Pegasus, full of confidence, netted again through Tanner on 80 minutes. Nimmins scored an unexpected goal for 'Bishops' with an overhead kick with five minutes remaining, but the university men emerged as worthy winners. Pegasus could claim to have shown that student leadership, properly applied, was still a vital force. On that April day forty years ago a dream had come true.

THE FOOTBALL ASSOCIATION CONNECTION

Dr 'Tommy' Thompson, later Professor Sir Harold Thompson, represented Oxford University on the FA Council (1941–70) and was FA Chairman for five years from 1976. John Tanner, scorer of the goal that won the Amateur Cup, also served on the FA Council (1970–87). Both have now passed away.

Denis Saunders, Pegasus's skipper at Wembley, was appointed House Master at the FA's National School when it opened at Lilleshall in 1984. Dr Ben Brown, who saved a penalty in the 1951 semi-final at Highbury, has served on the FA Council since 1987.

beefed-up tomatoes

Beef and Tomato. It's a tastier mouthful.

Batchelors

Cup a Soup

Barclays League

FIXTURE LIST

Season 1991-92

© The Football League Limited 1991 (Licence No. P11719)

Sat. 17th August

FIRST DIVISION

Arsenal *v* Queens Park Rangers ....
Chelsea *v* Wimbledon ....
Coventry City *v* Manchester City ....
Crystal Palace *v* Leeds United ....
Liverpool *v* Oldham Athletic ....
Manchester United *v* Notts County ....
Norwich City *v* Sheffield United ....
Nottingham Forest *v* Everton ....
Sheffield Wednesday *v* Aston Villa ....
Southampton *v* Tottenham Hotspur ....
West Ham United *v* Luton Town ....

SECOND DIVISION

Blackburn Rovers *v* Portsmouth ....
Brighton & Hove Albion *v* Tranmere Rovers ....
Bristol Rovers *v* Ipswich Town ....
Charlton Athletic *v* Newcastle United ....
Grimsby Town *v* Cambridge United ....
Middlesbrough *v* Millwall ....
Plymouth Argyle *v* Barnsley ....
Port Vale *v* Oxford United ....
Southend United *v* Bristol City ....
Sunderland *v* Derby County ....
Swindon Town *v* Leicester City ....
Watford *v* Wolverhampton Wanderers ....

THIRD DIVISION

A.F.C. Bournemouth *v* Darlington ....
Birmingham City *v* Bury ....
Bolton Wanderers *v* Huddersfield Town ....
Bradford City *v* Stoke City ....
Brentford *v* Leyton Orient ....
Chester City *v* Fulham ....
Peterborough United *v* Preston North End ....
Reading *v* Hull City ....
Stockport County *v* Swansea City ....
Torquay United *v* Hartlepool United ....
West Bromwich Albion *v* Exeter City ....

FOURTH DIVISION

Barnet *v* Crewe Alexandra ....
Blackpool *v* Walsall ....
Cardiff City *v* Lincoln City ....
Chesterfield *v* Maidstone United ....
Doncaster Rovers *v* Carlisle United ....
Gillingham *v* Scunthorpe United ....
Halifax Town *v* Northampton Town ....
Rochdale *v* York City ....
Rotherham United *v* Burnley ....
Scarborough *v* Mansfield Town ....
Wrexham *v* Hereford United ....

Sun. 18th August

THIRD DIVISION

Shrewsbury Town *v* Wigan Athletic ....

Tues. 20th August

FIRST DIVISION

Everton *v* Arsenal ....
Leeds United *v* Nottingham Forest ....
Notts County *v* Southampton ....
Sheffield United *v* West Ham United ....
Wimbledon *v* Sheffield Wednesday ....

SECOND DIVISION

Barnsley *v* Sunderland ....
Bristol City *v* Brighton & Hove Albion ....
Ipswich Town *v* Port Vale ....

Wed. 21st August

FIRST DIVISION

Aston Villa *v* Manchester United ....
Coventry City *v* Luton Town ....
Manchester City *v* Liverpool ....
Oldham Athletic *v* Chelsea ....
Queens Park Rangers *v* Norwich City ....

SECOND DIVISION

Derby County *v* Middlesbrough ....

Fri. 23rd August

SECOND DIVISION

Tranmere Rovers *v* Bristol Rovers ....

THIRD DIVISION

Wigan Athletic *v* Chester City ....

Sat. 24th August

FIRST DIVISION

Aston Villa *v* Arsenal ....
Everton *v* Manchester United ....
Leeds United *v* Sheffield Wednesday ....
Luton Town *v* Liverpool ....
Manchester City *v* Crystal Palace ....
Notts County *v* Nottingham Forest ....
Oldham Athletic *v* Norwich City ....
Queens Park Rangers *v* Coventry City ....
Sheffield United *v* Southampton ....
Tottenham Hotspur *v* Chelsea ....
Wimbledon *v* West Ham United ....

SECOND DIVISION

Barnsley *v* Brighton & Hove Albion ....
Bristol City *v* Blackburn Rovers ....
Cambridge United *v* Swindon Town ....
Derby County *v* Southend United ....
Ipswich Town *v* Middlesbrough ....
Leicester City *v* Plymouth Argyle ....
Millwall *v* Sunderland ....

183

Newcastle United v Watford ....
Oxford United v Grimsby Town ....
Portsmouth v Port Vale ....
Wolverhampton Wanderers v Charlton Athletic ....

Sun. 25th August

Tues. 27th August

Wed. 28th August

Fri. 30th August

Sat. 31st August

Tues. 3rd September

Bury v Peterborough United ....
Darlington v Bolton Wanderers ....
Fulham v West Bromwich Albion ....
Hartlepool United v Brentford ....
Hull City v Birmingham City ....
Leyton Orient v Bradford City ....
Preston North End v A.F.C. Bournemouth ....
Swansea City v Reading ....
Wigan Athletic v Stockport County ....

FOURTH DIVISION

Burnley v Chesterfield ....
Carlisle United v Rotherham United ....
Crewe Alexandra v Aldershot ....
Mansfield Town v Wrexham ....
Northampton Town v Doncaster Rovers ....
Scunthorpe United v Scarborough ....
Walsall v Rochdale ....
York City v Blackpool ....

Wed. 4th September

FIRST DIVISION

Aston Villa v Crystal Palace ....
Luton Town v Southampton ....
Manchester City v Nottingham Forest ....
Queens Park Rangers v West Ham United ....

SECOND DIVISION

Derby County v Blackburn Rovers ....
Leicester City v Grimsby Town ....
Millwall v Brighton & Hove Albion ....
Newcastle United v Plymouth Argyle ....
Oxford United v Middlesbrough ....

THIRD DIVISION

Exeter City v Torquay United ....
Huddersfield Town v Chester City ....
Stoke City v Shrewsbury Town ....

FOURTH DIVISION

Hereford United v Gillingham ....
Lincoln City v Barnet ....
Maidstone United v Cardiff City ....

Fri. 6th September

THIRD DIVISION

Stockport County v Torquay United ....

FOURTH DIVISION

Aldershot v Carlisle United ....

Sat. 7th September

FIRST DIVISION

Arsenal v Coventry City ....
Aston Villa v Tottenham Hotspur ....
Everton v Crystal Palace ....
Leeds United v Manchester City ....
Manchester United v Norwich City ....
Notts County v Liverpool ....
Oldham Athletic v Sheffield United ....
Queens Park Rangers v Southampton ....
Sheffield Wednesday v Nottingham Forest ....
West Ham United v Chelsea ....
Wimbledon v Luton Town ....

Bristol Rovers v Grimsby Town ....
Derby County v Barnsley ....
Ipswich Town v Southend United ....
Leicester City v Bristol City ....
Millwall v Cambridge United ....
Plymouth Argyle v Charlton Athletic ....
Port Vale v Swindon Town ....
Portsmouth v Brighton & Hove Albion ....
Sunderland v Blackburn Rovers ....
Tranmere Rovers v Newcastle United ....
Watford v Middlesbrough ....
Wolverhampton Wanderers v Oxford United ....

THIRD DIVISION

Bolton Wanderers v West Bromwich Albion ....
Chester City v A.F.C. Bournemouth ....
Darlington v Stoke City ....
Fulham v Swansea City ....
Hartlepool United v Leyton Orient ....
Huddersfield Town v Exeter City ....
Hull City v Bury ....
Peterborough United v Wigan Athletic ....
Preston North End v Bradford City ....
Reading v Birmingham City ....
Shrewsbury Town v Brentford ....

FOURTH DIVISION

Burnley v Crewe Alexandra ....
Cardiff City v Rochdale ....
Doncaster Rovers v Wrexham ....
Gillingham v Scarborough ....
Mansfield Town v Blackpool ....
Northampton Town v Barnet ....
Rotherham United v Hereford United ....
Scunthorpe United v Maidstone United ....
Walsall v Halifax Town ....
York City v Chesterfield ....

Fri. 13th September

SECOND DIVISION

Cambridge United v Derby County ....

FOURTH DIVISION

Crewe Alexandra v Mansfield Town ....
Halifax Town v Rotherham United ....

Sat. 14th September

FIRST DIVISION

Chelsea v Leeds United ....
Coventry City v Notts County ....
Crystal Palace v Arsenal ....
Liverpool v Aston Villa ....
Luton Town v Oldham Athletic ....
Manchester City v Sheffield Wednesday ....
Norwich City v West Ham United ....
Nottingham Forest v Wimbledon ....
Sheffield United v Everton ....
Southampton v Manchester United ....
Tottenham Hotspur v Queens Park Rangers ....

SECOND DIVISION

Barnsley v Ipswich Town ....
Blackburn Rovers v Port Vale ....
Brighton & Hove Albion v Watford ....
Bristol City v Tranmere Rovers ....
Charlton Athletic v Portsmouth ....
Grimsby Town v Plymouth Argyle ....
Middlesbrough v Leicester City ....

Newcastle United v Wolverhampton Wanderers ....
Oxford United v Millwall ....
Southend United v Bristol Rovers ....
Swindon Town v Sunderland ....

THIRD DIVISION

A.F.C. Bournemouth v Bolton Wanderers ....
Birmingham City v Peterborough United ....
Bradford City v Chester City ....
Brentford v Reading ....
Bury v Huddersfield Town ....
Exeter City v Hartlepool United ....
Leyton Orient v Darlington ....
Stoke City v Fulham ....
Swansea City v Preston North End ....
Torquay United v Shrewsbury Town ....
West Bromwich Albion v Stockport County ....
Wigan Athletic v Hull City ....

FOURTH DIVISION

Barnet v Doncaster Rovers ....
Blackpool v Cardiff City ....
Carlisle United v Lincoln City ....
Chesterfield v Scunthorpe United ....
Hereford United v Burnley ....
Maidstone United v Walsall ....
Rochdale v Northampton Town ....
Scarborough v Aldershot ....
Wrexham v Gillingham ....

Tues. 17th September

FIRST DIVISION

Crystal Palace v West Ham United ....
Manchester City v Everton ....
Sheffield United v Notts County ....

SECOND DIVISION

Barnsley v Leicester City ....
Blackburn Rovers v Watford ....
Bristol City v Millwall ....
Cambridge United v Wolverhampton Wanderers ....
Charlton Athletic v Sunderland ....
Grimsby Town v Portsmouth ....
Middlesbrough v Tranmere Rovers ....
Swindon Town v Bristol Rovers ....

THIRD DIVISION

A.F.C. Bournemouth v Shrewsbury Town ....
Birmingham City v Chester City ....
Bradford City v Bolton Wanderers ....
Brentford v Hull City ....
Bury v Fulham ....
Leyton Orient v Preston North End ....
Torquay United v Reading ....
Wigan Athletic v Huddersfield Town ....

FOURTH DIVISION

Barnet v Scunthorpe United ....
Blackpool v Gillingham ....
Carlisle United v Mansfield Town ....
Chesterfield v Walsall ....
Crewe Alexandra v Northampton Town ....
Halifax Town v Cardiff City ....
Rochdale v Rotherham United ....
Wrexham v Aldershot ....

Wed. 18th September

FIRST DIVISION

Chelsea v Aston Villa ....
Coventry City v Leeds United ....

Luton Town v Queens Park Rangers ....
Norwich City v Sheffield Wednesday ....
Southampton v Wimbledon ....

SECOND DIVISION

Brighton & Hove Albion v Port Vale ....
Newcastle United v Ipswich Town ....
Oxford United v Derby County ....
Southend United v Plymouth Argyle ....

THIRD DIVISION

Exeter City v Stockport County ....
Stoke City v Hartlepool United ....
West Bromwich Albion v Peterborough United ....

FOURTH DIVISION

Hereford United v York City ....
Maidstone United v Lincoln City ....
Scarborough v Doncaster Rovers ....

Fri. 20th September

FOURTH DIVISION

Aldershot v Halifax Town ....
Doncaster Rovers v Blackpool ....

Sat. 21st September

FIRST DIVISION

Arsenal v Sheffield United ....
Aston Villa v Nottingham Forest ....
Everton v Coventry City ....
Leeds United v Liverpool ....
Manchester United v Luton Town ....
Notts County v Norwich City ....
Oldham Athletic v Crystal Palace ....
Queens Park Rangers v Chelsea ....
Sheffield Wednesday v Southampton ....
West Ham United v Manchester City ....
Wimbledon v Tottenham Hotspur ....

SECOND DIVISION

Bristol Rovers v Oxford United ....
Derby County v Brighton & Hove Albion ....
Ipswich Town v Bristol City ....
Leicester City v Blackburn Rovers ....
Millwall v Newcastle United ....
Plymouth Argyle v Middlesbrough ....
Port Vale v Southend United ....
Portsmouth v Cambridge United ....
Sunderland v Grimsby Town ....
Tranmere Rovers v Barnsley ....
Watford v Charlton Athletic ....
Wolverhampton Wanderers v Swindon Town ....

THIRD DIVISION

Bolton Wanderers v Wigan Athletic ....
Chester City v West Bromwich Albion ....
Darlington v Brentford ....
Fulham v Leyton Orient ....
Hartlepool United v Birmingham City ....
Huddersfield Town v A.F.C. Bournemouth ....
Hull City v Torquay United ....
Peterborough United v Exeter City ....
Preston North End v Stoke City ....
Reading v Bradford City ....
Shrewsbury Town v Swansea City ....
Stockport County v Bury ....

FOURTH DIVISION

Burnley v Rochdale ....

Cardiff City v Scarborough ....
Gillingham v Barnet ....
Lincoln City v Chesterfield ....
Northampton Town v Carlisle United ....
Rotherham United v Maidstone United ....
Scunthorpe United v Crewe Alexandra ....
Walsall v Hereford United ....
York City v Wrexham ....

Fri. 27th September

THIRD DIVISION
A.F.C. Bournemouth v Fulham ....

FOURTH DIVISION
Halifax Town v Mansfield Town ....

Sat. 28th September

FIRST DIVISION
Chelsea v Everton ....
Coventry City v Aston Villa ....
Crystal Palace v Queens Park Rangers ....
Liverpool v Sheffield Wednesday ....
Luton Town v Notts County ....
Manchester City v Oldham Athletic ....
Norwich City v Leeds United ....
Nottingham Forest v West Ham United ....
Sheffield United v Wimbledon ....
Southampton v Arsenal ....
Tottenham Hotspur v Manchester United ....

SECOND DIVISION
Barnsley v Millwall ....
Blackburn Rovers v Tranmere Rovers ....
Brighton & Hove Albion v Bristol Rovers ....
Bristol City v Portsmouth ....
Charlton Athletic v Port Vale ....
Grimsby Town v Ipswich Town ....
Middlesbrough v Sunderland ....
Newcastle United v Derby County ....
Oxford United v Plymouth Argyle ....
Southend United v Wolverhampton Wanderers ....
Swindon Town v Watford ....

THIRD DIVISION
Birmingham City v Preston North End ....
Bradford City v Shrewsbury Town ....
Brentford v Bolton Wanderers ....
Bury v Hartlepool United ....
Exeter City v Reading ....
Leyton Orient v Huddersfield Town ....
Stoke City v Stockport County ....
Swansea City v Peterborough United ....
Torquay United v Chester City ....
West Bromwich Albion v Hull City ....
Wigan Athletic v Darlington ....

FOURTH DIVISION
Barnet v Cardiff City ....
Blackpool v Rotherham United ....
Carlisle United v Walsall ....
Chesterfield v Aldershot ....
Crewe Alexandra v Gillingham ....
Hereford United v Lincoln City ....
Maidstone United v York City ....
Rochdale v Doncaster Rovers ....
Scarborough v Burnley ....
Wrexham v Scunthorpe United ....

Sun. 29th September

SECOND DIVISION
Cambridge United v Leicester City ....

Fri. 4th October

SECOND DIVISION
Tranmere Rovers v Southend United ....

FOURTH DIVISION
Aldershot v Rochdale ....

Sat. 5th October

FIRST DIVISION
Arsenal v Chelsea ....
Aston Villa v Luton Town ....
Everton v Tottenham Hotspur ....
Leeds United v Sheffield United ....
Manchester United v Liverpool ....
Oldham Athletic v Southampton ....
Queens Park Rangers v Nottingham Forest ....
Sheffield Wednesday v Crystal Palace ....
West Ham United v Coventry City ....
Wimbledon v Norwich City ....

SECOND DIVISION
Bristol Rovers v Middlesbrough ....
Derby County v Bristol City ....
Ipswich Town v Oxford United ....
Leicester City v Charlton Athletic ....
Millwall v Blackburn Rovers ....
Plymouth Argyle v Swindon Town ....
Port Vale v Cambridge United ....
Portsmouth v Newcastle United ....
Sunderland v Brighton & Hove Albion ....
Watford v Grimsby Town ....
Wolverhampton Wanderers v Barnsley ....

THIRD DIVISION
Bolton Wanderers v Torquay United ....
Chester City v Stoke City ....
Darlington v Bury ....
Fulham v Brentford ....
Hartlepool United v Wigan Athletic ....
Huddersfield Town v Swansea City ....
Hull City v Exeter City ....
Peterborough United v Leyton Orient ....
Preston North End v West Bromwich Albion ....
Reading v A.F.C. Bournemouth ....
Shrewsbury Town v Birmingham City ....
Stockport County v Bradford City ....

FOURTH DIVISION
Burnley v Carlisle United ....
Cardiff City v Wrexham ....
Doncaster Rovers v Crewe Alexandra ....
Gillingham v Chesterfield ....
Lincoln City v Halifax Town ....
Mansfield Town v Maidstone United ....
Northampton Town v Blackpool ....
Scunthorpe United v Hereford United ....
Walsall v Barnet ....
York City v Scarborough ....

Sun. 6th October

FIRST DIVISION
Notts County v Manchester City ....

Fri. 11th October

THIRD DIVISION
Wigan Athletic v Reading ....

FOURTH DIVISION
Crewe Alexandra v Walsall ....

Sat. 12th October

SECOND DIVISION
Barnsley v Portsmouth ....
Blackburn Rovers v Plymouth Argyle ....
Brighton & Hove Albion v Ipswich Town ....
Bristol City v Watford ....
Cambridge United v Sunderland ....
Charlton Athletic v Bristol Rovers ....
Grimsby Town v Port Vale ....
Middlesbrough v Wolverhampton Wanderers ....
Newcastle United v Leicester City ....
Oxford United v Tranmere Rovers ....
Southend United v Millwall ....
Swindon Town v Derby County ....

THIRD DIVISION
A.F.C. Bournemouth v Hartlepool United ....
Birmingham City v Stockport County ....
Bradford City v Fulham ....
Brentford v Peterborough United ....
Bury v Preston North End ....
Exeter City v Darlington ....
Leyton Orient v Chester City ....
Stoke City v Bolton Wanderers ....
Swansea City v Hull City ....
Torquay United v Huddersfield Town ....
West Bromwich Albion v Shrewsbury Town ....

FOURTH DIVISION
Barnet v York City ....
Carlisle United v Scunthorpe United ....
Chesterfield v Rotherham United ....
Halifax Town v Gillingham ....
Hereford United v Aldershot ....
Maidstone United v Doncaster Rovers ....
Rochdale v Mansfield Town ....
Scarborough v Northampton Town ....
Wrexham v Burnley ....

Sun. 13th October

FOURTH DIVISION
Blackpool v Lincoln City ....

Tues. 15th October

FOURTH DIVISION
Northampton Town v Chesterfield ....

Fri. 18th October

SECOND DIVISION
Tranmere Rovers v Cambridge United ....

THIRD DIVISION
Stockport County v Chester City ....

FOURTH DIVISION
Aldershot v Rotherham United ....

Sat. 19th October

FIRST DIVISION
Chelsea v Liverpool ....
Coventry City v Crystal Palace ....
Everton v Aston Villa ....
Luton Town v Sheffield Wednesday ....
Manchester United v Arsenal ....
Notts County v Leeds United ....
Oldham Athletic v West Ham United ....
Sheffield United v Nottingham Forest ....
Southampton v Norwich City ....
Tottenham Hotspur v Manchester City ....
Wimbledon v Queens Park Rangers ....

SECOND DIVISION
Barnsley v Bristol City ....
Bristol Rovers v Plymouth Argyle ....
Charlton Athletic v Brighton & Hove Albion ....
Derby County v Portsmouth ....
Grimsby Town v Middlesbrough ....
Ipswich Town v Millwall ....
Leicester City v Wolverhampton Wanderers ....
Newcastle United v Oxford United ....
Port Vale v Sunderland ....
Swindon Town v Blackburn Rovers ....
Watford v Southend United ....

THIRD DIVISION
Birmingham City v Wigan Athletic ....
Bolton Wanderers v Fulham ....
Bradford City v Torquay United ....
Brentford v West Bromwich Albion ....
Darlington v Shrewsbury Town ....
Exeter City v Bury ....
Hartlepool United v Hull City ....
Leyton Orient v A.F.C. Bournemouth ....
Preston North End v Huddersfield Town ....
Reading v Peterborough United ....
Swansea City v Stoke City ....

FOURTH DIVISION
Barnet v Blackpool ....
Burnley v Walsall ....
Crewe Alexandra v Scarborough ....
Doncaster Rovers v Gillingham ....
Halifax Town v Chesterfield ....
Maidstone United v Rochdale ....
Mansfield Town v Cardiff City ....
Northampton Town v Scunthorpe United ....
Wrexham v Carlisle United ....
York City v Lincoln City ....

Tues. 22nd October

SECOND DIVISION
Cambridge United v Blackburn Rovers ....
Portsmouth v Plymouth Argyle ....
Tranmere Rovers v Watford ....
Wolverhampton Wanderers v Grimsby Town ....

Wed. 23rd October

SECOND DIVISION
Leicester City v Bristol Rovers ....
Millwall v Swindon Town ....
Newcastle United v Southend United ....
Oxford United v Charlton Athletic ....

Fri. 25th October

THIRD DIVISION
Huddersfield Town v Stockport County ....

FOURTH DIVISION
Rotherham United v York City ....

Sat. 26th October

FIRST DIVISION
Arsenal v Notts County ....
Aston Villa v Wimbledon ....
Crystal Palace v Chelsea ....
Leeds United v Oldham Athletic ....
Liverpool v Coventry City ....
Manchester City v Sheffield United ....
Norwich City v Luton Town ....
Nottingham Forest v Southampton ....
Queens Park Rangers v Everton ....
Sheffield Wednesday v Manchester United ....
West Ham United v Tottenham Hotspur ....

SECOND DIVISION
Blackburn Rovers v Grimsby Town ....
Brighton & Hove Albion v Swindon Town ....
Bristol City v Newcastle United ....
Cambridge United v Barnsley ....
Middlesbrough v Port Vale ....
Millwall v Derby County ....
Oxford United v Leicester City ....
Plymouth Argyle v Watford ....
Portsmouth v Ipswich Town ....
Southend United v Charlton Athletic ....
Sunderland v Bristol Rovers ....
Wolverhampton Wanderers v Tranmere Rovers ....

THIRD DIVISION
A.F.C. Bournemouth v Bradford City ....
Bury v Brentford ....
Chester City v Bolton Wanderers ....
Fulham v Preston North End ....
Hull City v Darlington ....
Peterborough United v Hartlepool United ....
Shrewsbury Town v Reading ....
Stoke City v Leyton Orient ....
Torquay United v Swansea City ....
West Bromwich Albion v Birmingham City ....
Wigan Athletic v Exeter City ....

FOURTH DIVISION
Blackpool v Wrexham ....
Cardiff City v Doncaster Rovers ....
Carlisle United v Crewe Alexandra ....
Chesterfield v Hereford United ....
Gillingham v Northampton Town ....
Lincoln City v Burnley ....
Rochdale v Halifax Town ....
Scarborough v Barnet ....
Scunthorpe United v Mansfield Town ....
Walsall v Aldershot ....

Tues. 29th October

SECOND DIVISION
Blackburn Rovers v Wolverhampton Wanderers ....
Charlton Athletic v Ipswich Town ....
Grimsby Town v Derby County ....
Plymouth Argyle v Cambridge United ....
Sunderland v Tranmere Rovers ....

Swindon Town v Bristol City ....
Watford v Millwall ....

Wed. 30th October

SECOND DIVISION
Brighton & Hove Albion v Leicester City ....
Bristol Rovers v Portsmouth ....
Southend United v Oxford United ....

Fri. 1st November

THIRD DIVISION
A.F.C. Bournemouth v Stockport County ....
Wigan Athletic v Swansea City ....

Sat. 2nd November

FIRST DIVISION
Arsenal v West Ham United ....
Coventry City v Chelsea ....
Liverpool v Crystal Palace ....
Luton Town v Everton ....
Manchester United v Sheffield United ....
Norwich City v Nottingham Forest ....
Notts County v Oldham Athletic ....
Queens Park Rangers v Aston Villa ....
Sheffield Wednesday v Tottenham Hotspur ....
Southampton v Manchester City ....
Wimbledon v Leeds United ....

SECOND DIVISION
Blackburn Rovers v Brighton & Hove Albion ....
Bristol Rovers v Port Vale ....
Cambridge United v Bristol City ....
Derby County v Tranmere Rovers ....
Grimsby Town v Charlton Athletic ....
Leicester City v Ipswich Town ....
Middlesbrough v Southend United ....
Millwall v Portsmouth ....
Oxford United v Barnsley ....
Plymouth Argyle v Wolverhampton Wanderers ....
Sunderland v Watford ....
Swindon Town v Newcastle United ....

THIRD DIVISION
Birmingham City v Torquay United ....
Bolton Wanderers v Reading ....
Bradford City v Brentford ....
Chester City v Preston North End ....
Darlington v Hartlepool United ....
Fulham v Hull City ....
Leyton Orient v Exeter City ....
Shrewsbury Town v Peterborough United ....
Stoke City v Huddersfield Town ....
West Bromwich Albion v Bury ....

FOURTH DIVISION
Blackpool v Scarborough ....
Cardiff City v Scunthorpe United ....
Carlisle United v Gillingham ....
Halifax Town v Burnley ....
Lincoln City v Aldershot ....
Maidstone United v Hereford United ....
Mansfield Town v Doncaster Rovers ....
Rochdale v Chesterfield ....
Rotherham United v Northampton Town ....
Wrexham v Barnet ....
York City v Walsall ....

Tues. 5th November

Barnsley v Middlesbrough ....
Bristol City v Plymouth Argyle ....
Charlton Athletic v Swindon Town ....
Ipswich Town v Sunderland ....
Port Vale v Derby County ....
Portsmouth v Leicester City ....
Tranmere Rovers v Millwall ....
Wolverhampton Wanderers v Bristol Rovers ....

THIRD DIVISION
Brentford v Birmingham City ....
Bury v Stoke City ....
Hartlepool United v West Bromwich Albion ....
Hull City v Shrewsbury Town ....
Peterborough United v Chester City ....
Preston North End v Wigan Athletic ....
Stockport County v Bolton Wanderers ....
Swansea City v Leyton Orient ....

FOURTH DIVISION
Aldershot v Blackpool ....
Barnet v Carlisle United ....
Burnley v York City ....
Crewe Alexandra v Maidstone United ....
Doncaster Rovers v Rotherham United ....
Gillingham v Cardiff City ....
Northampton Town v Mansfield Town ....
Scarborough v Wrexham ....
Scunthorpe United v Rochdale ....
Walsall v Lincoln City ....

Wed. 6th November

SECOND DIVISION
Brighton & Hove Albion v Grimsby Town ....
Newcastle United v Cambridge United ....
Southend United v Blackburn Rovers ....
Watford v Oxford United ....

THIRD DIVISION
Exeter City v Bradford City ....
Huddersfield Town v Fulham ....
Reading v Darlington ....
Torquay United v A.F.C. Bournemouth ....

FOURTH DIVISION
Hereford United v Halifax Town ....

Fri. 8th November

SECOND DIVISION
Tranmere Rovers v Plymouth Argyle ....

THIRD DIVISION
Stockport County v Shrewsbury Town ....
Swansea City v A.F.C. Bournemouth ....

FOURTH DIVISION
Aldershot v Cardiff City ....
Doncaster Rovers v York City ....

Sat. 9th November

SECOND DIVISION
Barnsley v Bristol Rovers ....
Brighton & Hove Albion v Middlesbrough ....

Bristol City v Sunderland ....
Charlton Athletic v Blackburn Rovers ....
Ipswich Town v Cambridge United ....
Newcastle United v Grimsby Town ....
Port Vale v Millwall ....
Portsmouth v Oxford United ....
Southend United v Swindon Town ....
Watford v Leicester City ....
Wolverhampton Wanderers v Derby County ....

THIRD DIVISION
Brentford v Wigan Athletic ....
Bury v Bolton Wanderers ....
Exeter City v Stoke City ....
Hartlepool United v Fulham ....
Huddersfield Town v Birmingham City ....
Hull City v Chester City ....
Peterborough United v Bradford City ....
Preston North End v Darlington ....
Reading v West Bromwich Albion ....
Torquay United v Leyton Orient ....

FOURTH DIVISION
Barnet v Halifax Town ....
Burnley v Mansfield Town ....
Chesterfield v Blackpool ....
Crewe Alexandra v Wrexham ....
Gillingham v Maidstone United ....
Hereford United v Rochdale ....
Northampton Town v Lincoln City ....
Scarborough v Carlisle United ....
Scunthorpe United v Rotherham United ....

Sat. 16th November

FIRST DIVISION
Aston Villa v Notts County ....
Chelsea v Norwich City ....
Crystal Palace v Southampton ....
Everton v Wimbledon ....
Leeds United v Queens Park Rangers ....
Manchester City v Manchester United ....
Nottingham Forest v Coventry City ....
Oldham Athletic v Arsenal ....
Tottenham Hotspur v Luton Town ....
West Ham United v Liverpool ....

SECOND DIVISION
Blackburn Rovers v Barnsley ....
Bristol Rovers v Watford ....
Cambridge United v Brighton & Hove Albion ....
Derby County v Ipswich Town ....
Middlesbrough v Charlton Athletic ....
Millwall v Wolverhampton Wanderers ....
Oxford United v Bristol City ....
Plymouth Argyle v Port Vale ....
Swindon Town v Portsmouth ....

Sun. 17th November

FIRST DIVISION
Sheffield United v Sheffield Wednesday ....

SECOND DIVISION
Sunderland v Newcastle United ....

Fri. 22nd November

SECOND DIVISION
Tranmere Rovers v Swindon Town ....

THIRD DIVISION

A.F.C. Bournemouth *v* Brentford ....
Wigan Athletic *v* Bury ....

FOURTH DIVISION

Halifax Town *v* Scarborough ....
Rotherham United *v* Walsall ....

Sat. 23rd November

FIRST DIVISION

Aston Villa *v* Leeds United ....
Everton *v* Notts County ....
Luton Town *v* Manchester City ....
Manchester United *v* West Ham United ....
Norwich City *v* Coventry City ....
Nottingham Forest *v* Crystal Palace ....
Queens Park Rangers *v* Oldham Athletic ....
Sheffield Wednesday *v* Arsenal ....
Southampton *v* Chelsea ....
Tottenham Hotspur *v* Sheffield United ....
Wimbledon *v* Liverpool ....

SECOND DIVISION

Bristol Rovers *v* Derby County ....
Charlton Athletic *v* Cambridge United ....
Grimsby Town *v* Millwall ....
Leicester City *v* Port Vale ....
Middlesbrough *v* Bristol City ....
Newcastle United *v* Blackburn Rovers ....
Oxford United *v* Brighton & Hove Albion ....
Plymouth Argyle *v* Sunderland ....
Southend United *v* Barnsley ....
Watford *v* Portsmouth ....
Wolverhampton Wanderers *v* Ipswich Town ....

THIRD DIVISION

Birmingham City *v* Exeter City ....
Bolton Wanderers *v* Preston North End ....
Bradford City *v* Swansea City ....
Chester City *v* Reading ....
Darlington *v* Peterborough United ....
Fulham *v* Stockport County ....
Leyton Orient *v* Hull City ....
Shrewsbury Town *v* Hartlepool United ....
Stoke City *v* Torquay United ....
West Bromwich Albion *v* Huddersfield Town ....

FOURTH DIVISION

Blackpool *v* Crewe Alexandra ....
Cardiff City *v* Northampton Town ....
Carlisle United *v* Hereford United ....
Lincoln City *v* Scunthorpe United ....
Maidstone United *v* Burnley ....
Mansfield Town *v* Gillingham ....
Rochdale *v* Barnet ....
Wrexham *v* Chesterfield ....
York City *v* Aldershot ....

Tues. 26th November

FIRST DIVISION

Tottenham Hotspur *v* Crystal Palace ....

Sat. 30th November

FIRST DIVISION

Arsenal *v* Tottenham Hotspur ....
Chelsea *v* Nottingham Forest ....

Coventry City *v* Southampton ....
Crystal Palace *v* Manchester United ....
Leeds United *v* Everton ....
Liverpool *v* Norwich City ....
Manchester City *v* Wimbledon ....
Notts County *v* Queens Park Rangers ....
Oldham Athletic *v* Aston Villa ....
Sheffield United *v* Luton Town ....
West Ham United *v* Sheffield Wednesday ....

SECOND DIVISION

Barnsley *v* Newcastle United ....
Blackburn Rovers *v* Middlesbrough ....
Brighton & Hove Albion *v* Plymouth Argyle ....
Bristol City *v* Charlton Athletic ....
Cambridge United *v* Oxford United ....
Derby County *v* Leicester City ....
Ipswich Town *v* Tranmere Rovers ....
Millwall *v* Bristol Rovers ....
Port Vale *v* Watford ....
Portsmouth *v* Wolverhampton Wanderers ....
Sunderland *v* Southend United ....
Swindon Town *v* Grimsby Town ....

THIRD DIVISION

Birmingham City *v* Bradford City ....
Brentford *v* Swansea City ....
Bury *v* A.F.C. Bournemouth ....
Darlington *v* Fulham ....
Exeter City *v* Chester City ....
Hartlepool United *v* Huddersfield Town ....
Hull City *v* Preston North End ....
Peterborough United *v* Torquay United ....
Reading *v* Stockport County ....
Shrewsbury Town *v* Bolton Wanderers ....
West Bromwich Albion *v* Stoke City ....
Wigan Athletic *v* Leyton Orient ....

FOURTH DIVISION

Barnet *v* Chesterfield ....
Blackpool *v* Halifax Town ....
Cardiff City *v* Rotherham United ....
Carlisle United *v* Maidstone United ....
Crewe Alexandra *v* Hereford United ....
Doncaster Rovers *v* Lincoln City ....
Gillingham *v* Aldershot ....
Mansfield Town *v* Walsall ....
Northampton Town *v* Burnley ....
Scarborough *v* Rochdale ....
Scunthorpe United *v* York City ....

Fri. 6th December

SECOND DIVISION

Tranmere Rovers *v* Portsmouth ....

Sat. 7th December

FIRST DIVISION

Aston Villa *v* Manchester City ....
Everton *v* West Ham United ....
Luton Town *v* Leeds United ....
Manchester United *v* Coventry City ....
Norwich City *v* Crystal Palace ....
Nottingham Forest *v* Arsenal ....
Queens Park Rangers *v* Sheffield United ....
Sheffield Wednesday *v* Chelsea ....
Southampton *v* Liverpool ....
Tottenham Hotspur *v* Notts County ....
Wimbledon *v* Oldham Athletic ....

SECOND DIVISION
Bristol Rovers v Cambridge United ....
Charlton Athletic v Barnsley ....
Grimsby Town v Bristol City ....
Leicester City v Millwall ....
Middlesbrough v Swindon Town ....
Newcastle United v Port Vale ....
Oxford United v Blackburn Rovers ....
Plymouth Argyle v Ipswich Town ....
Southend United v Brighton & Hove Albion ....
Watford v Derby County ....
Wolverhampton Wanderers v Sunderland ....

Fri. 13th December

SECOND DIVISION
Port Vale v Tranmere Rovers ....

THIRD DIVISION
Fulham v Reading ....
Stockport County v Peterborough United ....

FOURTH DIVISION
Halifax Town v Wrexham ....

Sat. 14th December

FIRST DIVISION
Arsenal v Norwich City ....
Chelsea v Manchester United ....
Coventry City v Sheffield Wednesday ....
Leeds United v Tottenham Hotspur ....
Liverpool v Nottingham Forest ....
Manchester City v Queens Park Rangers ....
Notts County v Wimbledon ....
Oldham Athletic v Everton ....
Sheffield United v Aston Villa ....
West Ham United v Southampton ....

SECOND DIVISION
Barnsley v Grimsby Town ....
Blackburn Rovers v Bristol Rovers ....
Brighton & Hove Albion v Newcastle United ....
Bristol City v Wolverhampton Wanderers ....
Cambridge United v Middlesbrough ....
Derby County v Plymouth Argyle ....
Ipswich Town v Watford ....
Millwall v Charlton Athletic ....
Portsmouth v Southend United ....
Sunderland v Leicester City ....
Swindon Town v Oxford United ....

THIRD DIVISION
A.F.C. Bournemouth v Birmingham City ....
Bolton Wanderers v Hull City ....
Bradford City v West Bromwich Albion ....
Chester City v Shrewsbury Town ....
Huddersfield Town v Darlington ....
Leyton Orient v Bury ....
Preston North End v Hartlepool United ....
Stoke City v Wigan Athletic ....
Swansea City v Exeter City ....
Torquay United v Brentford ....

FOURTH DIVISION
Aldershot v Doncaster Rovers ....
Burnley v Scunthorpe United ....
Chesterfield v Crewe Alexandra ....
Hereford United v Mansfield Town ....
Lincoln City v Scarborough ....
Maidstone United v Barnet ....

Rochdale v Blackpool ....
Rotherham United v Gillingham ....
Walsall v Northampton Town ....
York City v Cardiff City ....

Sun. 15th December

FIRST DIVISION
Crystal Palace v Luton Town ....

Wed. 18th December

FIRST DIVISION
Tottenham Hotspur v Liverpool ....

Fri. 20th December

FIRST DIVISION
Luton Town v Coventry City ....
Southampton v Notts County ....

SECOND DIVISION
Plymouth Argyle v Newcastle United ....
Port Vale v Wolverhampton Wanderers ....
Swindon Town v Ipswich Town ....

THIRD DIVISION
Birmingham City v Fulham ....
Peterborough United v Hull City ....
Reading v Hartlepool United ....
Torquay United v Preston North End ....

FOURTH DIVISION
Doncaster Rovers v Scunthorpe United ....
Wrexham v Walsall ....

Sat. 21st December

FIRST DIVISION
Arsenal v Everton ....
Chelsea v Oldham Athletic ....
Liverpool v Manchester City ....
Manchester United v Aston Villa ....
Norwich City v Queens Park Rangers ....
Sheffield Wednesday v Wimbledon ....
West Ham United v Sheffield United ....

SECOND DIVISION
Blackburn Rovers v Derby County ....
Brighton & Hove Albion v Millwall ....
Bristol Rovers v Bristol City ....
Charlton Athletic v Tranmere Rovers ....
Grimsby Town v Leicester City ....
Middlesbrough v Oxford United ....
Southend United v Cambridge United ....
Sunderland v Portsmouth ....

THIRD DIVISION
A.F.C. Bournemouth v Stoke City ....
Bolton Wanderers v Swansea City ....
Chester City v Wigan Athletic ....
Shrewsbury Town v Bury ....
Stockport County v Leyton Orient ....

FOURTH DIVISION
Aldershot v Burnley ....
Barnet v Mansfield Town ....
Blackpool v Carlisle United ....
Cardiff City v Crewe Alexandra ....
Chesterfield v Northampton Town ....

Gillingham v York City ....
Halifax Town v Maidstone United ....
Rotherham United v Lincoln City ....
Scarborough v Hereford United ....

Sun. 22nd December

FIRST DIVISION
Crystal Palace v Tottenham Hotspur ....
Nottingham Forest v Leeds United ....

SECOND DIVISION
Watford v Barnsley ....

THIRD DIVISION
Bradford City v Huddersfield Town ....
Brentford v Exeter City ....
West Bromwich Albion v Darlington ....

Thurs. 26th December

FIRST DIVISION
Aston Villa v West Ham United ....
Everton v Sheffield Wednesday ....
Leeds United v Southampton ....
Luton Town v Arsenal ....
Manchester City v Norwich City ....
Notts County v Chelsea ....
Oldham Athletic v Manchester United ....
Queens Park Rangers v Liverpool ....
Sheffield United v Coventry City ....
Tottenham Hotspur v Nottingham Forest ....
Wimbledon v Crystal Palace ....

SECOND DIVISION
Barnsley v Port Vale ....
Bristol City v Swindon Town ....
Cambridge United v Plymouth Argyle ....
Derby County v Grimsby Town ....
Ipswich Town v Charlton Athletic ....
Leicester City v Brighton & Hove Albion ....
Millwall v Watford ....
Newcastle United v Middlesbrough ....
Oxford United v Southend United ....
Portsmouth v Bristol Rovers ....
Tranmere Rovers v Sunderland ....
Wolverhampton Wanderers v Blackburn Rovers ....

THIRD DIVISION
Bury v Reading ....
Darlington v Birmingham City ....
Exeter City v Shrewsbury Town ....
Fulham v Torquay United ....
Hartlepool United v Bradford City ....
Huddersfield Town v Brentford ....
Hull City v A.F.C. Bournemouth ....
Leyton Orient v Bolton Wanderers ....
Preston North End v Stockport County ....
Stoke City v Peterborough United ....
Swansea City v Chester City ....
Wigan Athletic v West Bromwich Albion ....

FOURTH DIVISION
Burnley v Rotherham United ....
Carlisle United v Doncaster Rovers ....
Crewe Alexandra v Barnet ....
Hereford United v Wrexham ....
Lincoln City v Cardiff City ....
Maidstone United v Chesterfield ....
Mansfield Town v Scarborough ....
Northampton Town v Halifax Town ....

Scunthorpe United v Gillingham ....
Walsall v Blackpool ....
York City v Rochdale ....

Sat. 28th December

FIRST DIVISION
Aston Villa v Southampton ....
Everton v Liverpool ....
Leeds United v Manchester United ....
Luton Town v Chelsea ....
Manchester City v Arsenal ....
Notts County v West Ham United ....
Oldham Athletic v Nottingham Forest ....
Queens Park Rangers v Sheffield Wednesday ....
Sheffield United v Crystal Palace ....
Tottenham Hotspur v Norwich City ....
Wimbledon v Coventry City ....

SECOND DIVISION
Barnsley v Swindon Town ....
Bristol City v Port Vale ...._3-0.......................
Derby County v Charlton Athletic ....
Ipswich Town v Blackburn Rovers ....
Leicester City v Southend United ....
Millwall v Plymouth Argyle ...._2-1....................
Newcastle United v Bristol Rovers ...2-1...................
Oxford United v Sunderland ....
Portsmouth v Middlesbrough ....
Tranmere Rovers v Grimsby Town ....
Wolverhampton Wanderers v Brighton & Hove Albion .....

THIRD DIVISION
Bury v Birmingham City ....
Darlington v A.F.C. Bournemouth ....
Exeter City v West Bromwich Albion ....
Fulham v Chester City ....
Hartlepool United v Torquay United ....
Huddersfield Town v Bolton Wanderers ....
Hull City v Reading ....
Leyton Orient v Brentford ....
Preston North End v Peterborough United ....
Stoke City v Bradford City ....
Swansea City v Stockport County ....
Wigan Athletic v Shrewsbury Town ....

FOURTH DIVISION
Burnley v Doncaster Rovers ....
Carlisle United v Cardiff City ....
Crewe Alexandra v Rotherham United ....
Hereford United v Barnet ....
Lincoln City v Rochdale ....
Maidstone United v Aldershot ....
Mansfield Town v Chesterfield ....
Northampton Town v Wrexham ....
Scunthorpe United v Blackpool ....
Walsall v Scarborough ....
York City v Halifax Town ....

Sun. 29th December

SECOND DIVISION
Cambridge United v Watford ....

Wed. 1st January

FIRST DIVISION
Arsenal v Wimbledon ....
Chelsea v Manchester City ....
Coventry City v Tottenham Hotspur ....

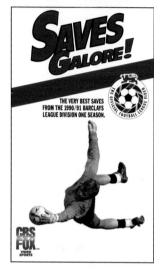

TBALL LEAGUE
JT NOW

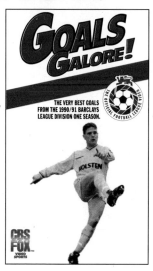

GOALS GALORE!

THE VERY BEST GOALS
FROM THE 1990/91 BARCLAYS
LEAGUE DIVISION ONE SEASON.

CBS
FOX
VIDEO
SPORTS

his season. It's action all the way.

NDING ON THE TERRACES.

Crystal Palace *v* Notts County ....
Liverpool *v* Sheffield United ....
Manchester United *v* Queens Park Rangers ....
Norwich City *v* Aston Villa ....
Nottingham Forest *v* Luton Town ....
Sheffield Wednesday *v* Oldham Athletic ....
Southampton *v* Everton ....
West Ham United *v* Leeds United ....

Blackburn Rovers *v* Cambridge United ....
Brighton & Hove Albion *v* Bristol City ....
Bristol Rovers *v* Leicester City ....
Charlton Athletic *v* Oxford United ....
Grimsby Town *v* Wolverhampton Wanderers ....
Middlesbrough *v* Derby County ....
Plymouth Argyle *v* Portsmouth ....
Port Vale *v* Ipswich Town ....
Southend United *v* Newcastle United ....
Sunderland *v* Barnsley ....
Swindon Town *v* Millwall ....
Watford *v* Tranmere Rovers ....

A.F.C. Bournemouth *v* Preston North End ....
Birmingham City *v* Hull City ....
Bolton Wanderers *v* Darlington ....
Bradford City *v* Leyton Orient ....
Brentford *v* Hartlepool United ....
Chester City *v* Huddersfield Town ....
Peterborough United *v* Bury ....
Reading *v* Swansea City ....
Shrewsbury Town *v* Stoke City ....
Stockport County *v* Wigan Athletic ....
Torquay United *v* Exeter City ....
West Bromwich Albion *v* Fulham ....

Aldershot *v* Crewe Alexandra ....
Barnet *v* Lincoln City ....
Blackpool *v* York City ....
Cardiff City *v* Maidstone United ....
Chesterfield *v* Burnley ....
Doncaster Rovers *v* Northampton Town ....
Gillingham *v* Hereford United ....
Rochdale *v* Walsall ....
Rotherham United *v* Carlisle United ....
Scarborough *v* Scunthorpe United ....
Wrexham *v* Mansfield Town ....

Fri. 3rd January

Aldershot *v* Scunthorpe United ....

Sat. 4th January

A.F.C. Bournemouth *v* Exeter City ....
Bolton Wanderers *v* Peterborough United ....
Bradford City *v* Bury ....
Chester City *v* Darlington ....
Fulham *v* Wigan Athletic ....
Huddersfield Town *v* Hull City ....
Leyton Orient *v* Shrewsbury Town ....
Preston North End *v* Reading ....
Stockport County *v* Brentford ....
Stoke City *v* Birmingham City ....
Swansea City *v* Hartlepool United ....
Torquay United *v* West Bromwich Albion ....

Burnley *v* Cardiff City ....
Chesterfield *v* Carlisle United ....
Halifax Town *v* Crewe Alexandra ....
Hereford United *v* Northampton Town ....
Lincoln City *v* Gillingham ....
Maidstone United *v* Blackpool ....
Rochdale *v* Wrexham ....
Rotherham United *v* Scarborough ....
Walsall *v* Doncaster Rovers ....
York City *v* Mansfield Town ....

Sat. 11th January

Arsenal *v* Aston Villa ....
Chelsea *v* Tottenham Hotspur ....
Coventry City *v* Queens Park Rangers ....
Crystal Palace *v* Manchester City ....
Liverpool *v* Luton Town ....
Manchester United *v* Everton ....
Norwich City *v* Oldham Athletic ....
Nottingham Forest *v* Notts County ....
Sheffield Wednesday *v* Leeds United ....
Southampton *v* Sheffield United ....
West Ham United *v* Wimbledon ....

Blackburn Rovers *v* Bristol City ......_4-0_
Brighton & Hove Albion *v* Barnsley ....
Bristol Rovers *v* Tranmere Rovers ....
Charlton Athletic *v* Wolverhampton Wanderers ....
Grimsby Town *v* Oxford United ....
Middlesbrough *v* Ipswich Town ....
Plymouth Argyle *v* Leicester City ....
Port Vale *v* Portsmouth ....
Southend United *v* Derby County ....
Sunderland *v* Millwall ....
Swindon Town *v* Cambridge United ....
Watford *v* Newcastle United ....

Birmingham City *v* Leyton Orient ....
Brentford *v* Stoke City ....
Bury *v* Swansea City ....
Darlington *v* Torquay United ....
Exeter City *v* Bolton Wanderers ....
Hartlepool United *v* Chester City ....
Hull City *v* Stockport County ....
Peterborough United *v* Fulham ....
Reading *v* Huddersfield Town ....
Shrewsbury Town *v* Preston North End ....
West Bromwich Albion *v* A.F.C. Bournemouth ....
Wigan Athletic *v* Bradford City ....

Barnet *v* Rotherham United ....
Blackpool *v* Burnley ....
Cardiff City *v* Hereford United ....
Carlisle United *v* Rochdale ....
Crewe Alexandra *v* Lincoln City ....
Doncaster Rovers *v* Halifax Town ....
Gillingham *v* Walsall ....
Mansfield Town *v* Aldershot ....
Northampton Town *v* York City ....
Scarborough *v* Chesterfield ....
Wrexham *v* Maidstone United ....

Fri. 17th January

Tranmere Rovers *v* Brighton & Hove Albion ....

Aldershot *v* Barnet ....

Sat. 18th January

FIRST DIVISION
Aston Villa *v* Sheffield Wednesday ....
Everton *v* Nottingham Forest ....
Leeds United *v* Crystal Palace ....
Luton Town *v* West Ham United ....
Manchester City *v* Coventry City ....
Notts County *v* Manchester United ....
Oldham Athletic *v* Liverpool ....
Queens Park Rangers *v* Arsenal ....
Sheffield United *v* Norwich City ....
Tottenham Hotspur *v* Southampton ....
Wimbledon *v* Chelsea ....

SECOND DIVISION
Barnsley *v* Plymouth Argyle ....
Bristol City *v* Southend United ....2-2.......................
Cambridge United *v* Grimsby Town ....
Derby County *v* Sunderland ....
Ipswich Town *v* Bristol Rovers ....
Leicester City *v* Swindon Town ....
Millwall *v* Middlesbrough ....
Newcastle United *v* Charlton Athletic ....
Oxford United *v* Port Vale ....
Portsmouth *v* Blackburn Rovers ....
Wolverhampton Wanderers *v* Watford ....

THIRD DIVISION
A.F.C. Bournemouth *v* Wigan Athletic ....
Bolton Wanderers *v* Hartlepool United ....
Bradford City *v* Hull City ....
Chester City *v* Brentford ....
Fulham *v* Shrewsbury Town ....
Huddersfield Town *v* Peterborough United ....
Leyton Orient *v* West Bromwich Albion ....
Preston North End *v* Exeter City ....
Stockport County *v* Darlington ....
Stoke City *v* Reading ....
Swansea City *v* Birmingham City ....
Torquay United *v* Bury ....

FOURTH DIVISION
Burnley *v* Gillingham ....
Chesterfield *v* Doncaster Rovers ....
Halifax Town *v* Scunthorpe United ....
Hereford United *v* Blackpool ....
Lincoln City *v* Wrexham ....
Maidstone United *v* Northampton Town ....
Rochdale *v* Crewe Alexandra ....
Rotherham United *v* Mansfield Town ....
Walsall *v* Cardiff City ....
York City *v* Carlisle United ....

Fri. 24th January

THIRD DIVISION
Wigan Athletic *v* Torquay United ....

FOURTH DIVISION
Doncaster Rovers *v* Hereford United ....

Sat. 25th January

THIRD DIVISION
Birmingham City *v* Bolton Wanderers ....
Brentford *v* Preston North End ....
Bury *v* Chester City ....

Darlington *v* Bradford City ....
Exeter City *v* Fulham ....
Hartlepool United *v* Stockport County ....
Hull City *v* Stoke City ....
Peterborough United *v* A.F.C. Bournemouth ....
Reading *v* Leyton Orient ....
Shrewsbury Town *v* Huddersfield Town ....
West Bromwich Albion *v* Swansea City ....

FOURTH DIVISION
Barnet *v* Burnley ....
Cardiff City *v* Chesterfield ....
Carlisle United *v* Halifax Town ....
Crewe Alexandra *v* York City ....
Gillingham *v* Rochdale ....
Mansfield Town *v* Lincoln City ....
Northampton Town *v* Aldershot ....
Scarborough *v* Maidstone United ....
Scunthorpe United *v* Walsall ....
Wrexham *v* Rotherham United ....

Tues. 28th January

FIRST DIVISION
Liverpool *v* Arsenal ....
Tottenham Hotspur *v* Oldham Athletic ....

SECOND DIVISION
Grimsby Town *v* Southend United ....

THIRD DIVISION
Swansea City *v* Darlington ....

Wed. 29th January

FIRST DIVISION
Nottingham Forest *v* Manchester United ....

SECOND DIVISION
Leicester City *v* Tranmere Rovers ....

Fri. 31st January

SECOND DIVISION
Cambridge United *v* Tranmere Rovers ....

THIRD DIVISION
Wigan Athletic *v* Birmingham City ....

FOURTH DIVISION
Cardiff City *v* Mansfield Town ....

Sat. 1st February

FIRST DIVISION
Arsenal *v* Manchester United ....
Aston Villa *v* Everton ....
Crystal Palace *v* Coventry City ....
Leeds United *v* Notts County ....
Liverpool *v* Chelsea ....
Manchester City *v* Tottenham Hotspur ....
Norwich City *v* Southampton ....
Nottingham Forest *v* Sheffield United ....
Queens Park Rangers *v* Wimbledon ....
Sheffield Wednesday *v* Luton Town ....
West Ham United *v* Oldham Athletic ....

SECOND DIVISION
Blackburn Rovers *v* Swindon Town ....

Brighton & Hove Albion v Charlton Athletic ....
Bristol City v Barnsley ....
Middlesbrough v Grimsby Town ....
Millwall v Ipswich Town ....
Oxford United v Newcastle United ....
Plymouth Argyle v Bristol Rovers ....
Portsmouth v Derby County ....
Southend United v Watford ....
Sunderland v Port Vale ....
Wolverhampton Wanderers v Leicester City ....

THIRD DIVISION
A.F.C. Bournemouth v Leyton Orient ....
Bury v Exeter City ....
Chester City v Stockport County ....
Fulham v Bolton Wanderers ....
Huddersfield Town v Preston North End ....
Hull City v Hartlepool United ....
Peterborough United v Reading ....
Shrewsbury Town v Darlington ....
Stoke City v Swansea City ....
Torquay United v Bradford City ....
West Bromwich Albion v Brentford ....

FOURTH DIVISION
Blackpool v Barnet ....
Carlisle United v Wrexham ....
Chesterfield v Halifax Town ....
Gillingham v Doncaster Rovers ....
Lincoln City v York City ....
Rochdale v Maidstone United ....
Rotherham United v Aldershot ....
Scarborough v Crewe Alexandra ....
Scunthorpe United v Northampton Town ....
Walsall v Burnley ....

Fri. 7th February

THIRD DIVISION
Stockport County v Huddersfield Town ....

FOURTH DIVISION
Crewe Alexandra v Carlisle United ....

Sat. 8th February

FIRST DIVISION
Chelsea v Crystal Palace ....
Coventry City v Liverpool ....
Everton v Queens Park Rangers ....
Luton Town v Norwich City ....
Manchester United v Sheffield Wednesday ....
Notts County v Arsenal ....
Oldham Athletic v Leeds United ....
Sheffield United v Manchester City ....
Southampton v Nottingham Forest ....
Tottenham Hotspur v West Ham United ....
Wimbledon v Aston Villa ....

SECOND DIVISION
Barnsley v Cambridge United ....
Bristol Rovers v Sunderland ....
Charlton Athletic v Southend United ....
Derby County v Millwall ....
Grimsby Town v Blackburn Rovers ....
Ipswich Town v Portsmouth ....
Leicester City v Oxford United ....
Newcastle United v Bristol City ....
Port Vale v Middlesbrough ....
Swindon Town v Brighton & Hove Albion ....

Tranmere Rovers v Wolverhampton Wanderers ....
Watford v Plymouth Argyle...

THIRD DIVISION
Birmingham City v West Bromwich Albion ....
Bolton Wanderers v Chester City ....
Bradford City v A.F.C. Bournemouth ....
Brentford v Bury ....
Darlington v Hull City ....
Exeter City v Wigan Athletic ....
Hartlepool United v Peterborough United ....
Leyton Orient v Stoke City ....
Preston North End v Fulham ....
Reading v Shrewsbury Town ....
Swansea City v Torquay United ....

FOURTH DIVISION
Aldershot v Walsall ....
Barnet v Scarborough ....
Burnley v Lincoln City ....
Doncaster Rovers v Cardiff City ....
Halifax Town v Rochdale ....
Hereford United v Chesterfield ....
Mansfield Town v Scunthorpe United ....
Northampton Town v Gillingham ....
Wrexham v Blackpool ....
York City v Rotherham United ....

Tues. 11th February

THIRD DIVISION
A.F.C. Bournemouth v Bury ....
Bolton Wanderers v Shrewsbury Town ....
Bradford City v Birmingham City ....
Chester City v Exeter City...
Fulham v Darlington ....
Huddersfield Town v Hartlepool United ....
Leyton Orient v Wigan Athletic ....
Preston North End v Hull City ....
Stockport County v Reading ....
Swansea City v Brentford ....
Torquay United v Peterborough United ....

FOURTH DIVISION
Aldershot v Gillingham ....
Burnley v Northampton Town ....
Chesterfield v Barnet ....
Rochdale v Scarborough ....
Rotherham United v Cardiff City ....
Walsall v Mansfield Town ....
York City v Scunthorpe United ....

Wed. 12th February

THIRD DIVISION
Stoke City v West Bromwich Albion ....

FOURTH DIVISION
Halifax Town v Blackpool ....
Hereford United v Crewe Alexandra ....
Lincoln City v Doncaster Rovers ....
Maidstone United v Carlisle United ....

Sat. 15th February

FIRST DIVISION
Arsenal v Sheffield Wednesday ....
Chelsea v Southampton ....
Coventry City v Norwich City ....
Crystal Palace v Nottingham Forest ....

Leeds United v Aston Villa ....

Liverpool v Wimbledon ....

Manchester City v Luton Town ....

Notts County v Everton ....

Oldham Athletic v Queens Park Rangers ....

Sheffield United v Tottenham Hotspur ....

West Ham United v Manchester United ....

SECOND DIVISION

Barnsley v Southend United ....

Blackburn Rovers v Newcastle United ....

Brighton & Hove Albion v Oxford United ....

Bristol City v Middlesbrough ....

Cambridge United v Charlton Athletic ....

Derby County v Bristol Rovers ....

Ipswich Town v Wolverhampton Wanderers ....

Millwall v Grimsby Town ....

Port Vale v Leicester City ....

Portsmouth v Watford ....

Sunderland v Plymouth Argyle ....

Swindon Town v Tranmere Rovers ....

THIRD DIVISION

Birmingham City v A.F.C. Bournemouth ....

Brentford v Torquay United ....

Bury v Leyton Orient ....

Darlington v Huddersfield Town ....

Exeter City v Swansea City ....

Hartlepool United v Preston North End ....

Hull City v Bolton Wanderers ....

Peterborough United v Stockport County ....

Reading v Fulham ....

Shrewsbury Town v Chester City ....

West Bromwich Albion v Bradford City ....

Wigan Athletic v Stoke City ....

FOURTH DIVISION

Barnet v Maidstone United ....

Blackpool v Rochdale ....

Cardiff City v York City ....

Crewe Alexandra v Chesterfield ....

Doncaster Rovers v Aldershot ....

Gillingham v Rotherham United ....

Mansfield Town v Hereford United ....

Northampton Town v Walsall ....

Scarborough v Lincoln City ....

Scunthorpe United v Burnley ....

Wrexham v Halifax Town ....

Fri. 21st February

SECOND DIVISION

Tranmere Rovers v Ipswich Town ....

FOURTH DIVISION

Aldershot v Mansfield Town ....

Sat. 22nd February

FIRST DIVISION

Aston Villa v Oldham Athletic ....

Everton v Leeds United ....

Luton Town v Sheffield United ....

Manchester United v Crystal Palace ....

Norwich City v Liverpool ....

Nottingham Forest v Chelsea ....

Queens Park Rangers v Notts County ....

Sheffield Wednesday v West Ham United ....

Southampton v Coventry City ....

Tottenham Hotspur v Arsenal ....

Wimbledon v Manchester City ....

SECOND DIVISION

Bristol Rovers v Millwall ....

Charlton Athletic v Bristol City ....

Grimsby Town v Swindon Town ....

Leicester City v Derby County ....

Middlesbrough v Blackburn Rovers ....

Newcastle United v Barnsley ....

Oxford United v Cambridge United ....

Plymouth Argyle v Brighton & Hove Albion ....

Southend United v Sunderland ....

Watford v Port Vale ....

Wolverhampton Wanderers v Portsmouth ....

THIRD DIVISION

A.F.C. Bournemouth v West Bromwich Albion ....

Bolton Wanderers v Exeter City ....

Bradford City v Wigan Athletic ....

Chester City v Hartlepool United ....

Fulham v Peterborough United ....

Huddersfield Town v Reading ....

Leyton Orient v Birmingham City ....

Preston North End v Shrewsbury Town ....

Stockport County v Hull City ....

Stoke City v Brentford ....

Swansea City v Bury ....

Torquay United v Darlington ....

FOURTH DIVISION

Burnley v Blackpool ....

Chesterfield v Scarborough ....

Halifax Town v Doncaster Rovers ....

Hereford United v Cardiff City ....

Lincoln City v Crewe Alexandra ....

Maidstone United v Wrexham ....

Rochdale v Carlisle United ....

Rotherham United v Barnet ....

Walsall v Gillingham ....

York City v Northampton Town ....

Fri. 28th February

SECOND DIVISION

Cambridge United v Bristol Rovers ....

THIRD DIVISION

Wigan Athletic v Fulham ....

FOURTH DIVISION

Crewe Alexandra v Halifax Town ....

Sat. 29th February

FIRST DIVISION

Arsenal v Nottingham Forest ....

Chelsea v Sheffield Wednesday ....

Coventry City v Manchester United ....

Crystal Palace v Norwich City ....

Leeds United v Luton Town ....

Liverpool v Southampton ....

Manchester City v Aston Villa ....

Notts County v Tottenham Hotspur ....

Oldham Athletic v Wimbledon ....

Sheffield United v Queens Park Rangers ....

West Ham United v Everton ....

SECOND DIVISION

Barnsley v Charlton Athletic ....

Blackburn Rovers v Oxford United ....

Brighton & Hove Albion v Southend United ....

Bristol City v Grimsby Town ....

Derby County *v* Watford ....
Ipswich Town *v* Plymouth Argyle ....
Millwall *v* Leicester City ....
Port Vale *v* Newcastle United ....
Portsmouth *v* Tranmere Rovers ....
Sunderland *v* Wolverhampton Wanderers ....
Swindon Town *v* Middlesbrough ....

Birmingham City *v* Stoke City ....
Brentford *v* Stockport County ....
Bury *v* Bradford City ....
Darlington *v* Chester City ....
Exeter City *v* A.F.C. Bournemouth ....
Hartlepool United *v* Swansea City ....
Hull City *v* Huddersfield Town ....
Peterborough United *v* Bolton Wanderers ....
Reading *v* Preston North End ....
Shrewsbury Town *v* Leyton Orient ....
West Bromwich Albion *v* Torquay United ....

FOURTH DIVISION
Blackpool *v* Maidstone United ....
Cardiff City *v* Burnley ....
Carlisle United *v* Chesterfield ....
Doncaster Rovers *v* Walsall ....
Gillingham *v* Lincoln City ....
Mansfield Town *v* York City ....
Northampton Town *v* Hereford United ....
Scarborough *v* Rotherham United ....
Scunthorpe United *v* Aldershot ....
Wrexham *v* Rochdale ....

Tues. 3rd March

THIRD DIVISION
Birmingham City *v* Swansea City ....
Brentford *v* Chester City ....
Bury *v* Torquay United ....
Darlington *v* Stockport County ....
Hartlepool United *v* Bolton Wanderers ....
Hull City *v* Bradford City ....
Peterborough United *v* Huddersfield Town ....
Shrewsbury Town *v* Fulham ....
Wigan Athletic *v* A.F.C. Bournemouth ....

FOURTH DIVISION
Barnet *v* Aldershot ....
Blackpool *v* Hereford United ....
Cardiff City *v* Walsall ....
Carlisle United *v* York City ....
Crewe Alexandra *v* Rochdale ....
Doncaster Rovers *v* Chesterfield ....
Gillingham *v* Burnley ....
Mansfield Town *v* Rotherham United ....
Northampton Town *v* Maidstone United ....
Scunthorpe United *v* Halifax Town ....
Wrexham *v* Lincoln City ....

Wed. 4th March

THIRD DIVISION
Exeter City *v* Preston North End ....
Reading *v* Stoke City ....
West Bromwich Albion *v* Leyton Orient ....

Fri. 6th March

SECOND DIVISION
Tranmere Rovers *v* Port Vale ....

THIRD DIVISION
Stockport County *v* Hartlepool United ....

FOURTH DIVISION
Halifax Town *v* Carlisle United ....

Sat. 7th March

FIRST DIVISION
Aston Villa *v* Sheffield United ....
Everton *v* Oldham Athletic ....
Luton Town *v* Crystal Palace ....
Manchester United *v* Chelsea ....
Norwich City *v* Arsenal ....
Nottingham Forest *v* Liverpool ....
Queens Park Rangers *v* Manchester City ....
Sheffield Wednesday *v* Coventry City ....
Southampton *v* West Ham United ....
Tottenham Hotspur *v* Leeds United ....
Wimbledon *v* Notts County ....

SECOND DIVISION
Bristol Rovers *v* Blackburn Rovers ....
Charlton Athletic *v* Millwall ....
Grimsby Town *v* Barnsley ....
Leicester City *v* Sunderland ....
Middlesbrough *v* Cambridge United ....
Newcastle United *v* Brighton & Hove Albion ....
Oxford United *v* Swindon Town ....
Plymouth Argyle *v* Derby County ....
Southend United *v* Portsmouth ....
Watford *v* Ipswich Town ....
Wolverhampton Wanderers *v* Bristol City ....

THIRD DIVISION
A.F.C. Bournemouth *v* Peterborough United ....
Bolton Wanderers *v* Birmingham City ....
Bradford City *v* Darlington ....
Chester City *v* Bury ....
Fulham *v* Exeter City ....
Huddersfield Town *v* Shrewsbury Town ....
Leyton Orient *v* Reading ....
Preston North End *v* Brentford ....
Stoke City *v* Hull City ....
Swansea City *v* West Bromwich Albion ....
Torquay United *v* Wigan Athletic ....

FOURTH DIVISION
Aldershot *v* Northampton Town ....
Burnley *v* Barnet ....
Chesterfield *v* Cardiff City ....
Hereford United *v* Doncaster Rovers ....
Lincoln City *v* Mansfield Town ....
Maidstone United *v* Scarborough ....
Rochdale *v* Gillingham ....
Rotherham United *v* Wrexham ....
Walsall *v* Scunthorpe United ....
York City *v* Crewe Alexandra ....

Tues. 10th March

FIRST DIVISION
Arsenal *v* Oldham Athletic ....
Liverpool *v* West Ham United ....
Notts County *v* Aston Villa ....
Wimbledon *v* Everton ....

SECOND DIVISION
Blackburn Rovers *v* Southend United ....
Cambridge United *v* Newcastle United ....
Grimsby Town *v* Brighton & Hove Albion ....

Middlesbrough v Barnsley ....
Plymouth Argyle v Bristol City ....
Sunderland v Ipswich Town ....
Swindon Town v Oldham Athletic ....

A.F.C. Bournemouth v Torquay United ....
Birmingham City v Brentford ....
Bolton Wanderers v Stockport County ....
Bradford City v Exeter City ....
Chester City v Peterborough United ....
Darlington v Reading ....
Fulham v Huddersfield Town ....
Leyton Orient v Swansea City ....
Shrewsbury Town v Hull City ....
Wigan Athletic v Preston North End ....

Blackpool v Aldershot ....
Cardiff City v Gillingham ....
Carlisle United v Barnet ....
Mansfield Town v Northampton Town ....
Rochdale v Scunthorpe United ....
Rotherham United v Doncaster Rovers ....
Wrexham v Scarborough ....
York City v Burnley ....

Wed. 11th March

Coventry City v Nottingham Forest ....
Luton Town v Tottenham Hotspur ....
Manchester United v Manchester City ....
Norwich City v Chelsea ....
Queens Park Rangers v Leeds United ....
Sheffield Wednesday v Sheffield United ....
Southampton v Crystal Palace ....

Bristol Rovers v Wolverhampton Wanderers ....
Derby County v Port Vale ....
Leicester City v Portsmouth ....
Millwall v Tranmere Rovers ....
Oxford United v Watford ....

Stoke City v Bury ....
West Bromwich Albion v Hartlepool United ....

Halifax Town v Hereford United ....
Lincoln City v Walsall ....
Maidstone United v Crewe Alexandra ....

Fri. 13th March

Stockport County v A.F.C. Bournemouth ....

Sat. 14th March

Aston Villa v Queens Park Rangers ....
Chelsea v Coventry City ....
Crystal Palace v Liverpool ....
Everton v Luton Town ....
Leeds United v Wimbledon ....
Manchester City v Southampton ....

Nottingham Forest v Norwich City ....
Oldham Athletic v Notts County ....
Sheffield United v Manchester United ....
Tottenham Hotspur v Sheffield Wednesday ....
West Ham United v Arsenal ....

Barnsley v Oxford United ....
Brighton & Hove Albion v Blackburn Rovers ....
Bristol City v Cambridge United ....
Charlton Athletic v Grimsby Town ....
Ipswich Town v Leicester City ....
Newcastle United v Swindon Town ....
Port Vale v Bristol Rovers ....
Portsmouth v Millwall ....
Southend United v Middlesbrough ....
Tranmere Rovers v Derby County ....
Watford v Sunderland ....
Wolverhampton Wanderers v Plymouth Argyle ....

Brentford v Bradford City ....
Bury v West Bromwich Albion ....
Exeter City v Leyton Orient ....
Hartlepool United v Darlington ....
Huddersfield Town v Stoke City ....
Hull City v Fulham ....
Peterborough United v Shrewsbury Town ....
Preston North End v Chester City ....
Reading v Bolton Wanderers ....
Swansea City v Wigan Athletic ....
Torquay United v Birmingham City ....

Aldershot v Lincoln City ....
Barnet v Wrexham ....
Burnley v Halifax Town ....
Chesterfield v Rochdale ....
Doncaster Rovers v Mansfield Town ....
Gillingham v Carlisle United ....
Hereford United v Maidstone United ....
Northampton Town v Rotherham United ....
Scarborough v Blackpool ....
Scunthorpe United v Cardiff City ....
Walsall v York City ....

Fri. 20th March

A.F.C. Bournemouth v Swansea City ....
Fulham v Hartlepool United ....
Shrewsbury Town v Stockport County ....
Wigan Athletic v Brentford ....

Cardiff City v Aldershot ....

Sat. 21st March

Arsenal v Leeds United ....
Chelsea v Sheffield United ....
Coventry City v Oldham Athletic ....
Crystal Palace v Aston Villa ....
Liverpool v Tottenham Hotspur ....
Manchester United v Wimbledon ....
Norwich City v Everton ....
Nottingham Forest v Manchester City ....
Sheffield Wednesday v Notts County ....
Southampton v Luton Town ....
West Ham United v Queens Park Rangers ....

SECOND DIVISION

Blackburn Rovers v Charlton Athletic ....
Bristol Rovers v Barnsley ....
Cambridge United v Ipswich Town ....
Derby County v Wolverhampton Wanderers ....
Grimsby Town v Newcastle United ....
Leicester City v Watford ....
Middlesbrough v Brighton & Hove Albion ....
Millwall v Port Vale ....
Oxford United v Portsmouth ....
Plymouth Argyle v Tranmere Rovers ....
Sunderland v Bristol City ....
Swindon Town v Southend United ....

THIRD DIVISION

Birmingham City v Huddersfield Town ....
Bolton Wanderers v Bury ....
Bradford City v Peterborough United ....
Chester City v Hull City ....
Darlington v Preston North End ....
Leyton Orient v Torquay United ....
Stoke City v Exeter City ....
West Bromwich Albion v Reading ....

FOURTH DIVISION

Blackpool v Chesterfield ....
Carlisle United v Scarborough ....
Halifax Town v Barnet ....
Lincoln City v Northampton Town ....
Maidstone United v Gillingham ....
Mansfield Town v Burnley ....
Rochdale v Hereford United ....
Rotherham United v Scunthorpe United ....
Wrexham v Crewe Alexandra ....
York City v Doncaster Rovers ....

Fri. 27th March

SECOND DIVISION

Tranmere Rovers v Leicester City ....

THIRD DIVISION

Stockport County v Fulham ....

FOURTH DIVISION

Aldershot v York City ....

Sat. 28th March

FIRST DIVISION

Aston Villa v Norwich City ....
Everton v Southampton ....
Leeds United v West Ham United ....
Luton Town v Nottingham Forest ....
Manchester City v Chelsea ....
Notts County v Crystal Palace ....
Oldham Athletic v Sheffield Wednesday ....
Queens Park Rangers v Manchester United ....
Sheffield United v Liverpool ....
Tottenham Hotspur v Coventry City ....
Wimbledon v Arsenal ....

SECOND DIVISION

Barnsley v Blackburn Rovers ....
Brighton & Hove Albion v Cambridge United ....
Bristol City v Oxford United ....
Charlton Athletic v Middlesbrough ....
Ipswich Town v Derby County ....
Port Vale v Plymouth Argyle ....
Portsmouth v Swindon Town ....
Southend United v Grimsby Town ....

Watford v Bristol Rovers ....
Wolverhampton Wanderers v Millwall ....

THIRD DIVISION

Bury v Wigan Athletic ....
Exeter City v Birmingham City ....
Hartlepool United v Shrewsbury Town ....
Huddersfield Town v West Bromwich Albion ....
Hull City v Leyton Orient ....
Peterborough United v Darlington ....
Preston North End v Bolton Wanderers ....
Reading v Chester City ....
Swansea City v Bradford City ....
Torquay United v Stoke City ....

FOURTH DIVISION

Barnet v Rochdale ....
Burnley v Maidstone United ....
Chesterfield v Wrexham ....
Crewe Alexandra v Blackpool ....
Gillingham v Mansfield Town ....
Hereford United v Carlisle United ....
Northampton Town v Cardiff City ....
Scarborough v Halifax Town ....
Scunthorpe United v Lincoln City ....
Walsall v Rotherham United ....

Sun. 29th March

SECOND DIVISION

Newcastle United v Sunderland ....

THIRD DIVISION

Brentford v A.F.C. Bournemouth ....

Tue. 31st March

SECOND DIVISION

Ipswich Town v Barnsley ....
Plymouth Argyle v Grimsby Town ....
Port Vale v Blackburn Rovers ....
Portsmouth v Charlton Athletic ....
Tranmere Rovers v Bristol City ....
Watford v Brighton & Hove Albion ....
Wolverhampton Wanderers v Newcastle United ....

THIRD DIVISION

Bolton Wanderers v A.F.C. Bournemouth ....
Chester City v Bradford City ....
Darlington v Leyton Orient ....
Fulham v Stoke City ....
Hartlepool United v Exeter City ....
Huddersfield Town v Bury ....
Hull City v Wigan Athletic ....
Peterborough United v Birmingham City ....
Preston North End v Swansea City ....
Shrewsbury Town v Torquay United ....
Stockport County v West Bromwich Albion ....

FOURTH DIVISION

Aldershot v Scarborough ....
Burnley v Hereford United ....
Cardiff City v Blackpool ....
Doncaster Rovers v Barnet ....
Gillingham v Wrexham ....
Mansfield Town v Crewe Alexandra ....
Northampton Town v Rochdale ....
Rotherham United v Halifax Town ....
Scunthorpe United v Chesterfield ....
Walsall v Maidstone United ....

Wed. 1st April

SECOND DIVISION
Bristol Rovers v Southend United ....
Derby County v Cambridge United ....
Leicester City v Middlesbrough ....
Millwall v Oxford United ....
Sunderland v Swindon Town ....

THIRD DIVISION
Reading v Brentford ....

FOURTH DIVISION
Lincoln City v Carlisle United ....

Fri. 3rd April

THIRD DIVISION
A.F.C. Bournemouth v Chester City ....
Wigan Athletic v Peterborough United ....

FOURTH DIVISION
Halifax Town v Walsall ....
Wrexham v Doncaster Rovers ....

Sat. 4th April

FIRST DIVISION
Chelsea v West Ham United ....
Coventry City v Arsenal ....
Crystal Palace v Everton ....
Liverpool v Notts County ....
Luton Town v Wimbledon ....
Manchester City v Leeds United ....
Norwich City v Manchester United ....
Nottingham Forest v Sheffield Wednesday ....
Sheffield United v Oldham Athletic ....
Southampton v Queens Park Rangers ....
Tottenham Hotspur v Aston Villa ....

SECOND DIVISION
Barnsley v Derby County ....
Blackburn Rovers v Sunderland ....
Brighton & Hove Albion v Portsmouth ....
Bristol City v Leicester City ....
Cambridge United v Millwall ....
Charlton Athletic v Plymouth Argyle ....
Grimsby Town v Bristol Rovers ....
Middlesbrough v Watford ....
Newcastle United v Tranmere Rovers ....
Oxford United v Wolverhampton Wanderers ....
Southend United v Ipswich Town ....
Swindon Town v Port Vale ....

THIRD DIVISION
Birmingham City v Reading ....
Bradford City v Preston North End ....
Brentford v Shrewsbury Town ....
Bury v Hull City ....
Exeter City v Huddersfield Town ....
Leyton Orient v Hartlepool United ....
Stoke City v Darlington ....
Swansea City v Fulham ....
Torquay United v Stockport County ....
West Bromwich Albion v Bolton Wanderers ....

FOURTH DIVISION
Barnet v Northampton Town ....
Blackpool v Mansfield Town ....
Carlisle United v Aldershot ....
Chesterfield v York City ....

Crewe Alexandra v Burnley ....
Hereford United v Rotherham United ....
Maidstone United v Scunthorpe United ....
Rochdale v Cardiff City ....
Scarborough v Gillingham ....

Fri. 10th April

SECOND DIVISION
Tranmere Rovers v Middlesbrough ....

FOURTH DIVISION
Aldershot v Wrexham ....

Sat. 11th April

FIRST DIVISION
Arsenal v Crystal Palace ....
Aston Villa v Liverpool ....
Everton v Sheffield United ....
Leeds United v Chelsea ....
Manchester United v Southampton ....
Notts County v Coventry City ....
Oldham Athletic v Luton Town ....
Queens Park Rangers v Tottenham Hotspur ....
Sheffield Wednesday v Manchester City ....
West Ham United v Norwich City ....
Wimbledon v Nottingham Forest ....

SECOND DIVISION
Bristol Rovers v Swindon Town ....
Derby County v Oxford United ....
Ipswich Town v Newcastle United ....
Leicester City v Barnsley ....
Millwall v Bristol City ....
Plymouth Argyle v Southend United ....
Port Vale v Brighton & Hove Albion ....
Portsmouth v Grimsby Town ....
Sunderland v Charlton Athletic ....
Watford v Blackburn Rovers ....
Wolverhampton Wanderers v Cambridge United ....

THIRD DIVISION
Bolton Wanderers v Bradford City ....
Chester City v Birmingham City ....
Darlington v Swansea City ....
Fulham v Bury ....
Hartlepool United v Stoke City ....
Huddersfield Town v Wigan Athletic ....
Hull City v Brentford ....
Peterborough United v West Bromwich Albion ....
Preston North End v Leyton Orient ....
Reading v Torquay United ....
Shrewsbury Town v A.F.C. Bournemouth ....
Stockport County v Exeter City ....

FOURTH DIVISION
Cardiff City v Halifax Town ....
Doncaster Rovers v Scarborough ....
Gillingham v Blackpool ....
Lincoln City v Maidstone United ....
Mansfield Town v Carlisle United ....
Northampton Town v Crewe Alexandra ....
Rotherham United v Rochdale ....
Scunthorpe United v Barnet ....
Walsall v Chesterfield ....
York City v Hereford United ....

Tues. 14th April

THIRD DIVISION
A.F.C. Bournemouth v Huddersfield Town ....
Torquay United v Hull City ....

Blackpool v Doncaster Rovers ....
Scarborough v Cardiff City ....

Wed. 15th April

SECOND DIVISION
Brighton & Hove Albion v Derby County ....
Southend United v Port Vale ....

Fri. 17th April

SECOND DIVISION
Cambridge United v Portsmouth ....

THIRD DIVISION
Brentford v Darlington ....
Swansea City v Shrewsbury Town ....

FOURTH DIVISION
Halifax Town v Aldershot ....

Sat. 18th April

FIRST DIVISION
Chelsea v Queens Park Rangers ....
Coventry City v Everton ....
Crystal Palace v Oldham Athletic ....
Liverpool v Leeds United ....
Luton Town v Manchester United ....
Manchester City v West Ham United ....
Norwich City v Notts County ....
Nottingham Forest v Aston Villa ....
Sheffield United v Arsenal ....
Southampton v Sheffield Wednesday ....
Tottenham Hotspur v Wimbledon ....

SECOND DIVISION
Barnsley v Tranmere Rovers ....
Blackburn Rovers v Leicester City ....
Bristol City v Ipswich Town ....
Charlton Athletic v Watford ....
Grimsby Town v Sunderland ....
Middlesbrough v Plymouth Argyle ....
Newcastle United v Millwall ....
Oxford United v Bristol Rovers ....
Swindon Town v Wolverhampton Wanderers ....

THIRD DIVISION
Birmingham City v Hartlepool United ....
Bradford City v Reading ....
Bury v Stockport County ....
Exeter City v Peterborough United ....
Leyton Orient v Fulham ....
Stoke City v Preston North End ....
West Bromwich Albion v Chester City ....
Wigan Athletic v Bolton Wanderers ....

FOURTH DIVISION
Barnet v Gillingham ....
Carlisle United v Northampton Town ....
Chesterfield v Lincoln City ....
Crewe Alexandra v Scunthorpe United ....
Hereford United v Walsall ....
Maidstone United v Rotherham United ....
Rochdale v Burnley ....
Wrexham v York City ....

Mon. 20th April

FIRST DIVISION
Arsenal v Liverpool ....
Aston Villa v Chelsea ....
Everton v Manchester City ....
Manchester United v Nottingham Forest ....
Notts County v Sheffield United ....
Oldham Athletic v Tottenham Hotspur ....
Queens Park Rangers v Luton Town ....
Sheffield Wednesday v Norwich City ....
West Ham United v Crystal Palace ....
Wimbledon v Southampton ....

SECOND DIVISION
Bristol Rovers v Brighton & Hove Albion ....
Derby County v Newcastle United ....
Plymouth Argyle v Oxford United ....
Port Vale v Charlton Athletic ....
Portsmouth v Bristol City ....
Sunderland v Middlesbrough ....
Tranmere Rovers v Blackburn Rovers ....
Watford v Swindon Town ....
Wolverhampton Wanderers v Southend United ....

THIRD DIVISION
Bolton Wanderers v Brentford ....
Chester City v Torquay United ....
Darlington v Wigan Athletic ....
Fulham v A.F.C. Bournemouth ....
Hartlepool United v Bury ....
Huddersfield Town v Leyton Orient ....
Hull City v West Bromwich Albion ....
Preston North End v Birmingham City ....
Reading v Exeter City ....
Shrewsbury Town v Bradford City ....
Stockport County v Stoke City ....

FOURTH DIVISION
Aldershot v Chesterfield ....
Burnley v Scarborough ....
Cardiff City v Barnet ....
Doncaster Rovers v Rochdale ....
Gillingham v Crewe Alexandra ....
Lincoln City v Hereford United ....
Rotherham United v Blackpool ....
Scunthorpe United v Wrexham ....
York City v Maidstone United ....

Tues. 21st April

FIRST DIVISION
Leeds United v Coventry City ....

SECOND DIVISION
Ipswich Town v Grimsby Town ....
Leicester City v Cambridge United ....

THIRD DIVISION
Peterborough United v Swansea City ....

FOURTH DIVISION
Mansfield Town v Halifax Town ....
Walsall v Carlisle United ....

Wed. 22nd April

SECOND DIVISION
Millwall v Barnsley ....

Fri. 24th April

Wigan Athletic v Hartlepool United ....

Crewe Alexandra v Doncaster Rovers ....

Sat. 25th April

FIRST DIVISION
Chelsea v Arsenal ....
Coventry City v West Ham United ....
Crystal Palace v Sheffield Wednesday ....
Liverpool v Manchester United ....
Luton Town v Aston Villa ....
Manchester City v Notts County ....
Norwich City v Wimbledon ....
Nottingham Forest v Queens Park Rangers ....
Sheffield United v Leeds United ....
Southampton v Oldham Athletic ....
Tottenham Hotspur v Everton ....

SECOND DIVISION
Barnsley v Wolverhampton Wanderers ....
Blackburn Rovers v Millwall ....
Brighton & Hove Albion v Sunderland ....
Bristol City v Derby County ....
Cambridge United v Port Vale ....
Charlton Athletic v Leicester City ....
Grimsby Town v Watford ....
Middlesbrough v Bristol Rovers ....
Newcastle United v Portsmouth ....
Oxford United v Ipswich Town ....
Southend United v Tranmere Rovers ....
Swindon Town v Plymouth Argyle ....

THIRD DIVISION
A.F.C. Bournemouth v Reading ....
Birmingham City v Shrewsbury Town ....
Bradford City v Stockport County ....
Bury v Darlington ....
Exeter City v Hull City ....
Leyton Orient v Peterborough United ....
Stoke City v Chester City ....
Swansea City v Huddersfield Town ....
Torquay United v Bolton Wanderers ....
West Bromwich Albion v Preston North End ....

FOURTH DIVISION
Barnet v Walsall ....
Blackpool v Northampton Town ....
Carlisle United v Burnley ....
Chesterfield v Gillingham ....
Halifax Town v Lincoln City ....
Hereford United v Scunthorpe United ....
Maidstone United v Mansfield Town ....
Rochdale v Aldershot ....
Scarborough v York City ....
Wrexham v Cardiff City ....

Sun. 26th April

Brentford v Fulham ....

Sat. 2nd May

FIRST DIVISION
Arsenal v Southampton ....
Aston Villa v Coventry City ....
Everton v Chelsea ....
Leeds United v Norwich City ....
Manchester United v Tottenham Hotspur ....
Notts County v Luton Town ....
Oldham Athletic v Manchester City ....
Queens Park Rangers v Crystal Palace ....
Sheffield Wednesday v Liverpool ....
West Ham United v Nottingham Forest ....
Wimbledon v Sheffield United ....

SECOND DIVISION
Bristol Rovers v Charlton Athletic ....
Derby County v Swindon Town ....
Ipswich Town v Brighton & Hove Albion ....
Leicester City v Newcastle United ....
Millwall v Southend United ....
Plymouth Argyle v Blackburn Rovers ....
Port Vale v Grimsby Town ....
Portsmouth v Barnsley ....
Sunderland v Cambridge United ....
Tranmere Rovers v Oxford United ....
Watford v Bristol City ....
Wolverhampton Wanderers v Middlesbrough ....

THIRD DIVISION
Bolton Wanderers v Stoke City ....
Chester City v Leyton Orient ....
Darlington v Exeter City ....
Fulham v Bradford City ....
Hartlepool United v A.F.C. Bournemouth ....
Huddersfield Town v Torquay United ....
Hull City v Swansea City ....
Peterborough United v Brentford ....
Preston North End v Bury ....
Reading v Wigan Athletic ....
Shrewsbury Town v West Bromwich Albion ....
Stockport County v Birmingham City ....

FOURTH DIVISION
Aldershot v Hereford United ....
Burnley v Wrexham ....
Doncaster Rovers v Maidstone United ....
Gillingham v Halifax Town ....
Lincoln City v Blackpool ....
Mansfield Town v Rochdale ....
Northampton Town v Scarborough ....
Rotherham United v Chesterfield ....
Scunthorpe United v Carlisle United ....
Walsall v Crewe Alexandra ....
York City v Barnet ....

It's what your body thirsts for

B & Q LEAGUE FIXTURES 1991-92

© The Scottish Football League 1991

Sat. 10th August

PREMIER DIVISION

Airdrieonians v Aberdeen ....
Dundee United v Celtic ....
Dunfermline Athletic v Heart of Midlothian ....
Falkirk v Motherwell ....
Hibernian v St Mirren ....
Rangers v St Johnstone ....

FIRST DIVISION

Clydebank v Dundee ....
Forfar Athletic v Ayr United ....
Kilmarnock v Stirling Albion ....
Meadowbank Thistle v Raith Rovers ....
Montrose v Hamilton Academical ....
Morton v Partick Thistle ....

SECOND DIVISION

Albion Rovers v Arbroath ....
Berwick Rangers v Stenhousemuir ....
Brechin City v Alloa ....
Clyde v East Fife ....
Cowdenbeath v Queen of the South ....
Queen's Park v Dumbarton ....
Stanraer v East Stirlingshire ....

Tues. 13th August

PREMIER DIVISION

Airdrieonians v Heart of Midlothian ....
Dundee United v St Mirren ....
Dunfermline Athletic v Celtic ....
Hibernian v St Johnstone ....
Rangers v Motherwell ....

FIRST DIVISION

Clydebank v Raith Rovers ....
Forfar Athletic v Dundee ....
Kilmarnock v Hamilton Academical ....
Montrose v Ayr United ....
Morton v Stirling Albion ....

Wed. 14th August

PREMIER DIVISION

Falkirk v Aberdeen ....

FIRST DIVISION

Meadowbank Thistle v Partick Thistle ....

Sat. 17th August

PREMIER DIVISION

Aberdeen v Dunfermline Athletic ....
Celtic v Falkirk ....
Heart of Midlothian v Rangers ....
Motherwell v Hibernian ....
St Johnstone v Dundee United ....
St Mirren v Airdrieonians ....

FIRST DIVISION

Ayr United v Clydebank ....
Dundee v Meadowbank Thistle ....
Hamilton Academical v Morton ....
Partick Thistle v Kilmarnock ....
Raith Rovers v Forfar Athletic ....
Stirling Albion v Montrose ....

SECOND DIVISION

Alloa v Albion Rovers ....
Arbroath v Stranraer ....
Dumbarton v Berwick Rangers ....
East Fife v Queen's Park ....
East Stirlingshire v Cowdenbeath ....
Queen of the South v Clyde ....
Stenhousemuir v Brechin City ....

Sat. 24th August

PREMIER DIVISION

Aberdeen v Celtic ....
Airdrieonians v Motherwell ....
Hibernian v Dundee United ....
Rangers v Dunfermline Athletic ....
St Johnstone v Heart of Midlothian ....
St Mirren v Falkirk ....

FIRST DIVISION

Ayr United v Raith Rovers ....
Clydebank v Montrose ....
Dundee v Hamilton Academical ....
Forfar Athletic v Morton ....
Meadowbank Thistle v Kilmarnock ....
Partick Thistle v Stirling Albion ....

SECOND DIVISION

Albion Rovers v Queen of the South ....
Berwick Rangers v Arbroath ....
Brechin City v East Fife ....
Clyde v Alloa ....
Cowdenbeath v Stenhousemuir ....
Queen's Park v East Stirlingshire ....
Stranraer v Dumbarton ....

Sat. 31st August

PREMIER DIVISION

Celtic v Rangers ....
Dundee United v Aberdeen ....
Dunfermline Athletic v St Johnstone ....
Falkirk v Airdrieonians ....
Heart of Midlothian v Hibernian ....
Motherwell v St Mirren ....

FIRST DIVISION

Hamilton Academical v Partick Thistle ....
Kilmarnock v Ayr United ....
Montrose v Forfar Athletic ....
Morton v Clydebank ....
Raith Rovers v Dundee ....
Stirling Albion v Meadowbank Thistle ....

Alloa v Queen's Park ....
Arbroath v Cowdenbeath ....
Dumbarton v Albion Rovers ....
East Fife v Stranraer ....
East Stirlingshire v Brechin City ....
Queen of the South v Berwick Rangers ....
Stenhousemuir v Clyde ....

Sat. 7th September

PREMIER DIVISION

Aberdeen v St Johnstone ....
Airdrieonians v Hibernian ....
Celtic v St Mirren ....
Dundee United v Dunfermline Athletic ....
Falkirk v Rangers ....
Heart of Midlothian v Motherwell ....

FIRST DIVISION

Ayr United v Partick Thistle ....
Clydebank v Kilmarnock ....
Hamilton Academical v Forfar Athletic ....
Montrose v Meadowbank Thistle ....
Morton v Dundee ....
Raith Rovers v Stirling Albion ....

SECOND DIVISION

Alloa v Queen of the South ....
Arbroath v East Stirlingshire ....
Berwick Rangers v Brechin City ....
Cowdenbeath v Albion Rovers ....
Dumbarton v Clyde ....
Stenhousemuir v East Fife ....
Stranraer v Queen's Park ....

Tues. 10th September

SECOND DIVISION

Clyde v Berwick Rangers ....

Sat. 14th September

PREMIER DIVISION

Dunfermline Athletic v Airdrieonians ....
Hibernian v Falkirk ....
Motherwell v Aberdeen ....
Rangers v Dundee United ....
St Johnstone v Celtic ....
St Mirren v Heart of Midlothian ....

FIRST DIVISION

Dundee v Ayr United ....
Forfar Athletic v Clydebank ....
Kilmarnock v Montrose ....
Meadowbank Thistle v Morton ....
Partick Thistle v Raith Rovers ....
Stirling Albion v Hamilton Academical ....

SECOND DIVISION

Albion Rovers v Stranraer ....
Brechin City v Dumbarton ....
Clyde v Arbroath ....
East Fife v Alloa ....
East Stirlingshire v Berwick Rangers ....
Queen of the South v Stenhousemuir ....
Queen's Park v Cowdenbeath ....

Tues. 17th September

SECOND DIVISION

Albion Rovers v East Stirlingshire ....
Berwick Rangers v Alloa ....
Brechin City v Clyde ....
Dumbarton v Arbroath ....
East Fife v Queen of the South ....
Stenhousemuir v Queen's Park ....
Stranraer v Cowdenbeath ....

Sat. 21st September

PREMIER DIVISION

Aberdeen v Hibernian ....
Celtic v Airdrieonians ....
Heart of Midlothian v Dundee United ....
Motherwell v Dunfermline Athletic ....
St Johnstone v Falkirk ....
St Mirren v Rangers ....

FIRST DIVISION

Ayr United v Meadowbank Thistle ....
Dundee v Kilmarnock ....
Hamilton Academical v Clydebank ....
Partick Thistle v Montrose ....
Raith Rovers v Morton ....
Stirling Albion v Forfar Athletic ....

SECOND DIVISION

Alloa v Stenhousemuir ....
Arbroath v Brechin City ....
Cowdenbeath v East Fife ....
East Stirlingshire v Dumbarton ....
Queen of the South v Stranraer ....
Queen's Park v Albion Rovers ....

Sat. 28th September

PREMIER DIVISION

Airdrieonians v St Johnstone ....
Dundee United v Motherwell ....
Dunfermline Athletic v St Mirren ....
Falkirk v Heart of Midlothian ....
Hibernian v Celtic ....
Rangers v Aberdeen ....

FIRST DIVISION

Clydebank v Stirling Albion ....
Forfar Athletic v Partick Thistle ....
Kilmarnock v Raith Rovers ....
Meadowbank Thistle v Hamilton Academical ....
Montrose v Dundee ....
Morton v Ayr United ....

SECOND DIVISION

Albion Rovers v Brechin City ....
Arbroath v Alloa ....
Cowdenbeath v Berwick Rangers ....
Dumbarton v East Fife ....
East Stirlingshire v Stenhousemuir ....
Queen's Park v Queen of the South ....
Stranraer v Clyde ....

Sat. 5th October

PREMIER DIVISION

Aberdeen v St Mirren ....
Airdrieonians v Rangers ....

Celtic *v* Heart of Midlothian ....

Falkirk *v* Dundee United ....

Hibernian *v* Dunfermline Athletic ....

St Johnstone *v* Motherwell ....

FIRST DIVISION

Ayr United *v* Stirling Albion ....

Clydebank *v* Meadowbank Thistle ....

Dundee *v* Partick Thistle ....

Forfar Athletic *v* Kilmarnock ....

Morton *v* Montrose ....

Raith Rovers *v* Hamilton Academical ....

SECOND DIVISION

Alloa *v* Dumbarton ....

Berwick Rangers *v* Albion Rovers ....

Brechin City *v* Cowdenbeath ....

Clyde *v* Queen's Park ....

East Fife *v* Arbroath ....

Queen of the South *v* East Stirlingshire ....

Stenhousemuir *v* Stranraer ....

Tues. 8th October

PREMIER DIVISION

Dundee United *v* Airdrieonians ....

Dunfermline Athletic *v* Falkirk ....

Motherwell *v* Celtic ....

Rangers *v* Hibernian ....

FIRST DIVISION

Kilmarnock *v* Morton ....

Montrose *v* Raith Rovers ....

Partick Thistle *v* Clydebank ....

Stirling Albion *v* Dundee ....

Wed. 9th October

PREMIER DIVISION

Heart of Midlothian *v* Aberdeen ....

St Mirren *v* St Johnstone ....

FIRST DIVISION

Hamilton Academical *v* Ayr United ....

Meadowbank Thistle *v* Forfar Athletic ....

Sat. 12th October

PREMIER DIVISION

Aberdeen *v* Airdrieonians ....

Celtic *v* Dundee United ....

Heart of Midlothian *v* Dunfermline Athletic ....

Motherwell *v* Falkirk ....

St Johnstone *v* Rangers ....

St Mirren *v* Hibernian ....

FIRST DIVISION

Ayr United *v* Forfar Athletic ....

Dundee *v* Clydebank ....

Hamilton Academical *v* Montrose ....

Partick Thistle *v* Morton ....

Raith Rovers *v* Meadowbank Thistle ....

Stirling Albion *v* Kilmarnock ....

SECOND DIVISION

Albion Rovers *v* Clyde ....

Arbroath *v* Queen of the South ....

Cowdenbeath *v* Alloa ....

Dumbarton *v* Stenhousemuir ....

East Stirlingshire *v* East Fife ....

Queen's Park *v* Berwick Rangers ....

Stranraer *v* Brechin City ....

Sat. 19th October

PREMIER DIVISION

Airdrieonians *v* St Mirren ....

Dundee United *v* St Johnstone ....

Dunfermline Athletic *v* Aberdeen ....

Falkirk *v* Celtic ....

Hibernian *v* Motherwell ....

Rangers *v* Heart of Midlothian ....

FIRST DIVISION

Clydebank *v* Ayr United ....

Forfar Athletic *v* Raith Rovers ....

Kilmarnock *v* Partick Thistle ....

Meadowbank Thistle *v* Dundee ....

Montrose *v* Stirling Albion ....

Morton *v* Hamilton Academical ....

SECOND DIVISION

Alloa *v* East Stirlingshire ....

Berwick Rangers *v* Stranraer ....

Brechin City *v* Queen's Park ....

Clyde *v* Cowdenbeath ....

East Fife *v* Albion Rovers ....

Queen of the South *v* Dumbarton ....

Stenhousemuir *v* Arbroath ....

Sat. 26th October

PREMIER DIVISION

Dunfermline Athletic *v* Dundee United ....

Hibernian *v* Airdrieonians ....

Motherwell *v* Heart of Midlothian ....

Rangers *v* Falkirk ....

St Johnstone *v* Aberdeen ....

St Mirren *v* Celtic ....

FIRST DIVISION

Dundee *v* Morton ....

Forfar Athletic *v* Hamilton Academical ....

Kilmarnock *v* Clydebank ....

Meadowbank Thistle *v* Montrose ....

Partick Thistle *v* Ayr United ....

Stirling Albion *v* Raith Rovers ....

SECOND DIVISION

Albion Rovers *v* Stenhousemuir ....

Arbroath *v* Queen's Park ....

Berwick Rangers *v* East Fife ....

Brechin City *v* Queen of the South ....

Clyde *v* East Stirlingshire ....

Cowdenbeath *v* Dumbarton ....

Stranraer *v* Alloa ....

Tues. 29th October

PREMIER DIVISION

Airdrieonians *v* Dunfermline Athletic ....

Dundee United *v* Rangers ....

FIRST DIVISION

Ayr United *v* Dundee ....

Clydebank *v* Forfar Athletic ....

Montrose v Kilmarnock ....
Morton v Meadowbank Thistle ....
Raith Rovers v Partick Thistle ....

Wed. 30th October

PREMIER DIVISION
Aberdeen v Motherwell ....
Celtic v St Johnstone ....
Falkirk v Hibernian ....
Heart of Midlothian v St Mirren ....

FIRST DIVISION
Hamilton Academical v Stirling Albion ....

Sat. 2nd November

PREMIER DIVISION
Aberdeen v Dundee United ....
Airdrieonians v Falkirk ....
Hibernian v Heart of Midlothian ....
Rangers v Celtic ....
St Johnstone v Dunfermline Athletic ....
St Mirren v Motherwell ....

FIRST DIVISION
Ayr United v Kilmarnock ....
Clydebank v Morton ....
Dundee v Raith Rovers ....
Forfar Athletic v Montrose ....
Meadowbank Thistle v Stirling Albion ....
Partick Thistle v Hamilton Academical ....

SECOND DIVISION
Alloa v Brechin City ....
Arbroath v Albion Rovers ....
Dumbarton v Queen's Park ....
East Fife v Clyde ....
East Stirlingshire v Stranraer ....
Queen of the South v Cowdenbeath ....
Stenhousemuir v Berwick Rangers ....

Sat. 9th November

PREMIER DIVISION
Celtic v Aberdeen ....
Dundee United v Hibernian ....
Dunfermline Athletic v Rangers ....
Falkirk v St Mirren ....
Heart of Midlothian v St Johnstone ....
Motherwell v Airdrieonians ....

FIRST DIVISION
Hamilton Academical v Dundee ....
Kilmarnock v Meadowbank Thistle ....
Montrose v Clydebank ....
Morton v Forfar Athletic ....
Raith Rovers v Ayr United ....
Stirling Albion v Partick Thistle ....

SECOND DIVISION
Albion Rovers v Alloa ....
Berwick Rangers v Dumbarton ....
Brechin City v Stenhousemuir ....
Cowdenbeath v East Stirlingshire ....
Queen's Park v East Fife ....
Stranraer v Arbroath ....

Tues. 12th November

SECOND DIVISION
Clyde v Queen of the South ....

Sat. 16th November

PREMIER DIVISION
Dundee United v Falkirk ....
Dunfermline Athletic v Hibernian ....
Heart of Midlothian v Celtic ....
Motherwell v St Johnstone ....
Rangers v Airdrieonians ....
St Mirren v Aberdeen ....

FIRST DIVISION
Hamilton Academical v Raith Rovers ....
Kilmarnock v Forfar Athletic ....
Meadowbank Thistle v Clydebank ....
Montrose v Morton ....
Partick Thistle v Dundee ....
Stirling Albion v Ayr United ....

SECOND DIVISION
Alloa v Clyde ....
Arbroath v Berwick Rangers ....
Dumbarton v Stranraer ....
East Fife v Brechin City ....
East Stirlingshire v Queen's Park ....
Queen of the South v Albion Rovers ....
Stenhousemuir v Cowdenbeath ....

Tues. 19th November

PREMIER DIVISION
Airdrieonians v Dundee United ....
Hibernian v Rangers ....

FIRST DIVISION
Ayr United v Hamilton Academical ....
Clydebank v Partick Thistle ....
Dundee v Stirling Albion ....
Forfar Athletic v Meadowbank Thistle ....
Morton v Kilmarnock ....
Raith Rovers v Montrose ....

Wed. 20th November

PREMIER DIVISION
Aberdeen v Heart of Midlothian ....
Celtic v Motherwell ....
Falkirk v Dunfermline Athletic ....
St Johnstone v St Mirren ....

Sat. 23rd November

PREMIER DIVISION
Airdrieonians v Celtic ....
Dundee United v Heart of Midlothian ....
Dunfermline Athletic v Motherwell ....
Falkirk v St Johnstone ....
Hibernian v Aberdeen ....
Rangers v St Mirren ....

FIRST DIVISION
Clydebank v Hamilton Academical ....
Forfar Athletic v Stirling Albion ....

Kilmarnock *v* Dundee ....
Meadowbank Thistle *v* Ayr United ....
Montrose *v* Partick Thistle ....
Morton *v* Raith Rovers ....

Albion Rovers *v* Cowdenbeath ....
Brechin City *v* Berwick Rangers ....
Clyde *v* Dumbarton ....
East Fife *v* Stenhousemuir ....
East Stirlingshire *v* Arbroath ....
Queen of the South *v* Alloa ....
Queen's Park *v* Stranraer ....

Sat. 30th November

PREMIER DIVISION

Aberdeen *v* Falkirk ....
Celtic *v* Dunfermline Athletic ....
Heart of Midlothian *v* Airdrieonians ....
Motherwell *v* Rangers ....
St Johnstone *v* Hibernian ....
St Mirren *v* Dundee United ....

FIRST DIVISION

Ayr United *v* Montrose ....
Dundee *v* Forfar Athletic ....
Hamilton Academical *v* Kilmarnock ....
Partick Thistle *v* Meadowbank Thistle ....
Raith Rovers *v* Clydebank ....
Stirling Albion *v* Morton ....

SECOND DIVISION

Alloa *v* East Fife ....
Arbroath *v* Clyde ....
Berwick Rangers *v* East Stirlingshire ....
Cowdenbeath *v* Queen's Park ....
Dumbarton *v* Brechin City ....
Stenhousemuir *v* Queen of the South ....
Stranraer *v* Albion Rovers ....

Tues. 3rd December

PREMIER DIVISION

Motherwell *v* Dundee United ....

FIRST DIVISION

Ayr United *v* Morton ....
Dundee *v* Montrose ....
Partick Thistle *v* Forfar Athletic ....
Raith Rovers *v* Kilmarnock ....
Stirling Albion *v* Clydebank ....

Wed. 4th December

PREMIER DIVISION

Aberdeen *v* Rangers ....
Celtic *v* Hibernian ....
Heart of Midlothian *v* Falkirk ....
St Johnstone *v* Airdrieonians ....
St Mirren *v* Dunfermline Athletic ....

FIRST DIVISION

Hamilton Academical *v* Meadowbank Thistle ....

Sat. 7th December

PREMIER DIVISION

Airdrieonians *v* Aberdeen ....

Dundee United *v* Celtic ....
Dunfermline Athletic *v* Heart of Midlothian ....
Falkirk *v* Motherwell ....
Hibernian *v* St Mirren ....
Rangers *v* St Johnstone ....

FIRST DIVISION

Clydebank *v* Dundee ....
Forfar Athletic *v* Ayr United ....
Kilmarnock *v* Stirling Albion ....
Meadowbank Thistle *v* Raith Rovers ....
Montrose *v* Hamilton Academical ....
Morton *v* Partick Thistle ....

Sat. 14th December

PREMIER DIVISION

Aberdeen *v* St Johnstone ....
Airdrieonians *v* Hibernian ....
Celtic *v* St Mirren ....
Dundee United *v* Dunfermline Athletic ....
Falkirk *v* Rangers ....
Heart of Midlothian *v* Motherwell ....

FIRST DIVISION

Ayr United *v* Partick Thistle ....
Clydebank *v* Kilmarnock ....
Hamilton Academical *v* Forfar Athletic ....
Montrose *v* Meadowbank Thistle ....
Morton *v* Dundee ....
Raith Rovers *v* Stirling Albion ....

SECOND DIVISION

Alloa *v* Stranraer ....
Dumbarton *v* Cowdenbeath ....
East Fife *v* Berwick Rangers ....
East Stirlingshire *v* Clyde ....
Queen of the South *v* Brechin City ....
Queen's Park *v* Arbroath ....
Stenhousemuir *v* Albion Rovers ....

Sat. 21st December

PREMIER DIVISION

Dunfermline Athletic *v* Airdrieonians ....
Hibernian *v* Falkirk ....
Motherwell *v* Aberdeen ....
Rangers *v* Dundee United ....
St Johnstone *v* Celtic ....
St Mirren *v* Heart of Midlothian ....

FIRST DIVISION

Dundee *v* Ayr United ....
Forfar Athletic *v* Clydebank ....
Kilmarnock *v* Montrose ....
Meadowbank Thistle *v* Morton ....
Partick Thistle *v* Raith Rovers ....
Stirling Albion *v* Hamilton Academical ....

SECOND DIVISION

Albion Rovers *v* Dumbarton ....
Berwick Rangers *v* Queen of the South ....
Brechin City *v* East Stirlingshire ....
Clyde *v* Stenhousemuir ....
Cowdenbeath *v* Arbroath ....
Queen's Park *v* Alloa ....
Stranraer *v* East Fife ....

Sat. 28th December

PREMIER DIVISION

Aberdeen v Celtic ....
Airdrieonians v Motherwell ....
Hibernian v Dundee United ....
Rangers v Dunfermline Athletic ....
St Johnstone v Heart of Midlothian ....
St Mirren v Falkirk ....

FIRST DIVISION

Ayr United v Raith Rovers ....
Clydebank v Montrose ....
Dundee v Hamilton Academical ....
Forfar Athletic v Morton ....
Meadowbank Thistle v Kilmarnock ....
Partick Thistle v Stirling Albion ....

SECOND DIVISION

Alloa v Berwick Rangers ....
Arbroath v Dumbarton ....
Clyde v Brechin City ....
Cowdenbeath v Stranraer ....
East Stirlingshire v Albion Rovers ....
Queen of the South v East Fife ....
Queen's Park v Stenhousemuir ....

Wed. 1st January

PREMIER DIVISION

Celtic v Rangers ....
Dundee United v Aberdeen ....
Dunfermline Athletic v St Johnstone ....
Falkirk v Airdrieonians ....
Heart of Midlothian v Hibernian ....
Motherwell v St Mirren ....

FIRST DIVISION

Hamilton Academical v Partick Thistle ....
Kilmarnock v Ayr United ....
Montrose v Forfar Athletic ....
Morton v Clydebank ....
Raith Rovers v Dundee ....
Stirling Albion v Meadowbank Thistle ....

SECOND DIVISION

Albion Rovers v Queen's Park ....
Berwick Rangers v Clyde ....
Brechin City v Arbroath ....
Dumbarton v East Stirlingshire ....
East Fife v Cowdenbeath ....
Stenhousemuir v Alloa ....
Stranraer v Queen of the South ....

Sat. 4th January

PREMIER DIVISION

Aberdeen v St Mirren ....
Airdrieonians v Rangers ....
Celtic v Heart of Midlothian ....
Falkirk v Dundee United ....
Hibernian v Dunfermline Athletic ....
St Johnstone v Motherwell ....

FIRST DIVISION

Ayr United v Stirling Albion ....
Clydebank v Meadowbank Thistle ....
Dundee v Partick Thistle ....

Forfar Athletic v Kilmarnock ....
Morton v Montrose ....
Raith Rovers v Hamilton Academical ....

Sat. 11th January

PREMIER DIVISION

Dundee United v Airdrieonians ....
Dunfermline Athletic v Falkirk ....
Heart of Midlothian v Aberdeen ....
Motherwell v Celtic ....
Rangers v Hibernian ....
St Mirren v St Johnstone ....

FIRST DIVISION

Hamilton Academical v Ayr United ....
Kilmarnock v Morton ....
Meadowbank Thistle v Forfar Athletic ....
Montrose v Raith Rovers ....
Partick Thistle v Clydebank ....
Stirling Albion v Dundee ....

SECOND DIVISION

Albion Rovers v Berwick Rangers ....
Arbroath v East Fife ....
Cowdenbeath v Brechin City ....
Dumbarton v Alloa ....
East Stirlingshire v Queen of the South ....
Queen's Park v Clyde ....
Stranraer v Stenhousemuir ....

Sat. 18th January

PREMIER DIVISION

Airdrieonians v Heart of Midlothian ....
Dundee United v St Mirren ....
Dunfermline Athletic v Celtic ....
Falkirk v Aberdeen ....
Hibernian v St Johnstone ....
Rangers v Motherwell ....

FIRST DIVISION

Clydebank v Raith Rovers ....
Forfar Athletic v Dundee ....
Kilmarnock v Hamilton Academical ....
Meadowbank Thistle v Partick Thistle ....
Montrose v Ayr United ....
Morton v Stirling Albion ....

SECOND DIVISION

Alloa v Arbroath ....
Berwick Rangers v Cowdenbeath ....
Brechin City v Albion Rovers ....
Clyde v Stranraer ....
East Fife v Dumbarton ....
Queen of the South v Queen's Park ....
Stenhousemuir v East Stirlingshire ....

Sat. 25th January

SECOND DIVISION

Alloa v Cowdenbeath ....
Berwick Rangers v Queen's Park ....
Brechin City v Stranraer ....
Clyde v Albion Rovers ....
East Fife v East Stirlingshire ....
Queen of the South v Arbroath ....
Stenhousemuir v Dumbarton ....

Sat. 1st February

Aberdeen *v* Dunfermline Athletic ....
Celtic *v* Falkirk ....
Heart of Midlothian *v* Rangers ....
Motherwell *v* Hibernian ....
St Johnstone *v* Dundee United ....
St Mirren *v* Airdrieonians ....

FIRST DIVISION

Ayr United *v* Clydebank ....
Dundee *v* Meadowbank Thistle ....
Hamilton Academical *v* Morton ....
Partick Thistle *v* Kilmarnock ....
Raith Rovers *v* Forfar Athletic ....
Stirling Albion *v* Montrose ....

SECOND DIVISION

Albion Rovers *v* East Fife ....
Arbroath *v* Stenhousemuir ....
Cowdenbeath *v* Clyde ....
Dumbarton *v* Queen of the South ....
East Stirlingshire *v* Alloa ....
Queen's Park *v* Brechin City ....
Stranraer *v* Berwick Rangers ....

Sat. 8th February

PREMIER DIVISION

Aberdeen *v* Hibernian ....
Celtic *v* Airdrieonians ....
Heart of Midlothian *v* Dundee United ....
Motherwell *v* Dunfermline Athletic ....
St Johnstone *v* Falkirk ....
St Mirren *v* Rangers ....

FIRST DIVISION

Ayr United *v* Meadowbank Thistle ....
Dundee *v* Kilmarnock ....
Hamilton Academical *v* Clydebank ....
Partick Thistle *v* Montrose ....
Raith Rovers *v* Morton ....
Stirling Albion *v* Forfar Athletic ....

SECOND DIVISION

Alloa *v* Brechin City ....
Arbroath *v* Clyde ....
Dumbarton *v* Stranraer ....
East Fife *v* Queen's Park ....
East Stirlingshire *v* Berwick Rangers ....
Queen of the South *v* Albion Rovers ....
Stenhousemuir *v* Cowdenbeath ....

Sat. 15th February

SECOND DIVISION

Albion Rovers *v* Dumbarton ....
Berwick Rangers *v* Alloa ....
Brechin City *v* Queen of the South ....
Clyde *v* East Fife ....
Cowdenbeath *v* East Stirlingshire ....
Queen's Park *v* Stenhousemuir ....
Stranraer *v* Arbroath ....

Sat. 22nd February

PREMIER DIVISION

Airdrieonians *v* St Johnstone ....

Dundee United *v* Motherwell ....
Dunfermline Athletic *v* St Mirren ....
Falkirk *v* Heart of Midlothian ....
Hibernian *v* Celtic ....
Rangers *v* Aberdeen ....

FIRST DIVISION

Clydebank *v* Stirling Albion ....
Forfar Athletic *v* Partick Thistle ....
Kilmarnock *v* Raith Rovers ....
Meadowbank Thistle *v* Hamilton Academical ....
Montrose *v* Dundee ....
Morton *v* Ayr United ....

SECOND DIVISION

Albion Rovers *v* East Stirlingshire ....
Arbroath *v* Queen's Park ....
Clyde *v* Berwick Rangers ....
Dumbarton *v* Brechin City ....
East Fife *v* Queen of the South ....
Stenhousemuir *v* Alloa ....
Stranraer *v* Cowdenbeath ....

Sat. 29th February

PREMIER DIVISION

Dundee United *v* Falkirk ....
Dunfermline Athletic *v* Hibernian ....
Heart of Midlothian *v* Celtic ....
Motherwell *v* St Johnstone ....
Rangers *v* Airdrieonians ....
St Mirren *v* Aberdeen ....

FIRST DIVISION

Hamilton Academical *v* Raith Rovers ....
Kilmarnock *v* Forfar Athletic ....
Meadowbank Thistle *v* Clydebank ....
Montrose *v* Morton ....
Partick Thistle *v* Dundee ....
Stirling Albion *v* Ayr United ....

SECOND DIVISION

Alloa *v* Stranraer ....
Berwick Rangers *v* Albion Rovers ....
Brechin City *v* Clyde ....
Cowdenbeath *v* East Fife ....
East Stirlingshire *v* Arbroath ....
Queen of the South *v* Stenhousemuir ....
Queen's Park *v* Dumbarton ....

Sat. 7th March

PREMIER DIVISION

Aberdeen *v* Heart of Midlothian ....
Airdrieonians *v* Dundee United ....
Celtic *v* Motherwell ....
Falkirk *v* Dunfermline Athletic ....
Hibernian *v* Rangers ....
St Johnstone *v* St Mirren ....

FIRST DIVISION

Ayr United *v* Hamilton Academical ....
Clydebank *v* Partick Thistle ....
Dundee *v* Stirling Albion ....
Forfar Athletic *v* Meadowbank Thistle ....
Morton *v* Kilmarnock ....
Raith Rovers *v* Montrose ....

SECOND DIVISION

Albion Rovers *v* Alloa ....

TUDOR CRISPS

BAGS OF ACTION

SPONSORS OF THE
SCOTTISH SCHOOLS
INTERNATIONAL
KIT FOR U15's & U16's

SPONSORS OF THE
TUDOR CRISPS CUP
PRIMARY SCHOOLS
SEVEN-A-SIDE
KNOCKOUT COMPETITION

Brechin City *v* Berwick Rangers ....
Clyde *v* Queen of the South ....
Dumbarton *v* East Stirlingshire ....
East Fife *v* Arbroath ....
Queen's Park *v* Cowdenbeath ....
Stranraer *v* Stenhousemuir ....

Sat. 14th March

PREMIER DIVISION

Celtic *v* Aberdeen ....
Dundee United *v* Hibernian ....
Dunfermline Athletic *v* Rangers ....
Falkirk *v* St Mirren ....
Heart of Midlothian *v* St Johnstone ....
Motherwell *v* Airdrieonians ....

FIRST DIVISION

Hamilton Academical *v* Dundee ....
Kilmarnock *v* Meadowbank Thistle ....
Montrose *v* Clydebank ....
Morton *v* Forfar Athletic ....
Raith Rovers *v* Ayr United ....
Stirling Albion *v* Partick Thistle ....

SECOND DIVISION

Alloa *v* Queen's Park ....
Arbroath *v* Albion Rovers ....
Berwick Rangers *v* Stranraer ....
Cowdenbeath *v* Clyde ....
East Stirlingshire *v* Brechin City ....
Queen of the South *v* Dumbarton ....
Stenhousemuir *v* East Fife ....

Sat. 21st March

PREMIER DIVISION

Aberdeen *v* Dundee United ....
Aidrieonians *v* Falkirk ....
Hibernian *v* Heart of Midlothian ....
Rangers *v* Celtic ....
St Johnstone *v* Dunfermline Athletic ....
St Mirren *v* Motherwell ....

FIRST DIVISION

Ayr United *v* Kilmarnock ....
Clydebank *v* Morton ....
Dundee *v* Raith Rovers ....
Forfar Athletic *v* Montrose ....
Meadowbank Thistle *v* Stirling Albion ....
Partick Thistle *v* Hamilton Academical ....

SECOND DIVISION

Albion Rovers *v* Queen's Park ....
Brechin City *v* East Fife ....
Clyde *v* Stranraer ....
Cowdenbeath *v* Berwick Rangers ....
Dumbarton *v* Alloa ....
Queen of the South *v* East Stirlingshire ....
Stenhousemuir *v* Arbroath ....

Sat. 28th March

PREMIER DIVISION

Aberdeen *v* Airdrieonians ....
Celtic *v* Dundee United ....
Heart of Midlothian *v* Dunfermline Athletic ....
Motherwell *v* Falkirk ....

St Johnstone *v* Rangers ....
St Mirren *v* Hibernian ....

FIRST DIVISION

Ayr United *v* Forfar Athletic ....
Dundee *v* Clydebank ....
Hamilton Academical *v* Montrose ....
Partick Thistle *v* Morton ....
Raith Rovers *v* Meadowbank Thistle ....
Stirling Albion *v* Kilmarnock ....

SECOND DIVISION

Alloa *v* Queen of the South ....
Arbroath *v* Cowdenbeath ....
Berwick Rangers *v* Dumbarton ....
East Fife *v* Albion Rovers ....
East Stirlingshire *v* Stenhousemuir ....
Queen's Park *v* Clyde ....
Stranraer *v* Brechin City ....

Sat. 4th April

PREMIER DIVISION

Airdrieonians *v* St Mirren ....
Dundee United *v* St Johnstone ....
Dunfermline Athletic *v* Aberdeen ....
Falkirk *v* Celtic ....
Hibernian *v* Motherwell ....
Rangers *v* Heart of Midlothian ....

FIRST DIVISION

Clydebank *v* Ayr United ....
Forfar Athletic *v* Raith Rovers ....
Kilmarnock *v* Partick Thistle ....
Meadowbank Thistle *v* Dundee ....
Montrose *v* Stirling Albion ....
Morton *v* Hamilton Academical ....

SECOND DIVISION

Albion Rovers *v* Cowdenbeath ....
Berwick Rangers *v* Stenhousemuir ....
Brechin City *v* Arbroath ....
Clyde *v* Alloa ....
East Fife *v* Dumbarton ....
East Stirlingshire *v* Stranraer ....
Queen of the South *v* Queen's Park ....

Tues. 7th April

PREMIER DIVISION

Dunfermline Athletic *v* Dundee United ....
Hibernian *v* Airdrieonians ....
Motherwell *v* Heart of Midlothian ....
Rangers *v* Falkirk ....

FIRST DIVISION

Dundee *v* Morton ....
Forfar Athletic *v* Hamilton Academical ....
Kilmarnock *v* Clydebank ....
Partick Thistle *v* Ayr United ....
Stirling Albion *v* Raith Rovers ....

Wed. 8th April

PREMIER DIVISION

St Johnstone *v* Aberdeen ....
St Mirren *v* Celtic ....

FIRST DIVISION

Meadowbank Thistle *v* Montrose ....

215

Sat. 11th April

PREMIER DIVISION

Aberdeen v Motherwell ....
Airdrieonians v Dunfermline Athletic ....
Celtic v St Johnstone ....
Dundee United v Rangers ....
Falkirk v Hibernian ....
Heart of Midlothian v St Mirren ....

FIRST DIVISION

Ayr United v Dundee ....
Clydebank v Forfar Athletic ....
Hamilton Academical v Stirling Albion ....
Montrose v Kilmarnock ....
Morton v Meadowbank Thistle ....
Raith Rovers v Partick Thistle ....

SECOND DIVISION

Alloa v East Stirlingshire ....
Arbroath v Queen of the South ....
Cowdenbeath v Brechin City ....
Dumbarton v Clyde ....
Queen's Park v Berwick Rangers ....
Stenhousemuir v Albion Rovers ....
Stranraer v East Fife ....

Sat. 18th April

PREMIER DIVISION

Airdrieonians v Celtic ....
Dundee United v Heart of Midlothian ....
Dunfermline Athletic v Motherwell ....
Falkirk v St Johnstone ....
Hibernian v Aberdeen ....
Rangers v St Mirren ....

FIRST DIVISION

Clydebank v Hamilton Academical ....
Forfar Athletic v Stirling Albion ....
Kilmarnock v Dundee ....
Meadowbank Thistle v Ayr United ....
Montrose v Partick Thistle ....

SECOND DIVISION

Albion Rovers v Brechin City ....
Arbroath v Alloa ....
Clyde v Stenhousemuir ....
Dumbarton v Cowdenbeath ....
East Fife v East Stirlingshire ....
Queen of the South v Berwick Rangers ....
Queen's Park v Stranraer ....

Sat. 25th April

PREMIER DIVISION

Aberdeen v Falkirk ....
Celtic v Dunfermline Athletic ....
Heart of Midlothian v Airdrieonians ....
Motherwell v Rangers ....
St Johnstone v Hibernian ....
St Mirren v Dundee United ....

FIRST DIVISION

Ayr United v Montrose ....
Dundee v Forfar Athletic ....
Hamilton Academical v Kilmarnock ....
Partick Thistle v Meadowbank Thistle ....
Raith Rovers v Clydebank ....
Stirling Albion v Morton ....

SECOND DIVISION

Alloa v East Fife ....
Berwick Rangers v Arbroath ....
Brechin City v Queen's Park ....
Cowdenbeath v Queen of the South ....
East Stirlingshire v Clyde ....
Stenhousemuir v Dumbarton ....
Stranraer v Albion Rovers ....

Sat. 2nd May

PREMIER DIVISION

Aberdeen v Rangers ....
Celtic v Hibernian ....
Heart of Midlothian v Falkirk ....
Motherwell v Dundee United ....
St Johnstone v Airdrieonians ....
St Mirren v Dunfermline Athletic ....

FIRST DIVISION

Ayr United v Morton ....
Dundee v Montrose ....
Hamilton Academical v Meadowbank Thistle ....
Partick Thistle v Forfar Athletic ....
Raith Rovers v Kilmarnock ....
Stirling Albion v Clydebank ....

SECOND DIVISION

Albion Rovers v Clyde ....
Alloa v Cowdenbeath ....
Berwick Rangers v East Fife ....
Brechin City v Stenhousemuir ....
Dumbarton v Arbroath ....
Queen's Park v East Stirlingshire ....
Stranraer v Queen of the South ....

List of Advertisers

Notes

Notes

Notes

Notes

Notes

Notes